EMPIRICAL FOUNDATIONS OF INFORMATION AND SOFTWARE SCIENCE III

A Continuation Order Plan is available for this series. A continuation order will bring delivery of each new volume immediately upon publication. Volumes are billed only upon actual shipment. For further information please contact the publisher.

EMPIRICAL FOUNDATIONS OF INFORMATION AND SOFTWARE SCIENCE III

Edited by

Jens Rasmussen

Riso National Laboratory
Roskilde, Denmark

Pranas Zunde

School of Information and Computer Science
Georgia Institute of Technology
Atlanta, Georgia

PLENUM PRESS • NEW YORK AND LONDON

Library of Congress Cataloging in Publication Data

Symposium on Empirical Foundations of Information and Software Science (3rd:
  1985: Roskilde, Denmark)
  Empirical foundations of information and software science III.

  "Proceedings of the Third Symposium on Empirical Foundations of Information and
Software Science, sponsored by the Riso National Laboratory and the Royal School of
Librarianship, held October 21–24, 1985, in Roskilde, Denmark"—T.p. verso.
  Includes bibliographies and index.
  1. Electronic data processing—Congresses. 2. Information retrieval—Congresses.
3. Computer software—Congresses. 3. Computer software—Congresses. I.
Rasmussen, Jens, 1926–   . II. Zunde, Pranas, 1923–   . III. Forsogsanlaeg Riso.
IV. Danmarks bibliogeksskole. V. Title.
QA75.5.S956 1985   005   87-12275
ISBN-13: 978-1-4612-9055-1   e-ISBN-13: 978-1-4613-1895-8
DOI: 10.1007/ 978-1-4613-1895-8

Proceedings of the Third Symposium on Empirical Foundations of Information
and Software Science, sponsored by the Riso National Laboratory and the Royal School of
Librarianship, held October 21–24, 1985, in Roskilde, Denmark

© 1987 Plenum Press, New York
Softcover reprint of the hardcover 1st edition 1987
A Division of Plenum Publishing Corporation
233 Spring Street, New York, N.Y. 10013

All rights reserved

No part of this book may be reproduced, stored in a retrieval system, or transmitted
in any form or by any means, electronic, mechanical, photocopying, microfilming,
recording, or otherwise, without written permission from the Publisher

SYMPOSIUM ADVISORY COMMITTEE

Dr. Harold Bamford, National Science Foundation; Joseph P.
Cavano, Rome Air Development Center; Dr. William Curtis,
Microelectronics and Computer Technology Corporation; Dr.
James W. Gault, U.S. Army European Research Office; Dr.
John J. O'Hare, Office of Naval Research; John R. Mitchell,
U. S. Army Institute for Research in Management Informa-
mation, Communications, and Computer Sciences; Dr. Edward
C. Weiss, Essex Corporation.

SYMPOSIUM ORGANIZING COMMITTEE

Dr. Jagdish C. Agrawal, Embry-Riddle Aeronautical University, Dayton, Florida; Jens Rasmussen, Ri'so National Laboratory, Roskilde, Denmark; Dr. Tefko Saracevic, Rutgers
University, New Brunswick, New Jersey; Dr. Williiam B.
Rouse, Dr. Vladimir Slamecka, and Dr. Pranas Zunde (chair-
man), all Georgia Institute of Technology, Atlanta, Georgia.

The organizers gratefully acknowledge partial funding of the symposium by
the U.S. Army Institute for Research in Management Information, Communications, and Computer Sciences, Atlanta, Georgia.

CONTENTS

Introduction   1

Database Management in Research Environment.   3
        K. Amano and T. Maeda

An Axiomatic Approach to Software Complexity Measures. 13
        P. Bollmann and H. Zuse

Systems Design and the Psychology of Complex Systems 21
        B. Brehmer

User Developed Prototype Systems 33
        S. Friis

The Text Environment and Data Base Management Systems. 45
        M.A. Heather and B.N. Rossiter

Validation of Software Under a Signal-Detection Theory Schema. . . 63
        M.H. Heine

Object-Oriented INTERLISP Programming Environment
        for Implementation of a Distributed Expert System. 73
        R.-D. Hennings and S. Schulze-Kremer

Combining Logging, Playback and Verbal Protocols:
        A Method for Analyzing and Evaluating Interactive Systems. . . 99
        P. Hietala

Analysis of the Needs for Computer Aids to
        Planning in Computer Programming 109
        J.-M. Hoc and A. Valentin

DEMON: A Model for the Monitoring of Decision Making. 123
        E. Hollnagel

On Initialization and Exitialization in Program Design 135
        P. Järvinen

Document Information System in Scientific Research 145
        T. Maeda and K. Amano

A Technique That Supports Evaluation and Design of User Interfaces . 155
        I. Mistrik and D.A. Nelson

The Term Association Thesaurus: An Information
        Processing Aid Based on Associative Semantics. 175
        A.P. Pejtersen, S.E. Olsen, and P. Zunde

Use of Computer Games to Test Experimental Techniques
        and Cognitive Models 187
    J. Rasmussen

Users' Opinion of Their Work, Language, and Computerized System. . . 197
    G. Sandström

Early Software Size Estimation: A Critical Analysis
        of the Software Science Length Equation and a
        Data-Structure-Oriented Size Estimation Approach 211
    A.S. Wang and H.E. Dunsmore

Software Systems for Managerial Work: Some Conclusions
        from Information Research. 223
    T. Wilson

Information and Its Relationship to Decision Making:
        The Information Profile and Other Quantitative
        Measures; A Brief Summary 231
    M.C. Yovits, A. de Korvin, R. Kleyle, and M. Mascarenhas

Information Science Laws and Regularities: A Summary. 243
    P. Zunde

Index. 271

INTRODUCTION

The monograph presents the proceedings of the Third Symposium on Empirical Foundations of Information and Software Sciences (EFISS) held at the Riso National Laboratory in Roskilde, Denmark, 23-25 October 1985. The EFISS series of meetings was initiated with the express purpose of exploring subjects and methods of scientific inquiry of empirical nature which are of common interest to information and software sciences. Furthermore, these meetings were expected to provide a cross-disciplinary forum for discussion of problems and exchange of research results of importance for the design and application of advanced information systems.

The previous two EFISS symposia took place at the Georgia Institute of Technology in Atlanta, Georgia, USA. The first meeting in 1982 focused on methods of experimental design and measurement techniques in information and software sciences. The second meeting was held in 1984 and its main theme was the value of information in prescriptive contexts, such as value of information for understanding and implementation of these messages, instructions, and commands. Specific examples of problems of this kind are the value of comments for the enhancement of understanding of computer programs, the value of information in assisting and guiding users of on-line interactive systems, and the value of lexical aids in information retrieval. In both symposia, contributed papers were considered on any other valid subject of empirical foundations of the said two sciences.

Although the first two EFISS symposia attracted also a fair number of contributors and attendees from overseas, their participation was not representative of the whole spectrum of, say, European activities in this field. Consequently, it was decided at the second meeting in Atlanta to organize EFISS symposia annually rather than every second year, alternating the symposia sites between USA and Europe. Thus the Third EFISS Symposium, the proceedings of which are being introduced here, was held in 1985 in Denmark as a European meeting, organized by the Riso National Laboratory and the Danish Royal School of Librarianship. The focus of that meeting was on empirical foundations of the design of advanced information systems. This broad focus was chosen in order to provide an opportunity to explore relevant areas of interest in the European scientific community. Furthermore, the topic of design of information systems was chosen to emphasize the interaction between software and information sciences and, for that purpose, papers were called also on empirical studies of users' needs and their behavior in suport of software specification and system design. An invited keynote address by Professor Berndt Brehmer, Psychological Institue of the Univsersity of Uppsala, served as an excellent way to introduce the psychological and other related empirical aspects under consideration.

In its last session, the Third EFISS Symposium addressed also the question what should be the main theme for the 1986 meeting in Atlanta, and it was agreed that the most timely topic is the evaluation of human-computer interfaces.

Last, but not least, we have the pleasure to acknowledge the assistance of the members of the Organizing Committee N. J. Belkin of the City University in London, U.K., M. H. Heine of the Newcastle upon Tyne Polytechnic, U.K., A. M. Pejtersen of the Royal School of Librarianship, Copenhagen, Denmark, and O. Platz of the Riso National Laboratory, Denmark, in the organization of the Symposium.

Two key persons without whose assistance the job of the editors would have been much more difficult also deserve our special thanks: Ms. Angela Jones of Georgia Institute of Technology, who type-setted the entire manuscript, and Mr. John Matzka of Plenum Publishing Corporation, who besides offering many helpful ideas, assisted in getting the figures and tables in a form ready for photo offset process. Their patience and untiring assistance to the editors in various iterations of proofing contributed a lot to the quality of the production of this volume.

Jens Rasmussen
Riso National Laboratory
Roskilde, Denmark

Pranas Zunde
Georgia Institute of Technology
Atlanta, Georgia, USA

DATABASE MANAGEMENT IN RESEARCH ENVIRONMENT

Kaname Amano*[1] and Takashi Maeda**

*Computing Center
 Hokkaido University
 Sapporo 060, JAPAN
**Department of Engineering Science
 Hokkaido University
 Sapporo 060, JAPAN

Abstract: Database management in a research environment is for assisting scientific researchers, who are often nonprofessional in database administration, in constructing their research-oriented database systems. Reported here is a support environment that takes advantage of a general-purpose Information Retrieval System (IRS) and Database Management System (DBMS) as basic softwares. Tools implemented as its integral part have made feasible rapid implementation of a working prototype followed by its iterative refinements. However, it is suggested that some further augmentations such as integration of IRS and DBMS, management of programs, and knowledge-based instruction are necessary.

INTRODUCTION

It is important in research environments that scientific researchers be able to construct their research-oriented information systems easily by themselves in their daily research activities (Kubo, 1981; Kubo, 1982). Though such a system may be intended for use in a specific field, it should be shared widely with other researchers not only because it may be useful in some other fields as well, but also because it may meet other requirements in addition to those originally expected.

This paper is concerned with a support environment for database construction and sharing by scientific researchers who are often nonprofessionals in database administration (Mochida et al., 1984; Amano et al., 1984; Amano and Mochida, 1985; Amano, Kaida and Mochida, 1986), and with the applicability of general-purpose commercial IRS and DBMS to such an environment.

A typical IRS or DBMS is too complicated for nonprofessionals. Convenient tools are needed for effective construction of database systems. A general-purpose IRS or DBMS with many tools available for users, but not

---

[1]Author's Present Address: Department of Applied Mathematics, Faculty of Engineering, Ehime University, Matsuyama 790, Japan.

with help facilities, is not said to be satisfactory. Each of these tools must be constructed as an integral part of an integrated support environment (Wasserman, 1982; Blum, 1983).

In this paper, first, we consider general features of database systems constructed in research environments together with difficulties encountered by their nonprofessional Database Administrators (DBAs). Then, we present a support environment for database construction and sharing which takes advantage of a general-purpose IRS (ORION) and DBMS (ADABAS) as basic software. Finally, some requirements for achieving further improvements are suggested.

DATABASE SYSTEMS IN A RESEARCH ENVIRONMENT

General Features

Research-oriented database systems are rather small in size, but must be adaptable to various requirements. They evolve with time in the progress of research. Adaptability and evolution are essentially important in a research environment. With this in mind, we examine features of such systems more specifically.

- Variety of Scientific Data. Various kinds of information must be dealt with such as bibliographies, documents, and observational, statistical, experimental, and designing data, etc., consisting of character strings, texts, numerical values, their tables, diagrams, images, etc.

- Nonprofessional DBA. A research-oriented system is designed, developed, and maintained by a small group of researchers, who are often non-expert of either computer systems or data processing.

- General-Purpose IRS and DBMS. General-purpose commercial IRSs and DBMSs, which have a potential for scientific application, are important since development and maintenance of a special-purpose IRS or DBMS are too laborious for scientific researchers. Note that IRSs and DBMSs are used not only for existing database management, but also for its construction.

- General-Purpose Machine. Merits of a special-purpose machine are evident. However, in scientific application, also general-purpose machines have some important merits: availability of various software libraries, convenience for database sharing, etc.

Research-oriented database systems are constructed and maintained by the DBA researchers themselves; then they should be responsible for their database management. However, a typical IRS or DBMS assumes that databases are administrated by full-time professional personnel, and its DBA interface is too complicated.

Non-Professional DBAs' Behavior and Difficulties

In many cases, requirements are indefinite and documents are not written for developing database systems. This is in part because nonprofessional DBAs lack experience. We must also take into account the fact that research-oriented systems have the following characteristics: adaptability and evolution; and the feature that the DBA group does all the work of requirement analysis, system design, development, and maintenance.

These features suggest that rigorous phase-oriented development methodologies are not necessarily suitable for research-oriented systems and that rapid implementation of a working prototype followed by its iterative refinement may be preferable. However, complicated procedures are involved in database construction; the following are main difficulties encountered by nonprofessional DBAs:

- Global Flow of Procedures. Many utility jobs must be executed in a specific order. Especially, it is difficult to find a restarting point when an error occurs.

- Usage of Job Control Language (JCL). Usually DBA interface involves much complicated usage of JCL due to batch processing.

- Data Definition with Data Definition Language (DDL).

- Data Loading. Data or programs in a specific format must be prepared.

DATABASE MANAGEMENT AT HUCC, AN EXAMPLE

Guiding Principle

HUCC is one of the largest university computer centers in Japan, which is connected to an inter-university computer network (Sugiura et al., 1982). It is shared with about a thousand academic researchers all over the country.

The guiding principle of the HUCC database management is as follows: HUCC assists its users by software and technical support in order that they can construct their database systems easily by themselves (Okino, 1982). A system satisfying the following conditions has been especially encouraged: usefulness in scientific research; openness to other users; and a prospect of continuous maintenance. However, of course, a system can be for private use by a user or group of users. See Table 1.

Method

The basic idea of our approach is to construct a support system for database construction and sharing by users with ORION and ADABAS as basic software. It consists of a database storing dictionary information of individual database systems and a set of command tools; the information is accessed in executing the commands of the system, and then necessary controls are made automatically.

ORION, which is supported by Hitachi Co., Ltd., is a typical IRS with an inverted file, and is superior in text retrieval.

Table 1. HUCC Database Classification

Class		DBA	User
Private			
Private DB (PDB)		Researcher(s)	Closed
Public			
User	DB (UDB)	Researcher(s)	Open
Center	DB (CDB)	HUCC	Open

ADABAS, which is supported by Software-AG of Far East, Inc., is a relational type DBMS with an inverted file. It has some suitable features for scientific application: variety of data types and structures; convenience of language interfaces; flexibility of data restructuring; etc.

The design principle of the support system is to enable rapid implementation of a working prototype followed by its iterative refinement by satisfying the following requirements:

- Detailed knowledge about the usage of ORION and ADABAS should not be required.

- Global flow of procedures should be clear, and data definition, loading, updating, restructuring and reconstruction, etc., can be easily done with a TSS terminal.

- Tools for DDL description and data loading should be provided.

- However, the support system should not hinder the use of original functions of ORION and ADABAS.

These have been realized by hiding unnecessary information from users, automatic generation of utility jobs, and screen control of VDT terminal with default values.

Support System

Figure 1 shows the general organization of HUCC DB SUPPORT. It consists of the following parts loosely connected: COMDBS, DATASE and ISIS DB GUIDE.

COMDBS (Controlling Monitor of Database Systems) is a central part of HUCC DB SUPPORT. It consists of an ADABAS database DBAT (Database Administration Table) and four system components HUCC DB MONITOR, ORION SUPPORT, ADABAS SUPPORT, and HUCC DB GUIDE. DBAT stores dictionary information of individual database systems such as database name, IRS or DBMS used, DBA and co-DBAs, calling procedure, guidance information for end users, etc. The system components are activated by the entrance commands HDBA, ORION, ADABAS, and HDB, respectively.

HUCC DB MONITOR creates and updates a DBAT record for each database, by which the following controls are made: restricting utility job execution and use of a database to co-DBAs and users authorized; checking its status of either private or public; and in service or in maintenance, etc.

ORION SUPPORT and ADABAS SUPPORT are for database construction and maintenance with ORION and ADABAS, respectively. As shown later, each user command corresponds to a logical work unit in which required utility jobs are generated in a specific order. This makes the global flow of procedures clear.

However, DDL description and data loading are yet laborious. Thus, some tools have been developed for ORION: DDL generator and standard input processors. DDL generator generates/updates a complicated DDL description from the minimum input into a template VDT screen. Standard input processors have the following three types: conversational type, which generates a template screen from the DDL description for data input/output; segment type for loading data consisting of labels and data of fixed length; and MARC type for data in a MARC format. As for ADABAS, these kinds of tools have been supported by Software-AG Far East, Inc., in response to the requirements of HUCC.

6

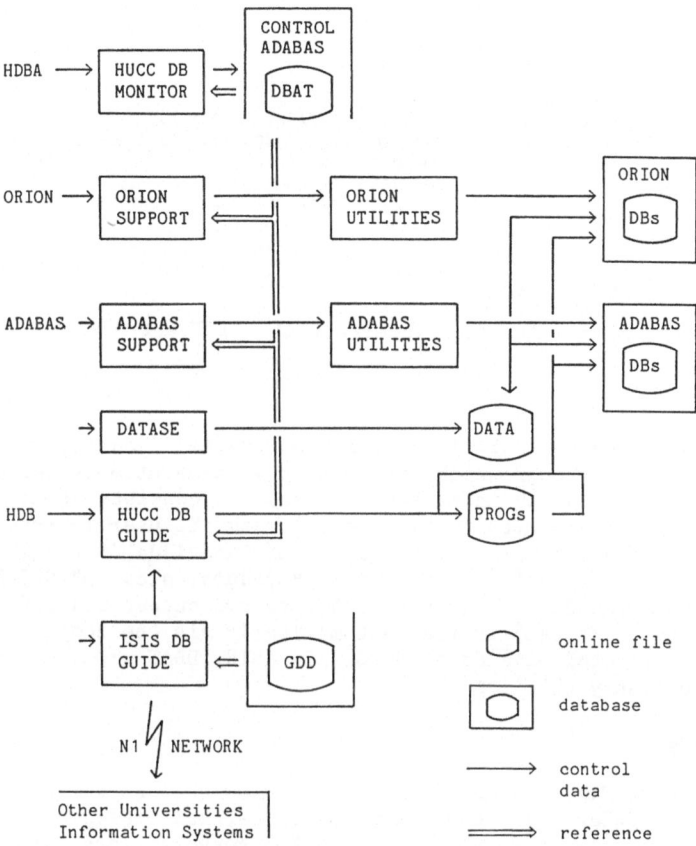

Figure 1. Organization of HUCC DB SUPPORT.

HUCC DB GUIDE is for end users of HUCC public databases. Their guidance information is available, which has been written in DBAT beforehand. If a system is assigned, its calling procedure is activated automatically.

It should be noted that COMDBS controls ADABAS operation, which needs a heavy overhead for managing many small databases. First, COMDBS activates and deactivates an ADABAS nucleus job for each database. The nucleus job for DBAT, which is called the control ADABAS at HUCC, is started automatically by Initial Program Loading (IPL). Second, it can deal with groups of different files as if each group were an independent database, which is called a logical database at HUCC.

DATASE (Data Storage and Edit System) is for creating and updating text data. It has the function of naive data definition and redefinition. Internal records are stored in a MARC format and then structural flexibility and high performance are achieved. Users can input data by each field or subfield in response to the prompting from the system. The stored data can be easily loaded into ORION and ADABAS. Counting word occurrence, KWIC indexing, data format transformation between MARC and segment types are also possible.

```
HDBA
DATABASE NAME ?ALGO
DBMS (ORION ADABAS) ?ORION
  :
ORION ALGO
        DEFINITION    1 HORALLOC   DATASET ALLOCATION
                      2 HORDDLG    DDL GENERATION (DESCRIPTION)
                      3 HORDDLC    DDL COMPILE
                      4 HORINIT    DATASET INITIALIZATION
        LOADING       5 HORINPUT   DATA INPUT AND UPDATING
                      6 HORLOAD    DATA LOADING AND INDEXING
        RETRIEVAL     7 HORRET     RETRIEVAL
        END           8 HOREND     END ORION COMMAND
WHICH COMMAND ?
```

Figure 2. User Interface of ORION SUPPORT.

ISIS (Integrated Scientific Information System) (Tanaka, 1983; Ishida, 1985) is a system through which information systems at many universities are viewed as a virtually integrated system. It consists of an ADABAS database, GDD (Global Database Dictionary), and its user interface DB GUIDE. GDD stores dictionary information of individual information systems such as guidance information, an access procedure, etc. DB GUIDE is equipped with commands for GDD retrieval, record output and information system calling. The call is made automatically via the computer network even if it is located outside of HUCC. In ISIS, DBAT may serve as a local Database Dictionary (LDD) of HUCC.

DBA Interface

Figure 2 and Figure 3 are examples of ORION SUPPORT and ADABAS SUPPORT, respectively. Underlines show the input parts, and messages from the system are simplified for saving space. Two conversational modes are available: system-initiative mode with the command menu for naive users and command-input mode for experienced users.

Each command tool has been implemented as an integral part of an integrated support environment, and users have only to accept, select, change or assign necessary parameters in response to the prompting from the system almost free from detailed syntax. This has made feasible the rapid implementation of a working prototype followed by its iterative refinement; first a prototype database system can be implemented by adopting default values, and then it is iteratively refined by testing behavior.


```
HDBA
DATABASE NAME ?ISIS
DBMS (ORION ADABAS) ?ADABAS
PASSWORD ?
MODE (PHYSICAL LOGICAL) ?LOGICAL
        AVAILABLE FILE RANGE IS 210-219
        END OF ADAFRM (TEMP STORAGE) C CODE = 0
  :
ADABAS ISIS
     1 HADAFDP    2 HADACMP    3 HADAFLD    4 HADADDM
     5 HADAMUP    6 HADACPL    7 HADADCU    8 HADAFDLT
     9 HADAULD   10 HADAFIX   11 HADAFLMD  12 HADADBMD
    13 HADAREP      HADAUSCR  15 HDBA      16 HADAEND
    17 HADANAT   18 HADASCR   19 HADASOAR  20 HADAGO
WHICH COMMAND ?
```

Figure 3. User Interface of ADABAS SUPPORT.

Prototyping has proved to be effective for developing interactive information systems (Blum and Houghton, Jr., 1982; Mason and Carey, 1983) in an environment where roles of user and developer are distinctly different. We have found that rapid implementation followed by iterative refinement may be effective also in an environment where users construct their database systems by themselves. It is not only because an iterative method is of least resistance for beginners, but also because a database system constructed in this way can be easily restructured or reconstructed.

The initial status of a database system is private. It becomes open to general users as a public database together with a calling procedure, if the status is changed to public.

TOWARD A MORE INTEGRATED SUPPORT ENVIRONMENT

To realize a more integrated support environment, the following three kinds of further augmentation will be required: integration of IRS and DBMS, management of programs; and knowledge-based instruction.

Integration of IRS and DBMS

IRSs and DBMSs now available have some specific advantages and disadvantages, respectively. The IRS is mainly for information retrieval of text data and not for data management. By contrast, the DBMS is mainly for management of formatted data and not for text data. The IRS usually lacks host language interface with Data Manipulation Language (DML) which is important in a research environment. These features hold true in the case of ORION and ADABAS.

However, these criterions are not decisively applied in actual selection of an IRS and a DBMS for construction of an information system. For example, HGEN (Iida, 1985), which is a typical scientific database system on genetic information, has adopted ORION for convenience of retrieval. But its interface between genetic codes and their analysis programs must have been implemented in an indirect manner via an external dataset. A document information system AIRIS (Maeda and Amano, 1986) is another example, which has applied ADABAS to text data.

Retrieval and management of formatted and textual data are often inseparable in scientific applications. Integration of the IRS and DBMS into an IRS/DBMS is needed.

Management of Programs

The IRS/DBMS could be applicable to the program management as well as data management, because programs are texts, i.e. informative texts for ordinary prescriptive texts (Zunde, 1984). We have intended to realize an integrated system for managing information on computational algorithms together with their source programs, and implemented a retrieval-oriented experimental system using ORION (Amano et al., 1984). However, programs have been stored in ordinary files outside of ORION due to some technical difficulties.

Note that programs are to be activated for processing data, though it does not mean that data are dependent on programs, and vice versa. Thus, a language interface equipped with the function of program execution is needed for further integration of data and programs in an information system.

Knowledge-Based Instruction

The more the coverage of an IRS or DBMS is extended, the more its user interface may be complicated. The IRS or DBMS should have knowledge about its usage in the system itself. That is to say, the interface should be realized as an expert system for database management rather than a simple self-documentation (Isomoto et al., 1983). For this purpose, present data dictionary systems are not necessarily sufficient (Allen, Loomis and Mannino, 1982).

In the case of HUCC DB SUPPORT, detailed instructions for constructing database systems have been embedded into the procedures of ORION and ADABAS SUPPORTs. They have reduced procedural errors greatly. However, if an error occurs, the system cannot diagnose its causes to yield a message for appropriate action for recovery. More flexibility will be achieved by including knowledge-based instructions.

CONCLUDING REMARKS

HUCC DB SUPPORT has been in practical use for several years, and produced a few tens of database systems. It is found that each tool should be implemented as an integral part of an integrated support environment and that rapid implementation of a working prototype followed by its iterative refinement is effective for research-oriented database systems; the former has made the latter feasible. To realize a more integrated support environment, three kinds of further augmentation will be required: integration of IRS and DBMS; management of programs; and knowledge-based instruction.

ACKNOWLEDGEMENTS

The authors wish to thank Ms. A. Mochida and T. Kaida (HUCC) for their support in system implementation, and Prof. M. Kitamura (Department of Engineering Science, Hokkaio University) for his careful reading and some comments on this manuscript.

REFERENCES

Allen, F. W., Loomis, M. E. S., and Mannino, M. V., 1982, "The Integrated Dictionary/Directory System", ACM Comput. Surv., 14, (2), pp. 245-286.

Amano, K., Chiba, M., Mochida, A., and Maeda, T., 1984, "An Approach Toward Integrated Algorithm Information System", Inform. Syst., 9, (3/4), pp. 197-206.

Amano, K., Kaida, T., and Mochida, A., 1986, "A Command Tool for Constructing Information Systems by Iterative Refinement", Trans. Inform. Process. Soci., Japan. (Submitted in Japanese.)

Amano, K., and Mochida, A., 1985, "A Supporting System for Effective Construction and Sharing of Scientific Databases by General Researchers", Inform. Process. Manage., (1985, in press).

Amano, K., Mochida, A., Kaida, T., Sugiura, T., and Sagara, T., 1984, "Support and Management for Construction of Scientific Databases by General Researchers", J. Inform. Process. Manage., 27, (9), pp. 787-799. (In Japanese.)

Blum, B. I., 1983, "An Information System for Developing Information Systems, <u>Proc. AFIPS National Comput. Conf.</u>, <u>52</u>, pp. 743–752.

Blum, B. I., and Houghton, Jr., R. C., 1982, "Rapid Prototyping of Information Management Systems, <u>ACM SISGSOFT Softw. Eng. Notes</u>, <u>7</u>, (5), pp. 35–38.

Iida, Y., 1985, "A Genetic Information Database (HGEN) and Its Usage", <u>HUCC Center News</u>, <u>17</u>, (2), pp. 66–81. (In Japanese.)

Ishida, H., ed., 1985, <u>Research on Widely Distributed Database Systems (with Different Machine Types) for Constituting an Integrated Scientific Information System</u>, Report for the Grant-in-aid for Developmental Scientific Research of the Ministry of Education, Science, and Culture in Japan (5888008). (In Japanese.)

Isomoto, Y., Ishiketa, T., Moriguchi, R., and Kakusho, O., 1983, "Knowledge Based DBMS for Nonprofessional Database Administrators", <u>Proc. IEEE COMPCOM Fall '83</u>, pp. 514–522.

Kubo, H., ed., 1981, <u>Research and Development of Scientific Database Systems at HUCC</u>, No. 1, Report for the Grant-in-aid for Developmental Scientific Research of the Ministry of Education, Science, and Culture in Japan (588018). (In Japanese.)

Kubo, H., ed., 1982, <u>Research and Development of Scientific Database Systems at HUCC</u>, No. 2, Report for the Grant-in-aid for Developmental Scientific Research of the Ministry of Education, Science, and Culture in Japan (588018). (In Japanese.)

Maeda, T., and Amano, K., 1986, "Document Information System in Scientific Research", in this volume.

Mason, R. E. A., and Carey, T. T., 1983, "Prototyping Interactive Information Systems, <u>Comm. ACM</u>, <u>26</u>, (5), pp. 347–354.

Mochida, A., Kaida, T., Sagara, T., and Amano, K., 1984, "A Management System for Practical Use of Databases at HUCC, <u>IPSJ WGSE</u>, <u>34</u>, pp. 55–60. (In Japanese.)

Okino, N., 1982, "On the Guiding Principle About Database Management at HUCC", <u>HUCC Center News</u>, <u>14</u>, (3), pp. 5–10. (In Japanese.)

Sugiura, T., Nagayama, T., Kaida, T., and Amano, K., 1982, "Outline of the Inter-university Computer Network (N-1 Network)", <u>HUCC Center News</u>, <u>14</u>, (1), pp. 11–23. (In Japanese.)

Tanaka, N., ed., 1983, <u>Research on the Service and Use of an Integrated Scientific Information System Composed of Widely Distributed Databases</u>, Report for the Grant-in-aid for Developmental Scientific Research of the Ministry of Education, Science, and Culture in Japan (57880007). (In Japanese.)

Wasserman, A. I., 1982, "Automated Tools in the Information System Development Environment", <u>Automated Tools for Information Systems Design</u>, Schneider, H.-J., and Wasserman, A. I., eds., IFIP North-Holland, Amsterdam, pp. 1–9.

Zunde, P., 1984, "Empirical Laws and Theories of Information and Software Sciences", <u>Inform. Process. Manage.</u>, <u>20</u>, (1-2), pp. 5–18.

AN AXIOMATIC APPROACH TO SOFTWARE COMPLEXITY MEASURES

P. Bollmann and H. Zuse

Technische Universität
Berlin, West Germany

Abstract: Basic concepts of an axiomatic approach to measuremesnt theory
are applied to software complexity measurement. In order to make valid
statements regarding such measurements, one has to know whether the appropriate scale is ordinal, interval or ratio. Criteria are derived for the
metric of McCabe on the basis of which one can determine which type of
scale it represents. It is shown that the proposed method can be applied
to other software complexity measures as well.

1. INTRODUCTION

The situation of the area of software complexity measures is characterized by two phenomena. First, there is an increasing number of proposed
measures and, second, there are no generally accepted criteria for determining what these measures really measure.

The result is a lot of contradicting measures of software complexity
and there is the problem of how to choose an appropriate measure. This
unsatisfactory situation has already been criticized by some authors
(Curtis, 1979). There have been some proposals to master these problems,
for example by introducing the measurement theory (Basili, 1980; Harrison
et al., 1982), in order to have an ordinal, an interval or a ratio scale.
But these retards have not been developed yet. Another approach deals with
software complexity measures from an axiomatic approach (Prather, 1984) by
defining criteria for software complexity measures.

In this paper an axiomatic approach is chosen and reflects the basic
concepts of measurement theory (Krantz et al., 1971). These concepts are
applied to the metric of McCabe (1976), but can be used with other measures
as well. A similar approach has already been developed for evaluation on
measures in information retrieval (Bollman, 1981; Bollman, 1984).

2. BASIC CONCEPTS OF MEASUREMENT THEORY

In this paragraph, basic concepts of measurement theory are introduced,
starting with the scale.

Definition 2.1: Let $A = (A, R_1, \ldots, R_n, o_1, \ldots, o_m)$ a relational system where A is a non-empty set of objects, R_i are ki-ary relations on A and o_j are closed binary operations on A. Let $B = (B, S_1, \ldots, S_n, o_1, \ldots, o_m)$ be a relational system where B is a non-empty set of formal objects (numbers, vectors, etc.), S_i are ki-ary relations on B and o_j are closed binary operations on B. Let $\mu: A \to B$ be a mapping. The triple (A, B, μ) is a scale iff for all i,j and for all $a, b, a_1, \ldots, a_{ki} \in A$.

$$R_i(a_1, \ldots, a_{ki}) \leftrightarrow S_i(\mu(a_1), \ldots, \mu(a_{ki}))$$

and

$$\mu(a \ o_j \ b) = \mu(a) \ o_j \ \mu(b).$$

The relational system A is often called the empirical or observed relational system. A is the set of objects being measured, R_i are the observed relations on A and o_j are observed binary operations. All this means that a measurement is a homomorphism. If we consider the situation for software complexity measures, we realize that the observed relational system is mostly neglected. Hence, software complexity measurement is mostly not a homomorphism. Therefore, it is not obvious what measures should measure and what they are really measuring. For that reason it is impossible to choose an appropriate measure.

But the problem still entails more consequences. If we have measurement values (for example, numbers), we want to make statements, to compare them, to compare arithmetic means and to make statistics. But not everything we can do with numbers is meaningful for measurement values. If two relational systems A and B are given there is, in general, not exactly one mapping μ. If we consider, for example, the measurement of length, we can do it in centimeters, meters, yards, miles, etc. In this case the following holds: if we have one measure we get all the others by multiplication by a positive constant and that all are measures. In the case of real scales, that is if B is the set of real numbers, Re, this leads to the well known classification of scales.

Definition 2.2: Let (A, B, μ) be a scale. A mapping g: $\mu(A) \to B$ is an admissable transformation iff $(A, B, g \circ \mu)$ is also a scale.

Definition 2.3: Let (A, B, μ) be a real scale. It is an ordinal scale, if every admissable transformation is a strictly increasing monotonic function and every strictly increasing monotonic function is an admissable transformation. In the case of a transformation $g(x) = \alpha x + \beta$, $\alpha > 0$, it is an interval scale and in the case of a function $g(x) = \alpha x$, $\alpha > 0$, it is a ratio scale.

Definition 2.4: A statement using measurement values is meaningful iff its truth value is invariant against admissable transformations.

The concept of meaningfulness will be illustrated by using examples of statements about software complexity measures.

Example 2.1 (Pressmann, 1982): Let P1 and P2 be two programs combined into one program P1 or P2 by the binary operation $\circ$ and let μ be a complexity measure. Pressmann demands that in this case the inequality

$$\mu(P1 \ \circ \ P2) \geq \mu(P1) + \mu(P2)$$

should hold.

This statement is not meaningful if we have an interval scale. Indeed, let $g(x)=\alpha x+\beta$, $\alpha>0$, be an arbitrary affine transformation. Then

$$\mu(P1 \circ P2)+\beta \geq \mu(P1)+\beta+\alpha\mu(P2)+\beta$$

may be wrong when

$$\mu(P1 \circ P2) \geq \mu(P1)+\mu(P2)$$

is true. It can be seen that the given inequality is true if we have a ratio scale.

Example 2.2 (Prather, 1984): In the paper of Prather, several axioms are introduced. Let Si be structured processes and p some predicate. The following axioms are discussed:

    i) $\mu(\text{begin},S1,\ldots,Sn,\text{ end}) \geq \Sigma\mu(Si)$

    ii) $2(\mu(S1)+\mu(S2)) \geq \mu(\text{if p then S1 else S2}) > \mu(S1)+\mu(S2)$

    iii) $2\mu(S1) \geq \mu(\text{while p do S1}) > \mu(S1)$

All these statements are not meaningful for an ordinal or interval scale, but they are meaningful for a ratio scale. These examples make obvious that very often strong measurement theoretics assumptions are made implictly. Therefore, it is necessary to have criteria regarding which type of scale is used. This, however, requires a measurement theoretic investigation of software complexity measures. To this end we will consider our observed objects, relations and binary operations.

In this paper we assume programs to be represented by their control flow graphs (McCabe, 1976), hence the set of observed objects P is the set of all control flow graphs.

The relation $\gtrsim$ means "not less complex than", i.e. $P \gtrsim P'$ means that P is not less complex than P'. We assume the following axioms to hold for $\gtrsim$ and for all $P,P',P''\epsilon P$.

    i) $P \gtrsim P$ (reflexivity)

    ii) $P \gtrsim P'$ and $P' \gtrsim P'' = P \gtrsim P''$ (transitivity)

    iii) $P \gtrsim P'$ or $P' \gtrsim P$ (completeness)

Hence $\gtrsim$ is assumed to be a weak order. If $P \gtrsim P'$ and $P' \gtrsim P$ holds, we will write $P \sim P'$ and call P and P' equivalent and if $P \gtrsim P'$ holds but not $P \sim P'$, we will write $P \cdot> P'$ and call P more complex than P'.

We will call $\gtrsim$ a viewpoint (Cherniavsky and Lakhuty, 1971) of complexity. A person, for example, may have a viewpoint of complexity. With every complexity measure, a viewpoint of complexity is connected. Choosing an appropriate measure means that it has the same viewpoint as the person or institution that performs the measurement.

As formal objects we have the real number Re with the relation $\geq$. If we restrict ourselves to ordinal scales a complexity scale is a triple $((P,\gtrsim), (\text{Re},\geq),\mu)$ with $\mu: P \to \text{Re}$ and for all $P,P' \in P$

$$P \gtrsim P' \leftrightarrow \mu(P) \geq \mu(P').$$

To get an interval scale the relational system has to be extended.

There are several possibilities, for example by using the concept of an algebraic difference structure (Krantz et al., 1971).

Definition 2.5: Let P be a non-empty set and $*\geq$ a quaternary relation on $P \times P$. $(P \times P, *\geq)$ is an algebraic difference structure iff for all P1,...,P6 $\in P$ and all sequences P1',P2',...,$\in P$ the following holds.

    i) $(P \times P, *\geq)$ is a weak order

    ii)   If (P1,P2) $*\geq$ (P3,P4) then (P4,P3) $*\geq$ (P2,P1)

    iii)   If (P1,P2) $*\geq$ (P3,P4) and (P2,P5) $*\geq$ (P4,P6) then (P1,P5) $*\geq$ (P3,P6).

    iv)   If (P1,P2) $*\geq$ (P3,P4) $*\geq$ (P1,P1) then there exists Q1,Q2 $\in P$, such that (P1,Q1) $*\sim$ (P3,P4) $*\sim$ (Q2,P2)

    v)   Every strictly bounded standard sequence P1',P2',... is finite. (P1',P2', ... is a strictly bounded standard sequence iff (P'i+1,P'i) $*\sim$ (P'2,P'1) for every i and not (P'2,P'1) $*\sim$ (P'1,P'1) and there exists Q1, Q2 $\in P$ such that (Q1,Q2) $*>$ (P'i,P'1) $*>$ (Q2,Q1)).

The following theorem holds (Krantz et al., 1971).

THEOREM: If $(P \times P, *\geq)$ is an algebraic difference structure then there exists a real valued function μ: $P \to$ Re such that for all P1,P2,P3,P4

    (P1,P2) $*\geq$ (P3,P4) iff $\mu(P1)-\mu(P2) \geq \mu(P3)- (P4)$.

    $g(x) = \alpha x + \beta, \quad \alpha > 0$

are all admissable transformations.

Given P1,P2,P3,P4, (P1,P2) $*\geq$ (P3,P4) means that the difference in complexity between P1 and P2 is not smaller than the difference between P3 and P4. In the next paragraph, for the metric of McCabe, a method will be given to describe these differences.

In order to obtain a ratio scale, the relational system of the ordinal scale has to be extended. To this end a binary operation is added (Krantz et al., 1971).

Definition 2.6: Let P be a non-empty set, $\gtrsim$ a binary relation on P and o a closed binary operation on P. The relational system $(P, \gtrsim, o)$ is a closed extensive structure if the following axioms hold for all P1,P2,P3,P4 $\in P$:

    i) $(P, \gtrsim)$ is a weak order

    ii)   P1 o (P2 o P3)~(P1 o P2) o P3 (weak associativity)

    iii)   P1 $\gtrsim$ P2 iff P1 o P3 $\gtrsim$ P2 o P3 iff P3 o P1 $\gtrsim$ P3 o P2 (monotonicity)

    iv)   If P1 $\gtrsim$ P2 then for any P3,P4 there exists a natural number k, such that

$$P1 \; o...o \; P1 \; o \; P3 \geq P2 \; o......o \; P2 \; o \; P4$$

k-times   k-times

THEOREM: Let $(P, \geq, o)$ be a closed extensive structure. Then there exists a mapping $\mu: P \to \text{Re}$ such that

    i) $P1 \geq P2 \leftrightarrow \mu(P1) \geq \mu(P2)$

    ii) $\mu(P1 \; o \; P2) = \mu(P1) + \mu(P2)$

for all $P1, P2 \in P$. μ is a unique up to multiplication with a positive real constant.

The problem remains how to define a binary operation between program control flow graphs. In this paper a sequential concatenation is applied which was already defined in Zuse (1985). Two control flow graphs P1 and P2 are concatenated by connecting P1 with P2 by a vertice after deletion of the end node of P1 and the start node of P2 (See Figure 1).

Of course there are other possibilities to define a binary operation. Further proposals are described in Zuse (1985).

In the following paragraph, the measuremeant theoretic approach is illustrated and a criterion is given whether the metric of McCabe may be used as ordinal, interval, or ratio scale.

3. CHARACTERIZATION OF THE METRIC OF MCCABE

3.1 The Metric of McCabe as an Ordinal Scale

The metric of McCabe is one of the most discussed software complexity measures. For a program control flow graph (McCabe, 1976) it is defined as

$$\mu(P) = V - N + 2$$

where V is the number of vertices and N is the number of nodes of P.

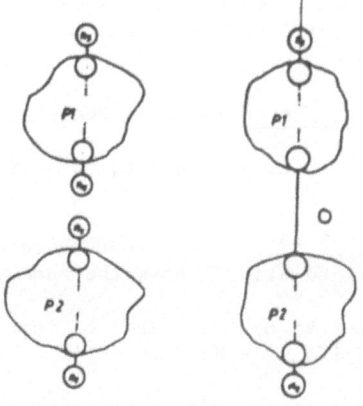

Figure 1. Concatenation P1 o P2 of P1 and P2.

To describe the metric of McCabe as an ordinal scale the notion of elementary viewpoint will be introduced.

Definition 3.1: Let $\succeq$ be a viewpoint. The binary relation $\succeq_e$ is an <u>elementary viewpoint</u> of $\succeq$ iff for all $P1,P2 \in P$ the following holds:

   i) $P1 \succeq_e P2 \rightarrow P1 \succeq P2$

   ii) $P1 \sim_e P2 \rightarrow P1 \sim P2$

For the metric of McCabe the following three elementary viewpoints are defined:

e_1: If P1 results from P2 whenever a node with a vertex is inserted in P2, then $P1 \sim_{e_1} P2$. Else P1 and P2 are not comparable with respect to e_1.

e_2: If P1 results from P2 whenever a vertex is inserted in P2, then $P1 \succeq_{e_2} P2$. Else P1 and P2 are not comparable with respect to e_2.

e_3: If P1 results from P2 by shifting a vertex then $P1 \sim_{e_3} P2$. Else P1 and P2 are not comparable with respect to e_3.

The elementary viewpoints e_1 and e_2 were already given by McCabe (1976). These three given elementary viewpoints can now be used to characterize the metric of McCabe.

THEOREM 3.1: Every mapping $\mu: P \rightarrow Re$ such that

   i) $P1 \sim_{e_1} P2 \rightarrow \mu(P1) = \mu(P2)$

   ii) $P1 \succ_{e_2} P2 \rightarrow \mu(P1) \rightarrow \mu(P2)$

   iii) $P1 \sim_{e_3} P2 \rightarrow \mu(P1) = \mu(P2)$

for all $P1,P2 \in P$, is a strictly monotonic increasing function of the metric of McCabe.

For the proof one has to show that the viewpoint of the metric of McCabe is the reflexive and transitive closure of the union of e_1, e_2, and e_3. The proof is contained in Zuse (1985). A similar theorem applied to evaluation measures in IRS can be found in Bollman and Cherniavsky (1981). A consequence of the theorem is that the metric of McCabe may be used as an ordinal scale by someone iff he agrees to the given elementary viewpoints, else it may not.

3.2   The Metric of McCabe as an Interval Scale

First a quaternary relation $*\succeq$ has to be defined on P. The following lemma is used.

Lemma 3.1: Let $P1,P2,P3,P4 \in P$. Then there exists $P'i$, $i=1,...,4$, such that $Pi \sim P'i$ and all $P'i$ have the same number of nodes.

Definition 3.2: Let Vi be the number of vertices of $P'i$, then $\overline{(P1,P2)} *\succeq \overline{(P3,P4)}$ iff $V1 - V2 \geq V3 - V4$.

It can be shown that $*\succeq$ is independent of the choice of the $P'i$. $*\succeq$ satisfies the axioms of the algebraic difference structure. Hence the metric of McCabe such that

$$(P1,P2) \; *\geq \; (P3,P4) \text{ iff } \mu(P1) - \mu(P2) \geq \mu(P3) - \mu(P4)$$

holds, may be used as an interval scale iff for a control flow graph with the same number of nodes the difference in the number of vertices is the only factor influencing the difference in complexity. Equivalent to this result is, that inserting a vertex to a program control graph always yields the same increase in complexity no matter how many vertices have already been inserted.

3.3 The Metric of McCabe as Ratio Scale

In this case it can be shown that $(P,\geq,o)$ where $\geq$ is the viewpoint of the metric of McCabe fulfills the axioms of a closed extensive structure. But the metric of McCabe does not fulfill additivity. From the theorem on closed extensive structures, we know that there exists a measure which is a strictly monotonic increasing function of the metric of McCabe which is additive. This function is $\mu-1$ where μ is the metric of McCabe. $\mu-1$ has already been used as an alternative to the metric of McCabe and for structured programs control graphs, it is the number of decision nodes. We may conclude that if someone has the same viewpoint as the metric of McCabe and concatenates control flow graphs in the above described way, he may use $\mu-1$ as a ratio scale.

4. CONCLUSIONS

In order to make statements with measurement values it is important to know whether the scale may be used as ordinal, interval, or ratio scale. For the metric of McCabe, criteria has been given to decide which type of scale it represents. This method can be applied to other software complexity measures as well. It can be seen that a measure is not an ordinal, interval, or a ratio scale per se, it depends on the situation in which it is used.

REFERENCES

Basili, V., 1980, Tutorial on Models and Metrics for Software Management and Engineering, Computer Society Press, Catalog No. EHO-167-7, COMSAC 80.

Bollmann, P., and Chierniavsky, V., 1981, "Measurement-Theoretical Investigation of the MZ-Metric", Information Retrieval Research, Oddy, R. N., Robertson, S. E., van Rijsbergen, C. J., and Williams, P. W., eds., Butterworth.

Bollman, P., 1984, "Two Axioms for Evaluation Measures in Information Retrieval", Research and Development in Information Retrieval, ACM, British Computer Society Workshop Series, pp. 233-246.

Cherniavsky, V., and Lakhuty, D. G., 1971, "On the Problem of Retrieval System Evaluation", Nauchno -Tekhnicheskaja Informacija, 2, (9). (In Russian.)

Curtis, B., 1979, "In Search of Software Complexity", Workshop on Quantitative Software Models for Reliability, pp. 95-106.

Harrison, W., Magel, K., Klucszny, R., and DeKock, A., 1982, "Applying Software Complexity Metrics to Maintenance", Computer, 15, (9), pp. 65-79.

Krantz, D. H., Luce, R. D., Suppes, P., and Tversky, A., 1971, <u>Foundations of Measurement</u>, Academic Press.

McCabe, T. J., 1976, "A Complexity Measure", <u>IEEE Transactions on Software Engineering</u>, <u>SE-2</u>, (4), December, pp. 308-320.

Prather, R. E., 1984, "An Axiomatic Theory of Software Complexity Measure", <u>The Computer Journal</u>, <u>27</u>, (4).

Pressmann, R. S., 1982, <u>Software Engineering: A Practitioner's Approach</u> McGraw Hill.

Zuse, H., 1985, <u>Messtheoretische Analyse von statischen Softwarekomplexitätsmassen</u>, TU-Berlin, Fachbereich Informatik. Dissertation im FB 20 (Ph.D. Thesis).

SYSTEMS DESIGN AND THE PSYCHOLOGY OF COMPLEX SYSTEMS

Berndt Brehmer

Uppsala University
Department of Psychology
Sweden

Abstract: This paper reviews the results from studies concerned with how
people learn to control complex dynamic systems. The results suggest that
people have considerable problems with such systems, especially when there
are delays in the system and when the system has a causal net structure.
The results also show some typical behavior tendencies in such systems that
create vicious circles that lead to failure to control the system. It is
concluded that systems designers cannot rely on operators to develop the
mental models they need to control complex systems, and that these make
important suggestions about what kinds of aids are needed to help the
operators learn the systems better.

INTRODUCTION

There is general agreement that system designers need to consider the
characteristics of those who have to operate the systems they design. This
is often expressed as the need to incorporate a model of the operator, or
user, in the design of the system.

I have no quarrel with those who think that systems will be better if
their designers consider the characteristics of the operators. But, I
think that the position that all will be well if we only had an adequate
model of the operator is misleading. This is because it reduces the
question of the relation between the man and the system to a problem of
controlling the behavior of the operator. However, from the operator's
point of view, the problem is quite the opposite: it is to control the
system, rather than to be controlled by the system.

To control the system, the operator needs a model of the system (Conant
and Ashby, 1970). A fundamental question about any system, therefore, is
whether it allows the operator to develop a good model of that system.

Technological systems are generally not designed with this in mind.
Most manuals tend to be written from the designer's point of view, and
ignore that the operator and designer have fundamentally different perspectives on the system (Rasmussen, 1985). The operator, therefore, is often
left no other alternative but to develop his own model on the basis of his
experience with the system.

To develop a model of a technological system is, however, not a very easy task. First, such systems tend to be opaque from the operator's point of view. Second, the operator often has no direct contact with the system (Brehmer, 1986). Thus, on the input side, the operator usually only gets some representation of the system, perhaps via a VDU, but he has no direct insight into how this representation is generated. On the output side, he communicates with the system via some device, such as a keyboard, but there is no direct relation between the operator's actual actions and what happens in the system, and he has no insight into how his keystrokes produce whatever effects they produce in the system.

The operator thus has to develop a model of the system from representations that may not have been designed to help him develop such a model. A fundamental question, therefore, is whether people are able to develop models and learn to control systems under these circumstances.

There is surprisingly little research on the problem of how people learn to control systems. There is certainly no dearth of studies of operators of specific systems, usually control room operators in nuclear power plants, or users of word processors. The results of the studies tend to be specific to the systems employed, however, and they have yielded little general knowledge about how people learn to control systems. Studies in cognitive psychology are of little help here, first because they tend to be concerned with very simple systems, and second, because they take a fundamentally different perspective: they are concerned with how the task controls the behavior of the person, rather than with how the person learns to control the task.

Recently, however, there has been some first attempts to study how people learn to operate complex systems. At present, this seems to be somewhat of a European speciality with research starting more or less independently in Bamberg (Dörner et al., 1983), Hamberg (Kluwe et al., 1984), Oxford (Broadbent and Aston, 1978), and Uppsala (Brehmer and Allard, 1985), but there are also some beginnings in the US (Kleinmuntz, 1985; Kleinmuntz and Thomas, 1985). All of these researchers employ complex, dynamic tasks. The actual tasks differ, however. Dörner and his associates dealt with a task which simulates the problems facing a mayor who has to run a town for a ten year period; Kluwe and his colleagues with an abstract task which requires the subjects to learn to control a system with 15 variables; Broadbent with how people learn to control a computer simulation of the British economy; Brehmer and Allard with fire fighting; and Kleinmuntz with medical diagnosis and treatment. In this paper, I will review some of the results of this research. I will concentrate on the Uppsala approach, and discuss the results of other researchers from the point of view of this approach.

THE UPPSALA APPROACH TO COMPLEX SYSTEMS: DYNAMIC DECISION MAKING

The best way to introduce our approach is to describe the general features of the experimental situation which we have been using. It is illustrated in Figure 1. The task is that facing a fire chief charged with the problem of putting out forest fires. He receives information about the fires from a spotter plane, which reports via an information system. He can fight the fires by issuing commands via a command system to his fire fighting units (FFUs), telling them where to go by giving them map references. The FFUs will then report back to him via the information system about their activities and their position. The subjects in our experiments receive all their information from a visual display, where the reports from the spotter plane and the FFUs' reports about their positions are given on a map, and the reports about the activities of the FFUs are given in a

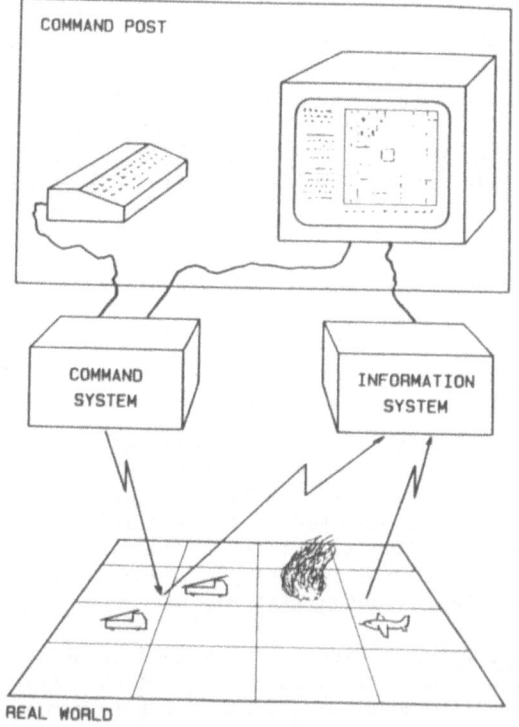

Figure 1. General Characteristics of the Situation Used in the DESSY Experiments.

table. Another table serves to remind the subjects of the commands they have issued. In addition, there is a weather report, which gives the general weather conditions, and the direction of the wind.

This situation has all the characteristics of a dynamic problem (Brehmer and Allard, 1985):

1. It requires a series of decisions.

2. The environment changes both spontaneously (the fire spreads) and, as a consequence of the decision maker's actions, the fire fighting units move around and the fire is or is not extinguished.

3. The time element is critical; it is not enough to make the correct decisions and to make them in the correct order, they also have to be made at the correct moment in time.

Note that the experimental situation also has all the characteristics of a modern technological system: the subject has no direct contact with the system, he only gets information via a representation of the system on the CRT, and he can only affect the system indirectly via the keyboard. The system is opaque; the subject does not see how the information is generated, or how his actions actually affect the fires he is trying to control.

23

A dynamic problem of this sort is interesting also because the standard normative theories for decision making do not apply (Brehmer and Allard, 1985); the models of the task embodied in these theories simply do not fit this kind of task. It is not possible to compute the correct course of action. This can only be found from a model of the system and, before the operators have developed such models, they will not be able to control the system. The research problem, therefore, is whether or not people are able to develop good mental models of this and similar tasks.

To study this problem, we have developed DESSY (Brehmer and Allard, 1985).

DESSY

DESSY (Dynamic Environment Simulation SYstem) is an interactive computer program which enables us to simulate any first order dynamic system at a level of complexity limited only by the capacity of the computer used for the experiments. DESSY enables us to vary all of the fundamental characteristics of a dynamic system. It is, of course, not self evident which these characteristics are, and the list is somewhat arbitrary. In our work, we have found the following list useful.

1. Complexity, which refers to the number of goals, the number of processes that must be controlled, and the number and characteristics of the means available for this control. In the DESSY experiments, the subjects have two goals: to prevent the fire from reaching the base where they are supposed to be located, and to put out the fire as soon as possible (with the obvious priority ordering). The number of processes to be controlled refers to the number of fires to be put out, and in most experiments, the number of fires has been two. The number of means refers to the number of FFUs, which is eight in most DESSY experiments. These units may differ with respect to efficiency, to further increase complexity.

2. Delays may occur anywhere in the system; in the information system as well as in the command system. It may make some difference to the operator where the delays occur, but generally, he cannot know the location of the delays. All he can do is to note that information, that his orders have been carried out will reach him after some delay.

3. The relation between the characteristics of the process to be controlled and the characteristics of the means is one of the most important aspects of a dynamic task for choosing the appropriate strategy for the task. In the case of DESSY, the process to be controlled, i.e., the fire, spreads exponentially. The fire fighting units, on the other hand, can only put out fire in one location at a time, so they follow a linear process. The problem facing the subjects in the DESSY experiments, then, is that of finding a way to control an exponential process with a linear one. The general requirement that such a strategy must meet can be formulated abstractly in the following terms: the subject must use his FFUs in such a way that the function relating the area extinguished by the FFUs to time intercepts the function relating the spread of the fire to time before the slope of the latter function exceeds that of the former function. Such an abstract formulation is not of very much help in choosing the actual commands, however.

These relations are, of course, a special case, but not necessarily uncommon. Exponential processes are quite frequent.
Indeed, all processes that involve something spreading over an
area tend to be exponential, such as, for example the process by
which weeds will spread in one's garden. However, there are also
other kinds of processes. For example, in the medical task used
by Kleinmuntz (1985), the disease follows a linear function, the
patient's state of health decreases linearly over time. The cure
follows a positive linear function, so here the strategic problem
is that of intercepting a negative linear process with a positive
linear process before the negative linear process has reached a
point of no return.

4. Rate of change is an important aspect both of the process to be
    controlled and the means. A dynamic task may be very fast, such
    as that of controlling a jet fighter in a low level attack, or
    very slow, such as that of controlling the economy of a country,
    with all sorts of intermediate cases, such as fire fighting.

    Presumably, the rate of change is important for determining
    whether or not the dynamics of the system are actually detected by
    the operator. It may be very much easier to detect the dynamics
    of a fast system than those of a slow system. A slow system may,
    therefore, be mistaken for a static system, and this may lead to
    inappropriate control strategies.

5. Delegation of decision making power. One of the principal means
    for handling the complexity of a real system is to impose a hier-
    archical organization. This makes it possible to delegate com-
    mand. This is the general principle according to which military
    command systems function.

    In DESSY, there are two levels of control: centralized control,
    where the fire chief assumes total responsibility, and decentral-
    ized control, where some decision making power is delegated to the
    FFU commanders. Centralized command is achieved by ordering the
    fire fighting units to go to a certain map reference, and start
    fighting the fire once they have reached their destination. De-
    centralized control involves ordering the units to go towards a
    certain destination and to starting fighting fire as soon as they
    encounter it.

    Decentralized control is useful when the subject is unable to
    predict the location of the fire, either because he is unable to
    predict the exponential spread of the fire or because there are
    delays in the system which make the subjects' information
    outdated.

6. Feedback quality. Feedback may not only be delayed, it can also
    have low quality, i.e., it may not give very accurate information
    about the state of the system. This may be because the informa-
    tion system has been designed to give only certain kinds of infor-
    mation or because the lower levels in the system do not want to
    feed back accurate information.

7. Probabilism or determinism. The systems modelled in experiments
    with complex systems may be modelled probabilistically or deter-
    ministically. DESSY is totally deterministic, as are the systems
    employed by Kluwe, Dörner and Broadbent. Kleinmuntz (1985), on
    the other hand, uses a probabilistic model, which, of course,
    makes sense in a medical context.

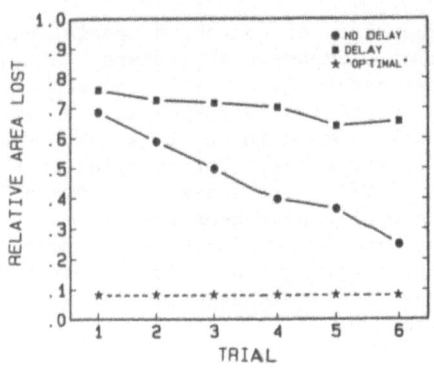

Figure 2. Typical experiments on the effects of
feedback delays on learning to control
the fires. The dependent variable is
the proportion of the total area that has
been burnt down at the end of a trial.
(Data from Brehmer and Allard, 1985.)

DESSY EXPERIMENTS

The details of the experiments are not important in the present context, and for those, I refer you to the original papers (Brehmer and
Allard, 1985, 1986). Let me just mention that the purpose of the experiments have been to study how people learn to control a complex dynamic
system rather than to study fire fighting as such, so the subjects in our
experiments have been students without any fire fighting experience rather
than professional fire fighters.

The results show that after having spent two hours a day with DESSY for
four days, the subjects' control over the system improves, but only if
there are no delays in the system. If there are even minimal delays, the
subjects' control over the system does not improve. This is somewhat dis-
concerting, since delays are probably a more common case than that of
immediate feedback. Figure 2 shows some typical results.

The results give no indication that the subjects actually develop predictive models of the system. This is shown by the fact that they persist
in sending the FFUs to the location of the fire at the time when the command is issued, rather than to the position where the fire will be when the
FFU gets there. Instead of a predictive model, the subjects seem to learn
some general heuristics, such as that they have to respond massively and
quickly, by sending as many FFUs as possible to a fire as soon as possible.
This may, of course, be seen as a primitive model of the relation between
the characteristics of the fire and the characteristics of the fire
fighting units.

Verbal protocols taken during the course of learning seem to yield
little information. This may be because the subjects simply do not have
the time to give very useful verbal reports or because the processes
involved are not of a kind that lends itself to verbalization.

THE HAMBURG APPROACH: CONTROL OF A COMPLEX ABSTRACT SYSTEM

In the experiments by Kluwe and his associates (Kluwe et al., 1984), subjects have to learn to control a system with 15 variables. For each variable, there is a target level, and the subject must learn to keep the 15 variables at their target level. The values of the variables change spontaneously over time, so the subjects must learn to predict the amount of change for each variable, and to compensate for the change by giving a series commands about quantities to add or subtract from the variables. On each trial, the subject may see only eight of the 15 variables, but he can influence all of them.

The results from the experiments by Kluwe and his associates show that the subjects learn to control the system over a practice period of 200 trials (Kluwe et al, 1984). The learning process is interpreted as a chunking process. The principle basis for the chunking process seems to be the magnitude of the compensation needed for the variables. Variables needing large compensations are detected first and chunked together. Subjects have greater problems learning to control variables that need positive compensations, i.e., variables to which they must add some value, than variables that need negative compensations, i.e., variables from which they need to subtract some value. This may be related to the finding in other contexts that relations with a positive slope are easier to learn than relations with a negative slope (Brehmer, 1974).

If the task is given the structure of a causal net, i.e., a structure where one variable influences another variable (that is, there are side effects), it becomes very much harder to learn than if the task follows a causal chain structure, i.e., a structure such that there are no side effects (Kluwe and Reimann, 1983).

Finally, Kluwe and Reimann (1983) found that asking the subjects to verbalize slows down the learning process. In these experiments this is hardly because the subjects do not have the time to verbalize; there is ample time for that. Instead, these results may mean that the knowledge acquired in these tasks is not primarily of a verbal nature. However, at the end of a 200 trial period, the subjects are able to give retrospective verbal accounts of what they have learned about the system, so it seems that although what is learned may not be verbalizable at first, the subjects later learn something about the system that they can verbalize. The actual nature of this learning process is obscure at the present time, however.

THE OXFORD APPROACH: LEARNING TO CONTROL A MODEL OF THE BRITISH ECONOMY

Broadbent and Aston (1978) studied subjects' ability to learn to control a computer model of the British economy. This is a complex task which involves a number of relations of different kinds. The results indicated that the subjects were able to improve their control over time, but that they were unable to verbalize what they had learned. Referring to Kluwe's results, this may simply mean that there was not enough practice in the Broadbent and Aston experiment.

THE BAMBERG APPROACH: BEING THE MAYOR OF A SMALL TOWN

Dörner's Lohausen task (Dörner et al., 1983) requires the subjects to learn to control a town in the role of mayor over a ten year period. This is a very complex task, which involves a number of different goals and a greater number of different relations. A striking feature of the results in the Lohausen experiments is that there are wide interindividual differences (as indeed there are also in the Uppsala and in the Hamburg experiments). Dörner (1980) has analyzed the behavior of subjects who fail to learn to control Lohausen in great detail. Dörner does not interpret these results as reflecting any underlying personality characteristics of the subjects who fail, but rather as indications of what may happen to anybody who starts to lose control of a system.

Dörner (1980) points out a number of primary mistakes that people are prone to make in complex systems. Among these are the following:

1. <u>Insufficient consideration of the time aspects of the task.</u> This refers to a tendency to ignore the dynamic aspects of the task, i.e., subjects ignore that the present state of the system is temporary, and that it has a history that should enable the subject to predict what will happen next. This is similar to the result in the DESSY experiments that subjects do not develop predictive models, but keep sending the fire fighting units to the destination where the fire is at the time when the command is issued.

2. <u>Inability to deal with exponential relations.</u> This is evident also in the DESSY experiments, but it should be pointed out, that so far we have no experiments that compare subjects' ability to deal with different kinds of relations. Therefore, we do not know the extent to which their problems are due to the exponential character of the relations compared to other aspects of the task. It may well be that the exponential character would be less of a problem if the task was simpler, e.g., if it only involved one process and one control variable. Results by Mackinnon and Wearing (1985) indicate that subjects are able to learn to control simple systems with some success.

3. <u>Thinking in causal series, rather than in causal nets.</u> This simply means that subjects have problems in taking side effects into account. Dörner's findings here agree with those of Kluwe and Reimann (1983), who found that subjects did not learn to control systems with a causal net structure to the same degree as they learned to control systems that involved only causal chains.

These three primary mistakes, as Dörner calls them, thus seem to have some generality.

Dörner (1980) also provides an interesting analysis of the actual behavior of subjects who do not learn to control the system.

Such subjects, Dörner maintains, are characterized by <u>thematic vagabonding,</u> i.e., they change their focus of interest from one control variable to another rapidly, rather than concentrate upon one strategy and try to make that strategy work, <u>encystment,</u> i.e., they concentrate on small details of the task, and lose the overall picture, they become <u>less and less willing to make decisions,</u> they tend to <u>delegate tasks that cannot be delegated,</u> and they <u>tend to blame others.</u>

Encystment is observed also in the DESSY experiments. Subjects in these experiments will concentrate upon one FFU and one fire, and ignore other units that could be used, and to do nothing about other fires. The other tendencies do not quite apply, but there is one finding in the DESSY experiments that is reminiscent of the tendency to blame others for one's failures, and this is that the subjects tend to interpret all delays in the system as evidence that the fire fighting units simply do not obey their commands, rather than as evidence of unavoidable delays in the information system (Brehmer and Allard, 1985). In the DESSY experiments, subjects tend not to delegate, but rather to assume more and more centralized control.

However, the DESSY experiments differ from those of Dörner et al., that in the DESSY experiments, delegation is the best policy, whereas in the Dörner experiments, subjects delegate tasks that they should have performed themselves. However, delegation in a hierarchical system obviously causes problems.

When total failure is imminent, the subjects may respond by an intellectual emergency reaction (Dörner, 1980). This means that the cognitive systems are organized to react quickly. Quick response is, of course, impossible if the intellectual level is too high, so the intellectual emergency reaction leads to more primitive cognitive functioning with a reduction in the level of reflection, reduction of the number of plans, increased stereotyping of reactions, decreased control over the execution of implementation of one's plans, increased willingness to take risks, and increased willingness to violate rules and regulations. Subjects suffering from the intellectual emergency reactions are, of course, more likely to destroy the system than to achieve control.

THE AUSTIN APPROACH: DIAGNOSIS AND TREATMENT OF PATIENTS

The subjects' task in Kleinmuntz's experiments (Kleinmuntz, 1985; Kleinmuntz and Thomas, 1985) is to diagnose a patient's disease and to pescribe a treatment. The patient's state of health decreases linearly over time. To find the state of the patient, the subjects must ask for tests. On the basis of the results of these tests, they may then prescribe treatments. These treatments may cure the patient,, which means that the patient's state of health will start increasing linearly. However, treatment may also have fatal side effects, i.e., the task requires thinking in terms of a causal net rather than in terms of a causal chain. Kleinmuntz's task differs from the other tasks employed in this kind of research in that there is random error in the task.

To make accurate diagnoses in Kleinmuntz's task, it is mainly important to find the relevant symptoms, it is not as important how the system information is actually used (Kleinmuntz, 1985). However, diagnosis is generally not as important as finding treatments. Because the patient is getting worse over time, treatments have to be found quickly and it may be more useful to select treatments at random than to try to diagnose the patients. A finding in these experiments is that subjects generally spend too much time diagnosing and too little time treating (Kleinmuntz and Thomas, 1985), i.e., a finding opposite to that of Dörner's, who found his subjects too willing to act, and unwilling to think, as conditions got worse.

Predictably, the subjects performed less well when the patient started out in a low state of health, i.e., when the subjects had little time to choose a treatment.

Introducing side effects also led to worse performance, as we would expect from the results of Dörner (1980) and Kluwe and Reimann (1983), who also found that subjects have problems thinking in terms of causal nets.

GENERAL CONCLUSIONS

As mentioned in the introduction, research on complex dynamic systems is only in its infancy. Yet, some interesting and generalizable results seem to emerge. These results give some preliminary indications of the problems people have in learning to control complex systems.

Some of these problems are tied to task characteristics: certain kinds

of tasks are simply harder to learn than other tasks. Other problems have
to do with behavioral characteristics, i.e., typical modes of behavior
under failure.

TASK CHARACTERISTICS

The most striking finding to emerge from the studies reviewed above is
that people have considerable problems with time dependent processes. The
subjects do not seem to use the historical information available to form
the notion that the present state of the system is part of a lawful change.
Instead, they use only the information at hand in deciding what to do.
That is, the subjects do not seem to develop predictive mental models of
dynamic aspects of these tasks, they only learn to react by means of general heuristics. This seems to be true in the DESSY experiments, as well
as in Dörner's experiments and in those of Kluwe and his associates (Kluwe,
personal communication). If the processes are exponential, the failures to
develop mental models becomes highly visible, but we do not know the extent
to which the actual characteristics of the processes are important; there
are no systematic studies on this problem.

Feedback delays have truly disastrous effects on the subjects' ability
to learn both in the DESSY experiments and in the task used by Broadbent
and Aston. This is not surprising; if the subjects do not develop
predictive models, they cannot handle feedback delays.

Finally, side effects, or causal nets, to put things more generally,
seem to create special problems. It should be possible, at least for
reasonably well defined systems, to develop ways to keep the operators
informed about possible side effects. In real systems one problem is that
the side effects are likely to turn up in places which had not been fore-
seen by the system designers, so it is not clear what one can do about this
(vide the problems the medical profession has with unexpected side effects
of treatments).

BEHAVIOR TENDENCIES

One general tendency in the DESSY experiments is that subjects seem
unable to utilize the possibility of reducing the complexity of the task by
relying on the hierarchical nature of the system, and to delegate some
decision making power to lower levels.

Dörner has documented a number of tendencies that tend to create
vicious circles, such as thematic vagabonding and encystment. The generality of these behavior tendencies is not known, but Dörner's results
should provide important guidelines for analyzing the behavior of subjects
also in other tasks.

IMPLICATIONS FOR SYSTEM DESIGNERS

The results reported above carry important implications for systems
designers. These results show that systems designers cannot rely upon the
operators to develop good mental models of complex systems. This implies
that we need to develop means that help the subjects develop such models,
or possibly means that eliminate the need for predictive models.

The results provide some hints about the kinds of aids the subjects may
need. First, since people seem to have problems in coping with the time
dependent aspects of the system, we need to develop information systems

that help the subjects realize and handle these time dependent aspects. An alternative will be to eliminate the need for predictions by having this function be performed by an information system. At the present time, we do not know what these aids need to do and what sorts of information people are able to use.

The results on verbalization suggest that information about the system may need to be communicated in nonverbal form, and that various graphic displays may prove useful. See Brehmer (1985) for a discussion of the need for such displays.

The results with respect to behavior tendencies also provide important clues to the systems designer. First, the problems subjects have in using the hierarchical nature of a system adequately suggest that these aspects of the system need to be regulated. That is, we need to decide what sort of commands can be issued by whom in the hierarchy. This also actualizes the corresponding problem of what kinds of information is needed on each level in the hierarchy. Clearly, if we give a higher level in the hierarchy the kind of information that is appropriate for a lower level we may invite the higher level to issue its commands on a lower level, and this may create problems, especially when there are delays in the system. Here is a whole new field of research where we have not even begun to have any ideas about what sorts of information systems that will be needed and what the characteristics of these systems have to be.

Second, the behavior tendencies that create vicious circles are of considerable interest to the systems designer. If there are such general tendencies, e.g., thematic vagabonding, it may be possible to design diagnostic systems that identify these tendencies when they occur, and prevent the current operator from further attempts to control the system and transfer control over the system to some other operator or level in the hierarchy.

Clearly then, the results of research on complex systems have important implications for systems designers, and will help these designers to create better systems. At the present time there is, of course, not very much evidence to rely upon; research on complex systems is only in its infancy. Moreover, we do not know what can be done to help people overcome the problems they have with complex systems. This should be an important field for cooperation among those researchers who are concerned with creating empirical foundations for software and information science.

ACKNOWLEDGMENT

Preparation of this paper was facilitated by grants from the Swedish Defense Research Institute and the Swedish Council for Research in the Humanities and Social Sciences.

REFERENCES

Brehmer, B., 1974, "Hypotheses About Relations Between Scaled Variables in the Learning of Probabilistic Inference Tasks", Organizational Behavior and Human Performance, 11, pp. 1-27.

Brehmer, B., 1985, "Man as an Operator of Systems", Communication in Health Care, W. Schneider and H. Peterson, eds., North-Holland, Amsterdam.

Brehmer, B. and Allard, R., 1985, <u>Dynamic Decision Making: A General Paradigm and Some Experimental Results</u>, Manuscript, Uppsala: Uppsala University, Department of Psychology.

Brehmer, B. and Allard, R., 1986, "Learning to Control a Dynamic System", <u>Learning and Instruction</u>, E. de Corte, et al., eds., North-Holland, Amsterdam.

Broadbent, D. and Aston, B., 1978, "Human Control of a Simulated Economic System", <u>Ergonomics</u>, <u>21</u>, pp. 1035-1043.

Conant, R. C. and Ashby, W. R., 1970, "Every Good Regulator of a System Must be a Model of that System", <u>International Journal of System Science</u>, <u>1</u>, pp. 89-97.

Dörner, D., 1980, "On the Problems People Have in Dealing with Complexity", <u>Simulation and Games</u>, <u>11</u>, pp. 87-106.

Dörner, D., Kreuzig, H., Reither, R., and Sträuder, T. H., 1983, <u>Lohausen</u>, Huber, Bern.

Kleinmuntz, D. N., 1985, "Cognitive Heuristics and Feedback in a Dynamic Decision Environment", <u>Management Science</u>, <u>31</u>, pp. 680-702.

Kleinmuntz, D. N. and Thomas, J. B., 1985, <u>The Value of Action and Inference in Dynamic Decision Making</u>, Technical Report 84/85-4-31, University of Texas, Graduate School of Business, Austin, TX.

Kluwe, R. H. and Reimann, H., 1983, <u>Problemlösen bei Vernetzten, Komplexen Problemen: Effekte der Verbalisierens auf die Problemlöseleistung</u>, Technical Report 1, Hochschule der Bundeswehr, Fachbereich Pädagogik, Abteilung Allgemeine Psychologie, Hamburg.

Kluwe, R. H., Misiak, C., and Reimann, H., 1984, <u>Lernvorgänge beim Umgang mit Systemen: Die Ausbildung Subjektiver Ordnungsstrukturen durch Erfahrung mit umfangreichen Systemen</u>, Technical Report 7, Hochschule der Bundeswehr, Fachbereich Pädagogik, Abteilung Allgemeine Psychologie, Hamburg.

Mackinnon, A. J. and Wearing, A. J., 1985, "Systems Analysis and Dynamic Decision Making", <u>Acta Psychologica</u>, <u>58</u>, pp. 159-172.

Rasmussen, J., 1985, <u>On Information Processing and Human-Machine Interaction. An Approach to Cognitive Engineering</u>, Elsevier, Amsterdam.

USER DEVELOPED PROTOTYPE SYSTEMS

Siv Friis

Lund University
Dept. of Information and Computer Science
Solvegatan 14 a
223 62 Lund, Sweden

Abstract: Prototyping is not new. It is just one technique among many used in systems design. What might be new is for what purpose prototyping is used. This purpose should be to achieve a more user controlled systems development and to give the future users a tool that will enable them to fully participate in not only the work with the requirements specifications, but also in the actual systems design. This paper describes a case study in which the future users designed prototype systems that acted as requirements specifications.

INTRODUCTION

Due to legislation, most computer-based information systems in Sweden are in some degree developed with the collaboration of the future users. Sometimes a few representatives, sometimes all of the users actually participate in the work of the systems analysis. Mostly in the requirements specifications.

These joint ventures are great time and personnel consumers. And, even though every effort is made to really catch the know-how of the users and the requirements for the future system, this is rarely achieved. One of the reasons for this, I believe, is that we, the systems analysts and data processing (DP) experts, do not let the users do more than just that - specify problems and requirements. We do not let them participate in the actual problem solving. We solve problems for them, even though the problems to be solved originate in the everyday reality of the users. The reason may be that we do not yet have facilities like VHLL, program generators, or even system generators that are adequate for user systems design. There is, however, in some computer environments tools like report and/or application generators and even simpler tools that will enable the non-expert user to build a small test database. Such facilities are adequate for designing small prototype systems by the users, if and when they are aided by DP experts.

In the PROTEVS project, we are concerned with the requirements specifications that are developed by the users. They design small prototype systems that act as requirements specifications. The procedure of this user prototyping is controlled by the users in collaboration with the researchers. The users come from all levels - management, secretaries, clerks, and assistants.

The prototype system can be used to improve the work with the requirements specifications and to further the communications between the users and the experts (Bally, Brittan, and Wagner, 1977; Friis, 1984; Järvinen, 1982; Rzewski, 1983). It serves not only as a specification for a future data system in communications with the DP experts; it is also a learning vehicle (Friis, 1984; Rzewski, 1983) for the users. It gives them the possibility to understand not only the possibilities of a computer-based information system, but also its constraints. And, since the users thus are able to work with, test, and evaluate the prototype systems in real situations, they are also participating in the actual problem solving.

The User Prototyping Concept

A prototype system is defined, as in Rzewski (1983), "as a small scale, inexpensive software/hardware artefact developed with a view to evaluating some aspects of the proposed information system". I should like to go further and state that the prototype system should be developed not only for the purpose of evaluation of a future system, but also as a means for better communications between users and DP experts.

This artefact can be built with the aid of pen and paper, punchcards, as described in Bally, Brittan, and Wagner (1977), wall graphs (Haug, 1976), verbal graphs, or with the aid of a computer. The prototype system described in this paper is a small scale model of a future data system, a model that should be designed by users and experts in collaboration, with users providing a simple conceptual/logical model and the DP experts implementing this model. The users can then perform tests on computers for modifications and improvement of the prototype. The basic idea for our systems design approach is one where the design is based on logical/conceptual data modelling (Sundgren, 1984), and the first "manual" prototype is a primitive conceptual model.

Prototyping is not new, it has been extensively used in systems design for quite some time. There are organizations that have special EDP departments that function as User Service Centers and where the DP experts design prototypes on requests of the users. Almost every conscientious EDP department of today use what is called a step-wise systems design, which is really some sort of prototyping. But these prototypes and/or system models are designed by the DP experts and as such they are still an interpretation of how the DP experts view the problem areas (Flensburg, 1979; Friis, 1984; Landmark and Gaupholm, 1983; Sandström, 1984). The DP experts are still doing the problem solving for the users.

As stated above, prototyping is just one technique among many used in systems design, whereas it might be new as for what purpose the prototyping is used in an EDP environment. The purpose might be to achieve a more process-oriented systems development (Nissen et al., 1982) and/or to give the future users a more understandable tool for their work with the requirements specification (Friis, 1984).

Data Systems As Social Systems

"Even the most mundane use of a computer is part of a system, and even the simplest such system does involve man, somehow", says Douglas T. Ross (1977), and argues that the computer is a tool designed by man, and as such, it is a social tool in that system. "So always there is a system. And always there is man either in that system, or at its boundary. So it is a social system." (Ross, 1977).

34

Any system that involves man is a social system. Whether we can argue that a computer-based information system is a social system must be given some thought. But we know, that every form of message or speech-act (Goldkuhl, 1981) originates from, or is received by man directly or indirectly. And every group of human beings with a common language is a social system.

Information, even in its most abstract form – numbers – is created by, and for, man and it is directed toward a certain environment, e.g., people in an everyday reality (Berger and Luckmann, 1967; Goldkuhl, 1981 and 1982; Ross, 1977; Ross and Schoman, 1977). An administrative office routine is an everyday reality with the accompanying professional knowledge and language. As many such realities it is exposed to changes, partly because the world in itself is changeable, partly because new tools for administrative management are developed. The computer is a new tool and a very effective tool when it comes to reshaping the everyday reality of people, since it has a language of its own – a formalized computer language. The participants of this reality are the users of the new tool/language.

The computer even has a double effect since it already has influenced the DP experts' way of viewing and interpreting the reality, because of the computers' formalized representations of messages. As a consequence, the DP experts are developing the new language for the users, because they have the knowledge of WHAT can be formalized and then, of course, HOW it should be formalized.

The users are thus confronted with a new language in their everyday reality. A language they have not developed themselves, but which they must fully comprehend to be able to participate fully in this new reality, and which is developed in consideration of a tool that has certain linguistic characteristics. This new reality can defeat those who do not have the ability to learn the new language. For those, that in spite of this, manage to remain in the new reality, it may mean nervous stress and uneasiness.

As long as these people, the users of the new tool, do not have adequate knowledge to design their own computer-based information systems, they should at least be allowed to participate in the work of the design. They ought to participate in the specifications of a future system, i.e., they must be allowed to state what the new reality should contain. Which means they ought to participate in the decisions of WHAT should be formalized in the new everyday reality to suit them and their reality – not the reality of the computer.

I can see here a certain advantage in considering a computer-based information system as a social system. It makes us further aware of the fact that there are people involved in such systems, and that it must be the people in the current situation that should develop any new systems and, hence, languages (Berger and Luckmann, 1967; Goldkuhl, 1981). In this way they might preserve the control of their everyday reality and ward off risks of reification of humans and humanization of machines. The users might even lose their fears of the experts and the computers (Rzewski, 1983). I believe that the only way to achieve this is to let the future users at every staff level participate in the systems design, in the actual problem solving of their everyday work problems – perhaps with the aid of a computer, if they should decide on that.

Research Method

In a research project where the perspective is that of the grassroots and where the procedure is tentative and uncertain at times – the concept of the action research should be adequate. It is recommended in action research that the actors as well as the researchers play an active and participative part in a research project (Swedner, 1978). These guidelines are very important to the PROTEVS project.

The difficult part in action research is the information/data collection, especially where the actors take part alternately. I have tried questionnaires in earlier projects, but found this method inadequate. It is very difficult to capture all the knowledge produced in a very active and sometimes confused situation when you ask questions about it some month later. In this project, I have instead used the method of participative and open observations. As Bubenko, Jr. (1982) so aptly puts it in an article where he actually advocates a more stringent data collection strategy and at the same time points out the difficulties of communicating with the actors/users in research projects of this kind:

"An increased formalization in collection of data naturally implies an improved communication between the researcher and the experts of the field. One objection to increased formalization might be that it would widen the gap between the experts and the ordinary users."
(Author's translation from Swedish)

In action research, where you want the actors to participate actively in the research project, you also want to communicate with them. My observations during the PROTEVS project have been noted in diary form, and I have discussed my notes openly with the actors.

USER DEVELOPED PROTOTYPE SYSTEM

In the PROTEVS project, I have had the opportunity to test the idea of user prototyping. The organization, where the tests took place, is one of the departments of a Local Government in Sweden. The reason for choosing this organization was that it was about to exchange its computer for a larger Tandem computer. Included in the software of the new computer were the programming tools ENABLE and ENFORM to load data into a database (ENABLE), and to retrieve, sort, and group data, format and print reports, and create new temporary files (ENFORM).

I was allowed to observe this "Tandem Project" during the planning and systems specifications phases of the data system for the new computer. At the same time, I had the opportunity to test my concepts of prototyping at two of the local district offices.

The users that participated in the PROTEVS project came from all staff levels of the district offices. The project proceeded during Summer and Autumn of 1984. Some of the users participated only partly, because of summer vacations, but their deputies often replaced them in the project. There were in all 23 users out of 51 that participated in the project, 8 from one office and 15 from another.

Some of the users were acquainted with computers in their daily work, but not very many. A selected few had been to one-day programming courses at the EDP department of the organization. The greater part of the users had no knowledge of computers. Little by little the number of users was decreasing and at the last test we were only ten people altogether.

We met six times, four times at the district offices, and twice at the EDP department of the organization. The meetings at the district offices were held separately with the two user groups. The duration of the meetings was approximately three hours.

I will not refer to any particular office in this report, because the procedures of the development of the prototype systems were almost identical at the two offices. The only major difference between the two groups was the number of participants and the chosen problem area.

We started the PROTEVS project at the end of June and the first four meetings were held during summer and early autumn. The first test with computers was held in October of the same year, and the second and last test was held in March of 1985. The users of the two groups met for the first time when we performed the first test of the system, though I had informed each group of the others progress and work.

The Procedure

Even though I had some notion of how to proceed with the project, since I had tried something similar in an EDP-course for users in another Local Government, the procedure of this test of user prototyping was not planned from the beginning. It developed during work, and, in short, the line of action was as follows.

After a short introduction of myself and of PROTEVS, and after a short presentation of my concept of user prototyping, at each of the two district offices, a loose plan for our joint activity was developed. I estimated that five to seven meetings would be adequate to produce a first model of a prototype system. As it turned out, we designed our first models in four meetings and then had two opportunities to test them on computers.

At the first meeting it was also agreed that I should act as instructor, when necessary or if it was requested by the users. This request came when we discussed some of the more common concepts pertaining to computers and systems design, e.g., systems development, requirements specifications, structured analysis, prototyping, programming, etc.

Together with the users, I then discussed some small manageable problem area suitable for user prototyping. I let the users select those which they thought had the highest priority. One of the offices selected a Safety Telephone routine. The telephones are installed in old peoples' service apartments. The other office selected a Deputy routine dealing with extra personnel.

The users were asked to study their problem areas carefully and to discuss them openly among themselves, then try to combine all ideas and problem statements in a structured written description of the current routine. For this work, the users asked for some techniques, and I demonstrated the following analyses and description techniques.

A) Flow Charts. I first showed them some very common flow chart symbols, which were easy to understand and to recognize. Some of the users had seen them before. I made the selection of symbols based on the clerical jobs the users had, and I told them so.

I also demonstrated deMarco's Data Flow Diagram bubbles for structured analysis (deMarco, 1978) and I even encouraged them to design their own models.

B) Verbal Graphs. Next we jointly developed some verbal graphs. We found that these graphs were useful when working on problem definition. The first draft of a verbal graph contained the concepts "Problem", "Cause", and "Area". This was later changed into "Symptom", "Cause", and "Goal/Objectives". After a short discussion of the "Symptom" concept which the users found too diffuse, we changed the "Symptom" concept back to "Problem".

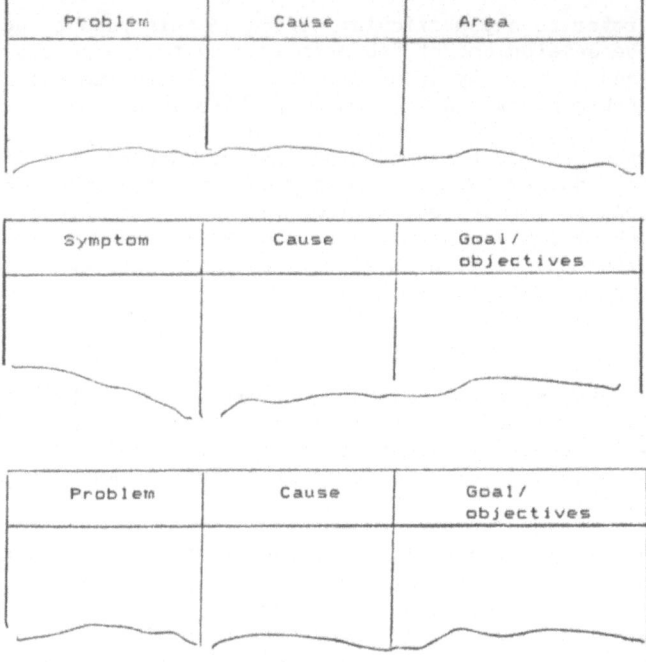

Figure 1. Design Evolution of the Verbal Graph.

This Chord model became our final choice of the verbal graph (See Figure 1.)

C) ISAC Graphs. As a last technique, I demonstrated ISAC graphs (Lundeberg, Goldkuhl, and Nilsson, 1978). This technique was almost at once rejected by both groups of users. They did not like it because the technique was too difficult, and they lost the general overview. They also lost track of the numberings and of the different levels of enlargements.

The users were supposed to do the mappings of the current problem areas all by themselves. We estimated they would need a week for this job.

All of the second meeting was devoted to the discussion of the analysis of the problem area (at both offices) which the users had done, and about the effects of the work. They had spent quite some time discussing the problem area – even free time – and they regarded the job done as important. It had affected their way of looking at the various subproblems of the problem area. The subproblems became more noticeable.

In line with the structured analysis the users had also recognized possible organizational changes of the routine. Another effect of the analysis was that at the same time the users spontaneously started to develop alternative solutions to the problems. I do not think this was solely because of the famous "Hawthorne effect" as Bubenko, Jr. (1982) states in his article. Rather it is more in line with the Swartout and Balzer (1982) discussion of how a person, in a work situation, instinctively looks for a solution the moment a problem is noticeable to him/her.

Since the users had already started to outline different solutions to their problems, the discussion of WHAT the prototype system should do and what information was needed, came up. What queries should the systems database be able to answer? This initiated a discussion about what information objects we needed for our prototype system, and that each system should have its own database. The users did not quite understand all this, so in the end I was asked to prepare a short lecture about "databases and such", for the next meeting.

The procedure was the same at each office. The only difference was in the techniques used for the structured analysis. One of the offices used only flow chart symbols, while the other used flow chart symbols and verbal graphs as well as models designed by themselves.

At the third meeting, I discussed how data might be organized in a database, why there are databases, and how the relational database model of Tandem was conceptually/logically organized.

The users had no difficulties in understanding the conceptual models. After a few demonstrations, they were able to sort out the necessary information objects and their attributes and the relationships between the objects for their own small prototype systems. I believe it came easy to them, because we spoke of a reality that was their own, and it seemed also easy for them to reason in the table form of the relational model, because in their daily work they often handle forms organized as tables. The mapping of the relations came out very easy as well.

Under my supervision, we then designed a small logical database which was very close to a relational model in third normal form (Bubenko, Jr., 1982). The users now had their first manual prototype, which I showed to one of the DP experts in the EDP department. For obvious reasons, I was not allowed to tamper with the actual database of the organization. According to our instructions, he built the physical test database in the Tandem DDL. He claimed it was not necessary to have the test database in third normal form, it was quite sufficient with a conceptual/logical model and descriptions of the records.

After the implementation of the test database, we started to load our computerized prototype systems using the tools ENABLE (for loading the database) and ENFORM (for programming and retrieval). Before that, I and a colleague of mine had written a manual for the programming tools in Swedish. It was requested by the users, since not many of them could understand computer technical English.

Under supervision of the researchers and the DP expert, the users had the opportunity to test their prototype systems on the computers. They were quite satisfied with them, although they wanted to modify and extend the systems. They were very quick to understand the tools.

The Results

An assessment of the two prototype systems was performed by the DP experts of the Tandem project. I intended to demonstrate the systems for them, but a hospital visit on my part came inbetween, so I had to "deliver" the prototype systems via the "development computer". Anyway, the DP experts treated the two systems as requirements specifications, which the systems actually were, and used them accordingly in their project.

A synthesis of the requirement specification of the ongoing Tandem project and the prototype system for the SAFETY Telephone System is now implemented on the organization's computer.

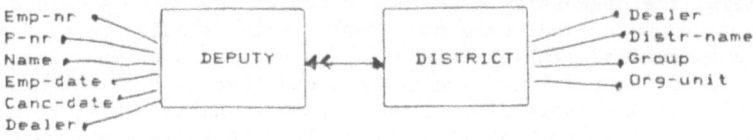

DEPUTY SYSTEM

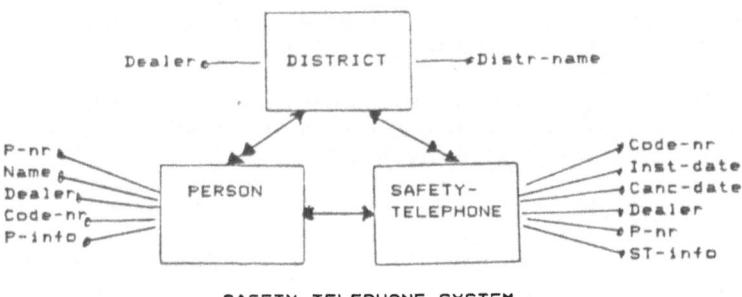

SAFETY TELEPHONE SYSTEM

Figure 2. The Two Prototype Systems.

The Deputy System was also accepted. It is being integrated into a current Personnel System of the organization, because the DP experts of the Tandem project recognized its potential. The two user groups were very pleased with the recognition.

CONCLUDING REMARKS

The Programming Tools

The tool ENABLE is designed to load a database and has a standard form in which you load your occurrences/records. This standard form depends on the attributes of the current relation of the database that you are working with. In our case, we actually had four relations, since we used the same DISTRICT relation for both systems (See Figure 2).

For the loading of our database we used fourteen instructions which are installed key-fashioned in the keyboard. Such a tool is very easy to learn, even for users with absolutely no prior experience with computers. You need no demonstration in advance, you just follow the instructions in the manual. The users commented on this and compared ENABLE to a programmed punch card machine.

ENFORM is a non-procedural query language kind of tool with a report generation facility as well. This tool was mainly used when we tested our prototype systems. You can use it to build-up report layouts and to create new temporary relations/files.

ENFORM is used as a traditional programming tool in the organization for just those reasons - to create temporary files and reports. But the EDP department cannot let the staff use ENFORM for traditional programming too often, because it is very time and workspace consuming, which to me indicates that tools of this kind should not be used for traditional programming, but should instead be used for user prototyping.

40

It also indicates that tools like these are a requirement for a computer environment where you want to practice user prototyping. As proven in the PROTEVS case, even tools as simple as these two are quite sufficient for building small scale prototype systems.

One cannot use ENFORM and ENABLE at the same time. You must exit one to enter the other. That was one of the disadvantages according to the users. They wanted to be able to correct or insert a record at the same time as they were using ENFORM for a certain screen or report layout.

Another disadvantage was that it is not possible to write the instructions in Swedish. On one occasion I familiarized the users with the idea of using legends and symbols, the way Apple does. The users agreed on the idea of symbols or legends as preferable to instructions in a foreign language. They found it quite confusing to write the instructions in English and the data in Swedish.

I believe that for prototyping in a large scale enterprise, there is a need for a VHLL that is easily accessible to non-expert users. And this VHLL must not be too dependent on a certain make of computers. In view of my theory stated above, it should also be designed to support the systems development approach of conceptual modelling.

User Prototyping

In this paper I have at some length discussed the role of the user without mentioning the EDP expert. This is not because I believe this to be unimportant. I think we are going toward a more user controlled systems design, at least in Scandinavia due to legislation about the forming of jobs and democratization of organizations. The control of the systems design process gives an increased influence on the design of the future jobs. This may change the future role of the DP expert towards more of a consulting role. Consulting in the sense of aiding, teaching (Friis and Nilsson, 1984) and, in case of user prototyping, building the physical databases and integrating the prototypes into the current system. The tasks and questions about safety and security systems and maintenance will still remain in the hands of the experts.

User controlled systems development depends very much on the ability of communication between the users and the DP experts. I see the prototypes as means for better communication (Date, 1977; Friis and Nilsson, 1984; Goldkuhl, 1981) as a sort of interpreter, between the two parties. As one of the users in the PROTEVS project spontaneously called out when we were discussing databases:

"Now I understand what the DP expert was saying the other day in the Tandem project, when he was talking of records and files and links!"

However, there are not only advantages with the prototyping concept, there are some disadvantages as well, and of some importance, that must be considered.

User prototyping is done beside one's daily work and this can be very time consuming for the users. To solve this problem, the users themselves feel they should be given extra time and, hence, extra staff for developments of this kind. It is my firm belief though, that any organization will think twice before they grant such a request.

Because of the time user prototyping takes from the time for one's daily work, one has to have wholehearted support from the management. This makes user prototyping very vulnerable. As an example I should like to mention what happened at one district office when I wanted to continue with user prototyping at two new district offices this summer. I intended to follow the same procedure as with the two earlier cases, which are described above, and it started out very well. Then, suddenly, something happened (outside the PROTEVS project) that was noted by the press, and one of the managers was blamed. This incident put the lid on the users' enthusiasm. They did not want to "stick their necks out", as one of the users said. We had to discontinue the project, at least temporarily.

Still, I find that due to work and experiences in the PROTEVS project, I can state that my theories about user prototyping are well founded, that the non-expert users can and will participate in the actual problem solving phases of systems development, and that they are able to design their own prototype systems. Provided the DP expert will help and teach them the necessary techniques.

The PROTEVS Model

I should like to point out once more that the PROTEVS model is only one way of achieving a more user controlled systems development. Another way might be to demonstrate and/or test "Standard Systems", perhaps even in combination with user prototyping. There are surely many more ways.

The PROTEVS model is, as stated above, still very vulnerable since it requires full support from the management. In fact, it is still administered by the management. It is also vulnerable because of the time it takes from the users' ordinary work.

The small number of users that actually participated in the user prototyping is, I believe, a consequence of lack of time and not lack of interest with the users. Still the actual success of the PROTEVS project might very well depend on factors such as:

- The great personal enthusiasm of the specific users,

- The fact that the users came from a work environment which is accustomed to office and business machines,

- The Local Governments' outlook on research projects,

- The researcher's enthusiasm and influence.

The work with user prototyping should, therefore, be continued. It is important that the PROTEVS model should be tested in different work environments, e.g., in a hospital, a farm, a school, or in a factory. And it should be tested on micro-computers as well.

ACKNOWLEDGEMENT

This report has been developed with the financial support from The Swedish Work Environment Fund.

REFERENCES

Bally, L., Brittan, J., and Wagner, K. H., 1977, "A Prototype Approach to Information System Design and Development", Information & Management, I, North Holland Publishing Co., pp. 21-26.

Berger, P. L. and Luckmann, T., 1967, The Social Construction of Reality,

Anchor Books, Doubleday and Company, Inc., Garden City, NY.

Bubenko, Jr., J., 1982, "En granskning av teori – och metodutvecklingen samt systemutvecklarens roll", DATA, 1/2, Sweden (In Swedish).

Date, C. J., 1977, An Introduction to Database Systems, Addison-Wesley Publishing Co., U.S.A.

deMarco, T., 1978, Structured Analysis and Systems Specifications, Yordon Inc., New York, NY.

Flensburg, P., 1979, Systemutveckling med människan i centrum, MOMS – Project, Dept. of Information and Computer Sciences, Lund University, Lund, Sweden (In Swedish).

Floyd, C., 1983, "A Systematic Look at Prototyping", Working Conference on Prototyping, Namur, Belgium.

Friis, S., 1984, "Prototyping and User Developed Requirements Specifications", Seventh Scandinavian Research Seminar on Systemeering, Helsinki, Finland.

Friis, S. and Nilsson, R., 1984, ENFORM och ENABLE i anslutning till användarutvecklade prototypsystem, Informationsbehandling-ADB, Lund, Sweden (In Swedish).

Goldkuhl, G., 1981, Datorbaserade Informationssystem och omvärldsuppfattning, SYSLAB WP No. 31/HUMOR, Stockholm University, Sweden (In Swedish).

Goldkuhl, G, 1982, "Humaninfologisk forskning – Att stödja människors arbete i informationssystemsammanhang", NordDATA 82, Gothenburg, Sweden (In Swedish).

Haug, T., 1976, NORSKE FOLKS administrative rationalisering, Seminar Documentation, Oslo, Norway (In Norwegian).

Järvinen, P., 1982, On Application-Sensitive and -Insensitive Properties of an Information System, University of Tampere, Finland.

Landmark, P., and Gaupholm, H. T., 1983, "A Pragmatic Approach to User Involvement in Systemeering", The 6th Scandinavian Research Seminar on Systemeering, Bergen, Norway.

Lundeberg, M., Goldkuhl, G., and Nilsson, A., 1978, Systemeering, Studentlitteratur, Lund, Sweden.

Nissen et al., 1982, User Oriented Information System – A Research Program, Dept. of Information and Computer Sciences, Lund University, Sweden.

Ross, D. T., 1977, "Guest Editorial, Reflections on Requirements", IEEE Transactions on Software Engineering, SE 3, (1), January 1977.

Ross, T. and Schoman, Jr., K. E., 1977, "Structured Analysis for Requirements Definition", IEEE Transactions on Software Engineering, SE 3, (1), January, 1977.

Rzewski, G., 1983, "Prototypes Versus Pilot Systems Strategies for Evolutionary Information System Development", Working Conference on Prototyping, Namur, Belgium.

Sandström, G, 1984, <u>Towards Transparent Data Bases</u>, Studentlitteratur, Lund, Sweden.

Sundgren, B., 1984, "Systemutveckling baserad pa Konceptuell modellering", <u>Statistisk Tidskrift</u>, <u>4</u>, Stockholm, Sweden (In Swedish).

Swartout, W. and Balzer, R., 1982, "On Inevitable Intertwining of Specification and Implementation, <u>Communications of the ACM</u>, <u>25</u>, (7), July 1982.

Swedner, H., 1978, <u>Sociologisk metod, En bok om kunskapsproduktion och förändringsarbete</u>, Liber Läromedel, Lund, Sweden (In Swedish).

THE TEXT ENVIRONMENT AND DATA BASE MANAGEMENT SYSTEMS

M. A. Heather* and B. N. Rossiter**

*Law School
 Polytechnic of Newcastle Upon Tyne
 England
**Computing Laboratory
 University of Newcastle Upon Tyne
 England

Abstract: Natural language text is the ordinary means for storing and communicating most forms of human knowledge. There are two major problems in
handling text. First, there is its bulk nature suggesting the need for the
use of advanced file handling techniques. Second, there is the problem of
dealing with the meaning. This second aspect requires that the file handling techniques must be based on some conceptual data model. Often text
is treated as free text, i.e., independent of its content, but it is convenient to identify classes of text such as loose text, speech text, short
text, and whole text as categories to be recognized on the road from
"machine-readable" form to "machine-understandable" form.

Thus, text like most real world data of any complexity and volume requires the use of database technology and, for economy of implementation,
the application of generalized Data Base Management Systems (DBMS). Of the
three primary DBMS models, the network, hierarchical and relational, the
hierarchical has so far been the most extensively used for text, but the
relational which has many general advantages, shows great promise for
textual applications, but still lacks proper software.

Examples are given of the use of DBMS in three diverse applications on
NUMAC at Newcastle involving textual data. In medicine, it has been found
that patient records cannot be adequately represented without the use of
descriptive text. In natural history on-line museum cataloging, there is
an analogous need for textual descriptions for full specification of speci-
mens. Law, on the other hand, is directly represented by text, so the data
modelling and management of law by machine can illustrate many of the features to be found in the text environment.

1. INTRODUCTION

1.1 The Importance of Text

A prime concern for software in advanced information processing is how
to handle text. For natural language text is at the core of human communications and information storage. Words form the elementary particles

of human understanding. Words have to be handled in a meaningful way by
machines in any automatic process intended to interact efficiently with
humans. Text is the natural form of expression for knowledge: data held
at the level of knowledge in other forms still normally require words for
interpretation and often for organization. Thus, computer programs require
extensive structured comment statements, graphical and tabular representations need captions, etc., digital versions of audio or visual materials
such as speech, music, pictures, designs, etc. usually need some language
textual characterization for storage and retrieval. Even the symbols in
mathematics need to be defined in natural language at some stage. Currently the programming languages used in knowledge engineering (such as
those of the LISP and PROLOG families) are based on atoms of text as
primitives.

1.2 Textual Information

Human knowledge is stored and communicated in documents mostly in the
form of full text natural language. However, textual information systems
are difficult to categorize. Classifications made to date tend to relate
to a particular task at hand. Thus, Sparck Jones and Kay (1973) distinguish fact retrieval from information retrieval; Radecki (1983) emphasizes
the distinction between discrete and continuous retrieval systems in developing a fuzzy-set theoretic approach to the subject; and Macleod and
Crawford (1983) stress the organizational differences between data base
management systems, document retrieval systems, and electronic filing
systems.

It is true that text is only one form of knowledge representation, and
cannot be isolated from other work on knowledge-based systems. Much of the
work around the world today is concentrated on the development of formal
methods to represent knowledge.[1] However, most of the world's knowledge is
stored in documents in full text natural language form. Any practical
knowledge-based or expert system involving any quantity of real world data
needs to be able to interact by automatic methods with documents already in
existence. This report is concerned with modelling the somewhat amorphous
structures to be found in full text for automatic machine handling of such
documents.

2. CLASSIFICATION OF TEXT

2.1 Textual Data Types

In order to deal with the enigmatic form of text, it is convenient to
make a classification into various textual data types. There are the two
main families of formal language and natural language. These may be further subdivided as in Figure 1. While formal non-numeric language is of
recent origin, the sub-categories of formal language in Figure 1 are well
developed and form the foundations of modern computer science. Natural
language on the other hand is of much more ancient origin, but is still far
from being understood by the machine. The sub-classification of natural
language in Figure 1 into data types is an obvious step toward machine
comprehension. For there are differences in the level of knowledge represented by different types of text such as 'loose text', 'short text', and
'whole text'. It may be convenient to distinguish these classes of text
before describing techniques of modelling them.

---

[1]Current work on knowledge formalism can be found in Proceedings of the
Workshop on Architectures for Large Knowledge Bases, Manchester University, 1984.

46

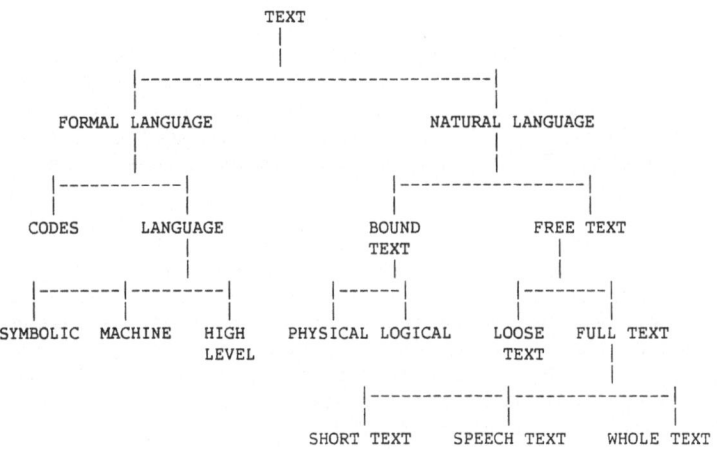

Figure 1. A Spectral Classification of Textual Data.

2.2 Types of Free and Bound Text

The terminology has not been standardized and 'full text' and 'free text' are used by some writers interchangeably. 'Free text' has no obvious or settled meaning, it may be used to describe the situation where a writer has no other constraints than those of natural language. Other than in this generic sense, it seems better not to encourage the use of 'free text' except perhaps when it is necessary to distinguish it from 'bound text'. 'Bound text' results from the use of language that is controlled in some manner. This control may be logical as in controlled vocabulary (the word 'thesaurus' is sometimes used in this sense) which is to be found frequently in information retrieval systems and computer based learning packages. Or the control may be physical as in fixed length fields. As machine data processing increases, the proforma (such as application forms for employment, insurance, etc.) are making more use of text which is controlled both physically and logically. Such combined control of words was previously only limited to oddities like crossword puzzles, but is now widespread in business and commerce.

Loose text consists of fragments of full text often to be found as extra words of explanation in a database that is not primarily in full text form. Thus, a personnel or bibliographic database, in addition to the text fields of NAME, ADDRESS, AUTHOR, TITLE, etc., may have notes in phrases or clauses which are not in full grammatical sentences. Explanations ancillary to graphs, diagrams, and figures often consist of loose text.

In Figure 1, 'free text' is divided into 'loose text' and 'full text'. 'Full text' is a generic term for textual expression at the ordinary knowledge level of human discourse. It comprises the categories 'short text', 'speech text', and 'whole text'. This is not an exhaustive list and it will be seen later that these categories themselves can be further subdivided.

Short text consists of an abbreviated form of full text. It is normally achieved by relaxing the strict rules of natural language. The form of communication is not expressly complete. It may take the form merely of suppressing some of the redundancy of language normally provided as a check. Short text usually relies on knowledge common to the writer and the reader. Syntactical shortening is possible because knowledge of normal forms of expression are common to the average reader of a given language. Semantic curtailment is more complicated, however, as it assumes a common knowledge of the subject matter. In terms of generative grammars, the semantic short text lies in the very context sensitive categories. The theoretical foundations of these are not yet very well explored. This makes the processing of short text at the semantic level more or less impossible at the present time.

In passing it might be noted that the syntactical short text relies on a common knowledge between the parties of the communication at the semantic level, while semantic short text implies pragmatic co-knowledge. This context-sharing between the communicator and the receiver is beyond the classical information theory of Shannon (Shannon and Weaver, 1949), which relies on long term ergodic processes to provide the overall independence needed for the application of statistical methods. Short text needs some metasignal theory such as proposed by Heine (1984).

However, these distinctions in the information-density spectrum of the various types of text are not merely of theoretical interest for they have some quite important consequences in practice. Thus in the UK the use of the teletex system PRESTEL has been smaller than was anticipated for general information, but it has become very popular for specialized users. The reason for this divergence may well lie in the characteristics of short text. Public teletex and videotex have been able to step into a ready made telematic network market place by using domestic television sets as terminal devices, but at the price of accepting the constraints. Communication from the user may even be limited to simple numeric keypads and communication to the user is normally restricted by the band widths and the physical format of the domestic television receiver 'window'. With the majority of sets currently available there is a maximum of about 150 words that can be displayed on one electronic page. The information providers on these systems have therefore tended to resort to short text. For the specialized user a considerable quantity of information can be conveyed in this way, particularly where the information is of a differential nature relating to changes, up-dates, etc. For the general user, however, the information in short text form may be quite unintelligible.

Whole text on the other hand is the ordinary full and free expression of language in written form and conforms to the accepted rules of such communication. The important difference between whole texts and loose or short text is at the semasiological level. Loose text is used for isolated scraps of information, short text either communicates information at a shallow level or acts as a mere pointer to a deeper level, but whole text tells the whole story. This wholesomeness comes not from completeness, for it may not be complete, but from its precision and level of reliability. Whole text is information at the level of knowledge. It is a matter of the level of specificity.

It is important to note that it is not just that short text is short and whole text is long. The difference relates more to the nature of the contents of a document. An abridgement or abstract may be in either short or whole text form. Brevity and conciseness are not necessarily synonomous. Often a short text form may be used, because there is neither the time nor intellectual energy available to produce an equivalent succinct whole text. On the other hand, speech text is at the level of specificity of whole text, but short text in form.

The power of human communication increases from left to right in Figure 1 across the different types of text, while the power of machine communication is in the reverse direction. Thus, the present state of human-machine communication has reached about half-way on this spectrum with high-level languages. The aim now it to bring the machine across the divide into natural language comprehension. One of the first steps is to handle these different classes of text. Here we are concerned only with written categories. These need to be integrated with other types such as speech text and graphics. Indeed other work carried out so far suggests that speech text is perhaps as broad a category as the more familiar 'high-level' group. Details have been omitted from the figure for these large family groups.

2.3 Full Text Processing

There are four principal phases to be considered in the handling of full text in an electronic medium. There is a transitional phase in converting the information from hard-copy documents into machine-readable form. Eventually, most documents may be written specifically for the electronic medium, and this will reduce to some extent logical problems on input. The second phase concerns the structuring of the textual data for systematic storage. The third phase relates to the interrogation and retrieval of information. The last phase involves the composition of the text in its final output form. The state of the art in electronic publishing is probably well represented by TEX (Knuth, 1979), and likewise in text processing by TROFF in the UNIX environment (Ossana, 1976). TEX can achieve sophisticated textual structures through defining elementary boxes such as single characters or rectangles which can be amalgamated into lists of boxes representing larger units such as a single page. However, TEX is orientated towards physical representation of text. Present methods in Information Retrieval on the other hand are mainly limited to considering documents as a collection of unstructured free text. Here we are concerned with the modelling that is required to handle the natural structure that is found in text. While it is necessary to draw upon the methods of Information Retrieval, the major emphasis is directed towards the techniques of modern data base technology. Electronic Publishing today is concerned with integrating text with other types of data such as numeric, graphic, etc. Such integration requires a structured approach to be applied to the text. The nature of electronic text and methods of handling it will be considered in the next section.

3. ELECTRONIC TEXT

3.1 Applications

Initially, computers were used solely for numeric applications by scientists and engineers. Thus, the early versions of languages such as FORTRAN were not designed to handle character strings at all. However, because linguistic forms of expression come more naturally to the human mind than numeric ones, it became necessary for the computer to deal with comment statements, captions, etc., and other forms of loose text. In business applications, text is more important and COBOL was developed with text fields for use by application programmers. As applications developed for handling natural languages for purposes such as computational linguistics and automatic translation, there was a need for the more powerful tools as in SNOBOL. All mainstream computer languages now incorporate basic string handling functions. Even comment statements are now recognized as an essential part of good structured software engineering. However, there are examples of loose text, or at the most short text. The limited extent to which these forms could represent human thoughts was acceptable because of the limitations of hardware. With the advent of more powerful machines and larger, cheaper storage devices, it has become possible to handle whole text by automatic means. There is then an immediate I/O problem because of the bulk and the complex structure of whole text, so that it cannot be held easily in fixed fields or as simple program data. A high level language can only cope with a small amount of text held in main memory. Even on a mainframe more than 0.5 Mbyte at a time soon becomes excessive. Flat file systems can handle large amounts of permanent data, if the structure is simple. Thus a telephone directory for the 500 million telephone subscribers in the World containing loose text in fields of name, number, address, etc., is well within present technology. On the other hand, whole text data of a much smaller quantity cannot be addressed in data fields in the same way and present commercial full text data bases are held and handled as free text with little regard to any structure.

Therefore, this combination of complexity and size require database techniques to model the structure and to provide reasonable performance for realistic quantities of text in applications of electronic publishing and in the electronic office. The approach adopted here, therefore, is from the standpoint of database technology. The emphasis is placed on the means of storage and the two other phases of input and output developed within that framework. The fundamental features of data base technology can be applied to text as data. It is necessary, therefore, to examine the possible data models (including those that may not yet get generally implemented) to assess their applicability for text.

3.2 Data Models

The simplest computer model for textual data is the free text model which penetrates no deeper than the level of 'FREE TEXT' in Figure 1. The free text model treats a collection of text as a continuous byte-stream without internal structure. Searching can be by sequential access or through indexes. Sequential methods are slow. Tests carried out on the Amdahl 5860 (a 12.5 MIPS machine) at NUMAC using the MTS context editor show that sequential searching of text can be carried out at the rate of 4Mb per CPU second. Thus, the search of a large text file of 100Mb would require at least 45 minutes elapsed time with 100 users connected to such a multiple-access system.

Searching by means of indexes is much faster, but the use of calculated indexes (by hashing, for example) requires a clear prespecification of key values that is not always appropriate for text. Physical indexes are expensive to build. Parallel methods now give faster access without the need to go through indexes, but require the purchase of specialized hardware (Agosti, 1983-4), and can also generally hold no more than typically 50Mb.

3.3 Specialized Text Systems

In the 1960's retrieval systems for text began to appear (Teskey, 1982). These typically were a suite of programs providing facilities to build indexes using inverted files. These indexes enabled retrieval using Boolean operators on all words and substrings in a text (excluding common words) or by means of a thesaurus. These systems offered various display features such as keyword in context (KWIC). Examples of these systems are STAIRS (IBM), STATUS (Harwell), SPIRIT (France), MISTRAL (Honeywell-Bull), GOLEM (Siemens), and QUOBIRD (Belfast). In the early 1970's more specialized text retrieval systems became available such as DIALOG (Lockheed's Bibliographic data base), MEDLARS (medical literature retrieval system of the US National Library of Medicine), and LEXIS (full text law retrieval). These systems began to incorporate some modern database management system techniques such as data fields and structures, and data directories and dictionaries.

3.4 Generalized DBMS for Text

The prime objective of a data base management system (DBMS) is to make application programs independent of the physical structure of the data. To achieve this objective, a conceptual schema or model needs to be defined as a global logical definition of the data structure. This schema relates to the physical definition by a series of mappings from the logical level to the physical level. The schema is protected from changes at the physical level by adjusting this mapping. Each user has his own view (external schema) of the data base which may be restricted. This is achieved by a series of mappings which provide security, logical data independence, etc., (Rossiter, 1984). The schemas are often classified into three main types: hierarchical, network, and relational (Date, 1981).

Hierarchical systems were developed as soon as magnetic tapes came into use as data could be easily organized physically in the form of nested trees. With the advent of magnetic disks, more sophisticated physical structures based on hierarchical data structuring have become possible and the ability to design complex systems has increased (e.g., IMS). The specialized text systems referred to above employ a hierarchical form of structure with relatively easy implementation.

Hierarchical systems are inadequate for complex commercial data processing because they only allow the modelling of one-to-many relationships. The network model, however, is more general allowing the modelling of many-to-many as well. The CODASYL model is a well known example which enables many-to-many relationships to be achieved in a number of ways. Many implementations of it exist (e.g., IDMS), and it has proved applicable to many administrative and commercial areas. To implement, however, a successful application of the network model needs the involvement of professional programming staff even for record retrieval because of the intimate knowledge that is required of the physical structure. In particular, network query languages are not suited to iterative searching and this may be the chief reason why the network model has not been used extensively for text. This is not to say that a network text programming initiative is impossible, but it would be a fairly major undertaking. Any user interface would always be of very complicated design and there would be the usual network constraint of having to define statically all the relationships.

The relational model (Codd, 1970) on the other hand offers the power of the network model, but with a simple and elegant method of data manipulation. However, problems arise with the relational systems that are in use today in handling the free text of the headings and content. A general survey of relational database systems was carried out in 1983 by Schmidt and Brodie (1983) to assess how closely the systems were adhering to the principles laid down by Codd and to compare their capabilities. While the use of text was not of primary interest in the report, it is possible by examining carefully the capabilities of the systems surveyed to extract information on their suitability for textual applications. The results are summarized in the table of Figure 2. Additions are given and marked by an asterisk (*) for known advances made since the report of Schmidt and Brodie was published.

In relational systems, variable length fields imply variable length records and vice versa for first normal form requires one occurrence of each field per record. Variable length records are possible on other models even with only fixed length fields, when it is possible to vary the number of the fixed fields. With text, the extreme variation of record size means setting the maximum field length at the largest can result in very poor storage utilization. The bulk nature of text, therefore, means that this wastage can be quite critical and most of the system storage

Product	Variable-length fields	Field Indexes	Word Indexes	Substring Search Facility
DBASE3*	only with special field	yes	no	only on fixed fields
INFO*	no	yes	{ only with a non-relational extension }	
INGRES	no (but data compression*)	yes	no	yes*
NOMAD	yes	yes	no	yes
ORACLE		yes	no	only end truncation
PRTV	no	yes	no	yes
QBE	yes (maximum 3200 bytes)	yes	no	yes, also patterns
RAPPORT	no	yes	no	only with RASQL
SYSTEM R	yes, special field type	yes	no	no

Figure 2. Analysis of Relational Systems for Text.
            (After Schmidt and Brodie)

available is occupied with blank space. Systems such as INGRES have introduced facilities such as data compression to deal with the limitation of
fixed length records. The compression is usually achieved by the use of a
blocking code to represent unused space in the fixed length fields. The
first column of Figure 2 indicates the efficiency with which data of mark-
edly varying length will be stored. Three systems, SYSTEM R, INGRES, and
NOMAD would provide efficient storage for the average textual record size
and QBE for small records only. The others would require a fixed maximum
length to be specified for each occurrence of data, the unused portion of
which would be wasted.

The second column indicates the speed with which data can be located in
large files, and all systems provide an indexing facility to assist in
this. However, as the third column shows, none allow index construction to
be programmed by the database designer to the extent that indexes can be
built on words contained within the text, which is required in this area.

Relational systems are in fact not too suited to indexing in the traditional manner using physical addresses for complex data. There is no real
concept of a 'global' index in relational data bases. A single index cannot readily be constructed for the various domains in the different relations across the data base. On the other hand, the relational approach
offers the possibility of logical indexing with the facilities for searching at various levels dynamically.

The last column indicates the ability to search for substrings contained within a textual string, and most systems have this ability (QBE, PRTV,
NOMAD, INGRES, and RAPPORT through the RASQL interface). In other systems
such as SYSTEM R, such a facility could be written by a user and placed in
a library of user functions. ORACLE only allows the facility to search for
the start of a data value using the PREFIX operator. These systems,

therefore, generally allow some ability to search for words contained within textual strings, but only in sequential mode, so response times would be extremely slow with large databases. Lorie (1981) of IBM Research, San Jose summed up the situation thus:

> "Finally, the extensions of data types to support non-formatted data completes the list of enhancements that could convert a classical relational system supporting data processing transactions into a system supporting a much wider class of applications".

He says of System R:

> "the normal maximum size of a field is 254 bytes, but there is a special field type CHAR (LONG) VARYING which allows up to 32767 bytes, but which gives intolerable restrictions and performance penalties in its use".

The three models of network, hierarchical and relational may be considered as the basic models in use today for practical purposes. However, other models have been proposed usually in order to incorporate more semantic features than can be included in the basic models in an attempt to model more closely the real world. These include RM/T (Codd, 1979), the Role Model (Bachman and Day, 1978; Bachman, 1980), the Basic Semantic Model (Schmid and Swanson, 1975), the Entity-Relationship Model (Chen, 1976), and the Borkin Semantic Model (Borkin, 1979).

General implementation of these models are not available in commercial packages, but they are useful for providing a more complete specification of a subject than can be obtained using the three basic models. So, if a more advanced model is employed, it is still necessary to map it on to one of the basic models while aiming to retain as much of the semantic detail as possible. The effectiveness of the E-R and Borkin models has been investigated as part of this work and a model of UK statutes using the Borkin Semantic Model is presented later in this report in Figure 5.

4. EXAMPLES OF TEXT IN DATA BASES

4.1 Numeric and Non-Numeric Data Bases

The proposition advanced here, therefore, is that proper text handling is a major requirement for database technology as many databases contain text as a natural means of human expression even where the primary data is other than textual. Since the late fifties, Newcastle has been a centre for electronic publishing, information retrieval, and large databases. There are at present on NUMAC (Northumbrian Universities Multiple Access Computers) at Newcastle a number of these databases built as research tools for daily use in some quite practical situations.

In the teaching hospital attached to the medical school a detailed database is daily maintained with full specification of the clinical condition of patients in the renal failure unit. Use is made of several hundred numeric parameters to record features of blood condition, effect of chemical therapy, description of surgical processes, and the effectiveness of treatment, etc. The level of specificity of the data means that this is really a knowledge base used as a support for clinical decision making including the selection for transplant operations. The data is in principle numeric, but it has been found that numeric fields alone are insufficient and for most of the parameters to be expressed fully natural language text is required. There is the further point that any database model for

```
MUSEUM-NUMBER = JH11.54;
TAXON-DETAIlS;
CATALOGUE = Palearctic;
  SCIENTIFIC-NAME = Pandion haliaetus;
  ENGLISH-NAME = Osprey;
  OLD-LABEL-NAME = Falco haliaetus;
  FAMILY = Pandionidae;
  VAURIE-NUMBER = 144NP;
COLLECT-DETAILS;
LOCATION = Loch Morlich, Glenmore, Highland Reg., Scotland, U.K.;
  COLLECTOR-NAME = Hewitson, W.C.;
  DATE-OF-COLL = 18 April 1850;
  YEAR-OF-COLL = 1850;
  ORIGINATION = Hewitson, W.C., Hancock, Albany, Hancock, J.;
  COLLECTION = Hancock, John;
EGG-DETAILS;
DESCRIPTION = 2 eggs with nest [& piece of trout];
  CONDITION = Eggs missing;
  LABEL-DETAILS = Eggs marked 'Glenmore, 18th April 1850, belong
  to nest', one also reads 'Sp. figd. by Hewitson 3rd ed. fig
  2 pl. 6.'. Note attached reads 'nest of Falco haliaetus taken
  by myself on the ruins of the old shooting box in Glen More.
  nr. Loch Morlick 1850. See journal. Two eggs were in [the]
  nest & we shot the old female & she had in her an egg full size
  but not shelled. The portion of stuffed trout was lying on the
  side of the nest when taken. This is only the lining of the
  nest the full diameter being twice this - the rest of the
  sticks which formed the outer part were an inch in diameter'
  ınitials are indecipherable but note is addressed to 'Albany
  Hancock Esq. - St. Mary's Terrace';
MISCELLANEOUS = Eggs stolen Aug. 1985, nest was left intact;
```

Figure 3.   Extract from Database of Natural
History Catalogue.

representing this type of record cannot have an exhaustive set of fields.
Sometimes a miscellaneous field is added to deal with limitations in the
classification chosen for the model. However, a miscellaneous field can
raise problems with other relationships in the model unless the contents of
such a field are independent of all other fields. In a medical database as
indeed in any research database the kind of information that does not fit
into the preexisting classification and which has to be relegated to a
miscellaneous field may be of the greatest significance.

    A similar example to the medical records is the extract from the cat-
alogue of the Hancock museum given in Figure 3. The catalogue is held in
machine readable form and this extract relating to an item in the orni-
thological collection is reproduced in the high level internal form of the
database. The generalized database management system SPIRES (Stanford
Public Information REtrieval System) is used for the catalog. SPIRES is a
fourth generation type high level systems package based on hierarchical
'B+' tree structures defined on meta-data principles and designed at Stanford. The hierarchic nature of the model can be seen from the indentation
structure of the printing of this extract. Numeric data is of very little
value here and most of the fields require text data. The fields which can
be specified with a single descriptor use loose text while for others the
cataloger has resorted to short text as in the field "LABEL-DETAILS". The
field names such as "LABEL-DETAILS", "DATE-OF-COL", "OLD-LABEL-NAME", etc.,
are examples of a high level formal language. They are descriptive meta-
text in the sense used by Zunde (1984).[2] It is clear from this example the

---

[2]Meta-text, however, does not have to be only in formal language. There
 are examples in the Law of loose, short and even whole meta-text, see
 Heather (1982).

An Act to consolidate the enactments relating to settled
land in England and Wales.   [9th April 1925]

*Powers of tenant for life and trustees of settlement under this Act conferred on trustees for sale
by Law of Property Act 1925 (c. 20), s. 28(1) and Forestry Act 1967 (c. 10), s. 5(4), Sch. 2
para. 1(1)-(3); applied by Land Registration Act 1925 (c. 21), ss. 40(2), 91(1)*
Words of enactment omitted under authority of Statute Law Revision Act 1948 (c. 62), s. 3
A dagger appended to a marginal note means that it is no longer accurate

Part I

General Preliminary Provisions

Settlements and Settled Land

1.—(1) Any deed, will, agreement for a settlement or other agreement, Act of Parliament, or other instrument, or any number of instruments, whether made or passed before or after, or partly before and partly after, the commencement of this Act, under or by virtue of which instrument or instruments any land, after the commencement of this Act, stands for the time being— *What constitutes a settlement.*

(i) limited in trust for any persons by way of succession; or

(ii) limited in trust for any person in possession—

   (*a*) for an entailed interest whether or not capable of being barred or defeated;

   (*b*) for an estate in fee simple or for a term of years absolute subject to an executory limitation, gift, or disposition over on failure of his issue or in any other event;

   (*c*) for a base or determinable fee or any corresponding interest in leasehold land;

   (*d*) being an infant, for an estate in fee simple or for a term of years absolute; or

(iii) limited in trust for any person for an estate in fee simple or for a term of years absolute contingently on the happening of any event; or

(iv) . . . .

(v) charged, whether voluntarily or in consideration of marriage or by way of family arrangement, and whether immediately or after an interval, with the payment of any rentcharge for the life of any person, or any less period, or of any capital, annual, or periodical sums for the portions, advancement, maintenance, or otherwise for the benefit of any persons, with or without any terms of years for securing or raising the same;

1

Figure 4 (Part A).   An extract from the printed version of UK Statues.

difficulty that any automatic parser would have if this short text was treated as whole text. Also, incorporated is a description taken from an original note made by the person claiming to be the collector of the eggs. There are also additions such as the words in square parentheses which seem to have been added later. The history and provenance of amendments and additions would be fairly obvious in handwritten documents and, therefore, much greater care has to be taken in the electronic medium to ensure that information is not lost or erroneously added. A major concern for any database is the problem of keeping the data up-to-date. Even here in this rather simple example of two eggs and a nest collected in 1850 it was necessary to add further information when the eggs were recently stolen in August 1985 in a burglary at the museum. This piece of information has creates or is for the purposes of this Act a settlement and is in this Act referred to as a settlement, or as the settlement, as the case requires:

Provided that, where land is the subject of a compound settlement, references in this Act to the settlement shall be construed as meaning such compound settlement, unless the context otherwise requires.

(2) Where an infant is beneficially entitled to land for an estate in fee simple or for a term of years absolute and by reason of an intestacy or otherwise there is no instrument under which the interest of the infant arises or is acquired, a settlement shall be deemed to have been made by the intestate, or by the person whose interest the infant has acquired.

(3) An infant shall be deemed to be entitled in possession notwithstanding any subsisting right of dower (not assigned by metes and bounds) affecting the land, and such a right of dower shall be deemed to be an interest comprised in the subject of the settlement and coming to the dowress under or by virtue of the settlement.

Where dower has been assigned by metes and bounds, the letters of administration or probate granted in respect of the estate of the husband of the dowress shall be deemed a settlement made by the husband.

(4) An estate or interest not disposed of by a settlement and remaining in or reverting to the settlor, or any person deriving title under him, is for the purposes of this Act an estate or interest comprised in the subject of the settlement and coming to the settlor or such person under or by virtue of the settlement.

(5) Where—

(*a*) a settlement creates an entailed interest which is incapable of being barred or defeated, or a base or determinable fee, whether or not the reversion or right of reverter is in the Crown, or any corresponding interest in leasehold land; or

(*b*) the subject of a settlement is an entailed interest, or a base or determinable fee, whether or not the reversion or right of reverter is in the Crown, or any corresponding interest in leasehold land;

the reversion or right of reverter upon the cesser of the interest so created or settled shall be deemed to be an interest comprised in the subject of the settlement, and limited by the settlement.

(6) Subsections (4) and (5) of this section bind the Crown.

[[1](7) This section does not apply to land held upon trust for sale.]

What is settled land.

2. Land which is or is deemed to be the subject of a settlement is for the purposes of this Act settled land, and is in relation to the settlement referred to in this Act as the settled land.

---

[1]S. 1(7) added by Law of Property (Amendment) Act 1926 (c. 11), Sch.

2

Figure 4 (Part B). An extract from the printed version of UK Statues.

been added as a MISCELLANEOUS sub-field of EGG-DETAILS although it might very well be argued that it belongs to COLLECT-DETAILS. This may not matter in a small record as in Figure 2, but in larger records, it may be quite critical to a user how the information is classified.

A full database model of a catalog record to hold the complete information about a museum exhibit, including details of the names and dates of the various curators who were responsible for it, descriptions and by whom they were applied, and so on would have to be very extensive. A more exhaustive example of this nature has actually been carried out at Newcastle for a legal database. In the Law this is necessary because precise information is required.

Act

be act:OBJECT					
act					
bt/physical		bt/logical	loose text	short text	short text
year*	chapter*	date	title	preamble	crossnote

Part

in.act:AGENT		in.act:OBJECT be part:OBJECT	
act		part	
bt/physical		bt/logical	loose text
year*	chapter*	number*	part-headings

Section

in.act:AGENT contains.part: agent		contains.part: object within.part: agent	in.act:OBJECT be section:OBJECT	
act		part	section	
bt/physical		bt/logical	bt/physical	whole text
year*	chapter*	number	number*	section-text

Subsection

in.act:AGENT contains.part: agent		contains.part: object within.part: agent	in.act:OBJECT within.part: object in.section: AGENT	in.section:OBJECT be section:OBJECT	
act		part	section	subsection	
bt/physical		bt/logical	bt/physical	bt/logical	whole text
year*	chapter*	number	number*	number*	subsection-text

Schedule

in.act:AGENT		in.act:OBJECT be schedule:OBJECT	
act		schedule	
bt/physical		bt/logical	loose text
year*	chapter*	number*	schedule-headings

Subschedule

in.act:AGENT		in.act:OBJECT in.schedule: AGENT	in.schedule:OBJECT be subschedule:OBJECT	
act		schedule	subschedule	
bt/physical		bt/logical	bt/logical	loose text
year*	chapter*	number*	number*	subschedule-headings

Figure 5 (Part A). A Linearized Representation of the Internal Structure of UK Statutes Using Borkin's Semantic Data Model.

4.2 Legal Database

Law has to be expressed in the medium of the day whether it is stone, wax parchment, or paper. Today the electronic medium is becoming very common in business and commerce and is particularly appropriate for law, because the computer can handle large quantities of data well and provide added value features such as centralized updating. One very important source of law is the statutes promulgated by governments. An extract from the printed version of a UK statute is given in Figure 4. This contains a

```
Paragraph
|in.act:AGENT|in.act:OBJECT |                |                     |
|            |in.sched:AGENT|                |   in.sched:OBJECT   |
|            |contains.sub- |contains.sub-   |                     |
|            |schedule:agent|schedule:object |   within.subschedule:|
|            |              |within.sub-     |         object       |
|            |              |schedule.agent  |   be paragraph:OBJECT|
|    act     |   schedule   |  subschedule   |       paragraph      |
| bt/physical|  bt/logical  |  bt/logical    |bt/physical|whole text|
|year|chapter|    number    |     number     | number |paragraph-|
|  * |   *   |      *       |                |    *   |  text    |
```

```
Subparagraph
|in.act:AGENT|in.act:OBJECT |                |                         |                |
|            |in.sched:AGENT|                |   in.sched:OBJECT       |                |
|            |contains.sub- |contains.sub-   |                         |                |
|            |schedule:agent|schedule:       |                         |                |
|            |              |object          |                         |                |
|            |              |within.sub-     |within.subschedule:      |                |
|            |              |schedule:agent  |        object           |                |
|            |              |                |in.paragraph:AGENT  |in.para-       |
|            |              |                |                    |graph:OBJECT   |
|            |              |                |                    |be subpara-    |
|            |              |                |                    |graph:OBJECT   |
|    act     |   schedule   |  subschedule   |      paragraph     |  subparagraph  |
| bt/physical|  bt/logical  |  bt/logical    |    bt/physical     | bt/   |whole   |
|            |              |                |                    | logical|text   |
|year|chapter|    number    |     number     |     number         | number |sub-   |
|  * |   *   |      *       |                |       *            |   *    |para-  |
|    |       |              |                |                    |        |graph  |
|    |       |              |                |                    |        |text   |
```

Figure 5 (Part B). A Linearized Representation of the Internal Structure
of UK Statutes Using Borkin's Semantic Data Model.

complex set of entity types including titles, preamble, headings, cross
notes, side notes, sections, schedules, paragraphs, etc., involving a
mixture of whole text, short text, and loose text.

In order to discover the law on a particular topic, the citizen or
lawyer needs to be able to find the relevant fragment, have it displayed
properly indented for good comprehension with the different types of text
distinguished, and to have identified and accessible its context and any
express or even implied part from elsewhere that may have bearing on the
meaning. A representation of the internal structure of a statute using
Borkin's Semantic Model referred to above is to be found in Figure 5. This
form of representation illustrates the difficulties involved in capturing
the structure in any simple model. This can be compared with the graphical
approach of the Chen Entity-Relationship model and a representation of the
same UK statutory structure using that model (Rossiter, 1985) or with the
hierarchical approach (Heather, 1985) where a discussion of the semiotic
significance of the surface structure of the text captured in these models
may also be found.

The computer representation of the statutory extract of Figure 4 is
given in Figure 6 using the same SPIRES hierarchical generalized database
management system as used in the museum catalog example above. The structure is mapped under complete automatic control using the typesetting information that is necessary to produce the ordinary printed version. To
display at a terminal one section of a statute, information is needed from
more than one record. There are three relevant records in Figure 6. The
crossheading information relates to the Part of the statute containing the
section and has to be held in a record which can be referenced by each section in that part. The footnotes also have to be dealt with in a separate

```
****
 ID = 192501810000000000001000000100000000;     RECNO = 1441;
ACCESS-NO = sif00034+ 1925 c.18 ,Part I,S 1 ,*1441;
ACT-TITLE = "SETTLED LAND ACT 1925 (c.'x18) '";
KIND = 2;     DATE = April 9, 1925;     TAPE = 1;   SCHSOURCE = PART;
MARG-N-OTHER = "'What constitutes a settlement.";
SECT-MAIN-TEXT = "!' 1.-(1) Any deed, will, agreement for a settlement
or other agreement, Act of Parliament, or other instrument, or any";
 SEQ = 1;    SECT-MAIN-TEXT = * number of instruments, whether made or passed
before or after, or partly before and partly after, the commencement of
this Act,  under or by virtue of which instrument or instruments any
land, after the commencement of this Act, stands for the time  being-;
 SEQ = 2;   HALF-I-SIN-I-SUB = " '(i) limited in trust for any persons by way of
succession; or";
 SEQ = 3;   HALF-I-SIN-I-SUB = " '(ii) limited in trust for any person in
possession-";
 SEQ = 4;   DBL-INDENT-LIST = " '(a) for an entailed interest whether or not
capable of being barred or defeated;";
 SEQ = 5;   DBL-INDENT-LIST = " <(b) for an estate in fee simple or for a term
of years absolute subject to an executory limitation, gift, or
disposition  over on failure of his issue or in any other event;";
 SEQ = 6;   DBL-INDENT-LIST = " '(c) for a base or determinable fee or any
corresponding interest in leasehold land;";
 SEQ = 7;   DBL-INDENT-LIST = " '(d) being an infant, for an estate in fee
simple or for a term of years absolute; or";
 SEQ = 8;   HALF-I-SIN-I-SUB = " 3(iii) limited in trust for any person for an
estate in fee simple or for a term of years absolute contingently on
the  happening of any event; or";
 SEQ = 9;   HALF-I-SIN-I-SUB = " '(iv) .........";
 SEQ = 10;   HALF-I-SIN-I-SUB = " '(v) charged, whether voluntarily or in
consideration of marriage or by way of family arrangement, and whether
immediately  or after an interval, with the payment of any rentcharge
for the life of any person, or any less period, or of any capital,
 annual, or periodical sums for the portions, advancement, maintenance,
or otherwise for the benefit of any persons, with or  without any terms
of years for securing or raising the same;";
 SEQ = 11;   CONT-TEXT = " 4creates or is for the purposes of this Act a
settlement and is in this Act referred to as a settlement, or as the
settlement, as the case requires:";
 SEQ = 12;   CONT-TEXT = " F Provided that, where land is the subject of a
compound settlement, references in this Act to the settlement shall be
construed as meaning such compound settlement, unless the context
otherwise requires.";
 SEQ = 13;   CONT-TEXT = " |(2)Where an infant is beneficially entitled to land
for an estate in fee simple or for a term of years absolute and by
 reason of an intestacy or otherwise there is no instrument under which
the interest of the infant arises or is acquired, a  settlement shall
be deemed to have been made by the intestate, or by the person whose
interest the infant has acquired.";
 SEQ = 14;   CONT-TEXT = " p (3) An infant shall be deemed to be entitled in
possession notwithstanding any subsisting right of dower (not assigned
by  metes and bounds) affecting the land, and such a right of dower
shall be deemed to be an interest comprised in the subject of  the
settlement and coming to the dowress under or by virtue of the
settlement.";
 SEQ = 15;   CONT-TEXT = " G Where dower has been assigned by metes and bounds,
the letters of administration or probate granted in respect of the
 estate of the husband of the dowress shall be deemed a settlement made
by the husband.";
```

Figure 6 (Part A).   The SPIRES Representation of the Extract From the UK Statute of Figure 4.

record. There is also a further record (not given here) for text in the
section omitted, such as the subsection:

"(iv)........................"

As we are mainly concerned here with the modelling aspect and mapping text
into databases, the output side is beyond the scope of this paper. The
input and output, however, are, of course, not entirely independent for it

```
SEQ = 16;   CONT-TEXT = " m (4) An estate or interest not disposed of by a
settlement and remaining in or reverting to the settlor, or any person
 deriving title under him, is for the purposes of this Act an estate or
interest comprised in the subject of the settlement and  coming to the
settlor or such person under or by virtue of the settlement.";
SEQ = 17;   CONT-TEXT = " ` (5) Where-";
SEQ = 18;   HALF-I-SIN-I-SUB = " T(a) a settlement creates an entailed interest
which is incapable of being barred or defeated, or a base or
determinable  fee, whether or not the reversion or right of reverter is
in the Crown, or any corresponding interest in leasehold land; or";
SEQ = 19;   HALF-I-SIN-I-SUB = "F(b)the subject of a settlement is an entailed
interest, or a base or determinable fee, whether or not the reversion
or  right of reverter is in the Crown, or any corresponding interest in
leasehold land;";
SEQ = 20;   CONT-TEXT ="Dthe reversion or right of reverter upon the cesser of
the interest so created or settled shall be deemed to be an interest
 comprised in the subject of the settlement, and limited by the
settlement.";
SEQ = 21;   CONT-TEXT = " `(6)Subsections (4) and (5) of this section bind the
Crown.";
SEQ = 22;   CONT-TEXT = " ` `D[[1]](7) This section does not apply to land held
upon trust for sale.`d";
TYPESUBSCH = ROMAN;    PARTLOW.SCT = 1;    PARTHIGH.SCT = 0;   CHAPTER.SCT = 0;
;
****
ID = 192501810000000000001000000000000000;     RECNO = 1440;
ACCESS-NO = sif00034+ 1925 c.18 ,Part I ,*1440;
ACT-TITLE = "SETTLED LAND ACT 1925 (c.`x18) `";
KIND = 10;    DATE = April 9, 1925;    TAPE = 1;    SCHSOURCE = PART;
PART-TEXT = "`PART I";
SEQ = 1;   PART-TEXT = " `General Preliminary Provisions";
SEQ = 2;   PART-SUBHEADING = " `Settlements and Settled Land";
TYPESUBSCH = ROMAN;    PARTLOW.SCT = 1;    PARTHIGH.SCT = 0;   CHAPTER.SCT = 0;
;
ID = 192501800000000000000000000000000000;     RECNO = 1439;
ACCESS-NO = sif00034+ 1925 c.18 ,0 ,*1439;
ACT-TITLE = "SETTLED LAND ACT 1925 (c.`x18) `";
KIND = 1;    DATE = April 9, 1925;    TAPE = 1;
SEQ = 1;   GEN-BOLD-TYPE = " `SETTLED LAND ACT 1925 (c.`x18) `";
SEQ = 2;   FOOTNOTE = " `[[1]]S.1(7) added by Law of Property (Amendment) Act
1926 (c.`x11), Sch.";
SEQ = 3;   FOOTNOTE = " `[[2]]Words inserted by Law of Property (Amendment) Act
1926 (c.`x11), Sch.";
SEQ = 4;   FOOTNOTE = " `[[3]]Words substituted by Law of Property (Amendment)
...
;
```

Figure 6 (Part B).   The SPIRES Representation of the Extract From the UK Statute of Figure 4.

is to be borne in mind that the basis is logical not physical. Thus Figure 4 is only one of many possible output forms that can be generated by
Figure 6. Which one is selected can be under user control.

5. CONCLUSIONS

Only a small part of the world's textual information is at present
stored in machine-readable structured form, although the quantity of
textual data on computer is increasing at a rapid rate due to the popularity of word-processing, computer type-setting, computer conferencing, electronic mail, office automation, etc. In order to make full use of this
information in textual form as a knowledge base, it is necessary to advance
the techniques for handling text automatically. File handling of structured text is at present inadequate for knowledge base purposes.

The aim of this paper has been to show that proper database technology
needs to be applied to text. This can only be achieved by the careful

design both of appropriate models to represent the structure of the text and of the software to implement these models. To this end it seems that due regard to textual data needs to be paid in the future by those engaged in the design of data models, DBMS packages, and even operating systems and new computer architectures.

6. ACKNOWLEDGEMENTS

We are grateful to the following persons whose data has been used in this study of textual databases. The clinical database has been designed and maintained by Dr. M. K. Ward and Mrs. J. Little of the Department of Medicine, Newcastle University. The extract from the natural history catalog was kindly provided by Mr. P. S. Davis and Mr. C. Brewer of the Hancock Museum, Newcastle University. It was only possible to construct an extensive legal database through the provision of data tapes from Her Majesty's Stationery Office. The printed version of the section from the Settled Land Act, 1925, is reproduced also by permission of the Controller of HMSO.

7. REFERENCES

Agosti, M., 1983-4, "Specialised Hardware for Data Base Management and Information Retrieval: A Classified Bibliography", ACM SIGIR Forum, 18, pp. 13-40.

Bachman, C. W., and Day, M., 1978, "The Role Concept in Data Models", Proceedings, 3rd International Conference on Very Large Data Bases, Tokyo.

Bachman, C. W., 1980, "The Role Data Model Approach to Data Structures", Proceedings, International Conference on Data Bases, University of Aberdeen.

Borkin, S. A., 1979, Equivalence Properties of Semantic Data Bases for Database Systems, Technical Report of Laboratory for Computer Science, MIT, TR-206.

Chen, P. P. S., 1976, "The Entity-Relationship Model - Towards a Unified View of Data", ACM Trans Database Systems, 1, p. 9.

Codd, E. F., 1970, "A Relational Model of Data for Large Shared Data Banks", Communications of ACM, 13, (6), pp. 377-387.

Codd, E. F., 1979, "Extending the Database Relational Model to Capture More Meaning", ACM Trans Database Systems, 4, pp. 397-434.

Date, C. J., 1981, An Introduction to Database Systems, Systems Programming Series, Addison-Wesley, 1, 3rd edition.

Heather, M. A., 1982, "Legal Structures for Law Machines", Artificial Intelligence and Legal Information Systems, C. Ciampi, ed., North Holland, London and Amsterdam.

Heather, M. A., 1985, "Semiotic Orders in Law", Second Annual Conference on Law and Technology. Legal Language, Computational Linguistics, and Artificial Intelligence, Houston.

Heine, M., 1984, "The Flow of Control in a Communication Process", Cybernetica, 27, pp. 57-64.

Knuth, D. E., 1979, TEX and METAFONT, New Directions in Typesetting,

Digital Press, Mass.

Lorie, R. A., 1981, Issues in Data Bases for Design Application, IBM
   Research Report RJ3176.

Macleod, I. A., and Crawford, R. G., 1983, "Document Retrieval as a
   Database Application", Inf. Technol. Res. & Dev., 2, (1), pp. 43-60.

Ossana, J. F., 1976, NROFF/TROLL, Computing Science Technical Report Number
   54, Bell Laboratories.

Radecki, T., 1983, "A Theoretical Background for Applying Fuzzy Set Theory
   in Information Retrieval", Fuzzy Sets and Systems, 10, (2), pp. 169-
   183.

Rossiter, B. N., 1984, "Introduction to Data Base Management Systems",
   Computer Physics Communications, 33, pp. 5-12.

Rossiter, B. N., 1985, "Full Text Data Base Management Systems: A Model
   and Implementation for Law", Proceedings Second International Congress
   LOGICA INFORMATICA DIRITTO, Florence.

Schmid, H. A., and Swanson, J. R., 1975, Proceedings ACM SIGMOD, International Conference on Management of Data.

Schmidt, J. W., and Brodie, M. L., 1983, Relational Database Systems:
   Analysis and Comparison, Springer-Verlag.

Shannon, C., and Weaver, W., 1949, The Mathematical Theory of Communication, Illinois.

Sparck Jones, K., and Kay, M., 1973, Linguistics and Information Science,
   Academic Press, New York.

Teskey, F. N., 1982, Principles of Text Processing, Ellis Horwood.

Zunde, Pranas, 1984, "Empirical Laws and Theories of Information and
   Software Science", Information Processing Management, 20, (1-2), pp.
   5-18.

VALIDATION OF SOFTWARE UNDER A SIGNAL-DETECTION THEORY SCHEMA

M. H. Heine

School of Librarianship & Information Studies
Newcastle upon Tyne Polytechnic
Newcastle upon Tyne NE1 8ST, United Kingdom

Abstract: The process of correcting errors in software appears at present to lack a general theoretical schema. Possible reasons for this are: (1) that software errors can be of fundamentally different types (e.g., errors due to incompatibility of source code with a given language-description; errors at run time; errors due to the "wrong output" being given); (2) that errors can have an existence that is 'imputed' rather than 'discovered'; (3) that debugging tends to be seen more as a theory-driven practice than an empiricism-driven one (i.e., centered on mismatch between program performance and program context); and (4) that the theory of software science has yet to accommodate, in a fully satisfactory way, the human-cognitive processes that create, evaluate, and use software. A schema of debugging in respect of one type of error, namely that arising from failure in the program specification itself, i.e., failure in program validity, is put forward. In this schema, different program options are seen (individually) as acting fallibly in respect of different units of input data, and seen also (together) as being applicable within different logical expressions. The latter are referred to as 'general tests'. A group of programs, serving to analyze the results of arbitrary attempts to tune (validate) a test-program is described. Last, a conjecture is offered as to the possible paradigmatic implications of the approach adopted for a science of information.

Paper originally presented under the title 'An Information Science Perspective on Detecting Errors in Software'.

1. INTERNAL AND EXTERNAL SOFTWARE ERRORS

Software errors may be divided into two categories: those defined in reference to a lack of conformity between a specification for the program and the program itself, and those defined in reference to an insufficiency in the program specification as judged by higher-order goals and as evident in mismatch between intended program output and actual output. We label these two error types as 'Type INT' and 'Type EXT' respectively, as suggested by the notions of 'Internal to specification' (closed-world errors) and 'External to specification' (open-world errors), respectively. More formally, we define:

1. TYPE 'INT' PROGRAM ERRORS: Errors that are internal to :

specification:

a. Program logic errors (incompatibility of source code with specification of program language, or incompatibility of object code with hardware), and

b. Run-time errors (errors arising from inconsistency in the program specification, or over-specification in respect of the ranges of data that are to be input to the program, etc.).

2. TYPE 'EXT' PROGRAM ERRORS: Errors that arise from incompatibility between intended and actual program performance. (Such errors are made, in effect, in recognition of deficiencies in the program specification, and are not associated with failure of the program to compile or run.)

Examples of these errors are readily imagined. Failure of a program to exit from a loop is clearly a Type INT error, as is failure of an instruction to execute because of incorrect initialization (either explicitly, or by default) of some variable. Examples of Type EXT errors, on the other hand, would be: (1) assertion by the program that a piece of encoded knowledge meets some external-to-program knowledge requirement, when it does not (or vice versa), and (2) the assertion by a program that an approaching object (in some informational world again external to the program) is 'hostile' when it is in fact friendly (or vice versa).

Our aim in this paper is to demonstrate that the theory of 'information storage and retrieval' (ISR) can be adapted so as to bear on the problem of software error-detection in respect of Type EXT errors. The possibility that ISR theory can also be applied to some types of Type INT error is not excluded, however. Some of the theory to which we shall appeal can be found in Heine (1984).

The possible technological value of such a development could reside, it is suggested, firstly, in improved conceptualization of software-error detection. Secondly, it might allow established theory of ISR to contribute to the software validation problem; and, thirdly, it could, by appeal to the philosophy and practice of underlined experimentation in ISR, bring a stronger influence of the classical, empirical sciences into software development and evaluation processes.

We also note and emphasize in this introduction a specific philosophical position in respect of the existence of Type EXT errors. This is that it is assumed that a Type EXT error exists (in some information state) prior to the execution of a test to establish the existence of that error. This may seem an obvious point, but it is suggested that some Type EXT errors might be seen to be of an a posteriori or imputational character, where the 'error' is asserted to exist in consequence of (i.e., arising from) an inspection of program output. For example, we might decide that a program telling us where to put down an oil well (or which drug to administer to a patient) was henceforth to be seen as 'in error' because we were now of the view that the program should have informed us how deep to put the well (or what drug dosage to administer). Thus, it seems to be an everyday truth that what a program specification could consist of, is usually influenced by analysis of the effects of previous versions of itself, just as program-writing itself against a fixed program specification is a process of iterative refinement. However, despite the everyday reality of such 'heuristics', we limit ourselves in this paper to some discussion of what would appear to be the more basic process of error detection against a fixed specification, and to cases where the errors are both of Type EXT, and <u>a priori</u> in character.

A final disclaimer is that we do not, in this paper, systematically review the literature of software-error detection in respect of the problem discussed; instead we set up at this time the fairly arbitrary 'pointers' to papers by authors such as Bending (1984), Dunn (1984), and Jain and Agrawal (1985), and the monograph by Deutsch (1982).

2. BASIC CONCEPTS

We first define a set of data structures, $j \in J$. These could be scalar-values or vectors, or more complicated data entities such as relations or matrices, tree-structures, lists, geometrical figures, or even programs.

Secondly, we define a <u>program under test</u>, U, and a cognitive system, V, that generates (specifies and constructs) and validates it.

Thirdly, we define a construct, C, <u>within V but external to U</u>, which serves as <u>criterion</u> against which each data-structure can be evaluated to True or False*. The evaluation process concerned is also seen as external to the program, and one imagines that it would usually be implemented with-in human-cognition or within a higher-order program acting as proxy for such cognition. Thus we see the construct C as existing <u>internally to a cognitive</u> process which is accessing (and also, as it happens, evaluating) the program being tested. The evaluation of C by the system V is in reference to a shell of (informational) existence, W, which could be termed "V's model of the World". (See Figure 1).

For example, suppose that the cognitive system V has constructed a data-structure j in reference to some industrial plant (e.g., a nuclear power plant). Moreover, V is prepared to assert that the industrial plant is either 'safe' or 'not safe' when described by j. (Let us say that the decision is 'safe'.)** Thus V maps the ordered pair (C,j) to the set {True,False}, and does so by reference to a knowledge shell W that it it-self generates.

Fourthly, we also define, in reference to the above criterion, a set of software tests, {TESTi} ($i \in I$). We think of these as <u>programmable options within the program V</u>, for example, they might be sub-routines to be called or not-called, or choices among main program branches. (The term 'tuning option' would perhaps be preferable to 'test', but as one is 'testing the tuning option' we prefer the simple term 'test'.) These tests exist to probe the program, U (not the external-to-program knowledge-World) in re-spect of C for any arbitrary data-structure j. For completeness, we note also the complication that the way a criterion is operationalized will ap-peal to further criteria that are transparent to this schema. (For ex-ample, in deciding that an industrial plant was safe, given some data-structure, a cognitive system choose to 'err on the safe side' or 'err on the dangerous side'.) Rather than explore this complication here, we pre-fer for the moment to note that once a 'criterion <u>has</u> been implemented by V on j, then tests can be selected by V which <u>themselves</u> will cause the pro-gram to 'err on the safe side', or etc. We exemplify this effect through a discussion of Recall and Precision effects in the following text.

---

*C is thus a logical criterion-variable existing within V but not U.
**For simplicity, we exclude discussion here of both <u>conflict of judgement</u> as between different cognitive systems, and <u>hindsight,</u> where - in both cases - fallibility in an assertion is recognized.

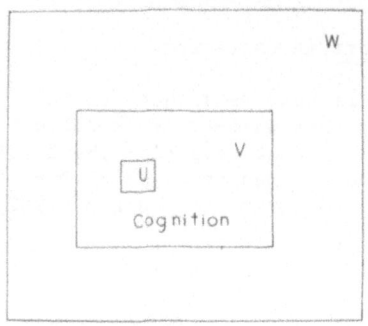

Figure 1. Three systems recognized by the
           paradigm given in the text. The
           innermost s..ell, U, is an algo-
           rithmic or information-processing
           shell, created and evaluated by
           a cognitive system V. The latter
           constructs U in order to facili-
           tate the functioning of U in an
           external-to-paradigm world which
           is modelled by W.

Such tests can be recognized as <u>fallible</u> (to differing extents) in the
sense that if TESTi leads to the assertion (by the program U) that an individual item of data, j, upholds C, then this assertion can be True or False
(within W) according to the external-to-program evaluation process referred
to above, i.e., evaluation by V. Similarly, the application of TESTi to
program U, by cognition V, could lead to the assertion by U that C is not
upheld, for some data-structure j. This too is a fallible assertion, and
will be adjudicated on, as such, by V appealing to C.

Thus our view of Type EXT software testing is that of evaluation of a
set of program options, each option being evaluated by program performance
in respect of a set of data-structures. (The members of this set are input
to the program under test, and are chosen by some cognitive system to be
representative of some problem of interest.) The program performance is
evaluated by a cognitive system (which is regarded in the simplest validation model as infallible), this system both adjudicating on the correctness
of the performance, and supplying both the program options and the test
data.

Fifthly, we note the possibility that some programs will be such, and
some tests will be such, that software tests can be applied jointly <u>in
logical expressions</u>. For example, we could choose to explore a program's
EXT validity by means of such 'composite' tests as:

        TEST7 AND (TEST8 or TEST10)

        TEST45 AND NOT TEST19.

We refer to such tests as 'general tests'. For such tests to exist, it
would seem to be necessary that the following condition should be met:

        that where two tests are ANDed, i.e., where both the program op-
        tions concerned are chosen for implementation, the program remains
        computable.

For our final set of constructs, we also define, conventionally from an ISR perspective, but unconventionally from a software-debugging perspective, the following measures of performance of individual or general tests. It is assumed that the testing of the program being validated has entailed inputting (to system U) each of the data-structures contained in J.

* Recall, R, is the probability that a data-structure which is evaluated to True by V, against C, is also evaluated to True by a general test.

* Precision, P, is the probability that a data-structure which is evaluated to True by a general test, is also evaluated to True by V against C.

* Fallout, F, is the probability that a data-structure which is evaluated to False by V against C, is evaluated to True by a general test.

* Generality, G, is the probability that a data-structure is evaluated to True by V against C.

* ELC-Recall, r_i, is the probability that a data-structure evaluated to True by V against C, is also evaluated to True by an <u>elementary logical conjunct</u>* of some of the tests, i.e., by a subset of the test-thesaurus.

* ELC-Precision, p_i, is the probability that a data-structure evaluated to True by an elementary logical conjunct of tests is also evaluated to True by V against C.

* ELC-Fallout, f_i, is the probability that a data-structure evaluated by V against C to False, is evaluated by an elementary logical conjunct of tests to True.

It is clear that any general test has Recall and Fallout values associated with it that can be derived by <u>summing</u> the ELC-Recall and ELC-Fallout values associated with the ELCs of which that test is a disjunction. That an arbitrary logical expression can always be expressed as a disjunction of ELCs is a standard result of logic theory (see for example Hohn (1966)). For given a set of ELCs (defined for some set of tests {TESTi|i∈I}), i.e., given:

{ $\forall$ L(TESTi) }, where the logical operator L can be either 'NOT', or be absent

— then any general test can be expressed as a <u>disjunction of a combination</u> of the members of this set.

We also note that there are <u>inherent limits</u> to the performance of a general test, associated with the values of the r_i and f_i. For example, suppose we denote the values of ELC-Recall and ELC-Fallout associated with

---

*An elementary logical conjunct is a logical expression, defined by all the members (or their negations) of a set of ELVs, and has the form of an ANDing of all the ELVs (or their negations). Thus, examples of ELCs, for the ELVs X, Y, and Z, are: X AND Y AND Z; X AND (NOT Y) and Z; (NOT X) and Y AND Z; etc. Note there are 2**n ELCs for a set of n ELVs, and 2**(2**n)-1 logical expressions (not all of which may be general tests) for this number of ELCs.

the all-negated ELC by ro and fo. Then the <u>maximum possible value of Recall</u> will be the value of the expression:

$$\Sigma ri \quad (ri \ not = ro).$$

and the maximum value of Fallout will be the value of:

$$\Sigma fi \quad (fi \ not = fi).$$

For otherwise (on the assumption that ro>0) the general test would need to assert that <u>all</u> data-structures input to the program could meet the criterion C, i.e., it would need to have the (trivial) tautological form:

$$TESTj \ OR \ NOT(TESTj), \quad J \ arbitrary.$$

The set of ri and fi values also determines a <u>maximum value for Precision</u> (which might or might not be 1). This value will be 1 if there exist one or more ELCs for which ri>0 and fi=0. Otherwise it has the value GR'/(GR'+ (1-G)F'), where R' and F' sum the ri and fi values respectively, for those ELC(s) for which ri/fi is a maximum.

Lastly, here, we note that a 'syntax-free' characterization of the action of a set of tests (contingent on U) may be defined as follows. First, generate <u>all possible</u> general tests for some subset of the repertoire of program options that the program-validator (V) estimates to be optimum and, secondly, map each general test to some outcome space of interest. The latter could be the Precision-Recall outcome space, or the Recall-Fallout outcome space, for example, of the outcome spaces of P, R, or F (say) taken individually. This having been done, various characterizations of the set of individual tests can be defined. For example, one might conceive of 'the center-of-mass of the resulting distribution (of general tests)'.

3. SOME PROGRAMS TO ANALYZE TEST DATA

Suggested by the preceding schema, a set of programs was written with a view to assisting in the understanding of the interactions between general software tests of Type EXT and general programs to which they could be applied, and possibly to suggest new theory. These programs have not yet been applied in a formal experiment.

All the programs assume that data have been collected from a validation experiment, and that the data determine a set of ordered pairs of values of the random vector (ri,fi), or else corresponding frequency-pairs. This set itself is unordered except that the final pair of values is (ro,fo) (or the corresponding pair of frequency-values). Each ELC derived from the component tests is associated with one such pair of values. An example makes this clearer. Suppose we try to tune a program using two tuning options T1 and T2. The ELCs derived from these options are: T1 and T2; T1 AND NOT(T2); NOT(T1) AND T2; NOT(T1) and NOT(T2). Suppose also that J comprises 20 data-structures, of which a cognitive system determines 5 to be True against C, and 15 to be False against C. Then if the ELC 'T1 AND NOT(T2)', say, evaluates 3 of the 5 C-True structures to U-True, and 3 of the 15 C-False structures to U-True, the (ri,fi) probability-pair associated with this ELC will be (0.6,0.2).

The analysis programs at present assume that all conceivable test-expressions, for a given set of individual program tests, are general tests, i.e., they lead to computable programs, but it is planned to relax this assumption in the future (so that only those test-expressions that do lead to computable programs are analyzed).

The programs are named as follows, the common prefix 'CLCST' signifying 'Context-Logic Centered Software Testing':

CLCST.OPTIM
CLCST.SURFACES
CLCST.FOLD1
CLCST.FOLD2
CLCST.LIMITS

Outlines of the specifications of these analysis programs are as follows:

1. CLCST.OPTIM This identified various <u>optimal general tests</u>, subject to 4 criteria, and for n=1 to 4. The criteria are:

   * Minimum value of Marczewski-Steinhaus metric (P+R-2PR)/ (P+R-PR);

   * Maximum value of Euclidean distance from the point R=0, P=0 to (R,P), i.e., $SQRT(R**2 + P**2)$;

   * Maximum value of 'Retrieval Power', i.e., $GR(1-G)(1-F)$;

   * Maximum value of Precision, P, i.e., $GR/(GR+(1-G)F)$.

2. CLCST.SURFACES This program: (1) identifies the distribution of all general tests* and related marginal distributions; (2) evaluates statistics for these distributions; and (3) identifies an optimal ranking of the ELCs (by the ratio ri/fi, $fi>0$).

3. CLCST.FOLD1 and CLCST.FOLD2 These identify the effect on general test performance of (a) varying n (from 1 to 4), and (b) altering the individuation of tests, where k tests are used from a choice of n, $0<k<n<5$.

4. CLCST.LIMITS This program evaluates the <u>inherent limits</u> to test performance for a given set of tests, in terms of R, P, and other criterion variables.

Illustration of Program Action

To illustrate the functioning of the program CLCST.SURFACES, for example, we assume that experimental data has been obtained on the effects of inputting 928 test data-structures to a program, 14 of which have been evaluated to True by an extra-program cognitive agent in reference to some criterion. (For example, 928 map-coordinates have been input to an expert system which advises on whether or not to drill for oil at a given coordinate-pair location, and it is assumed to be known that oil is present at (and only at) 14 of these locations.) We assume that 4 tuning actions attempting to validate the program against that criterion have been defined, along with <u>rules</u> to give meaning to the application of those tests in conjunction, disjunction, and negation. Sixteen ELCs are thus determined. The arbitrary (ri,fi)-data pertaining to these ELCs is assumed to be as follows:

---

*An internal option also allows for all general tests <u>but excluding those containing a disjunction with the all-negated ELC.</u>

ri=(2,1,0,1,2,0,0,3,1,1,0,1,0,1,0,1)
fi=(0,0,1,1,0,2,0,4,0,0,2,2,1,1,4,896)

The data here are in pairs, are in frequency rather than probability form, and are in a program-recognized order. The last pair relates to (ro,fo), i.e., to the all-negated ELC:

NOT(TEST1) AND NOT(TEST2) AND NOT(TEST3) AND NOT(TEST4), i.e.,
NOT (TEST1 OR TEST2 OR TEST3 OR TEST4).*

Then the distributions of all possible general tests, under these conditions, over the RP and RF outcome spaces are as shown in Figure 2, as output by CLCST.SURFACES. As mentioned above, this program also computes the marginal distributions (for R, P, and F) and evaluates such statistics as the center-of-mass of the random vector (R,P).

4. PARADIGMATIC IMPLICATIONS

It is hoped that the preceding 'information science view' of the software validation problem will prove useful in practice. However, it should be our concern, it is suggested, to look more deeply at its significance as a schema per se. We offer the following brief comments by way of tentative contributions here.

We recap that our schema involves three information-processing 'worlds' or 'systems', as we showed in Figure 1. The three systems are such that W encloses V, and V encloses U, i.e., the model is a shell one. It is also a pragmatic schema in that it is centered on the middle shell, V. Cognition is viewed as having two modes, corresponding to the modeling (knowledge-construction) of the real World of which it is a part (and upon which it is dependent), i.e., W-construction, and the construction of processes that facilitate the interactions of it with that World, i.e., U-construction. We could, if we liked, refer to these as "outward-looking" and "inward-looking" modes, respectively. System U comprises one or several information-processing systems that are 'known' to the cognitive system, V, i.e., are accessible to it in all or some senses of this term (i.e., definable, controllable, and usable by V). System U includes conventional software, but might usefully include also any complete algorithmic schema, or set of algorithms.

System or shell V may be regarded as 'intelligent', i.e., autonomous but with an incompletely-defined control structure. (We follow Heine (1984) in seeing intelligence as simply a semiotic property, and associated with incompleteness in description.) It is this shell that we might associate with our minds, and with our propensity to generate (semiotic) worlds within the real-World.

System W, in contrast to system U, is only partly dependent on system V, i.e., on the cognition part of our reality. (This is notwithstanding that W is created by V.) This system is accessible to V, but the constructions that make it up are influenced in a way that does not form part of the specification of W by V. (We might say that the values of the constructs are accessible to V, but not determined by V, or that the language

---

*This ELC has evaluated one data-structure to True when that data-structure was judged (externally to the program) to meet some specified criterion (there being 14 such units), and it evaluated 896 data-structures to True when the data-structures had been judged (externally to the program) not to meet that criterion (there being 914 such data-structures).

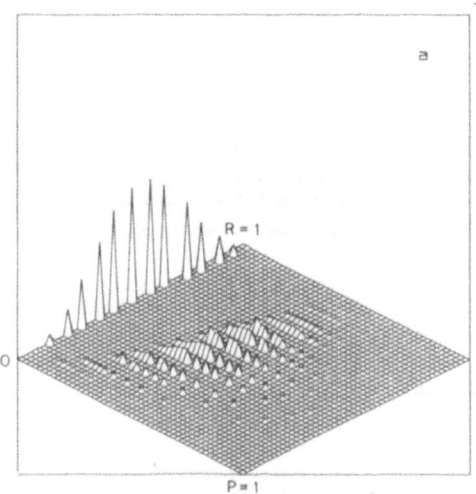 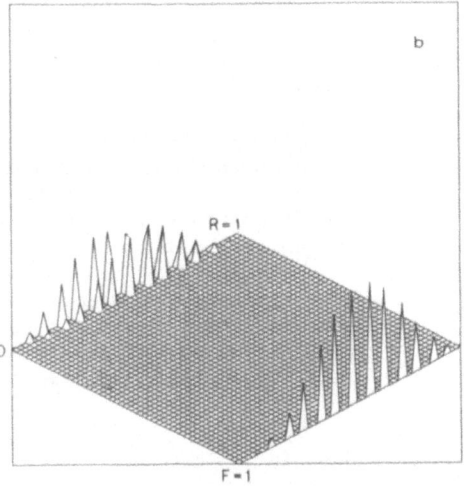

Figure 2. Distributions of a General Software Test: 'a' shows the
distribution of all possible general tests over the Recall-
Precision outcome space, for the arbitrary data given in
the text: whereas 'b' shows their distribution over the
Recall-Fallout outcome space. The more effective general
tests, according to these criteria, are those associated
with high P and R values, and low F values.

but not the content of system W is specified by V.) The concept of an
external 'real-World' is a necessary one, since V has created W as a model
of 'something', and since W only reacts with a system external to V –
rather than fully specifies that system. Such a view is necessary in order
to explain the intelligent actions of V (and thus the incompleteness of our
portrayal of V, and V's self-portrayal). Thus we see a necessary paradox
consisting in the assertion that a real-World exists that is not fully
knowable.

We suggest that such a paradigm could recognize intercommunication between several systems of type V, for the effects of same would be evident
locally within shells W and V, possibly facilitated by U. This would be to
introduce a social cognitive system, and we might agree that systems W' and
W" local to systems V' and V", could be seen to converge through cognitive
negotiation between systems V' and V"; i.e., that a consensus as to an optimum and common form for the W-systems could be sought for cognitive-
social advantage.

Within the paradigm, we might also sensibly see the cognitive systems V
as self-adapting (in response to data-flow from systems W), but more essentially we seem obliged to recognize incompleteness in definition, i.e., intelligence, to provide a control-mechanism for such adaptation. As already
stated, we see the origins of 'intelligent action' as ultimately semiotic
in character.

Clearly, such a schema can be provisional and an outline only, and
would benefit from refinement. We note here, finally, some points which
might assist in its development:

1. The schema is a 'pragmatic' one, in the sense of this term offered
   by Durkheim (and arguably, also William James and Ernest Mach).
   The notion of a priori absolute truth, as a (hypothetically) knowable property of cognition, is rejected. Instead, truths are seen

as local to cognitive being, i.e., to a system such as that represented by 'V'. Possibly it would be feasible to reconcile the
"monads" of Leibniz with systems of the latter type?

2. Possibly, existence-shell V could be identified with Popper's
    'Third World' but this would seem to be a precarious step, for
    the schema as a whole is in essence a disavowal that any worlds
    other than those of information-processing can be meaningfully de-
    scribed, even if their existence is regarded as certain.

3. The concept of 'knowledge' in the schema is replaced by that of
    'process' and 'data', the definition of the latter depending on the
    prior definition of the former, but this is perhaps now a conven-
    tional view within software science.

ACKNOWLEDGEMENTS

The author acknowledges, with thanks, the helpful comments and criti-
cisms by delegates to the EFISS3 conference in regard to an earlier version
of this paper.

REFERENCES

Bending, M. J., 1984, "HITEST: A Knowledge-Based Test Generation System",
    IEEE Design & Test of Computers, 1, pp. 83-92.

Deutsch, M. S., 1982, Software Verification and Validation: Realistic
    Project Approaches, Prentice-Hall.

Dunn, L. N., 1984, "IBM's Engineering Design System Support for VLSI Design
    and Verification", IEEE Design & Test of Computers, 1, pp. 30-40.

Heine, M. H., 1984, "The Flow of Control in a Communication Process",
    Cybernetica, 27, pp. 57-64.

Hohn, F. F., 1966, Applied Boolean Algebra, 2nd Ed., Macmillan, UK.

Jain, S. K., and Agrawal, V. D., 1985, "Statistical Fault Analysis", IEEE
    Design & Test of Computers, 2, pp. 38-44.

OBJECT-ORIENTED INTERLISP PROGRAMMING ENVIRONMENT FOR IMPLEMENTATION OF A

DISTRIBUTED EXPERT SYSTEM

Ralf-Dirk Hennings and Steffen Schulze-Kremer

Freie Universität Berlin
Fachbereich Kommunikationswissenschaften
Arbeitsbereich Informationswissenschaft
Malteser Strasse 74-100   L 625
D-1000 Berlin 46

Abstract: Commencing with a short review of the MONSTRAT-concept (i.e., a model of MOdular functions based on Natural information processes for STRAtegic problem Treatment, the paper deals in its first part with aspects of distribution and autonomy of all the experts involved in these processes, the requirements of complexity, the challenge of parallelism, and, finally, the limitations of closed systems.

Foundational characteristics of open systems are explained, fitting very well into the MONSTRAT-concept.

Then, consequences for an implementation are considered including a direct claim for object-oriented programming environments.

Finally, a prototype implementation is presented, thus leading to key insights into the mechanisms, and giving us better programming capabilities on our INTERLISP-system for implementing a distributed expert system.

The paper concludes with an outlook to future aspects of our work.

1. THE MONSTRAT-APPROACH

The problem of a general model of information systems which uses basic concepts in a way that in reality could be represented by human or techno- logical components has led to the MONSTRAT-approach.

Experience and research with people seeking specific information, in- termediaries, and interaction between both, have revealed some basic func- tions which have to be fulfilled by any information provision mechanism. The modelling of these functions followed approaches of Artificial Intelli- gence, where systems are constructed out of separate experts, which are responsible for a specific task. The communication among these experts can be realized by different models. This led to a model of "MOdular functions based on Natural information processes for STRAtegic problem Treatment (MONSTRAT)".

The MONSTRAT-model of an intellectual architecture of the information provision mechanism within an information system is thought of as an interactive process between an information seeking (IS), normally a user, and an information providing (IP) mechanism being realized by modular components, each of which might be represented by

- computerized or computer-aided function(s) within a mainframe unit or on distributed systems

- human function(s) by a single dedicated person

- social function(s) being dealt with in a social mono- or hetero-functional group.

The basic modules which are graphically represented in Figure 1 can be specified in different manners. The informal description in Chapter 1 is only a short repetition of other earlier papers given for easier understanding of the following parts, omitting a lot of details which can be found (Wersig, 1982; Seeger, 1982; Belkin, Seeger, and Wersig, 1983; Wersig and Hennings, 1984; Hennings, 1984; and Hennings and Munter, 1985(d)).

They have been verified by means of a simulation with human beings (Belkin, Hennings, and Seeger, 1984; Seeger, Belkin, and Hennings, 1983; Seeger and Hennings, 1983; Hennings, 1983(b); Hennings et al., 1983(f); Belkin, 1983; and Hennings, 1983(d)).

All those functions which should be provided by computer-assistance must be described very formally. Until now, some have been elaborated in more detail (Wolf-Zweifler, 1984; Straube, 1985; Hennings, 1982; Hennings, 1983(a); Hennings, 1983(c); Hennings 1984(b); Hennings, 1984(c); Hennings et al., 1985), but a lot of work still has to be done.

1.1 Input Function (Input Analyst (IA))

Regardless of how the interaction should be started, interaction requires input from the IS-mechanism into the IP-mechanism. To be processed and "understood" internally by the IP-mechanism, this input has to be transformed into an appropriate internal representation and then analyzed according to certain aspects like language and language level being used, and linguistic skills being indicated. This is the task of the Input Analyst (IA).

1.2 Analytical Functions

The analytical functions have to analyze the transformed input according to different tasks. Investigation of "natural information processes" so far revealed the following functions.

Problem Description (PD). The Problem Description (PD) function of the information mechanism is concerned with describing or modelling the user's problematic situation (Wersig, 1979) or anomalous state of knowledge (Belkin, 1980) in such a way that it is capable of discovering the type of problem which has brought the user to the mechanism, and so that the mechanism can identify the topic(s), the type, the structure and its context. This categorization is necessary because different problem types might require different strategies for retrieval from the mechanism's data base.

A topical function is evident; by type of problem, we mean, for instance, procedural or decision making or learning; by structure, coherent or unstructured state of knowledge, gap in knowledge or need for establishing relations, and so on, is meant.

provision mechanism within an information system is thought of as an interactive process between an information seeking (IS), normally a user, and an information providing (IP) mechanism being realized by modular components, each of which might be represented by

- computerized or computer-aided function(s) within a mainframe unit or on distributed systems

- human function(s) by a single dedicated person

- social function(s) being dealt with in a social mono- or hetero-functional group.

The basic modules which are graphically represented in Figure 1 can be specified in different manners. The informal description in Chapter 1 is only a short repetition of other earlier papers given for easier understanding of the following parts, omitting a lot of details which can be found (Wersig, 1982; Seeger, 1982; Belkin, Seeger, and Wersig, 1983; Wersig and Hennings, 1984; Hennings, 1984; and Hennings and Munter, 1985(d)).

They have been verified by means of a simulation with human beings (Belkin, Hennings, and Seeger, 1984; Seeger, Belkin, and Hennings, 1983; Seeger and Hennings, 1983; Hennings, 1983(b); Hennings et al., 1983(f); Belkin, 1983; and Hennings, 1983(d)).

All those functions which should be provided by computer-assistance must be described very formally. Until now, some have been elaborated in more detail (Wolf-Zweifler, 1984; Straube, 1985; Hennings, 1982; Hennings, 1983(a); Hennings, 1983(c); Hennings 1984(b); Hennings, 1984(c); Hennings et al., 1985), but a lot of work still has to be done.

1.1 Input Function (Input Analyst (IA))

Regardless of how the interaction should be started, interaction requires input from the IS-mechanism into the IP-mechanism. To be processed and "understood" internally by the IP-mechanism, this input has to be transformed into an appropriate internal representation and then analyzed according to certain aspects like language and language level being used, and linguistic skills being indicated. This is the task of the Input Analyst (IA).

1.2 Analytical Functions

The analytical functions have to analyze the transformed input according to different tasks. Investigation of "natural information processes" so far revealed the following functions.

Problem Description (PD). The Problem Description (PD) function of the information mechanism is concerned with describing or modelling the user's problematic situation (Wersig, 1979) or anomalous state of knowledge (Belkin, 1980) in such a way that it is capable of discovering the type of problem which has brought the user to the mechanism, and so that the mechanism can identify the topic(s), the type, the structure and its context. This categorization is necessary because different problem types might require different strategies for retrieval from the mechanism's data base.

A topical function is evident; by type of problem, we mean, for instance, procedural or decision making or learning; by structure, coherent or unstructured state of knowledge, gap in knowledge or need for establishing relations, and so on, is meant.

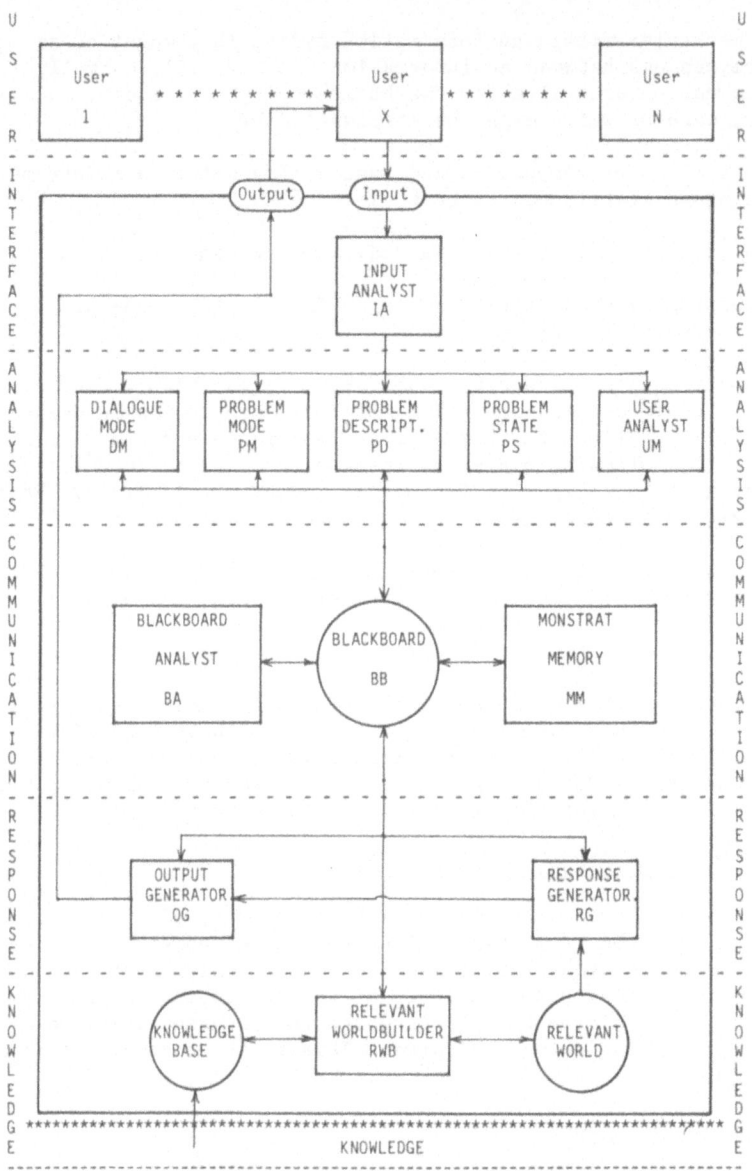

Figure 1. MONSTRAT: MOdular Functions Based on Natural
Information Processes for STRAtegic Problem
Treatment.

Problem State (PS). Another function must provide information of where
in the problem treatment process the user is located. This function is
necessary because users at different points in the problem treatment process will require different kinds of information, and different kinds of
responses from the mechanism. For example, a person just beginning to
understand a problem might require help in shaping the problem itself,
whereas a person with a well-defined problem might require only a factual
response. We call this the Problem State function (PS).

Problem Mode (PM). Related to the problem state is the Problem Mode
function (PM) which provides mechanisms for choosing the appropriate model

of response: that is, of knowing what it is capable of doing, and of selecting the appropriate capability for the given situation. Thus, capabilities of a general information provision mechanism might be problem specification, fact retrieval, advice or comparative evaluation, role reinforce-
ment, and so on. An important aspect of this function is, that the mechanism be able to recognize situations for which it is not appropriate, for
which it has no well suited capabilities, and that it be able to respond
accordingly.

User Model. The state and mode functions are closely related to the
user's problem treatment activity and to how that activity relates to the
mechanism's problem treatment capabilities. In addition to this type of
knowledge, there is a requirement for knowledge of specifics of the situation, related to details of the user and the problem the user is facing.
If we consider the interaction between mechanism and user as a cognitive
communication system, then we see that one of the primary functions of the
mechanism must be to develop a model of the user, especially of the user's
intentions, situation, preferences, and, perhaps, beliefs. That is, a
model of what the user is like, and therefore, of what the user is likely
to need. Thus, the User Model function (UM) is concerned with developing a
description of the user and the user's intentions.

For instance, if it is known that the user is a beginning research
student, this will be of great help to the mechanism in choosing an appropriate response. The response in such a case is likely to be quite different than the type of response, even in the same general subject area,
that would be appropriate for an experienced research or an interested
lay-person.

1.3 Synthetical Functions

The four "experts" mentioned above constitute the more analytically
working functions. The following modules are responsible for the generation of "solutions" - as far as they exist - of the problem treatment
process, i.e., a response of the IP- to the IS-mechanism.

Relevant World Building (RWB). The response is based upon the mechanism's model of the world: that is, its knowledge or database, and will
depend upon the mechanism's perception of what aspects of its world are
relevant to the particular user in the particular situation. Thus, a major
function must be the interaction of the mechanism with the knowledge resource to decide upon a partition of the world relevant to this situation.
This function we call the Relevant World Builder (RWB).

The function will have a set of strategies for interaction with the
knowledge base, the choice of strategy being dependent upon knowledge of
the whole situation. Again, if there appears to be no part of its world
relevant to the situation, the mechanism must be able to inform the user,
and to suggest alternative strategies or treatment modes.

Response Generation (RG). It is insufficient for the purposes of the
mechanism to provide only a representation of the Relevant World to the
user. Therefore, the mechanism must be able to interpret that relevant
world in terms of what the mechanism knows of the user and the user's situation, so that the mechanism can generate an appropriate response. This
function, depending to a great extent upon information provided by the
other functions, we call the Response Generator (RG).

Dialogue Mode (DM). In order for the mechanism to accomplish the previous functions, it is necessary for it to interact appropriately with the
user. This will be accomplished via some form of dialogue, but the

specific kind of interaction used in any context will depend upon the circumstances of the situation. Dialogue is used to elicit information from
the user, which is then used by the information mechanism to help it accomplish its functions; dialogue is used to help the user and the mechanism in
problem formulation; and, dialogue is used to inform the user and the mechanism of one another's progress, intentions, perceptions of the other, and
of the problem, and so on. In general, dialogue is used to help both the
mechanism and the user to manage the user's problem effectively. The
Dialogue Mode function (DM) is to determine the type of dialogue
appropriate to the given context.

For different types of users in various problem states and with various
types of problems, different modes of dialogue will be appropriate. For
instance, at some states a natural-language interaction in an informal mode
might be appropriate (in, say, initial problem description by the user with
as yet nebulous perceptions of the problem), in others, interactive graphic
interaction might be preferred (in, say, representation of the mechanism's
perception of the user's anomalous state of knowledge for a user who pre-
fers multi-dimensional to linear representations).

1.4 Output Function

Last, but not least, the Output Generation function (OG) converts the
structures which the other functions have achieved into some form which the
user can understand, in a way that is appropriate to the immediate situation (in response to the dialogue function).

1.5 Auxiliary-Functions

As far as a blackboard is used for communication, a function is necessary: the Blackboard Analyst (BA). This module is responsible for a well
ordered blackboard.

Another function is responsible for the various administrative or log-
istic details appropriate to the situation, such as cost of the service,
etc. It is called System (SYS).

For internal reasons, a documentation has to be guaranteed. For this
purpose, a Mechanismus/MONSTRAT Memory (MM) function must be installed.

We believe that the functions we have enumerated (see Figure 1):

Input Analyst	(IA)
Problem Description	(PD)
Problem Mode	(PM)
Problem State	(PS)
User Model	(UM)
Dialogue Mode	(DM)
Relevant World Builder	(RWB)
Response Generator	(RG)
Output Generator	(OG)

and three auxiliary functions:

Blackboard Analyst	(BA)
Memory Mechanism	(MM)
System	(SYS)

constitute the minumum functions required of a general information mechanism, if it is to carry out its task of helping a user to manage problems
appropriately.

In the following part, some issues in the context of an implementation are considered.

2. ASPECTS OF DISTRIBUTION AND AUTONOMY

One of the basic ideas of the MONSTRAT-concept is distribution of the whole problem-treatment processes among various autonomous "experts", which might be computer-assisted as well as human and societal functions.

As far as an implementation is concerned, the concept of "experts" is used synonymous to "function" and "module".

Designing a software system for simulation processes like this focused our attention on a lot of problems.

First of all, there is a problem of a well suited distribution of knowledge. Related to the various tasks, the experts must have access to functions and data not only on a global level, but also locally. Additionally, they must be able to organize and execute the distribution of information units on their own.

This depends on variables which may be clustered either according to more formal aspects or with regard to the contents of the information-units or -messages.

In our first approach, we analyzed mainly the formal capabilities of the experts: number of messages per time unit, length of messages, mean time-intervals between messages, routing of the messages, and clusters of message-passing, etc.

On the other hand, we became aware that content-dependent distribution of information units is a very difficult task: after initializing, a certain distribution of knowledge must be established, related to the different tasks each expert has to fulfil, because each expert is an individual specialist in non-overlapping (sub)fields of expertise.

Thus, all experts must do their tasks mainly based on individual knowledge, which normally contains little experience from other experts. As a consequence, a lot of decisions must be verified based on a subset of all accessible knowledge within the distributed system, only. And no expert is really capable of judging or evaluating partial results of others.

Under certain circumstances, this may lead to a so-called positive feedback, where wrong results of some experts are amplified by others, such that the whole system output becomes wrong.

Whether this can be avoided might depend on weighting functions and on an incremental optimization process of the whole throughput. Especially, the knowledge bases and inference procedures must be "tuned" such that hypotheses with only little evidence at the beginning get the chance to improve the position within a certain time interval (Mlodinow and Stamatesku, 1984).

Summing up: It is of high importance that all experts get the right knowledge tailored to their certain tasks with a minimum overhead of multiple representations of equivalent expertise. This demand is a challenge not only for the design process of an expert system, but also the whole life cycle of each expert, i.e., the different stages of:

- identification, i.e., determining problem characteristics;

- conceptualization, i.e., finding concepts to represent knowledge;

- formalization, i.e., designing structures to organize knowledge;

- implementation, i.e., formulating entitites that embody knowledge;

- testing, i.e., validating these entities and the inference procedures;

- maintaining, i.e., fixing and eliminating bugs/errors;

- updating, i.e., integrating new knowledge into the subsystem; and

- evaluation, i.e., analyzing partial and whole systems output.

Especially the latter must be done from time to time for improving and tuning the knowledge bases and/or starting a redesign of parts or the whole system.

Autonomy is a second requirement strongly related to the first mentioned aspect of distribution in an information provision mechanism or expert system.

In this paper, autonomy should be a notion for operating/acting independently, using global and local information.

Especially in a MONSTRAT-environment, the availability of information depends on communication mechanisms because knowledge must be distributed to more than one active counterpart.

Thus, we have tried to formalize various communication processes during problem treatments. In the first approach, we separated and described some patterns of the flow of information by means of action/action-schemata in Belkin, Seeger, and Hennings (1984).

These schemata use a finite set of information (messages) types, i.e., QUESTION, ANSWER, HYPOTHESIS, FACT, RULE, etc., which are the basic entities for describing certain patterns of interaction, and can also be used for describing different modes of communication.

When communication is done in a direct mode between two experts, then the receiver of a message can react in several ways:

- Either the receipt of the whole message can be rejected totally with or without time delay; or

- Alternatively, the receipt of the whole message can be accepted and reaction takes place either immediately or with time delay due to special conditions, which includes passing to other experts too.

Overall, message-reception in the direct mode seems to be a more "passive" process, which may be implemented under optimal conditions in one cycle of interaction. Thus, the procedure is best described by the attribute "direct" because sender(s) and receiver(s) are involved in one phase.

Alternatively, communication can be implemented by means of a so-called blackboard, i.e., a global storage medium for all involved experts. In this case, message passing is done in an indirect mode because sending and receiving needs more than one cycle: the first step involves the transfer of the internal message-representation to the blackboard. Then, in a second step, all potential receivers must scan the content of the black-board and search for messages which might be relevant for them.

Thus, the procedure is best described by the attribute "indirect" because two phases can be distinguished: first, active processes of the sender(s), then active processes of the receiver(s).

Especially the latter mode of communication might be differentiated according to similar action-patterns as explained above:

- Either the receiver has decided not to seek new messages or only with time-delay because of certain conditions such as overloading, etc.

- Or the potential receivers are doing their task and searching for new messages initiating reactions immediately or with some time delay.

Summing up: When different active processes should do tasks with autonomy, they must have specialized individual knowledge. This tackles the flow of information which can be described by action/action schemata.

On the other hand, direct and indirect modes of communication within distributed expert systems must be distinguished.

These aspects are important in the context of global information. But autonomy — as defined above — depends on local information too.

This tackles the question, how an "individual environment" with "personal" functions and data can be realized.

Two features seem to be necessary characteristics:

(1) No mutual <u>access</u> to "personal" procedures and data between the various experts.

(2) But controlled <u>inheritance</u> of information in form of procedures and data, if necessary.

Both are related to the concept of autonomy in contrasting aspects: The first guarantees real individual operation: each expert is responsible for his own set of functions and data, and no external can use it uncontrolled. If regular exchange is wanted, then it can be triggered by means of messages, which allow a protocol-defined communication.

On the other hand, a long-range exchange can be planned by means of inheritance mechanisms which allow the spreading of information in a controlled manner.

3. CONSIDERATION OF COMPLEXITIES, PARALLELISM, AND EXTENSION

Very important issues, with regard to an implementation following the MONSTRAT-concept, have been dedicated to problems of complexity on various levels.

3.1 Complexity of Computer Time and Space

Much research in Artificial Intelligence seems often to pay only little attention to this very important aspect of Computer Science as Goldberg and Pohl (1982) pointed out in 1982. In a lot of other areas, results from the so-called complexity theory have strongly influenced developments, especially in operations research, circuit design, operating systems, and scheduling theory.

Complexity theory has its roots in computability theory of the logicians Gödel, Post, Turing, and Church, who constructed different mathematical models of computation. From these famous results, the undecidability of first order logic was derived by the latter in 1936.

This theorem says that it is impossible to construct an algorithm which, given a formula in first order logic, will determine whether the formula is valid or not. On the other hand, there are semi-decision procedures, i.e., algorithms that will recognize valid formulas, when sufficient computer time and space (memory) is available, which compute endlessly on invalid formulas.

In this context, the amount of computer resources plays an important role, because, by means of certain estimation procedures, it is possible to calculate not only the worst, but also the best case behavior of all algorithms.

The measurement takes into account the maximum (minimum) number of computer calculations and their maximum (minimum) time needed, thus providing a worst or best bound of time of the very algorithms with regard to the length of the input given as function of N, the number of elements.

Similar functions can be used for the amount of needed computer space, where in a lot of cases it is possible to reduce the amount of time by extending the amount of space and vice versa.

Now, the main point of complexity theory is the following statement assuming a serial model of computation:

A problem is considered intractable, iff all known algorithms that can solve the problem have time/space complexity growing as fast or faster than an exponential function, i.e., they have the above mentioned input length N in their exponent.

Conversely, algorithms for tractable problems have a polynomial time/space complexity.

Without going too much into the details, because they can be found in various books (e.g., Aho, Hopcraft, and Ullman, 1975), an extension of this model of measurement should be mentioned, which was investigated by Karp (1972) and Cook (1971).

They defined two subclasses of so-called Yes/No-problems (i.e., problems the solutions of which can be given by the answer "Yes" or "No" or equivalents):

P   the class for which there exists deterministic solutions with polynomial bounds in time (and space), where "deterministic" means that each step of execution is well defined, and

NP the class of Yes/No-problems with non-deterministic solutions the worst case behavior of which being also bounded by polynomials in time/space (therefore NP), where "non-deterministic" means that at certain points of computation there are (theoretical) mechanisms being able to select a feasible step among several alternatives which lies on the path to an optimal solution with polynomial amount of time/space, iff one exists.

Only in a few cases was it possible to construct real non-deterministic mechanisms, but, nevertheless, it is a theoretical aid which allows a description and an estimation of the complexity overall.

Now, Karp and Cook and many others afterwards were able to describe deterministic transformation processes between certain problems which worked in polynomial bounded time and space, such that the following statement holds:

A Yes/No problem is NP-complete, iff it is in NP and any problem in NP is polynomial reducable to it. Two problems are said to be polynomial reducable if there exists a function f computable deterministically in polynominal time, such that given an input I for the first and an algorithm to solve the problem, f(I) is an instance of the second problem and the algorithm works too.

Now, what of this theory is relevant for building information/expert systems using methods from Artificial Intelligence?

Using first order logic, hundreds of problems are proven to be either NP-complete in time or space. Among those are, for instance, quantified propositional logic (extending propositional logic by quantification over propositional variables), and propositional satisfiability (i.e., given a formula in conjunctive normal form, an assignment for the variables, for which the formula is true, must be found), as well as subproblems from Go and Checkers.

And there is strong evidence that those problems remain intractable, i.e., can be solved only by exponential amount in space/time. If, on the other hand, one of these problems would be solved in polynomial time, all others would be solved, too, because they are contained in NP. In such a case, we would derive the result $P = NP$, i.e., both classes of problems are equivalent.

On this background Newell stated in 1981:

All intelligent activity is based on search and search and deduction are the most important methods in AI which mainly suffer from combinational explosion most of their algorithms, the question is whether there is a chance to solve large problems in an acceptable amount of time and space, at all.

Especially the above mention problems, which are basics in the context of expert systems and inference mechanisms, should make all expert systems builders aware of internal limitations of the procedures which they are going to use, thus leading in many cases to completely inefficient solutions.

On the other hand, there is strong evidence that acceptable solutions might exist if either special cases are studied or heuristics, i.e., "rules of thumb" are used such that coping with these problems must not be hopeless!

And, of course, counter-examples might help to prevent researchers from investing a lot of effort going into the wrong direction.

3.2 Parallelism in Brain-, Soft-, and Hardware

The question arises, whether parallelism might help to handle these complex tasks of simulating intelligent behavior. Some important ideas from J. A. Feldman (1985) should first be summarized.

He complains that the general questions of intelligence and its simulation has not been touched, though in Artificial Intelligence a lot of progress has been made.

Comparing only the speed of modern computers/processors and the basic active elements of human beings, there is a big gap: the firing of neurons is in the millisecond range whereas computers operate in nanoseconds.

Looking at human response times in various situations, the difference becomes even more remarkable: simple tasks as naming a picture or deciding whether a certain sound is a noun takes about half a second!

Thus, though the speed of information processing on the neuron-level is very low, difficult problems of vision and language can be solved in about 100 time-units of firing neurons.

AI-programs, on the other hand, need for significant simple tasks much more time.

But, of course, the brain works in parallel, and most computers sequential.

And there is still another difference to be mentioned: neurons can send only a few bits of information to one another and not big symbolic expressions as are commonly used in Artificial Intelligence.

Thus, "the computational richness" must be in the connections among the units Feldman concludes.

If the brain is used as a model, a lot of connections per unit are possible. Considering the total number of neurons within about 100 billions, another limitation is obvious: Vision might have a million parallel inputs: thus any algorithm requiring N^2 units cannot be used!

Additionally, no new units can be generated and eventually no new connections, which seems to be a strong limitation of modelling.

Then, in the above mentioned paper, some examples of visual models, natural-language application, and knowledge representations are given, where the underlying basic algorithms, and how the basic elements of knowedge are represented, are central issues.

A lot of cooperative research seems to be necessary until basic answers may be found.

Nevertheless, the research is oriented towards the development of parallel computers consisting of about 100 processors (e.g., Butterfly multiprocessor of BBN with 128 processors), to simulate a network of 20,000 units.

Questions of how to partition the network seem to be easier than how to monitor and modify the behavior. But breaking a problem in a lot of parallel solvable units is still another problem which occurred in the context of the development of methods for parallel computation on parallel processors.

Now, why do we summarize those ideas on parallelism?

The main reason is, that among all different developments of mainframe-computers of the 'next' generation, two lines seem to be dominant.

On one side, there are large vector-processors using pipelining, operating mainly on simple instruction- and multiple data-streams such that a lot of operations can be executed in parallel.

The other line seems to be the development of the 5th generation of (mainframe) computers, where much effort is dedicated to the development of new inference mechanisms (catchword: PROLOG), convenient interfaces for potential users, etc.

The question arises, whether a model like MONSTRAT, where parallelism is an intrinsic feature realized by the concept of various independent experts who only communicate their results (either directly to one another or via a blackboard), can be more easily implemented on one of these architectures. Especially, because all experts are characterized by independence and autonomy as far as their individual work is concerned.

As mentioned above, these two attributes express that they must be able to operate independently using local and global data but communicate their various results on a current level of attainment via a blackboard mechanism or directly, where a <u>decentralized</u> architecture with a finite extentable set of <u>independent</u> processors each of which operate on multiple instruction- and multiple data-streams, is needed.

Thus, neither of the above mentioned directions of development seem to cover these requirements very well.

We think that the best basis would be an "ensemble" of various different machines (e.g., LISP-, PROLOG-machines, Graphic-Systems, etc.) each of which being an independent hard- and software environment dedicated to special tasks with a limited but very large set of communication lines to each other including the blackboard.

Of course these lines must have at least the capacity of local area networks, thus providing a backbone of a very fast communication mechanism where "solutions" are the outcome of various different resources being able to assemble local results to one or more global results.

This concept seems to us better suited for coping with those issues being the basis of problem treatment with computer assistance than central architectures.

The design of such systems must be an incremental process, where from level-to-level more functions of the whole molecular system, until then being done by human beings, can be simulated sufficiently well, such that they can be replaced by non-human system mechanisms.

Thus, when enough insight in all the different aspects of human problem treatment is gained,, a whole system could be established operating totally independent in certain fields of knowledge.

3.3 Closed vs. Open Systems

A third aspect of this discussion touches the limitations of closed systems. MONSTRAT has an underlying open system concept, therefore, we refer to a discussion of some issues by Carl Hewitt (1985), where he claims for open systems, i.e., systems of interconnected and independent computers. He pointed out that those systems are subject to quite different limitations and constraints than the computer systems of the past, and can be characterized by:

- Continuous change and evolution, i.e., addition of new computers, users, software, such that the system must be able to change as the components and demands placed upon them change;

- Arms-length relationships and decentralized decision making, i.e., there are only limited possibilities of access to the various resources, thus implying a decentralized decision making;

- Perpetual inconsistencies among knowledge bases because of privacy and discretionary concerns;

- Need for negotiation among system computers because no system component directly controls the resources to another, where the various parts must have arguments to persuade one another to provide a certain capability; and

- Inadequacy of the closed-world assumption, i.e., information about the world is relatively incomplete such that it is not sufficient to search within local storage for certain instances of knowledge.

All these properties are interdependent and necessary. From these demands the conjecture of inconsistency is derived,, which depends on the dispersed asynchronous nature of human knowledge. It says that the axiomatizations of human knowledge of all physical systems are uniformly inconsistent in practice which has to do with four different contexts:

- environmental, because there are always relations to different physical systems;

- spatiotemporal, because knowledge about history is comprised;

- terminological, because predicates used in axiomatizations seem to be problematic in practice; and

- evidential, because there is always metaknowledge in the context of various issues.

From these aspects, he formulated the need of so-called message-passing semantics, because meaning is communication-based, not logic-based.

He argues for mechanisms which are able to apply due-process reasoning, because there is always conflicting information and contradictory beliefs in reality such that logical proof methods are in a certain sense inadequate as reasoning instruments.

Hewitt concludes his paper with some information-processing principles for the future.

Under the concept of reflection, the following minimum capabilities should be included:

- history of its own behavior;

- representation of its own information-processing procedures;

- knowledge of the relationship between its previous behavior and current procedures; and

- representation of its procedures for interacting with the external world.

Additionally, the following features should be encompassed:

- serendipity, i.e., a certain kind of learning capabilities;

- pluralism, i.e., different kinds of truth within the whole system;

- accessibility, i.e., availability of all local and global knowledge;

- parallelism of all resources;

- due-process reasoning as explained above;

- reflection in theory and practice with mutual fertilization; and

- reasonableness, i.e., efficient use of conflicting information and inconsistent beliefs.

Hewitt has collected a lot of ideas which fit very well into the whole MONSTRAT-discussion. Some of these claims and characteristics have been described in the context of the development of our general information provision mechanism.

Especially his claim for an open systems design with the above mentioned features might help to simulate human behavior in all its complexity and parallelism.

4. PROBLEMS OF IMPLEMENTATION: NEED OF OBJECT-ORIENTED ENVIRONMENTS

From the short discussion of several important aspects of distributed expert systems, it becomes obvious that a lot of our efforts are centered around the problem of well suited software for implementing these communication and information provision mechanisms.

With our questions in mind, we focused our attention on LISP and, especially, an object-oriented programming environment.

The latter aspects of the previous chapter have direct consequences to an implementation.

Open systems characterized by inconsistencies, incompleteness and various contexts cannot be modelled adequately with first order logic. Thus, current logic programming methods may be insufficient for developing intelligent systems. Especially PROLOG has adopted a very strong form of closed world assumptions (in most versions) as it incorporates negation as failure. That means if an entry is not found, then it is treated as false.

Additionally, there are no message-passing mechanisms, and due-process reasoning seems also to be impossible.

PROLOG is strongly based on first-order logic augmented with set theory. An extension to omega-order logic (Rudin, 1981) seems to extend some limitations, because quantification over functions and predicates is allowed, thus including the complete lambda calculus as a sublanguage (which is the basis of LISP-dialects), though the functions are often not the same as in the theory of lambda calculus. (E.g., objects can change their state while the identity is retained. This is not allowed in lambda calculus (Christaller and DiPrimio, 1984).)

With this background, the whole discussion LISP vs. PROLOG should not be decided definitely. But a strong impetus is givens towards LISP, perhaps with embedded PROLOG-features.

Nevertheless, the above mentioned requirement of parallelism and accessibility seems to uncover a limitation of several LISP environments, because they employ only dynamic scoping, i.e., binding all variables with relation to the run-time. Often, however, it is necessary to have a clearer cut situation by means of lexical scoping as it is implemented in some LISP-dialects and most other (higher) programming languages.

In INTERLISP there is a FUNARG-mechanism which allows integrating a lexical scoping into the programming environment.

On the background of the above itemized questions of open systems, a message-passing mechanism is needed for various active elements using a defined protocol. Additionally, a very well defined environment of variables and functions is needed, such that all processes can act independently, because parallelism by means of various distributed computers is not available for us today.

In our programming environment, we can simulate parallelism only by means of several independent LISP-processes which communicate on operating system level.

Unfortunately, this is a very time consuming procedure because it must be done by sending/receiving of state vectors with the aid of assembler routines (Schulze-Kremer, 1985(b)).

Thus, we are mainly operating in a sequential environment where an efficient and save mechanism for message exchange is needed.

For this purpose, an object-oriented mechanism is very well suited. In such an environment we can create a finite set of entities called <u>objects</u> which are able to communicate with one another by sending and receiving <u>messages</u>.

Thus, executing programs means that objects send messages to other objects (including themselves) which in turn send messages containing (parts of) the result, until a final stage is reached.

Today, many more or less different approaches are implemented in various LISP-dialects, though the first non-LISP realization of object-oriented programming was done in SIMULA. From those early ideas, a lot of other implementations emerged. A very famous object-oriented system became SMALLTALK and the flavor-system of ZetaLISP for LISP-Machines and SYMBOLICS 36XX. Other implementations are LOOPS in INTERLISP-D and ORBIT as well as OBJTalk in FranzLISP.

Unfortunately, there is no suitable implementation for SIEMENS BS2000-INTERLISP, i.e., our programming environment. Therefore, we decided to develop our own system. Until now we have had two implementations, one of which will be presented shortly in the next chapter, (Schulze-Kremer, 1985(a); Spade, 1985).

5. INTERLISP FLAVOR-SYSTEM

To implement the MONSTRAT-concept we will use an object-oriented programming system in INTERLISP (Version 4) called INTERLISP Flavor-System.

The main facilities of flavor-systems enable you to define two kinds of objects, generic and individual, which can be used in simulations to represent real objects of the world in an abstract manner.

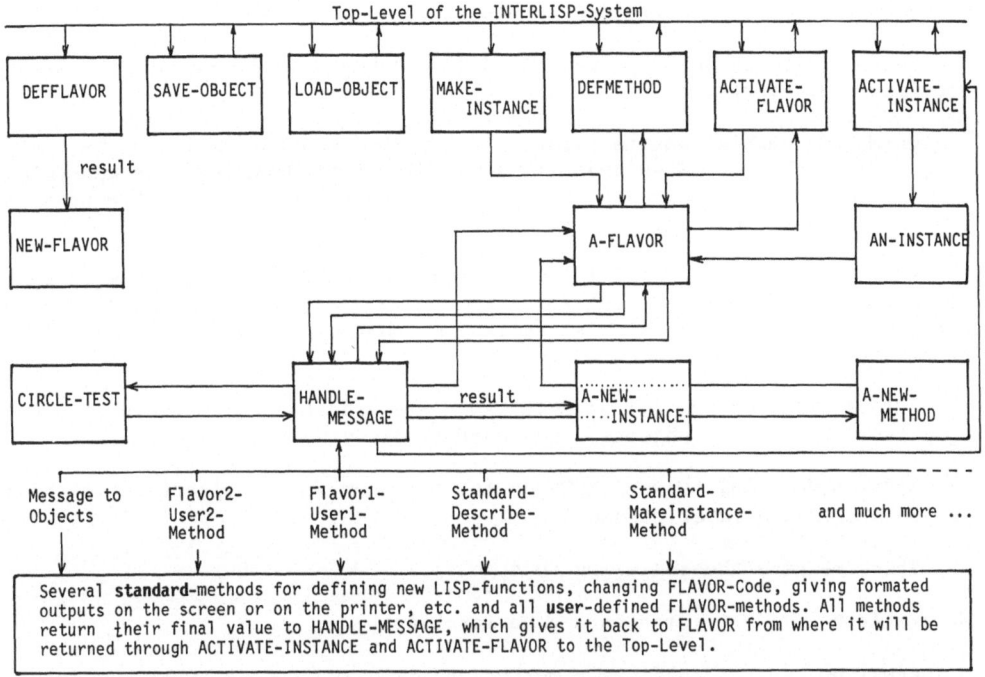

Figure 2.   Top-Level Dependencies.

Every object is characterized by its name, its specific variables, its values, and by so-called methods. The latter give the object procedural knowledge in addition to its data storing capabilities.

The user is free to choose values for all of these characteristics of an object.

Moreover, both kinds of objects can receive and send messages. This is their way to communicate with the programmer or - how we shall see later on - with each other.

For a simulation, we are going to use generic objects, as we want to represent a class of objects of the real world, e.g., COMMUNICATOR might be a generic object for all beings who communicate by the same communication methods.

In addition to this, every new generic object can inherit specific variables and methods from other generic objects. By the aid of this feature, you are easily able to build hierarchic structured graphs, even with circularities in the network.

Generic objects are also called flavors because you can mix them just like flavors and according to your own taste.

Individual objects, often called instances, represent specific objects of a generic object. They are the "active" actors in simulation, which interact with the programmer or with each other.

In the following part, we are going to explain seven of the main functions of our Flavor-system, which are necessary for providing generic and individual objects and creating methods.

The function DEFLAVOR is made to define a new generic object with its specific characteristics.

DEFMETHOD enables you to create a new method and to fix it to the body of a generic object. When creating a new flavor by DEFLAVOR, you can refer to other existing flavors, which may pass on characteristics to the new flavor or inherit characteristics from the new flavor.

MAKE-INSTANCE creates individual objects. All you have to type in is the name of the generic object which should be used, and the name of the new instance. Later on, its values can be updated by standard methods, if necessary.

ACTIVATE-FLAVOR and ACTIVATE-INSTANCE are used to activate generic, respectively individual objects, in a comfortable manner.

SAVE-OBJECTS and LOAD-OBJECTS do the file serving: objects and methods can be stored and later reloaded.

Thus, we have the following functions:

- **DEFLAVOR**   creates a generic object

-ʹ **DEFMETHOD**   defines a method and relates it to a generic object

- **MAKE-INSTANCE**   creates an individual object of a generic object

- **ACTIVATE-FLAVOR**   activates a generic object

- **ACTIVATE-INSTANCE**   activates an individual object

- **SAVE-OBJECTS**   stores all objects with their characteristics, values, and methods in a file

- **LOAD-OBJECTS**   reloads a flavor-file

The next picture (Figure 2) shows the full range of dependencies between the various functions.

With the exception of creating new flavors and handling flavor-files, each task will be executed by sending a special message either directly or indirectly to a flavor.

Given a certain FLAVOR, it passes the specific environment, together with the incoming message, to HANDLE-MESSAGE.

HANDLE-MESSAGE has three responsibilities:

(1) Splitting the message into selector and arguments;

(2) Calling a method-function which matches the given selector. It may be standard-, system-, or user-defined;

(3) Evaluation of the very method or a negative reply, if there is none.

Tasks, which operate in networks where circularities may occur, usually call CIRCLE-TEST to prevent endless loops.

Now, let us take a look at some of the special features of the Inter-LISP Flavor-System.

For the implementation of the system, we use FUNARGS to represent environments of objects.

FUNARGS are functional expressions consisting of a LISP-Function with a permanent but local set of parameters. Thus, a mixing up of any user-defined toplevel- or property-data with data of the objects can be prevented.

Inheritance is another matter. We simulate inheritance by storing and removing the very items. This saves time, especially, when you are seeking a certain method throughout large networks of flavors.

So, methods are known by inherited method-names where method-definitions must not be stored at different places related to different objects. This saves a lot of memory capacity.

The whole Flavor-System requires only four global variables:

- one containing a list of all existing flavors;

- one for recording circle graphs; and

- two for the flavor-file package.

To specify a method not only by its selector, but also by the very flavor the method belongs to, a second argument viewed-as, followed by the name of the flavor, can be used.

Again, the reactions of the specified method will be evaluated, or a negative reply results.

All INTERLISP trace facilities can be used. Additionally, there is a class-variable named BLACKBOARD, that allows you to program your own tracer.

Another interesting feature is the possibility to define an instance and a flavor with the same name. Which of these objects should be activated can be determined by the use of ACTIVATE-INSTANCE and ACTIVATE-FLAVOR.

In addition, one instance can have several names, which might be useful, for example in certain simulations.

Concerning the topological structure of flavor graphs, we have the following features: You can generate any directed network of flavors, especially circle graphs, without limitations. Addition can be done, flavor-upward and -downward, related to the previous flavor network, even simultaneously.

To see what the structure of a certain network looks like you have to ask for "relations" between the flavors. Then a graphical network analysis is done and presented on the screen.

In order to make the operation with INTERLISP Flavor-System as effective as possible, there are UNDO facilities for several events, abbreviations for frequently used functions, commands to modify comfortably objects and networks, and a special user function ALL-FLAVORS to apply messages to every existing flavor at once.

```
---> (ACTIVATE-FLAVOR COMMUNICATOR give methods)

   ---> (HANDLE-MESSAGE give methods)
          with the environment of FLAVOR COMMUNICATOR !

      ---> (EVAL methods)

      <--- EVAL = (ask answer talk-to reset)

   <--- HANDLE-MESSAGE = (ask answer talk-to reset)

<--- ACTIVATE-FLAVOR = (ask answer talk-to reset)

(ask answer talk-to reset)
```

Figure 3.   Message Passing While Calling
Generic Object COMMUNICATOR.

To send more than one message to an object simultaneously (this means one message immediately after another) you can concatenate these messages by the separator word and.

Last, but not least, networks of a very complex structure can be composed out of smaller subunits which may be linked later. Therefore, the function LOAD-OBJECTS has a special argument.

Now, how does this message-passing work?

The first line in Figure 3 represents the input at top-level of INTER-LISP. This input means that the generic object COMMUNICATOR is asked to tell how many and what methods it has.

COMMUNICATOR passes the question to the LISP-function HANDLE-MESSAGE (as each flavor must do) and gives its arguments to this function. Additionally, the flavor passes its own specific environment to HANDLE-MESSAGE.

In this environment, all information concerning the flavor COMMUNICATOR is stored.

Now HANDLE-MESSAGE reacts on the selector "give" and returns the value of "methods" of the actual environment.

```
---> (ACTIVATE-INSTANCE TIM give name)

   ---> (COMMUNICATOR give name)
          with the environment of INSTANCE TIM !

      ---> (HANDLE-MESSAGE give name)
             with the environment of INSTANCE TIM and
             the environment of FLAVOR COMMUNICATOR !

         ---> (EVAL name)

         <--- EVAL = TIM

      <--- HANDLE-MESSAGE = TIM

   <--- COMMUNICATOR = TIM

<--- ACTIVATE-INSTANCE = TIM

TIM
```

Figure 4.   Message Passing While Calling
individual object TIM.

```
---> (ACTIVATE-INSTANCE TIM talk-to TOM)

    ---> (ACTIVATE-INSTANCE TIM ask TOM name)

  <--- "My name is TIM ! What's your name ?"

      ---> (ACTIVATE-INSTANCE TOM answer TIM name)

    <--- "My name is TOM !"

        ---> (ACTIVATE-INSTANCE TIM ask TOM hobby)

      <--- "I like writing LISP-programs, do you ?"

          ---> (ACTIVATE-INSTANCE TOM answer TIM hobby)

        ....
(This continues until no more subjects are to be discussed. The
dialogue is terminated by the following statement:)
        ....

        <--- "Ok., good-bye !"
```

**Figure 5. Message Passing During a (small-)talk
Between TIM and TOM.**

Thus, each flavor can use the same message handler. The result will be
returned to ACTIVATE-FLAVOR, which will make an output on the screen or on
the printer.

In Figure 4 you can see a similar invocation, but in this case with an
instance, named TIM, activated at Top-level.

The way of message passing between objects and HANDLE-MESSAGE is the
same as before except that the object TIM also has its own environment
which contains specific bindings.

Now HANDLE-MESSAGE can refer to this environment in addition to that of
flavor COMMUNICATOR. It finds the correct answer and returns it step-
by-step to Top-Level.

Figure 5 shows a more complicated event, where some methods work together: ask, answer, talk-to, and, although hidden, reset. Both TIM and
TOM are instances of flavor COMMUNICATOR.

The calls of COMMUNICATOR and HANDLE-MESSAGE have been omitted.

So what you can see is how TIM and TOM pass messages to each other and
answer them until their internal list of subjects (they can talk about) is
empty.

In Figure 5, TIM and TOM are individual objects of the generic object
COMMUNICATOR.

With these explanations, the presentation is terminated. We are firmly
convinced that these are the software-mechanisms by means of which the decentralized MONSTRAT-concept might be implemented. Although details are
rather complicated, we hope that a "problem-solving discussion" among
several modules of an expert-system can be simulated.

For more details of the INTERLISP Flavor-System see our references.

6. OUTLOOK

After having studied two questions which are related to autonomy (in our sense), i.e, the flow of information and the modes in the inter-expert-communication, a third problem is of great relevance: How it is possible to realize an individual environment of procedures and data? For this issue a solution was presented in section 5.

In this context, two features seem to be absolutely necessary: No mutual access from one expert to "individual" procedures and data of others, but controlled inheritance of procedures/data between them.

Both requirements are related to the concept of autonomy. The first guarantees real individual decision-making on the basis of individual data and procedures. The second allows (under certain conditions) that (computer-)time and space can be saved, such that complexity can be lowered.

As mentioned in section 2, the design of a software environment is one step towards realization of a MONSTRAT-system. By means of the mechanisms explained before, we see a good chance of realizing a small kernel within the near future.

The first version is going to contain the following experts:

- Input Analyst for partial analysis of the user input (without a complete syntactical analysis) and transformation into an internal representation;

- Problem Description as focus-mechanism to the very problem;

- User Model for a description of several user profiles;

- Blackboard as central message exchange medium maintained by a so-called Blackboard Analyst;

- Relevant World Builder who assembles the knowledge base;

- Response Generator for all inference processes;

- Output Generator as output medium to the user; and a

- MONSTRAT Memory for recording the systems behavior, overall.

The knowledge base operates mainly on rules, subject is advice taking/giving during the search processes for old deposits of various industrial and non-industrial matters (Hennings and Spade, 1985).

In the first phase of this procedure, the main question was, whether the underground, especially the groundwater, is contaminated and why. For this purpose at the Bundesgesundheitsamt Berlin, a research team has studied many various chemical procedures which help to answer the above raised question, when they are applied in a more or less defined sequence.

With this background, we have formulated several sets of rules which describe parts of the whole process and can be dedicated to the several experts.

Our main concern today is to get experience with the means of a object-oriented programming environment in INTERLISP, where all experts are independent and autonomous instances of the class EXPERT augmented by some special methods for their individual purposes.

An indirect communication-mode is realized with a blackboard as a global memory mechanism. Messages are the only way to communicate within the system.

All experts can make use of individual knowledge within their individual environment. For this purpose LISP is very well suited, as pointed out above.

7. REFERENCES

Aho, A. V., Hopcroft, J. E., and Ullman, J. D., 1975, The Design and Analyst of Computer Algorithms, Addison-Wesley.

Belkin, N. J., 1980, "Anomalous States of Knowledge as a Basis for Information Retrieval", Canadian Journal of Information Science, 5, pp. 133-143.

Belkin, N. J., 1983, MONSTRAT-Simulation V. Statistical Evaluation of the MONSTRAT Simulation. Projekt INSTRAT, Internal Report, April 1983 (A 5/83).

Belkin, N. J., Hennings, R.-D., Seeger, T., Wersig, G., and Windel, G., 1983, "Mass-Informatics and Their Implication for Everyday Life, Proceedings of the International Federation for Information Processing Meeting in Paris, September 19-23, 1983", Information Processing, pp. 583-587.

Belkin, N. J., Hennings, R.-D., and Seeger, T., 1984, "Simulation of a Distributed Expert-based Information Provision Mechanism", Information Technology: Research, Development, Applications, 3, (3), 1984.

Belkin, N. J., Seeger, T., and Wersig, G., 1983, "Distributed Expert Problem Treatment as a Model for Information System Analysis and Design", Journal of Information Science, 5, pp. 153-167.

Brooks, H. M. and Belkin, N. J., "Using Discourse Analysis for the Design of Information Retrieval Interaction Mechanisms", Proceedings of the Sixth Annual International ACM SIGIR Conference, New York.

Christaller, T., and DiPrimio, F., 1983, Franco: A Poor Man's Flavor System, Institute Dalle Molle (ISSCO), Universite de Geneve, May 1983.

Cook, S. A., 1971, "The Complexity of Theorem Proving Procedures", Third Annual ACM Symposium on Theory of Computing, May 1971.

Feldmann, J. A., 1985, "Connections", BYTE, April 1985.

Goldberg, A., and Pohl, I., 1982, "Is Complexity Theory of Use to AI", Artificial and Human Intelligence, A. Elithorn and R. Banerji, eds., Elsevier Science Publications.

Hennings, R.-D., 1982, MONSTRAT-Designbericht 1. Allgemeine Uberlegungen zur MONSTRAT-Modellbildung und Klassifikation von Wissen bei Expertensystemen, Freie Universität, Projekt INSTRAT Interner Bericht (B 1/82), Berlin, November 1982.

Hennings, R.-D, 1983(a), MONSTRAT-Designbericht 2. Statische und dynamische Aspekte der Modellbildung des MONSTRAT-Systems, Freie Universität, Projekt INSTRAT (B 2/83), Berlin, April 1983.

Hennings, R.-D, 1983(b), <u>MONSTRAT-Simulation IV. Übergreifende Auswertung</u>, Freie Universität, Projekt INSTRAT (A 4/83), April 1983.

Hennings, R.-D, 1983(c), <u>MONSTRAT-Designbericht 3. Grundlegende Ansätze der Implementierung von MONSTRAT1 mit INTERLISP</u>, Freie Universität, Projekt INSTRAT Interner Bericht (B 3/83), Berlin, June 1983.

Hennings, R.-D, 1983(d), <u>MONSTRAT-Simulation VI. Results and Discussion</u>, Freie Universität, Projekt INSTRAT, Interner Bericht, Berling, August 1983.

Hennings, R.-D, 1983(e), <u>MONSTRAT-Designbericht 4. Zum Design und zur Spezifizierung/Implementierung eines Expertensystems – Verteilte Problembehandlung unter Nutzung von erweiterbaren zielgerichteten Produktionsregel-Hierarchien</u>, Freie Universität, Projekt INSTRAT (B 4/83), Berlin, October 1983.

Hennings, R.-D. et al., 1983(f), <u>MONSTRAT-Simulation III. Register und Materialien</u>, Projekt INSTRAT, Internal Report (B 3/83), June 1983.

Hennings, R.-D. and Wersig, G., 1984, "The Intellectual Architecture of Information Systems. A Broad Range Research Agenda", <u>Representation and Exchange of Knowledge as a Basis of Information Processes. Proceedings of the Fifth International Research Forum in Information Science (IRFIS 5), September 5-7, 1983</u>, J. J. Dietschmann, ed., North-Holland, Amsterdam, u.a., Heidelberg.

Hennings, R.-D., 1984(a), <u>Informationssysteme und Problembewältigung III. Informationsvermittlungsmechanismen als konstruktive Aufgabe. Abschlußbericht des BMfT-Projektes INSTRAT (Informationssysteme als informationspolitisches Gestaltungspotential und gesellschaftliche Entwicklungsstrategie – Informationswissenschaftliche Grundlagen organisierter Information unter Kommunikation als Komponenten individueller und gesellschaftlicher Problembewaltigung)</u>, Berlin, February 1984, (Bundesministerium für Forschung und Technology (BMFT) Postfach 200706, 5300 Bonn 2).

Hennings, R.-D., 1984(b), <u>MONSTRAT-Designbericht 5. Aufgabenstellungen und Teillösungen für das MONSTRAT1-System. Teil 1: Analytische Experten</u>, Freie Universität Berlin, Arbeitsbereich Informationswissenschaft, Interner Bericht, Berlin, 1984.

Hennings, R.-D., 1984(c), <u>MONSTRAT-Designbericht 6. Aufgabenstellungen und Teillösungen für das MONSTRAT1-System. Teil 2: Synthetische Experten</u>, Freie Universität Berlin, Arbeitsbereich Informationswissenschaft, Interner Bericht, Berlin.

Hennings, R.-D. et al., 1985, <u>MONSTRAT-Designbericht 7. Aufgabenstellungen und Teillösungen für das MONSTRAT1-System. Teil 3: Praxis-Exkurs: Detail-Implementierungen</u>, Freie Universität Berlin, Arbeitsbereich Informationswissenschaft, Interner Bericht, Berlin, 1985.

Hennings, R.-D., 1985(a), <u>The Use of Expert Systems in Industry</u>, Paper prepared for a Joint Symposium VDI-Technology Centre/GOFI: Integrated Information Systems for Administration and Industry, April 10-12, 1985, Cairo, Egypt.

Hennings, R.-D., 1985(b), "Neue optische Technologien für Information und Kommunikation", <u>Nachrichten für Dokumentation</u>, <u>36</u>, (3), pp. 137-143.

Hennings, R.-D., 1985(c), "Expertensysteme für industrielle Nutzung",

Nachrichten für Dokumentation, 36, (4), und VDI-Verlag: Künstliche Intelligenz: Wesen und Bedeutung neuer Computerleistungen. Sammelband einer Vortragsreihe des VDI-Technologiezentrums, Berlin, 1985.

Hennings, R.-D., 1985(d), "Expertensysteme: Grundlagen, Entwicklungen, Anwendungen, Trends", ARTIFICIAL INTELLIGENCE 1: Expertensysteme, R.-D. Hennings, H. Munter, and Reihe, eds., MathWare-Verlag, D-1000 Berlin 61, Katzbachstraße 14, 352 Seiten, (DM 39, 90), Berlin.

Hennings, R.-D. and Spade, F., 1985, Materialien zur Projektierung eines Expertensystems für die Beurteilung des Kontaminationspotentials von Altlaststandorten, Freie Universität Berlin, Arbeitsbereich Informationswissenschaften.

Hewitt, C., 1979, "Control Structure as Patterns of Passing Messages", Artificial Intelligence: An MIT Perspective, P. H. Winston and R. H. Brown, eds., Cambridge et al., 2, pp. 433-465.

Hewitt, C., 1985, "The Challenge of Open Systems", BYTE, April 1985.

Karp, R. M., 1972, "Reducibility Between Combinatorial Problems", Complexity of Computer Computations, Miller and Thatcher, eds., Plenum Press, NY.

Rudin, L., 1981, Lambda-Logic, Technical Report 4521, California Institute of Technology, Pasadena, CA, May 1981.

Schulze-Kremer, S., 1985(a), INTERLISP Flavor-System, Freie Universität Berlin, Arbeitsbereich Informationswissenschaft, Berlin.

Schulze-Kremer, S., 1985(b), INTERLISP Exit and Entry, Freie Universität Berlin, Arbeitsbereich Informationswissenschaft, Berlin.

Seeger, T., ed., 1982, Information Systems as Collectives of Cooperating Functional Experts, Proceedings of a Workshop, Berlin, 1981, FUB-IFP 5/82, Freie Universität Berlin, Fachbereich Kommunikationswissenschaft, Arbeitsbereich Informationswissenschaft, Berlin, 1982.

Seeger, T., Belkin, N. J., Hennings, R.-D, and Wersig, G., 1983, MONSTRAT-Simulation I. Das operationalisierte MONSTRAT-Konzept, Projekt INSTRAT, Internal Report (A 1/83), April 1983.

Seeger, T. and Hennings, R.-D., 1983, MONSTRAT-Simulation II. Die Anlage der Simulation, Projekt INSTRAT, Internal Report (A 2/83), April 1983.

Siemens, A. G., 1983, INTERLISP: Interaktives Programmiersystem BS2000, December 1983.

Spade, F., 1985, Implementierng einer exemplarischen objekt-orientierten Umgebung in INTERLISP, Free University Berlin, Institute of Information Science, Berlin.

Stamatescu, I. O., and Mlodinow, L. D., 1984, An Evolutionary Procedure for Machine Learning, Max-Planck-Institut für Physik und Astrophysik, München, bzw. Freie Universität Berlin, Institut für Theorie der Elementarteilchen, Berlin.

Straube, A., 1985, Beschreibung und Modellierung von Dialogstrukturen, Magisterarbeit, Freie Universität Berlin.

Wersig, G., 1979, "The Problematic Situation as a Basic Concept of

Information Science in the Framework of the Social Sciences - A Reply to N. Belkin," New Trends in Informatics and Its Terminology, FID 568, VINITI, Moscow, pp. 48-57.

Wersig, G., 1982, "MONSTRAT: The Intellectual Architecture of Information Systems", Cybernetics and System Research, R. Trappl, ed., Amsterdam et al., pp. 837-841.

Wolf-Zweifler, D. B., 1984, Gesprächsanalyse und Probleme der Verständigung in wissenstransferierender Beratungssituation, Magisterarbeit, Freie Universität Berlin.

COMBINING LOGGING, PLAYBACK AND VERBAL PROTOCOLS: A METHOD FOR

ANALYZING AND EVALUATING INTERACTIVE SYSTEMS

Pentti Hietala

University of Tampere
Department of Mathematical Sciences
Computer Science, P.O. Box 607
SF-33101 Tampere 10, Finland

Abstract: In this paper we describe a method that can be used in the
analysis and evaluation of interactive systems. This method is a combination of three techniques: logging, playback, and verbal protocols. We
have employed the method in the evaluation of an interactive program verification system. This evaluation involved users on two levels of expertise: on one hand, novices taking a course on program verification; and on
the other hand, subjects already familiar with verification. The system
stored the commands of the test subjects into a log file while the test
subjects were working on a given problem. Directly after the first session, a second one followed where the previous session was shown in playback on the terminal to the test subjects and they were asked to verbalize
their work retrospectively. According to our tests the above procedure
turned out to be a convenient way of obtaining data for system evaluation
as well as data on the mental models formed by the subjects of the system.
It is especially useful in early design phases eliciting user opinions,
e.g., on prototype versions which then can be used for iterative design.
In our case, the collected information has been utilized in the design of a
new version of the verification system. In addition, the combined method
can be useful in teaching, which is also demonstrated through our
experiments.

1. INTRODUCTION

    The recent proliferation of interactive systems has not been accompa-
nied by an evolution of appropriate methodologies to deal with these
systems. For example, we are still in need for methods to support the
design of these systems as well as the evaluation of the final products.
Methodologies dealing with interactive systems should take into account the
fact that the users of the system will ultimately decide its usability.
Considering the evaluation phase, this means that it should be more clearly
recognized that assessment of the system should especially address the
system fit to human capabilities.

    There are several traditional techniques to be employed in studying and
evaluating interactive human-computer systems, e.g., questionnaires, interviews, and verbal protocols. Computers can also be used to collect and
analyze data from the user sessions with the system (logging and

monitoring). In this paper, we discuss studies where we combined three well-known methods, namely logging, playback, and verbal protocols. This combined method was applied in the evaluation of a prototype version of an interactive program verification system. We were interested whether the prototype fulfilled its design goals and whether the system was suitable for teaching verification issues. The evaluation took place in a rather early stage of system development so it was possible to utilize these results in the further development of the system.

In our opinion, the emphasis on verbal protocols in connection with logging and playback can provide benefits that have not been recognized hitherto. In particular, presenting the working sessions to the test subjects in playback can produce unique aspects for evaluation purposes. The combined method allows the users to work in their own familiar working place which reduces distortion from environmental issues (due to the experiment). The method helps to reveal the cognitive fit of the system and elicits useful suggestions for improvement of the system. The approach is a rather fast and inexpensive compared to laboratory tests with special equipment.

This paper is organized as follows. In the next section, we give a brief overview of various available evaluation techniques and discuss the relation of the proposed method to these techniques. Then we describe our experiments with the combined method and the results obtained. We conclude with some recommendations concerning the use of the method.

2. ON THE EVALUATION OF INTERACTIVE SYSTEMS

In this section we briefly outline several evaluation techniques and discuss also the combined method and its relationship to these more traditional ones.

2.1 Overview of Evaluation Methods

"Know the user" is one of the most-used maxims in the design and evaluation of interactive software. There are also various other guidelines to direct the designer and the evaluator in his work (Shneiderman, 1980). However, it is sometimes very difficult to apply these suggestions to the system at hand and obtain relevant guidance. Getting to know the user can be accomplished by collecting information by questionnaires and interviews. This information about the user can be collected before, during, or after the actual use of the system. These queries should be carefully administered and fitted to the background and experience of the respondents. The above methods are, as Root and Draper (1984) note, somewhat user-indifferent, programmer-dominated methods, where the actual behavior of the user is dictated by the investigators' set of questions.

Logging user activities and monitoring his work afterwards is another way of evaluating how the system is used. Gaines (1981) has advocated the guideline "Log user activities" where logging means recording user keystrokes into a file and analyzing this data for obtaining frequencies of the most common slips or wrong paths that the user has been taking. This kind of analysis can be very sophisticated, as evidenced by the human-computer interface evaluation of USS Carl Vinson System (Yoder, MacCracken, and Akscyn, 1984). Logging data can also be useful in the design of new systems, e.g., in designing editors (Good, 1985).

Furthermore, it is possible to conduct the monitoring in modern laboratory environments using advanced video/recording equipment. Users can be observed from another room through a one-sided glass wall and the observations can be recorded in real-time on computer. For example, Neal and Simons (1983) describe a "Playback program" developed at the IBM Human Factors Center in San Jose which collects performance data of the user interface. In the analysis phase the experimenter can pace through the user's actions after the session. However, this is carried out mainly by the experimenter alone, although "there are occasions when the playback is done immediately after a session with the user present in order to obtain supplementary information about the user's thoughts or reasons for particular actions while performing the task" (Neal and Simons, 1983).

Monitoring can be seen as a way of finding out the tactics of the user, but it is very difficult to infer from his log data the strategies he is using. In our opinion, we need to incorporate the user more closely into the process of evaluation. One possibility is to utilize a standard method of cognitive psychology, verbal protocols, in order to obtain a more accurate picture of the subject's problem-solving.

By verbal protocols (also known as the "thinking aloud" method) we mean users verbalizing their mental behavior while performing or just after the task. Ericsson and Simon (1980, 1984) provide an in-depth study of verbal protocols as data. There are, however, problems with the verbal protocol method (O'Malley, Draper, and Riley, 1984). First, it is not clear whether there is a direct connection between verbal reports and mental processes (Bainbridge, 1979). At least, some tasks are easier to verbalize than others. People also tend to rationalize their actions more when giving a verbal report. Secondly, there is the question whether having to make a verbal report changes the task and thus invalidates any generalization of the findings (i.e., the experimental situation is not ecologically valid). In the model of Ericsson and Simon (1980), they found no difference between silent and vocalizing groups doing the same task. On the other hand, Bainbridge (1979) notes that sometimes the performance may change to a more efficient one, perhaps due to the fact that the situation forces concentration on task components. Finally, as Lewis (1982) points out, the thinking aloud technique does not lend itself to a benchmark kind of assessment with pass-fail ratings, but is useful in a "find and fix" investigation where specific information about design features and how they work is needed.

2.2 The Combined Method

In this paper, we propose a combination of logging, playback, and verbal protocols to be used in addition to the above mentioned methods. Our basic assumption is that the user of the interactive system is a thinking and "cognitive" human being whose assessment and judgement of the system should be appreciated. So, when analyzing the interaction between the system and the user, we should employ a method that elicits user comments.

In our opinion, the emphasis on verbal protocols in connection with logging and playback can provide benefits that have not been recognized hitherto. In this method the test subject is working in his own familiar environment. The system is set to operating in a monitoring (or logging) mode where the keystrokes of the subject are stored into a file. The system is also capable of playbacking the session from the log file, which should be done directly after the session. In this retrospective session, the subject is supposed to verbalize his thoughts and problem-solving processes at the same time as the corresponding part of the previous session is reached on the terminal screen.

Hoc and Leplat (1983) have used a similar method (aided subsequent verbalization) as the combined method in a study of a sorting task. They compared this method to simultaneous verbalization and to unaided subsequent verbalization, and concluded that for their type of logical task the aided subsequent verbalization was the most favorable. Their approach, however, was more directed towards analyzing user behavior, while we would also like to point out the possibilities offered by the above kind of experimental setting for evaluation and teaching purposes.

We argue that the combined method is suitable for analyzing strategies in complex situations in which there are many possible solution paths, but not necessarily one single path over the others. In this kind of situation, the task-solving process requires most of the energy of the subject, so valuable comments for the evaluation purposes can be more easily obtained in the retrospective sessions. Important evaluation issues often tend to be of an elusive, temporary nature. Thus they cannot be recorded in a post-mortem interview, but need the reproduction of the actual situation to be reborn. In the retrospective session one can also infer more clearly the deficiencies in the system that were hindering the task-solving process. In our experiments, this kind of evaluation was used as a "find and fix" method where we hoped that the subject was able to see more general views than in the actual work situation.

Considering the combined method and the study of the behavior of the test subjects we can note that the combined method avoids, in part, the difficulties with concurrent thinking and verbalization. However, it contains problems due to the retrospectiveness, e.g., to what amount the information stays in the memory of the respondent. The exact reproduction of the real situation by showing it in playback to the subjects can alleviate this difficulty. There are also other problems, such as the fact that people tend to rationalize over one's earlier behavior. We think that drawing on the work of Ericsson and Simon (1980) the investigator can manage these situations and design his probes so that the above problems can be avoided.

The third use of the combined method is in teaching, as a tutoring method, because reviewing the completed session can be rewarding to the test subject, too. Moreover, the investigator can support the learning process of the subject by suggesting good strategies. Thus the method can be seen as an extension to those uses of playback sessions where the students replay scripts of keystrokes that the instructor has previously saved (Brown and Sedgewock, 1984). Because it is possible to edit the log files, student sessions can be modified and reused for instructional purposes later on, e.g., for demonstrating how to avoid errors.

The combined method can be employed in the traditional "objectivistic" fashion (the investigator observing and recording the actions of the research subject), or to support the "actional approach" (the investigator also communicating with the research subject). These two basic approaches to empirical research are discussed more closely in Hietala et.al. (1985). The combined method can easily be augmented to produce data, for monitoring purposes, e.g., data on the times that the subjects have spent during each of their activities. In the I3V system, each action of the user (while in the log mode) is time-stamped. We have not yet, however, utilized the data obtained this way. One reason for this was the difficulty to define appropriate time measures, e.g., for a set of "core" verification tasks, as is often done in the evaluation studies of text editors. In our opinion this difficulty is mainly due to the inherent nature of program verification as a problem-solving task, which makes it more difficult to divide a verification task into distinct subtasks. The nature of problem-solving seems also to lead to bigger tasks than what is the case if we consider routine task-solving. However, the questions of an appropriate time measuring for verification tasks and "what kind of process the actual process of verification really is" are interesting topics for further research.

The combined method approach is rather fast and inexpensive, if compared to laboratory tests with special equipment. Our method requires modification of the software of the system involved, but if the system is modularized (especially the input/output handling), this may not be a big problem. In our experiment instrumenting the system to support data gathering and re-input was quite straightforward. Some modern systems provide features (e.g., the tee-command in Unix or the system audit trail facility in modern workstations (Goldberg, 1984)) which would significantly assist the implementation of the method.

3. A CASE STUDY: EVALUATING AN INTERACTIVE SYSTEM

In this section we describe how we have applied the method introduced in the previous section. The combined method was employed as one among several analysis and evaluation methods in the evaluation of a prototype version of a verification support system. The evaluation took place on two occasions: (1) during a course for university students who were learning to verify programs with the help of the system; and (2) in separate sessions with users already familiar with verification. We first discuss the environment briefly and then the actual experiments and results in more detail.

3.1 The Setting

The System. The system we wanted to evaluate was a program verification support system called I3V (an Interactive system for Incremental and Iterative program Verification). It emphasizes program proof-building as a user-driven process, where the system assists this process by employing the paradigm of direct manipulation. The proof for a program can be built incrementally and the system supports iterations in this process. The theory for the system is described in Back (1983) and the user interface issues in Back and Hietala (1984). A prototype version of the system is running on the mainframe (DEC2060) of the University of Tampere.

The evaluation of the prototype version of the I3V system involved students of a verification course as well as a group of experienced users. Here we discuss the evaluation from the point of view of the combined method. The overall evaluation of the I3V system has been reported in greater detail in Hietala (1985c).

The Verification Course. The course in March-April 1984 consisted of 30 hours of lessons in four week's time. After that the students had one and a-half week for a take-home final exercise. The nature of the lessons was mainly lectures at the beginning of the course, but near the end there were also demonstrations and test sessions with the system. There were six third-year undergraduate students who participated in the course. Their only previous experience with verification was some anecdotal examples on the introductory programming course.

The combined method was used on two occasions during the course: during the third week and at the final evaluation session after the course. On each of the occasions the students solved specific problems while the I3V system was in the logging mode. The sessions were then unfolded with the teacher also present. These sessions took about 2-3 hours (one hour for the working session and the rest for the evaluation session).

The combined method was employed as one among several other methods for studying the students and their learning as well as their assessments of the I3V system: the others were exercises, examinations, questionnaires, and course diaries. The impact of the I3V system for teaching program verification has been reported in Hietala (1985b) and a detailed description of the verification course has been given in Hietala (1985a).

Experienced Users. So far there have been five experienced users participating in our experiments. They were mainly graduate students having previous experience with program verification (four with the same methodology as applied in the I3V system). Some of them had seen demonstrations of an earlier version of the system, but during our experiments most of them saw the system for the first time. Computer science, and also mathematics, had been the main subjects of their earlier studies. Their background in logic was also extensive. Their working experience included mostly teaching at the universities, but some also had industrial experience.

The exercises given the students during the verification course were replicated with the experienced users (in two three-hour sessions in one day for each experienced user). They were also given the same materials as students in the course. However, these sessions were the first time they actually used the system.

3.2 Experiments and Results

The I3V system provided a mode where the user commands were recorded with a time-stamp into a log file specified at the start of the session. In another mode the commands of the session were fetched from that log file. After each command the system would then require an additional keystroke in order to continue the session, which made it possible to control the pacing speed in the playback session.

In the test situation the subjects were instructed to switch to the logging mode and were aware that after one hour's work there would be a follow-up session with the playback system and the teacher. In this latter session they were supposed to verbalize the mental processes they applied in the previous session. They were also encouraged to express their opinions about the system and its user interface. Moreover, when the session advanced to a point where something exceptional happened, they were prompted by questions like "Why did you do that?". The teacher's role in the session was slightly more interruptive than Ericsson and Simon (1980) require. This was because we wanted primarily to obtain evaluation information about the system. It should also be noted that in this retrospective session the questions did not alter the actual behavior of the subject. In the sessions there was an educational aspect involved as well: we wanted the students to learn better ways of using the system to verify programs.

Experiments. The log-playback facility of the I3V system was used twice during the course (these two exercises were replicated for the experienced users). In the first of these terminal exercises we wanted to know whether the system assisted the test subjects to find the inconsistencies between program text and program specifications (i.e., invariants embedded in the program text). They were given an example program, which had incomplete invariants for the program task at hand (they were told that if they found any inconsistences they should use the I3V facilities to change and modify program invariants). During the verification they were supposed to run into these trouble spots and try to modify them.

In the second terminal exercise (at the end of the student course) we wanted to know how well the system assisted the users in inventing new program invariants, now assuming that the program code and the entry and exit invariants were correct. The test subjects were requested to add the crucial loop invariants to the program using the I3V system's assistance (e.g., in browsing and manipulating the program).

Results. The instructional goal of the first terminal exercise was to
introduce the modification facility of the I3V system by means of a
problem, where the test subjects were supposed to verify a given program
which contained (without them knowing it) incomplete invariants. This
succeeded rather well: all students "got stuck" in the corresponding
locations and, during the playback session with the instructor, the
procedure needed for modification was explained, now maybe with more
emphasis to them than when it was covered during the lectures.

The experienced users started their work with the system for the first
time in this exercise, so they tended to have troubles with the system.
However, they also seemed to find rather easily the inconsistent spots in
their example program.

The second terminal exercise concentrated on the I3V features supporting iterative verification: the test subjects were supposed to "fill-in"
the missing invariants in the program and to adjust their suggestions for
the invariants so that they were strong enough. The I3V system seemed to
support rather well this kind of activity which is essential to practical
verification. Moreover, the playback sessions showed that the verification
strategies of the students had not yet matured; most of them did not have a
clear strategy to approach the problem, nor did they utilize all the possibilities provided by the system. However, it must be mentioned that "invariant inventing using the system" had not been exercised earlier during
the course.

The experienced users managed clearly better in this exercise and got
more locations of the program verified and more appropriate invariants
invented.

The terminal exercises in which the combined method was employed seemed
to produce evaluation comments from the novice of a far better quality than
those in their diaries (Hietala, 1985a). Instead of just pointing out
errors or shortcomings in the system behavior, the students also gave alternatives and motivations for their comments. From the evaluation point
of view, comments of the experienced users were not significantly more
insightful than those of the students.

The evaluation comments obtained in the terminal exercise sessions have
been used to facilitate the further development of the I3V system. We
think that this kind of design process is appropriate for interactive systems, although it is not a generally accepted and adhered to design principle (Gould and Lewis, 1985). In our case, we obtained a large number of
development suggestions from the two groups of test subjects (Hietala,
1985a). The most important areas for further work seemed to be the following: more versatile ways of pacing in the program to be analyzed; more
flexible ways to organize and manipulate the information on the terminal
screen; and, most urgently, facilities for developing the program and the
proofs together. Some of these suggestions have already been included in
the next version of the verification system.

Results from the terminal exercises indicate that the experienced users
acted more purposefully than the novices; the experienced users seemed to
have a plan for advancing in the program, e.g., advancing from the goal
(exit assertions) to the initial conditions. This claim, however, needs
more elaboration. The I3V system gives the user possibilities to choose
rather freely his cognitive strategy to approach the verification. In the
terminal exercises it turned out to be an asset that the system did not
force the subjects to use a rigid ordering in which one should move in the

program. The reason is that in this kind of situation (with a problem-solving nature) there exist various alternative "good" strategies.

The analysis of problem-solving strategies in verification is a very interesting area for further research. Our preliminary experiments with the combined method demonstrated, on one hand, the suitability of the method to tasks described above, and, on the other hand, several important issues were revealed which need to be taken into account in future experiments. For example, the need for a greater amount of time (than one hour that we used) is indispensable for this kind of performance investigation. Also the study of the entire programming process, not just "slices of it", would be more appropriate, but would also require much more time; and a verification environment capable of also supporting the entire process. Careful selection of exercises and, in the case of evaluation sessions, detailed early preparation of the probes made by the investigator is of utmost importance.

4. CONCLUSIONS

The evaluation of interactive systems is a demanding task, mainly due to the fact that the system should provide cognitive fit to the capabilities of its users. Questionnaires, monitoring and verbal protocols, to name a few techniques, are all necessary means to evaluate these systems, but each of them has certain drawbacks that should be taken into account when applying them.

In this paper, we have proposed that combining logging, playback and verbal protocols could be beneficial in evaluating interactive software, and demonstrated this in a case study. The advantages obtained in carrying out evaluation in this manner are the following: the method is unobtrusive to the subjects; it can be inexpensive and easy to realize; it can support eliciting of relevant evaluation information by reproducing the actual work situation; and is capable of bringing out knowledge of the users' mental models and problem-solving processes. In our opinion, this method should be especially considered when devising the evaluation techniques for the early phases in the design of interactive software, and would, together with other methods, provide useful information for further development of the system.

However, the work reported in this paper must be seen as the first step in the investigation of the usefulness of the combined method. Additional work is needed to provide means to bring the log data to bear in a more versatile manner in the playback sessions. It is also necessary to carry out more extensive experiments in order to get more data about the use of the method.

ACKNOWLEDGEMENTS

This work was supported by the Academy of Finland. The constructive comments of Marja Vehviläinen on an earlier version of this paper are gratefully acknowledged.

REFERENCES

Back, R. J. R., 1983, "Invariant Based Programs and Their Correctness", Automatic Program Construction Techniques, Biermann, Guiho, and Kodratoff, eds., MacMillan, Section IV, pp. 1-22.

Back, R. J. R., and Hietala, P., 1984, "A Simple User Interface for Interactive Program Verification", Proceedings of INTERACT'84: First IFIP Conference on Human-Computer Interaction, B. Shackel, ed., London, September 4-7, 1984, 1, pp. 114-118.

Bainbridge, L., 1979, "Verbal Reports as Evidence of the Process Operator's Knowledge", International Journal of Man-Machine Studies, 11, pp. 411-436.

Brown, M. H., and Sedgewick, R., 1984, "Progress Report: Brown University Instructional Computing Laboratory", Proceedings of the Fifteenth SIGCSE Technical Symposium on Computer Science Education, Philadelphia, February 16-17, 1984. ACM SIGCSE Bulletin 16, 1, February, 1984, pp. 91-101.

Ericsson, K. A., and Simon, H. A., 1980, "Verbal Reports as Data", Psychological Review, 87, pp. 215-251.

Ericsson, K. A., and Simon, H. A., 1984, Protocol Analysis: Verbal Reports as Data, MIT Press, Cambridge, Mass.

Gaines, B. R., 1981, "The Technology of Interaction-Dialogue Programming Rules", International Journal of Man-Machine Studies, 14, pp. 137-150.

Goldberg, A., 1984, Smalltalk-80: The Interactive Programming Environment, Addison-Wesley, Reading, Mass.

Good, M., 1985, "The Use of Logging Data in the Design of a New Text Editor", Human Factors in Computing Systems, L. Borman and B. Curtis, eds., CHI'85 Conference Proceedings, San Francisco, CA, April 14-18, 1985, pp. 93-98.

Gould, J. D., and Lewis, C., 1985, "Designing for Usability: Key Principles and What Designers Think", Comm. ACM, 28 (3), pp. 300-311.

Hietala, P., 1985, A Course on Program Verification, University of Tampere, Department of Mathematical Sciences, Report A137.

Hietala, P., 1985, "Teaching Program Verification With the Help of an Interactive Program Verification", Proceedings of WCCE/85: World Conference on Computers in Education, K. Duncan and D. Harris, eds., Norfolk, Virginia, July 29 - August 2, 1985, pp. 561-566.

Hietala, P., 1985, "On the Evaluation of a Support System for Interactive Program Verification", Preprints of the Second IFAC/IFIP/IFORS/IEA Conference on Analysis, Design, and Evaluation of Man-Machine Systems, G. Johannsen, G. Mancini and L. Märtensson, eds., Varese, Italy, September 10-12, 1985, pp. 198-203.

Hietala, P., Järvinen, P., Mäkinen, E.., and Tyllilä, P., 1985, "On Two Approaches to Computer Science Research and on Their Symbiosis", 20th Anniversary Book of the Faculty of Economics and Administration, University of Tampere, Acta Universitatis Tamperensis, Ser. A, 190, pp. 317-338.

Hoc, J-M., and Leplat, J., 1983, "Evaluation of Different Modalities of Verbalization in a Sorting Task", International Journal on Man-Machine Studies, 18, pp. 286-306.

Lewis, C., 1982, Using the "Thinking Aloud" Method in Cognitive Interface Design, IBM, T. J. Watson Research Center, Research Report RC 9265.

Neal, A. S., and Simons, R. M., 1983, "Playback: A Method for Evaluating the Usability of Software and its Documentation", Human Factors in Computing Systems, A. Janda, ed., CHI'83 Conference Proceedings, Boston, December 12-15, 1983, pp. 78-82.

O'Malley, C., Draper, S., and Riley, M., 1984, "Constructive Interaction: A Method for Studying User-Computer-User Interaction", Proceedings of INTERACT'84: First IFIP Conference on Human-Computer Interaction, B. Shackel, ed., London, September 4-7, 1984, 2, pp. 1-5.

Root, R. W., and Draper, S., "Questionnaires as a Software Evaluation Tool", Human Factors in Computing Systems, A. Janda, ed., CHI'83 Conference Proceedings, Boston, December 12-15, 1983, pp. 83-87.

Shneiderman, B., 1980, Software Psychology: Human Factors in Computer and Information Systems, Winthrop, Cambridge, Mass.

Yoder, E., MacCracken, D., and Akscyn, R., 1984, "Instrumenting a Human-Computer Interface for Development and Evaluation", Proceedings of INTERACT'84: First IFIP Conference on Human-Computer Interaction, B. Shackel, ed., London, September 4-7, 1984, 2, pp. 309-314.

ANALYSIS OF THE NEEDS FOR COMPUTER AIDS TO PLANNING IN COMPUTER PROGRAMMING

Jean-Michel Hoc and Annette Valentin

Groupement Scientifique du CNRS
"Activités Cognitives et Conduites Complexes"
EPHE - Laboratoire de Psychologie du Travail
41, rue Gay-Lussac F - 75005 PARIS

Abstract: This paper is devoted to the psychological analysis of the needs for computer aids to planning in computer programming, in relation to the development of computer-aided software factories. Two methodologies are presented and illustrated by empirical results: experimental assessment of a prototype, and observational study in a traditional environment. The complementarity of these methodologies is emphasized.

INTRODUCTION

Programming is obviously a planning task, in as much as it implies the elaboration of a procedure before getting feedback from execution. But planning must not be restricted to this simple way of regarding at anticipation. Anticipation itself may lead the subject to remove execution details. This removal allows the subject to use schematic representations, which are remote from the details, and to elaborate instructions in an order which is sometimes very different from the order of execution.

The limited capacity of the human operator's processors and his (or her) high level knowledge lead and permit him (or her) to construct and use schematic representations during the planning process (Hoc, 1982; Adelson et al., 1984). Nevertheless, this cognitive skill must not be confused with the ability to follow a strictly top-down programming strategy. Schematic representations may be elaborated as abstract constructs from detailed representations. Hence, planning processes very often put top-down and bottom-up components into action (Hayes-Roth and Hayes-Roth, 1979).

Solving a problem in a situation where immediate execution is possible induces a prospective strategy which generates actions in the order of execution. But planning may permit the subject to construct the program in the reverse order, by following a retrospective strategy, as is the case in some forms of mathematical problem-solving. Moreover, the subject may think more in terms of static properties or relations between objects than in terms of the dynamic operation of a device (human or machine).

In designing a computer program, the multiplicity of knowledge domains involved must be emphasized. Planning may take place in diverse and separate subject's knowledge domains, called Representation and Processing Systems (RPS) by Hoc (1977): knowledge of the problem domain, of the programming language, of the editor, etc. RPS are brought into play in the same kind of heterarchical way, as in the Hayes-Roth and Hayes-Roth's (1979) "opportunistic" planning model using "specialists", or Stefik's (1981) artificial planning system, using constraints propagation.

For some years, software engineering has made considerable progress in the implementation of computer aids to programming. For example, program editors have become more and more powerful and are not only aids to the final steps of programming (program development) but also to the very first steps in designing programs (problem analysis). To design suitable computer-aided software engineering environments of this kind, it is important to consider the need for diverse types of computer aids, especially for planning and for shifting easily from one RPS to another.

Satisfactory design and assessment of these types of aids underline the need for a better understanding of the cognitive strategies in elaborating programs. From this perspective, observational studies and individual protocol analyses are very useful in formulating reasonable hypotheses to be tested later by suitable experimental designs.

In order to provide the designer of the programming aids with useful information as rapidly as possible, these observational and experimental studies may be carried out in two complementary ways: the observation of programming behavior (1) using a prototype and (2) in traditional environments.

This paper is devoted to the use of these two methodologies and their complementary goals in studying planning strategies. It examines:

- The main results of an experimental evaluation of a prototype of interactive computer aids in program design, developed by CRIN (the MAIDAY environment: Guyard and Jacquot (1984)), with an automatic recording of professional programmers' behavior on a VDT (Hoc, in preparation).

- The principles of an observational study, in progress, of professional programmers in a traditional environment, the aim of which is to formulate recommendations for designing the computer-aided environment CONCERTO, developed by CNET (André, 1985).

In the first study the emphasis is put on the interaction between the characteristics of the programming tools, the types of problems to be solved with the tools, and the subjects' planning strategies. It deals, in particular, with the use of schematic representations and the implementation of a retrospective strategy. The second study is concerned more with the problem of shifting from one RPS to another, and the corresponding need for multi-window displays and access to information.

EVALUATION OF A PROTOTYPE: THE MAIDAY ENVIRONMENT

The Tools: A Language (MEDEE) and its Editor (MEDEDIT)

The tools have been designed within the framework of a structured and top-down programming method: the "deductive method" (Pair, 1979), which presents the following properties:

- It is definitional, in that it leads to the definition of relations between objects, as in the case of algebraic variables, as opposed to assigning values to computer variables.

- It is retrospective, in that it first defines the results in
  relation to intermediary results, and then defines these intermediary results in relation to the data (the definitions are
  introduced in reverse order, in contrast to the order of
  execution).

- It is of a top-down, modular, and structured programming kind.

The language MEDEE. Relative to these properties, the basic unit of
the language is the definition of objects, as can be seen in the left-hand
column of Table I, which presents a MEDEE algorithm for calculating a test
group mean, standard deviation, and size. There are three types of definitions (not all of them are listed in the table):

- simple definitions (logical and algebraic formula, readings,
  and printouts), e.g., mean=total/size; result=print(mean,
  stdev,size).

- conditional definitions (case structures), e.g., a: if cond1
  then a=...if cond2 then a=...if...else a=....

- iterative definitions, e.g., total: total=0 for x in data
  repeat total=∂total+x.

Each object must be defined only once. Consequently, in recursive formula, each element of a series is a distinct object: the sign '∂' is used
to differentiate the previous element from the current one.

Several objects may be defined conditionally or iteratively (last elements of series). In this case, everything on the right of 'then' and 'repeat' is expressed separately in the form of labelled modules. Thus, the
algorithm can be seen as a tree of modules and analogical terms from genealogy, such as 'father' and 'son' module, are used.

The structure of printout, conditional, and iterative definitions is
implied by the definitional character of the language. Contrary to the
corresponding traditional program instructions, the user must express the
objects defined by the structure.

The Editor MEDEDIT. The editor is stratified into four levels:

- environment: access to algorithms;

- algorithm: access to modules of an algorithm;

- module: access to definitions in a module; and

- definition: access to components of a definition.

At present, the two first levels are very poor. In the future, at the
environment level, tools should permit the subject to use old algorithms
wholly or partly in designing a new one. In the same way, at the algorithm
level tools should be designed to enable modules to be shifted within the
algorithm. At the moment existing tools mainly concern the two last
levels.

A multi-window display is used, with dedicated keys. The central part
of the display is a vertical scrolling zone (98 lines, 24 of which are visible through the window), where the accepted definitions of the current
module are listed, as in the Table I format. Surrounding this zone, five
other zones are devoted to displaying respectively: the current level;

111

TABLE I

MEDEE Algorithm for Calculating a Test Group Mean, Standard-Deviation, and Size. (In each column, the number above the line indicates the order of writing in following a retrospective strategy).

PRINCIPAL		
Definitions	**Types**	**Comments**
1 result=print(mean,stdev,size) 5 mean=total/size 7 stdev=sqrt((sqrs-total pow 2)/ size) /size) 9 total,sqrs,size:INI for x in data repeat OBSERVATION	result(edit) 2 mean(real) 3 stdev(real): 'standard deviation' 4 size(integer) 6 total(real): 'sum of ob- servations' 8 sqrs(real): 'raw sum of squares' 10 x(real): 'observation'	11 INI:'initializes' 12 OBSERVATION: 'processes an observation'

OBSERVATION		
13 total=∂total+x 14 sqrs=∂sqrs+x pow 2 15 size=∂size+1		

INI		
16 total,sqrs,size=0		

messages from the system; the definition currently being validated (temporary storage); the list of objects which may be defined in the current module; and the entry being composed from the keyboard.

Three types of functions are available:

- editing functions (e.g., parsing a definition),

- control functions (e.g., checking contextual consistences),

- 'clever' functions (e.g., aids in initializing recurrent objects, updating a list of objects to be defined in each module).

The user is guided by explicit scripts of a question-answer kind. In Table I, the numbers indicate the order of the entries when following a retrospective strategy. But the scripts do not impose this kind of strategy: in a module, the definitions may be composed in an arbitrary order. Nevertheless, a 'son' module cannot be defined before entering the definition module which uses it in the 'father' module.

The most important script is the definition-creation one:

- the user enters the definition from the keyboard into the zone of composition,

- if the definition is syntactically correct, it is transferred from this zone to the temporary storage zone,

- then, the system asks for comment and type of each unknown object (not yet introduced in the module or its ancestry),

- if the definition uses modules, the system asks for comment on each module, and

- if there is no contextual inconsistency, the definition is accepted and transferred, with all other information, to the module (as in Table I).

Method and Hypotheses

Method. Ten professional programmers, having learned the language at the University, agreed to devote 15 hours to solving two programming problems interactively with the editor (without using pencil and paper). Several problems were chosen to assess the tools in various situations, some of them favorable and others not.

There were four types of problems which combined two classification dimensions: the result of a preliminary study, with the same subjects, which aimed at inferring classification criteria used by programmers confronted with problem statements without solving them (Hoc, 1983).

The first dimension is planning direction, which may be prospective (generating instructions by following the order of execution) or retrospective (reverse order). The second dimension is planning guidance type: the program structure may be derived from data or results structure (declarative guidance), or inherent in the procedure (procedural guidance).

Consequently, the four types of problems were the following:

- prospective declarative: the program structure is derived from data structure (e.g., certain business problems in which the organization of input files is a strong constraint),

- prospective procedural: the expression of a procedure follows a symbolic execution (e.g., word processing problems),

- retrospective declarative: the program structure is derived from the structure of the results (e.g., certain business problems in which the organization of output files is a strong constraint),

- retrospective procedural: the program is elaborated by running through a database of definitions of variables, from the required results back to the data (e.g., statistical problems).

Declarative and procedural problems were solved by two independent groups of subjects. But each subject solved a prospective and a retrospective problem. Problem order was balanced. All the problems were as equivalent as possible, with regard to the complexity of optimal algorithms (depth of the tree of modules, number of modules, objects, and definitions).

All the keyboard entries were recorded. Individual protocol analyses were carried out to identify the programming strategies and the most frequent and persistent difficulties encountered. Due to the small number of subjects, the aim of the work was exploratory and no statistical test was performed. It has led instead to the formulation of reasonable hypotheses and to a methodology which can be automated in order to test them on larger samples. We will focus this short paper on the main results concerning planning. The other results and a detailed presentation will be found in Hoc (in preparation).

Hypotheses. In the limited framework of this paper, three main hypotheses are emphasized:

Hypothesis 1: In this language (MEDEE), with this editor (MEDEDIT), conditional or iterative structures must be expressed in a definitional form (expression of the objects to be defined by the structure). This form introduces a kind of a priori justification of a possibly complex part of the algorithm, by the goals (objects to be defined). The tools employed were expected to induce retrospective strategies and as a result to create a lot of difficulty with the prospective problems, but less difficulty with the retrospective ones.

Hypothesis 2: Among the prospective problems, the procedural one was expected to be the most difficult, relative to the definitional nature of the language (expressing static definitions as opposed to dynamic operations). The retrospective declarative problem was expected to be the easiest.

Hypothesis 3: The editor was expected to create a lot of planning difficulties. When writing higher level modules, the subject is supposed to express mainly schematic representations. But the language and the editor introduce the constraints of expressing precise conditional or iterative definitions before access is available to low-level modules. Also the only access to the algorithm is a limited window on detailed parts of it. This restriction was expected to cause the subject difficulty: namely in updating the representation of the overall structure of the algorithm, and in shifting from one part to another (e.g., in dealing with interactions between subproblems).

114

Main Results and Discussion

The tools clearly induced retrospective strategies, whatever the type of problem (55% to 70% of the objects are used in defining other objects before being themselves defined). Nevertheless, a lot of difficulties were encountered when the problem was of a prospective type (especially the procedural one in contrast to the retrospective declarative problem):

- the time spent on prospective problems was one third longer than on retrospective ones,

- the strategy was more bottom-up (modifications of 'father' modules after writing the 'sons'),

- the conceptualization of the problem was more difficult (more errors in the representation of the problem, more introduction of inappropriate objects before choosing the right ones),

- using the language was more difficult.

It is interesting to explore possible aids for retrospective strategy, in as much as an editor can provide a greater amount of memory aids for a retrospective strategy than for a prospective one. The editor can know more about the subject's goals in the former case than in the latter. The analysis of protocols shows how some extra aids could be used to successfully implement a retrospective strategy, even on prospective problems.

For example, an important reason for the difficulties observed on the prospective procedural problem was the limited set of data structures in the language, as in classical procedural languages. In a procedural language, this lack of data structures has a less blocking effect, since the subject can be guided by the structure of the dynamic execution of the procedure, by following a prospective strategy. In a definitional language such as MEDEE, inducing a retrospective strategy, guidance by the structures of the objects is necessary.

In the course of top-down program design, when writing highest level modules, the subjects' representations of the problems were fuzzy and difficult to express with the precision imposed by the language. These difficulties are possibly explained by the fact that the strategies were rather depth-first than breadth-first (defining each branch of the tree in its entirety before turning to another one, instead of defining the whole problem at each abstract level before going down to the next one). Generalization strategies were very often observed (by restricting the problems to simpler ones, with simpler trees, at first before gradually introducing the complexity). As a result some schematic expressions of conditional and iterative definitions to be detailed later in the course of the design should be introduced.

A purely top-down programming strategy cannot always be followed: it must be articulated with some bottom-up components. A plan is a hypothesis which is tested by detailing it. In the case of invalidation, detected in a module, a plan (a higher level module) must be modified and, at the same time, the design of the current module carried on. The subjects frequently had to modify the plan in order to carry on the current module. The complexity of the modification procedures with the editor and the lack of simultaneous display of modules created long interruptions with perturbations in working memory as the thread of the principal process was lost.

In general, analysis of the diverse types of modifications and their contexts has led to a proposal of extra editing functions. These will make the modifications easier, by minimizing interruption and working memory load.

In planning, the subjects very often had to shift for information purposes between schematic levels of representation and detailed ones, while the screen showed the subject a small window in a detailed part of his algorithm. Some errors observed revealed that subjects were unable to keep the overall structure of the algorithm in working memory. It seems that they needed a parallel updated presentation of this overall structure, with possibilities of zooming in on its detailed parts. This was especially the case when an object, defined in one module, was used in a collateral one.

Consequently, the need for parallel access to information in planning seems to be clear.

This kind of study, on a prototype, suffers from lack of reference to work situations (or other computer-aided situations) which can:

- provide an external and comparative evaluation,

- possibly allow the subject to get around the difficulties, by leaving him freer to choose the means he wants; only then appropriate hints can be obtained how to design aids.

The second part of this paper presents a complementary methodology: the observational study of program design behavior in work situations. This project is in progress and we will only illustrate this methodology with a single subject's protocol.

OBSERVATIONAL STUDY IN A TRADITIONAL ENVIRONMENT: RECOMMENDATIONS FOR THE CONCERTO ENVIRONMENT

Aim of the Study

This study aims at providing information on differences between usual programming environments and the future CONCERTO work station, so that ergonomic approaches can be suggested. The following CONCERTO environment features are to be emphasized:

- A multi-window display should permit parallel access to several documents. The study must provide information on the suitable number and dimensions of windows, as well as on the management of a necessarily limited number of windows, according to different needs for document availability and access mode.

- Direct showing-off techniques are planned. The study will examine the various common showing-off schemata and their relative importance. For graphic needs: circling, ticking off, writing brackets, etc.

- A consistent command language is desired. The study will try to define generalizable functions from analogous scripts followed when performing different types of tasks.

- A syntactic editor would perform three kinds of function: syntactical control, text or graphic display presentation, and more or less abbreviated program representations. The study must provide precise suggestions concerning the modalities of these different functions.

Observational Methodology

The aim of the study is incompatible with any analysis of gross performance measures on large samples. It requires a fine grain analysis of a small number of individual protocols. This kind of methodology will also enable us to justify the usability of the suggested computer aids, by their actual functions in the development of programming strategies.

The subjects are four professional programmers working in a service firm. In order to interpret the sources of individual differences, we conducted a preliminary interview on the subjects' educational background, professional experience, and work environment. Two subjects are beginners (less than 6 months in the firm after graduating) and two experts (3 and 5 years). Data analysis is in progress and we will focus on part of the analysis of an expert's protocol.

The individual observation of each subject takes place in the course of quite long programming tasks (about 4 to 5 days), from going through the dossier until debugging, with thinking aloud instructions. Verbal reports are recorded and used to infer goals and implicit processes or intermediary results. The other types of behavior are directly coded (sequence of actions on documents, showing-off modalities, and access modes).

The verbal reports are very useful in hierarchically decomposing the protocol into multi-level episodes (Table II). At the uppermost level, the protocol is divided into several macro-episodes corresponding to general topics (goals and objects), which are verbalized and very often introduced by readily identifiable transition words. Then, these macro-episodes are themselves decomposed into episodes and sub-episodes down to the fourth and last level corresponding to the coded actions. Each action refers to the RPS within which it is mainly generated, so as to regroup cognitively connected actions on different documents. Knowledge of programming language syntax, of editor handling, of problem domain, etc., are examples of RPS.

Data Analysis in Progress

At present, analysis is guided by the main aspects of the CONCERTO work station, relative to document consultation behavior throughout the protocols, whatever the kind of episode: routine or problem-solving. Later, programming strategies will be characterized, so that an interpretation framework for relevant aids can be proposed. This will stress functions independently of the specific information distribution on those documents used in the observed situations. This analysis of strategies will only concern those crucial parts of protocols where problems are actually encountered.

Certain results from one of the expert subjects are presented in order to illustrate the methodology. Interruption periods have been removed from the protocol (representing 60% of the total time spent on the project; 80% of this time is due to system latencies).

The implications of these results for work-station design are shown, but results from the other protocols will be used to evaluate inter-individual variability.

Multi-window Display. For each episode, corresponding to a short-term goal (5 to 15 minutes), the number of documents handled is computed. A document is defined by its physical medium, except when it is displayed on the screen, where several documents must be distinguished by their objects. For each document, the consulting time and the delay between two successive

Table II

Part of a Protocol. Episode 2.2.1 – 10h38 to 10h44 – "problem about zones not restored to zero (RTZ)" Belongs to Macro-Episode "program modifications after verification". Legend: S codes "screen", L: "listing", Syst. CMD: "system command", FC.TA20: "content of the file TA20" and SP.TA20: "source program for processing the file TA20".

	Time	Action	Goal	Document	Precision	Production	Showing-off	RPS
1	10,38 10,38	seize	calls the program	S.Syst.Cmd	S.SP.TA20	prog display		system
2	10,38 10,39	read	zones not restored to zero	L.FC.TA20	Page 1	error summary	circles	problem
3	10,39 10,39	read	looks for informa-tion	S.SP.TA20	zones RTZ	ill Def. pb	points out	editor
4	10,39 10,40	plan	zones restored are wrong ones					problem
5	10,40 10,41	seize	duplicates lines	S.SP.TA20				editor
6	10,41 10,41	seize	modifies copied lines	S.SP.TA20				syntactic
7	10,41 10,41	read	looks for zones not restored	S.SP.TA20	zones RTZ		points out	editor
8	10,41 10,42	seize	duplicates lines	S.SP.TA20				editor
9	10,42 10,43	seize	modifies copied lines	S.SP.TA20				syntactic
10	10,43 10,44	read	verifies the modi-fications	S.SP.TA20	pb zones	problem solved		problem

consultations are calculated, so that the needs for parallel presentation and availability of information can be assessed. The documents access modes are also analyzed.

In 55% of the episodes, the subject uses only one output document (two to three documents in 30%, and none in 15% of the episodes). In 52% of the episodes, he uses two input documents (three to four in 30%, and none in 18% of the episodes). The relevant span of a document can be inferred from showing-off behaviors, and is short for input documents. These input documents are used for a shorter time than output ones, and the discrepancy between two successive consultations is larger. In the observed situation the size of output documents is A4 and there is no evidence to support a recommendation reducing this size. In 72% of the episodes, for this subject, an A3 screen would have been sufficient: A4 for one output document, and A4 divided in two to four input documents.

Direct Showing-off Techniques. Distributions (time and frequency of use) of the diverse showing-off modalities are examined in relation to document processing types.

Common editing functions are implemented by the subject: search by keywords, area names, etc. In this protocol, 25% of the actions are performed using showing-off techniques (nicking, arrowing, circling, etc.) It seems useful, therefore, to plan this kind of facility, with the possibility of erasing marks (e.g., from one version of a document to another). The subject very often follows the lines with his finger: a rule would be very useful on the screen.

Consistent Command Language. A search for analogous scripts in different episodes is conducted.

In this protocol, three kinds of scripts are recurrent. First, personal showing-off techniques are used in the same way whatever the document: equivalent coding schemata must be respected and consistent from one document to another. For example, circled windows for large parts of documents, and inverse video for small ones. Second, after each interruption, the subject always has to sum up the current goal and the preceeding actions. Consistent aids are expected for these summing up scripts. Third, the subject re-uses old programs, files, etc., very often. Consistent aids have to be designed, whatever the kind of document, for retrieving and modifying information.

Syntactic Editor. In CONCERTO the editor is designed with a particular stress on programming language syntax. In order to delimit the relative role of the corresponding RPS, each RPS's frequency of occurrence and time of use are calculated. In this way, improvements to the editor can be suggested so that aids to other RPSs can be provided. Here, comparisons between experts and beginners are necessary in order that aids relative to the level of expertise may be designed.

In this expert's protocol, only 20% of the actions take place in the language RPS. So, for this kind of subject (expert) the usefulness of a syntactic editor is relative. Aids must be provided for other RPS. The analysis of documents consulted in parallel with the program points out the need for graphic and abbreviated representations of the program. The editor has to manage them, especially for aiding summing up episodes after interruptions.

CONCLUSION

Emphasis is placed on the complementarity of the two methodologies referred to: evaluation of a prototype and observational study of a traditional work situation.

Assessment of a prototype makes process tracing easier: automatic recordings of protocols are very often available and the necessary interactions between the subject and the system make certain covert behaviors explicit. A prototype may provide the subject with new tools permitting him to implement very interesting new strategies, but certain profound difficulties may appear and may be related to the fact that the prototype is only a skeleton of the final system. In the studied example (assessment of MAIDAY environment), there is a contrast between the very fine grain aids for a retrospective strategy, even incomplete, and the lack of aids in processing schematic representations of the program and in rapid shifting between representations, which is useful in planning. In addition, certain effective strategies may be blocked.

In an observational study of a work situation, the subject is freer in his choice of strategy, and, therefore, a larger variety of strategies may be described to point to possible computer aids. This kind of situation may be a reference for the evaluation of a prototype, in pointing out improvements and deteriorations. But observations are less controlled and often very tedious to obtain, and also certain kinds of interesting strategies may not be implemented for lack of necessary aids.

Consequently, these two kinds of studies are complementary and their results must be compared.

ACKNOWLEDGEMENT

The studies presented in this paper are supported by ADI (French National Agency for Informatics), and by CNET (French National Research Center for Telecommunications). One of them has been done with the collaboration of CRIN (Informatics Research Center at Nancy) and some observations have been collected at SEMA (Software Engineering Department).

REFERENCES

Adelson, B., Littman, D., Ehrlich, K., Black, J., and Soloway, E., 1984, "Novice-Expert Differences in Software Design", INTERACT'84, London, September 1984, 2, p. 187.

André, E., 1985, CONCERTO: An Integrated and Flexible Software Development Environment, Research Report, CNET, Lannion.

Guyard, J., and Jacquot, J. P., 1984, "MAIDAY: An Environment for Guided Programming with a Definitional Language", Proceedings of the 7th International Confserence on Software Engineering, Orlando, FL.

Hayes-Roth, B., and Hayes-Roth, F., 1979, "A Cognitive Model of Planning", Cognitive Science, 3, p. 275.

Hoc, J. M., 1977, "Role of Mental Representation in Learning a Programming Language", International Journal of Man-Machine Studies, 9, p. 87.

Hoc, J. M., 1982, "Le Role Organisateur de la Planification dans la Résolution de Probléme", Journal de Psychologie, 87, p. 409.

Hoc, J. M., 1983, "Une Méthode de Classification Préalable des Problèmes d'un Domaine pour l'Analyse des Stratégies de Résolution," <u>Le Travail Humain</u>, <u>46</u>, p. 205.

Hoc, J. M., in preparation, "Towards Effective Computer Aids to Planning in Computer Programming: Theoretical Concerns and Empirical Evidence Drawn from Assessment of a Prototype", <u>Theoretical Perspectives and Empirical Illustrations in Human-Computer Interaction</u>, T. R. G. Green, J. M. Hoc, D. Murray, and G. van der Veer, eds., Academic Press, London.

Pair, C., 1979, "La Construction des Programmes", <u>RAIRO Informatique</u>, <u>13</u>, p. 113.

Stefik, M., 1981, "Planning with Constraints (MOLGEN: Part 1 & 2)", <u>Artificial Intelligence</u>, <u>16</u>, p. 111.

DEMON: A MODEL FOR THE MONITORING OF DECISION MAKING

Erik Hollnagel

Senior Lecturer   and Computer Resources International
Psychological Laboratory   Copenhagen, Denmark
University of Copenhagen
Copenhagen, Denmark

Abstract: This paper describes the basic principles for a decision monitoring model (DEMON). The background is the growing interest for the metacognitive functions in decision making that controls strategy selection and
resource monitoring. The purpose of the DEMON model is externally to monitor decision making to determine the cognitive load. This is done through
a modelling of the metacognitive control, in particular the changes in the
goal network of the decision making system. The paper describes the ratio-
nale of the model, and gives an outline of its basic functional modules.
The present version of the model is aimed at off-line analysis of specific
event sequences, and focuses on resource monitoring rather than strategy
selection.

INTRODUCTION

    The progress in computer science and Artificial Intelligence, particu-
larly the interest in Expert Systems and the various 'Fifth Generation'
projects, has led to an increased interest in modelling human cognition
(Alty et al., 1985; Hollnagel et al., 1986). This is matched by a growing concern for cognitive modelling as (a) a potential solution for designing more advanced man-machine systems (MMS), (particularly in process control (Abbott, 1982)) and (b) to improve the understanding and measurement
of human action and, consequently, erroneous actions. Much of the interest
has focused on particular cognitive functions, such as decision making,
problem solving, diagnosis, and strategy generation - and many of these
are, of course, intimately related.

    The focus has thus generally been on the cognitive functions that are
the immediate or direct constituents of behaviour, and which we can observe
and experience directly. These functions are all characteristics of purposeful behaviour. In addition, there also is a growing interest for cognitive functions that, although they are not direct constituents of behavior, are just as important for purposeful action. These are the metacognitive functions, which are the higher order (secondary or mediate)
cognitive functions that guide and control the more immediate actions.

Cognition and Metacognition

The difference between cognition and metacognition is probably best explained by an example. Take, for instance, decision making. This is generally described as a series of steps that the decision maker or decision making system (DMS) has to go through, each step being a cognitive function on its own. The following is a generic set of decision steps (Fischhoff, 1986):

Option Generation: Identifying possible courses of action (and inaction).

Value Assessment: Evaluating attractiveness or aversiveness of the consequences of each action.

Uncertainty Assessment: Assessing the likelihood of each consequence actually happening.

Option Choice: Integrating these considerations using a defensible (rational) decision rule to select the best (optimal) action.

These steps must, of course, be preceded by an awareness of the need to make a decision and followed by the execution of the chosen action. A more comprehensive series of steps is the following (Hollnagel, 1985):

Activation: Becoming aware of or alerted to the need of making a decision.

Preparation: Making observations, collecting data, and identifying the alternatives.

Deliberation: Evaluating the alternatives and interpreting their consequences.

Decision: Choosing an alternative.

Execution: Planning for the execution, monitoring the execution and post-decisional evaluation.

The number of steps as well as their names may vary slightly between different models and fields of application, but the core remains essentially the same. We shall use the last list, since it is most convenient for the domain of the DEMON model.

Normative decision theory prescribes how a rational decision should be made, i.e., what the steps should be and in which order they should be carried out. Descriptive decision theory, in contrast, does not require that the decision maker goes through the steps in any particular order, or even that he goes through them at all. Steps may be repeated, and actual decision making is normally an iterative rather than a strict sequential process. Several descriptive decision models (e.g., Rassmussen (1974)) make a virtue of pointing out that the decision maker can use shortcuts or shunts, and that this in fact is the rule rather than the exception (Dreyfus, 1980). To do so, however, requires that the decision maker not only is engaged in making the decision, but also that he keeps an eye on how he does it, i.e., a secondary or metacognitive function in addition to the primary function of making the decision.

Another argument for the necessity of metacognitive functions is the simple fact that we only rarely engage in a single activity. Instead we are continuously occupied with several things and try to achieve several goals simultaneously. (It is, perhaps, only in the isolation of a psychological laboratory that single tasks ever occur.) In addition, the environment is far from stable, and we are frequently interrupted in an activity by other events. So even in the pursuit of a single goal it is necessary to keep track of what happens in the environment. To engage in more than one activity obviously requires a higher-level, monitoring function which must be carried out in support of, hence in addition to, the primary functions.

For the purpose of this paper and the development of the DEMON model, metacognition is defined as the higher-order cognitive functions that control and support the execution of the cognitive functions that can be observed and experienced in purposeful behaviour. If we use <u>attention</u> as an operational criterion we can say that attention is directed <u>at</u> cognitive functions <u>by</u> metacognitive functions. The latter can therefore, by definition, <u>not</u> be experienced, but their existence can be deduced from the way cognitive functions appear. In this context we shall focus on the metacognitive functions that <u>control</u> behaviour. Other types of metacognition, for instance memory management, will not be considered.

THE MODELLING OF METACOGNITION

We shall here remain with decision making, primarily because it attracts considerable interest in both basic and applied research. But rather than consider decision making as such, we shall consider the metacognition of decision making - in other words, the <u>monitoring</u> of decision making. This has the very practical reason that we need to know more about this to design MMSs, since decision making is one of the activities that occurs across the interface, and one where computers may be of substantial help.

The goals for metacognition in a decision making system (DMS) can very briefly be stated as follows (Reason, 1985):

1. <u>Decide if the situation is relevant for the ready application of existing rules.</u>

    To do this the DMS must first identify and characterize the current situation. It must be determined whether it is familiar and, therefore, safe to use the normal procedures (which implies the skipping of steps), or whether it is unfamiliar so that greater caution is called for. The characterization must be used to select or construct an appropriate decision strategy. This function must, of course, precede the beginning of the decision and may be seen as the initial phase of decision making (and as decision making in itself). But more importantly it must also be regularly repeated, to prevent the continued application of a strategy when the circumstances have changed, i.e., when it is no longer appropriate. If the DMS fails to do so, the result may be functional fixation and a deterioration or break-down of the decision making.

2. <u>Direct the limited cognitive resources (attention and memory) toward critical aspects of the problem space.</u>

    The DMS must determine whether the selected stragey can be carried out as required, i.e., whether the needed resources are available. This means that decision making must be monitored continuously. Conditions may change, while the decision is being made, so that it becomes impossible to implement the strategy although it is still appropriate. The resources may, for instance, have changed (time has become shorter, other activities have interfered) or the priorities of the decision criteria (or the order of goals) may have changed, so that less capacity is available for carrying out the chosen strategy.

Obviously, these considerations are valid for any DMS, a computer as well as a human decision maker. But, whereas they are explicitly applied in computers, being an integral part of system design and programming, they have not received much attention in the study of human decision making. Some work has been done on the explicit choice of a strategy, for decision making or problem solving, but only at the beginning of the decision. And, although it is generally recognized that there are strict limits to human information processing capacity, and that these limits furthermore may vary under changing environmental conditions such as stress, these facts have not been properly incorporated in existing models and descriptions of decision making.

A complete analysis of the metacognition of decision making must, of course, consider both of the above points (strategy selection and resource monitoring). Here I will, however, only consider resource monitoring since that is the primary purpose of the proposed model. To analyze metacognition in decision making it is an advantage to consider both man and machine in the same way as Decision Making Systems, using the same terminology (since the ultimate goal is the much wider field of MMSs). As we furthermore are dealing with cognitive functions, it is reasonable to use a terminology that emphasizes the cognitive aspects, as propsoed by Cognitive Systems Engineering (Hollnagel and Woods, 1983).

RESOURCE MONITORING IN METACOGNITION

A necessary although not sufficient condition for a successfully completed decision is that no unforeseen difficulties prevent the DMS from carrying out the decision as planned. Such difficulties may be of various types. External events may, for instance, interrupt or suspend the decision making, priorities and/or decision criteria may change due to changes in the environment, or the DMS may simply be incapable of carrying out the decision as prescribed by the strategy because it has assessed the resource requirements incorrectly.

To describe decision making as information processing puts some requirements to the system that carries out the information processing. This is particularly clear in the normative decision theories, but also quite obvious in the descriptive approach taken here. A detailed understanding of resource demands and monitoring must refer to established theories of human cognitive capacity. There is general agreement about a number of basic facts, although there may be considerable difference between models and theories for detailed phenomena. The following is a useful summary description of the human cognitive system:

The evidence is overwhelming that the system is basically serial in its operation: that it can process only a few symbols at a time and that the symbols being processed must be held in special, limited memory structures whose content can be changed rapidly. The most striking limits on subject's capacities to employ efficient strategies arise from the very small capacity of the short-term memory structure (four chunks) and from the relatively long time (five seconds) required to transfer a chunk of information from short-term to long-term memory (Simon, 1981, p. 96).

Other limitations apply to complex cognitive functions such as learning and adaptation, but these need not concern us here since we are mainly interested in the simpler types of human information processing. The following are the most important of the limitations in human cognitive functioning that directly affect the way decisions are made:

Speed of Processing: Humans are limited in terms of the general speed of sequential processing. This is probably a combined effect of limitations in information retrieval and recall, of limitations on attention, and of inefficient cognitive 'algorithms' or strategies. On the whole, humans must be considered as slow algorithmic information processors.

Limited Attention: Human cognitive systems are limited both with regard to the span of attention, i.e., the number of things that can be attended to simultaneously, and the duration of attention, i.e., the time attention can be sustained unbroken.

Short-Term Memory Capacity: Humans are limited in the number of items they can remember temporarily, i.e., without committing them to the more permanent long-term memory. This is generally referred to as the number of STM chunks - the 'magical' number seven (Miller, 1956).

Limited Goal Stack: This differs from both the limited attentional span and the limitation in number of STM chunks. It refers instead to the limitation of the number of goals (or purposes) that can be simultaneously active without disruption. In computational terms it refers to the stack depth for goals, and is thus clearly a metacognitive rather than cognitive function.

Transfer Between Short-Term and Long-Term Memory: This limitation refers to the storing as well as retrieval of information. In both cases the process is relatively slow, and furthermore generally outside conscious control, hence a form of metacognition.

Resource Requirements in Decision Making

If we consider the generic description of the different steps in decision making (see above) in relation to the five types of limitations listed here, we can characterize the steps in the following way:

Activation: This step is of short duration and processing demands are low. It puts requirements to STM-LTM transfer (remembering the current activity) and may increase the number of goals (goal stack capacity).

Preparation and Deliberation: Both these steps may be of long duration and processing demands are normally high. They put requirements to attention, speed of processing, STM capacity, and the transfer of information between STM and LTM.

Decision: This step is of short duration and demands for processing capacity are moderate. It puts requirements to STM capacity, transfer between STM and LTM, attention, and the goal stack (since it essentially adds a new goal).

Execution: Execution is of relatively long duration, but processing demands are low. In the essential part of execution - monitoring of performance - requirements are to sharing of attention and manipulation of the goal stack (switching of goals).

The requirements are applicable irrespective of the nature of the DMS, i.e., whether it is a man or a machine. But they are probably more crucial for human decision makers, for two reasons. The first is that the human capacity for simple 'algorithmic' information processing is strictly limited compared to the capacity of computers. The second is that the monitoring of this capacity is, at best, implicit in human decision makers, whereas it is an explicit feature of the design of artificial DMSs. In other words, human decision making may easily be degraded by the limitations in human information processing capacity and this degradation may not be detected in time for the decision maker to recover the decision. The decision maker may, for instance, recall information incompletely, miss or transpose steps in processing, apply the right rules to the wrong information, etc. In short, we should expect to find many of the same 'mechanisms' that are used to describe human error in general (Rasmussen et al., 1981).

In one sense very little can be done about that. Since human decision makers are not explicitly designed and built there are few opportunities for modifying their functioning. The main avenue is, in fact, to develop appropriate decision rules and try to make sure they are used. One way of doing that is to construct computerized or intelligent decision support systems that can assist the human decision maker (Hollnagel, Mancini and Woods, 1986). One of their functions could be to offer special assistance in cases where the capacity limits of the human decision maker are either approached or broken, since that might prevent decision errors. Or they might assist by reducing the requirements to algorithmic human information processing and instead take advantage of the heuristic modes of cognition (Norman, 1985). In either case, however, it is necessary in some way to monitor <u>externally</u> the cognitive load of the decision maker to make a timely counteraction possible. We are, therefore, faced with the problem of how such external monitoring is possible.

THE STRUCTURE OF THE DEMON MODEL

To monitor an activity requires that a suitable indicator or measure for the state and development of that activity exists. In addition, one must also have a set of clear definitions of what the limits are, i.e., a set of criteria to determine whether or not the envelope of normal performance has been transgressed. In the case of monitoring cognitive functions the basis must be taken in a model of these functions. The model, as well as the limited values, must be derived from knowledge about how the human cognitive system functions in the range of tasks under consideration. With reference to the aspects mentioned above, we can suggest a number of essential elements of the model, and data from experimental psychology can provide us with a set of tentative limits.

Ideally, monitoring should take place as the process in question evolves, i.e., in real time. At the present stage of development this is, however, not possible. The main reason is that input to the model must be highly categorized, hence requires considerable pre-processing. This pre-processing is impossible to carry out in real time, since it basically involves the transformation of continuous (cognitive) functioning into a description of discrete steps using well-defined categories - similar to the difference between understanding spoken natural language and correctly written texts.

Instead the model will be used in an off-line fashion where the pre-processing of the input is bypassed, in the sense that input is in the form required by the model. Input can be event records from actual decisions or synthesized event descriptions (worst-case scenarios, for instance). Since input will be in a discrete form, there is no need to run the model as a continuous process, hence no problem with timing, speed of processing, etc. If the model does not work under these simplifed conditions there is little reason to belive that it will work under more realistic, hence more difficult conditions.

Model Assumptions

The model is based on some assumptions about human cognition, i.e., about human beings as natural cognitive systems (Hollnagel, 1985). These assumptions can either be taken for granted, or argued at great length from a philosophical, epistemological or ontological basis. For the sake of brevity, I will take the first approach, and describe the assumptions in terms of the functioning of cognitive systems in general. The list reads as follows:

Cognitive processing during decision making is controlled by the goals of the cognitive system. This I take to be self-evident.

Decision making never occurs in isolation, but always as a part of another activity/decision. This is also self-evident. A consequence is that there must always be multiple goals for the system. Some of these goals must furthermore exist prior to the beginning of the decision, hence be given or defined externally rather than by the DMS itself.

Decision making is controlled by the goal with the highest priority for the DMS; goal priority may change during decision making. The first part of this assumption is trivial, but the second part is not. The priority of decision goals have an impact on decision criteria, hence on how decision strategies are chosen and modified.

These assumptions have some consequences for the functional structure of the model, particularly with regard to the nesting or imbedding of actions and the way goal priorities can change. Since decision making is controlled by goals, the goal network becomes an important part of the model. We shall, therefore, consider this in more detail.

The Nesting of Goals and Actions

The assumption that decision making always is part of other activities/ decisions has parallels in other domains, most notably in the general theory of problem solving (Newell and Simon, 1972). Here it is expressed in terms of dividing a problem into subproblems, which can be further divided into sub-subproblems, etc. This recursive procedure is also characteristic of a later model for cognitive skills, the GOMS model (Card, Moran, and Newell, 1980).

In our case nesting means that even though each decision can be considered by itself as the pursuit of its goals, there must also be a higher level monitoring of the set of unfinished decisions corresponding to the remaining goals. The set of remaining goals is, of course, structured, but not necessarily as a hierarchy. For the time being we shall refer to it as a network (since each goal must be related to at least one other goal), and discuss the structure of the network in relation to the priorities of the goals.

This higher level monitoring or metacognition is logically necessary because the DMS, as a cognitive system, is goal directed, hence must work in an orderly fashion towards achieving its goal. It is furthermore a reasonable assumption that there is a direct connection between the complexity of the goal network and cognitive capacity. In order to function efficiently the DMs must either be constantly aware of or be able to recall effortlessly the goal set. The metacognitive function thus involves the use of memory (STM), hence requires part of the cognitive capacity (Simon, 1981). Consequently, the more complex the goal network is the higher is the cognitive load of the DMS.

The formation of subgoals and subproblems is recursive, as shown by the original GPS Model (Newell and Simon, 1972). Recursive functions are attractively simple, but have the nasty consequence of eating up memory. This is true for any cognitive system, computers as well as humans. The depth to which nesting takes place, the level of recursion, is therefore an important parameter for a DMS. In relation to metacognition and decision making it refers to the stack depth for goals. The limited stack depth, therefore, becomes an important capacity measure for metacognition and for the external monitoring of the cognitive load in decision making.

Goal Changes From Interrupts

So far we have assumed that nesting occurs as a logical part of decision making, whereby the decision (hence the overall goal) is divided into subdecisions (hence subgoals). In this sense nesting is a natural consequence of the chosen strategy and simply reflects a way of handling the limited cognitive capacity. Another type of nesting occurs as a result of a time-out, for instance in process environments. Time-out means that a suspended goal needs to be resumed to avoid disruption of the orderly progress of the decision. The goal may, for instance, have been suspended earlier because cognitive capacity was insufficient and because it was not crucial to reach it at the time. But the priority of it may, gradually or abruptly, have increased so that it now requires attention. In principle this development is predictable, and such time-outs may indeed be triggered by metacognition, i.e., be internal rather than external interrupts.

A different type of nesting occurs as a consequence of external interrupts where an unforeseen event alerts the DMS. This must logically establish the temporary new goal of investigating the cause of the interrupt. Depending on how important this turns out to be it may lead to the establishing of a new goal with a higher priority, or the goal structure may remain unaffected by the disturbance. If a new goal is established, it may not be logically related to the existing set of goals, but rather exist on its own, i.e., as the root of a new network. In terms of the DMS it will be a conflicting goal, and the pursuit of it must be coordinated with the pursuit of the other goals.

Generally speaking, interrupts in ongoing activity will lead to a reconfiguration of the goal network. For external interrupts this is likely to increase the goal stack and the goal network, and to push down the current goals, i.e, forcing a change in priorities. For internal interrupts this is more likely to be handled by the existing goal structure (since they in principle are predictable) and thus reconfigure the goal network rather than increase it.

Goal and Strategies

It is essential to understand the selection of and changes in strategies in decision making. Strategies are derived from goals in the sense that a strategy is chosen because it is expected (or believed) to lead to the goal. Consequently, changes in strategies occur as a result of changes in goals rather than the other way around. We must, therefore, consider how goals may change, and how this can be described by the model.

As we have seen above, goals can be introduced in different ways as a result of either nesting or interrupts. An important distinction is whether goals are permanent or temporary. A goal is permanent if it is integrated in the goal network, hence functionally related to other goals (e.g., as a subgoal). A goal is temporary if it is not a member of the existing goal network, but rather leads to a suspension (and potential disruption) of ongoing activity. Put differently, permanent goals lead to activity which can be subsumed under the current strategy, while temporary goals force a change to a new strategy. A temporary goal may, for instance, occur in error recovery or as a result of external events (abrupt changes in the environment).

In order to fulfill the two functions of metacognition, strategy selection and resource monitoring, it is necessary to map the goal network and monitor the changes in the goal stack. The limited size of the goal stack is an important factor in decision making and the number of active and remaining goals must be explicitly represented in the model. It must thus be able to account for how the ordering of decision goals change as a result of external events. A more complex goal structure will increase the demands to information processing, attention, STM capacity, and STM-LTM transfer. Consequently, metacognition will compete with cognition for cognitive capacity.

The Elements of the Model

Turning to the actual decision monitoring (DEMON) model we can describe its main elements using the framework of cognitive systems engineering. According to this, cognitive systems are characterized by being goal oriented, using heuristic knowledge, being adaptive, and having the ability to plan. With regard to metacognition in decision making, goal orientation is the most conspicuous characteristic. The model must, therefore, have the following characteristics.

Goal Network: The DMS, and, therefore, also the DEMON model, must have a representation of the goal network. This is a representation of the active and remaining goals and how they are related. Goals can be either synergistic (goal - subgoal) or antagonistic (competing or rivaling goals). The network need not itself be a strict hierarcy but may have subsets which, considered by themselves, are hierarchies, at least within a given time interval. The goals may be considered as separate objects, to use a current analogy from computer science.

A particular feature of the goal network is goal priority. This describes the relative importance of the goals to each other and identifies the goal that currently has the highest priority, i.e., the node in the network that currently controls action. In terms of synergistic goals (goal - subgoal) the priorities are straightforward: the subgoal must obviously have the highest priority, since it would otherwise not have been established (i.e., it is necessary to achieve the parent goal). In terms of antagonistic goals the priorities may be more difficult to specify, but they are essential to the implementation of a strategy since, by definition, the goal with the highest priority is the one that is carried out.

Another feature of the goals is the concept of inheritance. This refers to the relation between synergistic goals (goals - subgoals). Inheritance is important as a way of defining the context of the subgoal by referring to the conditions under which it was created. The context is necessary to select the proper strategy but it is normally more efficient to provide it implicitly rather than explicitly. Inheritance also permits a tracing through the goal network to identify the conceptually higher-level goals that guide the decision. (Synergistic goals are thus analogous to some of the ideas in Multilevel Flow Modelling (Lind, 1985)).

Goal Stack Size: As mentioned above, the size of the goal stack is an important parameter in the model. It is assumed that the goal stack is strictly limited and that errors in decision making will occur when the limits are exceeded. It, therefore, becomes important to monitor the changes in the goal stack so approaches to the limit are detected, since it may prevent the occurrence of critical situations. This in turn requires a description of how the development of an event can produce changes in goal priorities.

Model Input

Since the DEMON model monitors decision making as a function of how the event develops, the input to the model must be a description of the event. As mentioned above, this description will be in the form of a sequence of discrete steps that refer to well def'ned categories. In other words, we must be able to make a grammatical analysis of the cognitive functions in decision making. This requires a definition of the elementary actions and the correct ways in which they can be related. In analogy with psycholinguistics we are thus referring to a parsing of actions.

If we refer to the (very limited) set of steps in decision making described before we may, purely as an example, define the possible transitions between steps:

    (Activation, Preparation)
    (Preparation, Deliberation)
    (Deliberation, (Decision, Preparation, Activation))
    (Decision (Execution, Deliberation))
    (Execution, (Nil, Activation))

The element 'Nil' indicates the successful completion of a decision. An example of a grammatical decision sequence would be: Activation – Preparation – Deliberation – Preparation – Deliberation – Decision – Execution – Nil. An ungrammatical sequence would be one that contained, e.g., the sequence – Decision – Preparation. If we furthermore assumed that (sub)goals were created as a consequence of the Activation step, this very simple grammar could be used to generate sequences of nested (synergistic) decisions, hence to trace the development of the goal network.

Model Overview

This simplified example makes it clear that the model must interpret the input with the same classification that was used to produce it. To be of any real use, the classification would certainly have to be more specific than the example given here, but that is no serious obstacle. Another essential element of the DEMON model is, therefore, a representation of a suitable grammar of actions. The model does not require one particular grammar (corresponding to a particular theory of decision making), but only that a consistent principle of action analysis is available as a reference. This means that the DEMON model can be applied to input from different sources – as long as the basis for categorization is known.

In computational terms the DEMON model contains four basic modules:

(a) An input analyzer, which processes the input stream (discrete event description),

(b) A goal network builder, which constructs and updates the goal network based on the input. The network must, of course, also contain the set of initial goals that provide the overall guidance for the DMS.

(c) A stack size estimator, which analyzes the goal network and monitors the cognitive load.

(d) A next step predictor, which basically serves to detect the occurrence of antagonistic goals. This module makes use of inheritance
to generate descriptions of synergistic goals.

Lacking here are the modules for building strategies and monitoring
strategies, as well as a module for backtracking to be used, e.g., in error
recovery. However, even in its first version the DEMON model can be used
to analyze available event descriptions (real or hypothetical). In this
way, it serves as an external, although off-line, monitoring of decision
making, hence as a model of the metacognitive functions of the DMS, and
produces as output an estimation of the cognitive load on the system. It
thereby demonstrates one way of answering the need for an improved understanding of metacognitive functions.

REFERENCES

Abbott, L. S., ed., 1982, Proceedings of Workshop on Cognitive Modelling
of Nuclear Plant Control Room Operators, NUREG/CR-3114, Dedham, MA,
August 15-18.

Alty, J., Elzer, P., Holst, O., Smart, G., Johannsen, G., and Savory, S.,
1985, Literature and User Survey of Issues Related to Man-Machine
Interfaces for Supervision and Control Systems, ESPRIT P-600, Computer
Resources International, Copenhagen.

Card, S. K., Moran T. P. and Newell, A., 1980, "Computer Text-Editing: An
Information-Processing Analysis of a Routine Cognitive Skill",
Cognitive Psychology, 12, pp. 32 and 74.

Dreyfus, S., 1980, Formal Models vs. Human Situational Understanding:
Inherent Limitations on the Modelling of Business Expertise, (Draft
Report), Berkeley, CA: University of California, Operations Research
Centre.

Fischhoff, B., 1986, "Decision Making in Complex Systems", Intelligent
Decision Support in Process Environments, E. Hollnagel, G. Mancini & D.
Woods, eds., Springer Verlag, Heidelberg.

Hollnagel, E., 1984, "Inductive and Deductive Approaches to Modelling of
Human Decision Making", Psyke & Logos, 5 (2), pp. 288 and 301.

Hollnagel, E., 1986, "Cognitive System Performance Analysis", Intelligent
Decision Support in Process Environments, E. Hollnagel, G. Mancini and
D. Woods, eds., Springer Verlag, Heidelberg.

Hollnagel, E., Mancini, G., and Woods, D., eds., 1986, Intelligent Decision
Support in Process Environments, Springer Verlag, Heidelberg.

Hollnagel, E. and Woods, D., 1983, "Cognitive Systems Engineering: New
Wine in New Bottles", International Journal of Man-Machine Studies, 18,
pp. 583 and 600.

Lind, M., 1986, Representing Goals and Functions of Complex Systems: An
Introduction to Multilevel Flow Modelling, Aalborg University Center,
Aalborg, Denmark.

Miller, G. A., 1956, "The Magical Number Seven, Plus or Minus Two: Some Limits on our Capacity to Process Information", _Psychological Review_, _63_, pp. 81 and 97.

Newell, A. and Simon H. A., 1972, _Human Problem Solving_, Prentice-Hall, Englewood Cliffs, NJ.

Norman, D. A., 1986, "New Views of Information Processing: Implications for Intelligent Decision Support Systems", _Intelligent Decision Support in Process Environments_, E. Hollnagel, G. Mancini, and D. Woods, eds., Springer Verlag, Heidelberg.

Rasmussen, J., 1974, _The Human Data Processor as a System Component. Bits and Pieces of a Model_, Riso-M-1722, Riso National Laboratory, Roskilde, Denmark.

Rasmussen, J., Pedersen, O. M., Carnino, A., Griffon, M., Mancini, G., and Gagnolet, P., 1981, _Classification System for Reporting Events Involving Human Malfunctions_, Riso-M-2240, Riso National Laboratory, Roskilde, Denmark.

Reason, J., 1986, "Recurrent Errors in Process Environments: Some Implications for the Design of Intelligent Decision Support Systems", _Intelligent Decision Support in Process Environments_, E. Hollnagel, G. Mancini, and D. Woods, eds., Springer Verlag, Heidelberg.

Simon, H. A., 1981, _The Sciences of the Artificial (2nd Ed.)._, The MIT Press, Cambridge, MA.

ON INITIALIZATION AND EXITIALIZATION IN PROGRAM DESIGN

P. Järvinen

University of Tampere
P. O. Box 607
SF-33101 Tampere, Finland

Abstract: The control structures "if then else", "while do" and others
have played a central role in program design so far. Crockett paid attention to process functions instead of control functions and proposed the
triform structure: initialization, process, and exitialization.

In this paper, the triform structure is more elaborated. Operations
research literature shows that some preparation efforts are always required
before (initialization) and after (exitialization) the process proper.
They (initialization and exitialiation) are, however, neglected from around
the process of a single part when similar parts are repetitively produced
in the same production run. Hence, we propose that initialization and exitialization should always surround the program body and every iteration in
the program. This result is also applied to improve Nassi and
Shneiderman's structured flowchart technique and Warnier's LCP methodology.

1. INTRODUCTION

One of the most important problems in software engineering is how to
derive a program structure from a programming problem. In their review
articles Yourdon (1977), Parker (1978) and Bergland (1981), considered many
software development and design methodologies: structured programming,
modular programming, structured design (Stevens, Myers, and Constantine,
1974), HIPO – Hierarchy plus Input, Process and Output (Katzan, 1976), LCP
– Logical Construction of Programs (Warnier, 1974), JSP – Jackson Structured programming (Jackson, 1975), the constructive proof-of-correctness
discipline (Dijkstra, 1976; Gries, 1976), etc. Crockett (1981) then developed a new approach, triform programs, and recently Zave (1984) presented the operational approach. Zave describes a situation as follows:
"Some of the most serious problems of software development were identified
years ago, but continue to resist practical solutions".

The control structures ("if then else", "while do" and others) (see
Ledgard and Marcotty, 1975) have played a central role in program design so
far. Instead of control functions, process functions have rarely been analyzed. Crockett's triform structure of process functions: initialization,
production, and completion (here later called exitialization according to
Wills (1982)); seems to be a promising exception (see Appendix I). Most
components of the program structure are thus called as process functions,

which means that the program control function(s) must be removed from the process function modules and placed in, at least, one separate control module.

Crockett was not the first to propose the idea of the triform structure. The three primitives of structured programming (sequence, alternation, and iteration) were supplemented by Nassi and Shneiderman (1973) with the fourth one, where the program body was surrounded by begin and end.

The triform structure was also combined with two primitives of structured programming in LCP-methodology (Warnier, 1974). According to Canning (1974), LCP has two basic control structures. The alternation structure has three parts: (1) some initialization orders; (2) the IF ... THEN ... ELSE ... switch; and (3) some exitialization orders. The repetition structure also has three parts: (1) some initialization orders; (2) a DO ... UNTIL ... loop; and (3) some exitialization orders. The third primitive, sequence, was embedded either into some initialization orders (1) or into some exitialization orders (3).

Where are the initialization and exitialization functions coming from? We think that Crockett's fine idea of the triform structure requires more elaboration. In this paper, our aim is to analyze the triform structure more thoroughly by considering its 'precedents' in other sciences. It will be shown that some initialization operations are needed before performing separate tasks at a certain machine (e.g., computer) and some exitialization operations are also necessary after completion of the task. Hence, our reasoning will be done on the ground of analogy instead of examples used by Crockett.

In this paper we address the following questions:

(1) What kind of evidence can be produced for the triform structure?

(2) Where can the triform structure be found?

(3) How could the triform structure improve some program design methodologies (if correctly applied)?

By reviewing various methods for sequencing and scheduling problems in operations research (in Section 2) we shall show that initialization and exitialization exist at different levels, and they are often neglected from around a single task when the same task is repeatedly performed in the same production run. When these and other results are applied to program design, it will be shown (in Section 3) that initialization and exitialization always surround the program body and each iteration structure. But there are no arguments for such a claim that initialization and exitialization should surround the alternation structure.

2. ON INITIALIZATION AND EXITIALIZATION

In this section, we shall do a historical review of initialization and exitialization in operations research literature. In their famous book, Introduction to Operations Research, Churchman, Ackoff, and Arnoff (1975) mentioned these functions in connection with planning parts production. The costs were called the setup and takedown costs and they were counted per run. They included four major components:

(1) Office Setup. Before anything is done in the shop, the Production Planning Department must plan the production and the Standards Department must prepare necessary drawings and

control forms.

(2) Shop Setup Cost. This cost consists of the cost of actually adjusting the production equipment to perform the required operations, the cost of the scrap which is involved in making adjustments at the beginning of the run, and the cost of setting up the quality inspection procedure.

(3) Shop Takedown Costs. This involves the cost of entering the finished parts in stock and performing the necessary paper work attached thereto.

(4) Office Takedown. This is the cost of the analysis performed by the Cost Analysis Section.

Components (1) and (4) refer to management subfunctions and components, (2) and (3) to initialization and exitialization of production run. During one run many similar parts are produced and components (2) and (3) are counted only once.

Initialization and Exitialization functions can also be found in sequencing and scheduling. Conway, Maxwell, and Miller (1967) proposed an important distinction between sequencing and scheduling: the former is concerned only with the ordering of operations on a single machine, while the latter is a simultaneous and synchronized sequence on several machines. The processing time, $p(i,j)$, is the amount of time that is required for machine $m(i,j)$ to perform the operation. Where setup is assumed to be independent of sequence, setup time can be included in the processing time $p(i)$. This assumption does not always hold. Then the flow-times (the total times that the jobs spend in the shop), $F<i>$, depend on how the jobs are ordered. The flow times are then

$F<1> = s<0,1> + p<1>$

$F<2> = F<1> + s<1,2> + p<2>$

. . . .

$F<i> = F<i-1> + s<i-1,i> + p<i>$

. . . .

where numbers inside of < > mean order numbers and $s<0,1>$ is the time required to bring the facility from idleness to a state ready to process the first job in sequence and $s<i-1,i>$ is the time to change over from the $(i-1)$-th job to the i-th job and $p<i>$ is the processing time of the i-th job. If we have n jobs in the single machine shop and if the setup times are order dependent, then the maximum flow time is minimized by minimizing the sum of the n setup times. The problem of minimizing the sum of the setup times corresponds to what is usually called the travelling salesman problem.

Ashour (1972) uses somewhat different terms in defining various time components of the processing time of an operation, i.e.

(1) The Job Transportation Time -- the time required to transport the job from one machine to another according to the pre-specified machine ordering;

(2) The Machine Setup Time -- the time required to prepare the machine for performing that operation;

(3) The Operation Running Time -- the time required to perform the job on a particular machine; and

(4) The Machine Teardown Time -- the time required to reset the machine after the operation has been completed. Note that also Ashour connects initialization (setup) and exitialization (teardown) to the use of a certain machine.

We can finish this section by concluding that the following findings concerning initialization and exitialization have been presented in operations research literature:

(a) initialization and exitialization exist both at the management and performance levels;

(b) they were neglected from around a single part, when similar parts were produced in the same production run;

(c) initialization and exitialization (and changeover times) are order dependent, when several jobs are performed in the single machine; and

(d) initialization and exitialization depend both on the job to be performed and on the machine to be used.

3. ON PROGRAM DESIGN METHODOLOGIES

In this section, we analyze some program design methodologies to determine whether initialization and exitialization are correctly used or not. Nassi and Shneiderman (1973) proposed four symbols, i.e. the process

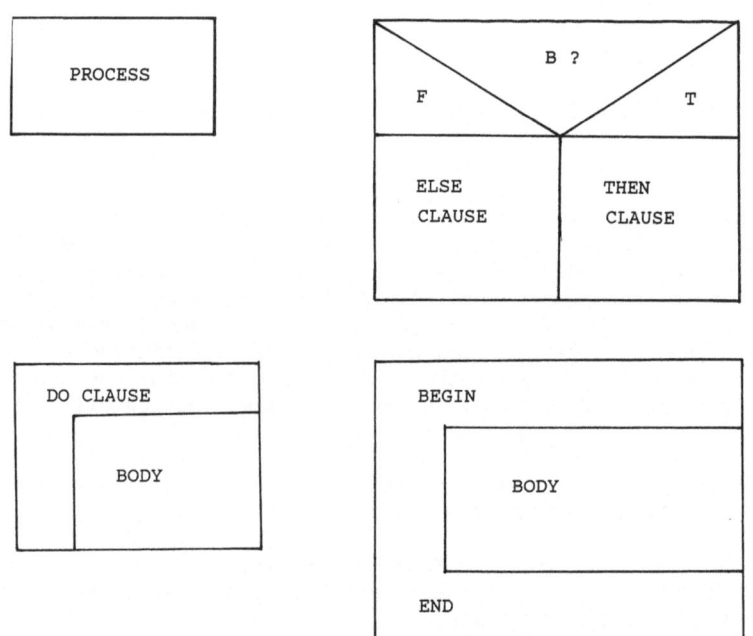

Figure 1. The Process, Decision, Iteration, and BEGIN-END Symbols.

symbol, the decision (alternation) symbol, the iteration symbol, and the BEGIN-END symbol, as the notational basis for representing most operations in a program (see Figure 1). The BEGIN-END symbol was included for representing block structure and for performing some of the functions of the START and END blocks in earlier flowcharting systems. "The BEGIN-END symbol (Figure 1) was used to represent the BEGIN-END statement pair as found in ALGOL or PL/I. This symbol is akin to the brackets that many programmers draw in the left margin of their programs to indicate nested groups of statements. This technique enables the programmer to easily recognize the scope of his declarations and the logical structures in his program. The body of the BEGIN-END symbol is a structure of arbitrary complexity." (Nassi and Shneiderman, 1973).

Nassi and Shneiderman gave four examples of how to use the symbols in Figure 1. But there was no application of the BEGIN-END symbol. So we cannot with certainty say whether the initialization and exitialization were included in BEGIN and END or not. But, on grounds of the results in Section 2, we propose that they should be included in BEGIN and END.

Warnier's (1974) LCP-methodology emphasizes that the structure of input and output data determines the structure of the program. If input data consist of hierarchical, repetitive, or alternative subsets, the program will then contain hierarchical, repetitive, or alternative structures, respectively. According to Canning's interpretation, LCP consists of two control structures: alternation (initialization, if then else, exitialization) and repetition (initialization, do until, exitialization). We say here 'interpretation', because Warnier (1974, p. 24) writes: "If an input data subset is of repetitive structure, so is the corresponding program subset. A program of repetitive structure always includes a repetitive subset preceded by a subset 'begin' to be executed 1 time and followed by a subset 'end' to be executed 1 time within the set." Warnier doesn't clearly speak about what is the content of 'begin' and 'end'. As an example, Figure 2 shows the structure of the program for a statistical report of the employees of a firm having several plants with many units.

According to Warnier (1974, p. 47) "a data set of alternative structure is a set within which there are one or many subsets whose presence or utilization is random. If there are several, they are mutually exclusive. A program set of alternative structure is a set which includes two or more mutually exclusive sub-sets whose execution is random and the subsets 'begin' and 'end' to be executed once within the set."

Appendix II contains both the flowchart and the sorted list of instructions of a program producing a periodic report of customer's accounts. In the program of Appendix II there are two nested iterations: the outer one

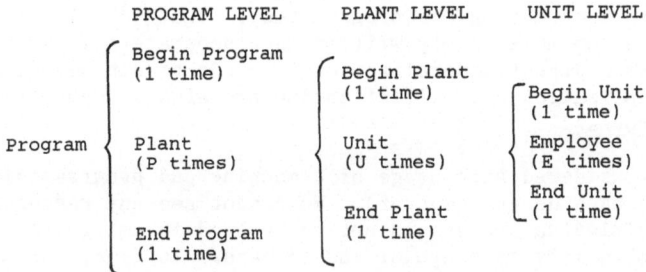

Figure 2. The structure of a Statistical Report Program.
(Warnier, 1974; p. 25)

between blocks 040-120 and the inner one between blocks 070-100. For the iterations there are some initialization and exitialization operations. In the same program there are also two IF-sentences for alternation, in blocks 010 and 070. (Note that other IFs are controlling the terminations of iterations.) But, having thoroughly studied the sorted list of instructions we came to the conclusion that there are no instructions for initializing and for exitializing these IFs for alternation. After looking at all the examples in Warnier's book (1974), we found neither any initializing nor exitializing instructions intended to IFs for alternation.

Orr (1977) has slightly modified Warnier's diagrams. He also connects 'begin' and 'end' both to repetition and to alternation. In my opinion, the former is correct, but the latter is not. To demonstrate, we take Orr's example of extracting statistical data from a file of employees of a university. A staff member is counted as either teaching faculty or nonteaching faculty or nonfaculty (Appendix III). There is in Appendix III 'begin' for repetition (initialize totals for zero) and 'end' for repetition (print totals for university), and 'begin' for alternation (check staff member's data), and 'end' for alternation (get next staff member's data, check if all fac. members processed). 'Begin' for alternation is a condition of IF-statement and 'end' of alternation belongs, in fact, to the terminating condition of repetition. Orr does not show any proper content for 'begin' and 'end' of alternations in other applications presented in his book either .

In conclusion, we can say that:

- the Nassi and Shneiderman structured flowchart technique can be improved a little by incorporating initialization and exitialization in the BEGIN-END symbol; and

- Canning's and Orr's interpretation of Warnier's 'begin' 'end' are correct in connection with repetitions, but we cannot find any arguments for their usage in connection with alternations.

4. DISCUSSION

Our analysis concerning program design methodologies in Section 3 was based on the results picked up from operations research literature. We considered a computer as a machine and a program as a job to be processed with the machine. Our argumentation rested upon analogy.

On the grounds of the results in Section 2, and their applications in Section 3, we propose that initialization and exitialization should always surround the program body and every iteration in the program. We have strong empirical evidence for the former part of the proposal from our programming course. In every student's program there was initialization and exitialization surrounding the program body. Instead initialization and the exitialization were rarely written as a separate 'paragraph' around an iteration. As a direct generalization from our result we propose that, as a rule, initialization and exitialization are always connected with discontinuous processes.

We have considered here usage of a machine and programs directing operations with a machine (a computer). We cannot see any reason why initialization and exitialization should not be applied in using resources other than machines, namely to manpower and to data. In fact, use of data resources always seems to imply initialization (e.g., OPEN the file) and exitialization (e.g., CLOSE the file). However, more research needs to be done on this topic.

REFERENCES

Ashour, S., 1972, "Sequencing Theory", Lecture Notes in Economics and Mathematical Systems, 69, Springer-Verlag, Berlin.

Bergland, G. D., 1981, "A Guided Tour of Program Design Methodologies", Computer, 14, (10), pp. 13-37.

Canning, R. G., 1974, "Improving the System Building Process", EDP ANALYZER, 12, (12).

Churchman, C. W., Ackoff, R. L, and Arnoff, E. L., 1957, Introduction to Operations Research, Wiley, New York.

Conway, R. W., Maxwell, W. L., and Miller, L. W., 1967, Theory of Scheduling, Addison-Wesley, Reading, Mass.

Crockett, D. W., 1981, "Triform Programs", Comm. ACM, 24, pp. 344-350.

Dijkstra, E. W., 1976, A Discipline of Programming, Prentice-Hall, Englewood Cliffs, NJ.

Gries, D., 1976, "An Illustration of Current Ideas on the Derivation of Correctness Proofs and Correct Programs", IEEE Trans. Software Eng., SE-2, pp. 238-244.

Jackson, M. A., 1975, Principles of Program Design, Academic Press, London.

Katzan, Jr., J., 1976, Systems Design and Documentation: An Introduction to the HIPO Method, van Nostrand, New York.

Ledgard, H. F., and Marcotty, M., 1975, "A Genealogy of Control Structures", Comm. ACM, 18, pp. 629-639.

Nassi, I., and Shneiderman, B., 1973, "Flowchart Techniques for Structured Programming, SIGPLAN Notices, 8, (8), pp. 12-26.

Orr, K. T., 1977, Structured Systems Development, Yourdon Press, New York.

Parker, J., 1978, "A Comparison of Design Methodologies, ACM SIGSOFT - Software Engineering Notes, 3, (4), pp. 12-19.

Stevens, W. G., Myers, G. J., and Constantine, L. L., 1974, "Structured Design", IBM Systems Journal, 14, pp. 115-139.

Warnier, J.-D., 1974, Logical Construction of Programs, H. E. Stenfert Kroese, B. V., Leiden.

Wills, J. A., 1982, "On Triform Programs (Technical Correspondence)", Comm. ACM, 25, pp. 389-390.

Yourdon, E., 1977, "The Choice of New Software Development Methodologies for Software Development Projects", National Computer Conference, pp. 261-265.

Zave, P., 1984, "The Operational Versus the Conventional Approach to Software Development", Comm. ACM, 27, pp. 104-118.

APPENDIX I

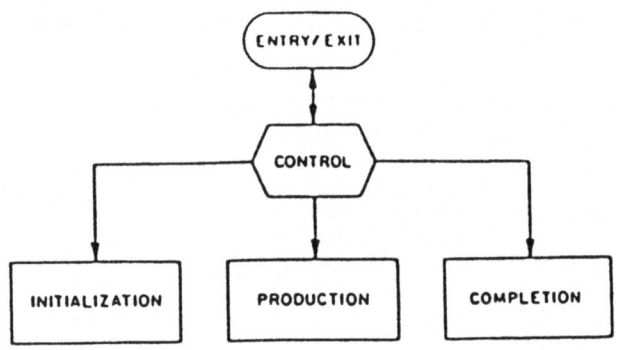

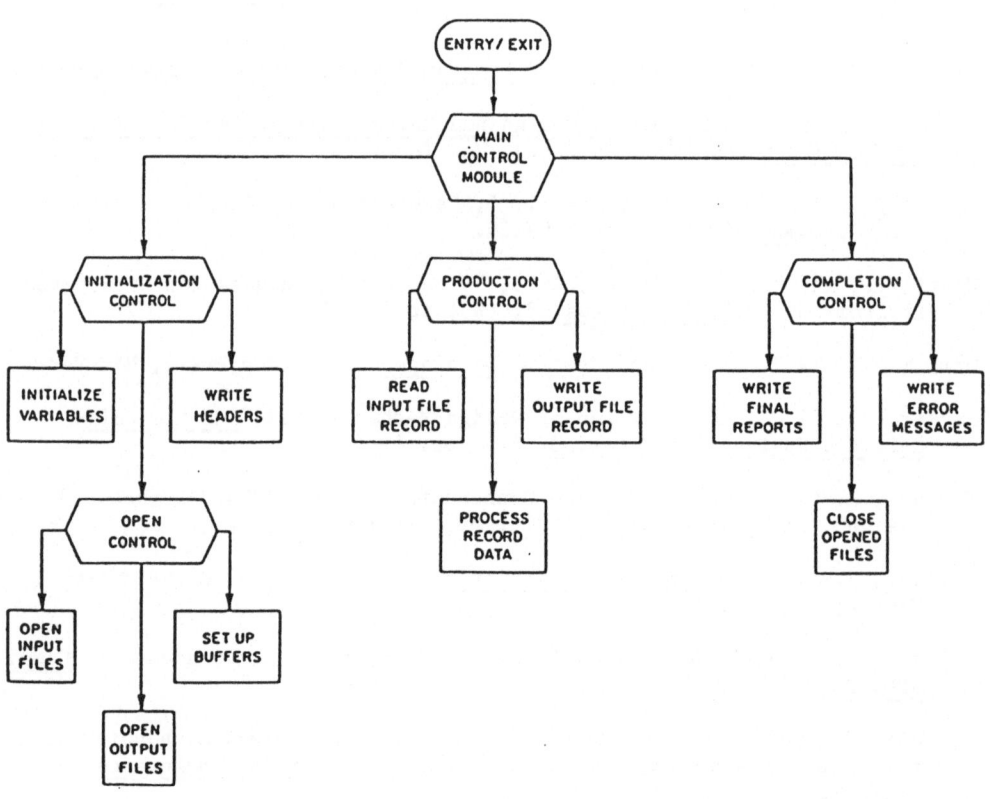

APPENDIX II

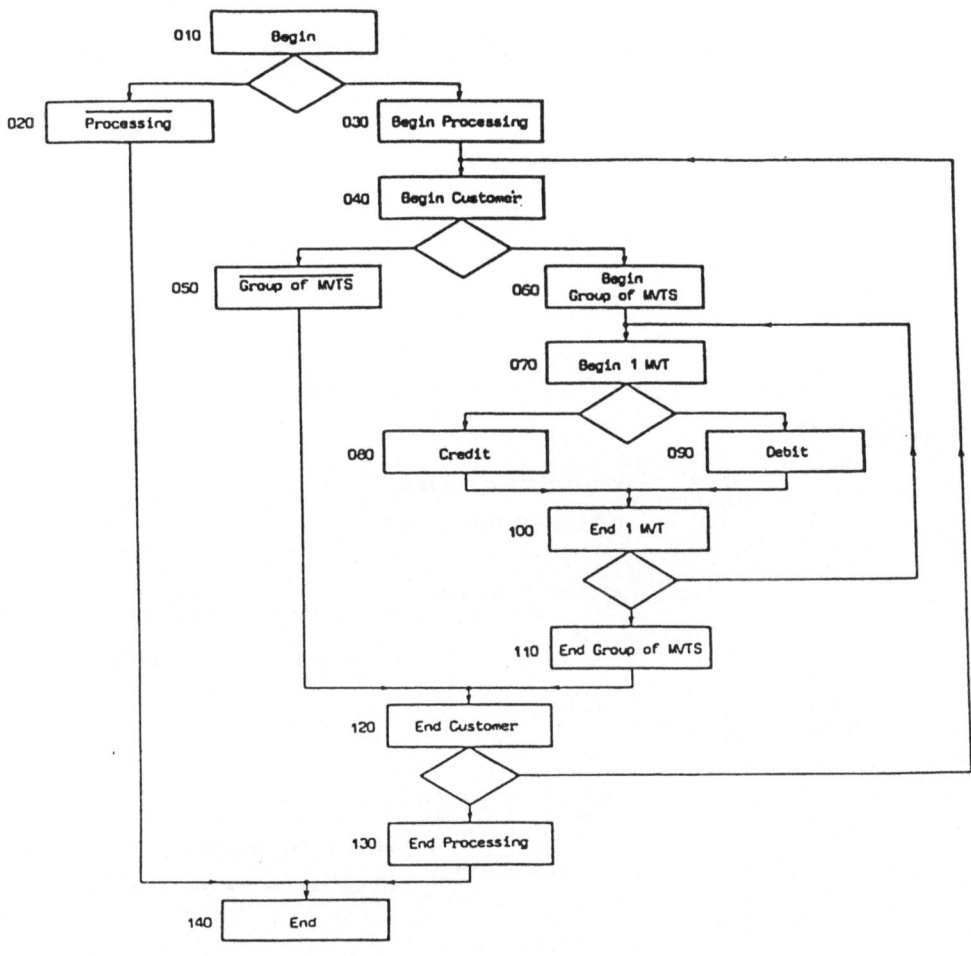

The sorted list of instructions:

010 — Read
    If $\overline{EOF}$ 030
020 —   140
030 — Spaces to print area
040 — Cust N° to Reference Cust N°
    Old balance to working field
        „   „   ref field
    Edit Cust N°
    Print and restore print area
    Read
    If Cust N° = Ref. Cust N°   060
050 —   120
060 — Clear debit total
    Clear credit total
070 — Edit MVT N°
    If code DB   090

080 — Add credit to CR total
    Edit credit   100
090 — Add debit to DB total
    Edit debit
100 — Print and restore print area
    Read
    If cust N° = ref Cust N°   070
110 — Subtract DB total from
    working field
    Add CR total to working field
    Edit DB total
    Edit CR total
120 — Edit old balance
    Edit new balance
    Print and restore print area
    If $\overline{EOF}$ 040

APPENDIX III

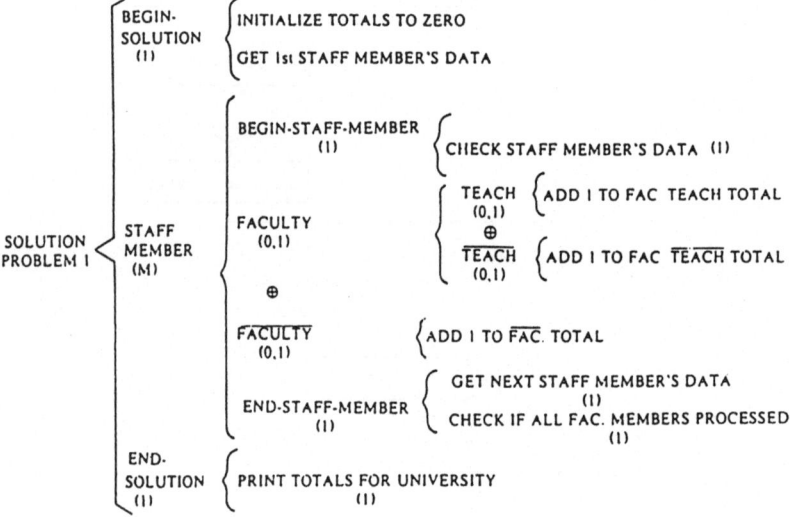

DOCUMENT INFORMATION SYSTEM IN SCIENTIFIC RESEARCH

Takashi Maeda* and Kaname Amano**

*Department of Engineering Science
Hokkaido University
Sapporo 060, Japan
**Computing Center
Hokkaido University
Sapporo 060, Japan

Abstract: Scientific documents consist of bibliographic and textual information as well as complicated information such as figures, tables, graphs,
and images. A future scientific information system will be connected to a
huge integrated database and constructed as a scientific workstation with
advanced functions for data processing of various forms of multi-media
knowledge information. Such an information system requires some specific
abilities for processing of non-coded information of variable length,
set-valued information and structural information, in addition to usual
coded elementary information.

In this paper, we discuss design and implementation problems in constructing a document information system, as a prototype of such information
systems, with the function of text processing, a typical example of complicated information processing. Future directions of an advanced scientific
information system are also suggested.

INTRODUCTION

Scientific documents such as memos, reports, papers, and books in scientific working environments consist, in general, of not only bibliographic
and textual information, but also complicated information such as figures,
tables, graphs, and images. From a viewpoint of information science, the
document can be considered as an arrangement with some order and structure
of various representations of conceptual and factual objects. That is, the
document may be construed as a knowledge information representation with
some reasonable structure of multi-media knowledge information as a whole.

Future scientific information systems will be connected to a huge integrated database including information of such documents, and a variety of
facts and statistical information. In order to handle various forms of
multi-media knowledge information, it has also to be constructed as a scientific workstation with various functions such as creation, analysis,
storage, retrieval, transformation, processing, and synthesis together with
devices for simple and easy input/output.

Basic problems in designing such a multi-media information system, are those of modelling of multi-media information and its processing (Meyrowitz and van Dam, 1982). Some specific features required for such a system include, at least, flexible representation, storage, content retrieval and processing of (1) non-coded information of variable length, (2) set-valued information, and (3) structural information, in addition to coded elementary information (Bancilhon and Richard, 1984; Gardarin, 1984; Lum et al., 1985; Rabitti, 1985). An attempt of constructing such an information system by applying technologies of general-purpose information retrieval system (IRS) and database management system (DBMS) will encounter some difficulties, since these systems have not been taking into account such complicated data structures (Crawford, 1981).

In this paper, we discuss design and implementation problems in constructing a document information system with the function of text processing, a typical example of complicated information processings including the above three characteristic features, using a commercial DBMS under a supporting system for database construction at Hokkaido University Computing Center (Amano and Mochida, 1985; Amano and Maeda, 1985). The next section is concerned with the design of a document information system which will be dealing mainly with textual information in a scientific working environment. Implementation problems of the system will be considered in the third section. Finally, future directions of the advanced scientific information system are suggested in the last section.

DOCUMENT INFORMATION IN SCIENTIFIC WORK

There are various forms of documents such as memos, reports, papers, books, etc., in a scientific working environment. A document information system, which is an important resource of information in such an environment, has great utility value first as an information tool and second as a research subject. We consider the design of a document information system as effective in these two aspects. Then, a plan and design of an advanced scientific information system as described in the previous section will be developed with an extension and evolution of such a document information system.

In the following, guidelines for the design of the scientific document information system are considered from a viewpoint of serving scientific work as an important information resource. The document may include some rare data such as memos, notes, references to other works, letters, various figures, computer programs, manuscripts, etc. It should be desirable to deal with and process these various forms of scientific data in the system as well as other formatted data (Stonebraker et al., 1983). Such an integrated system for management and manipulation of formatted and unformatted data and for the usage of the database in public and in private will be required in a scientific working environment. The following effects in the scientific work may be expected of such an information system:

- effective use of accumulation of (a piece of) knowledge;

- systematic acquisition and dissemination of knowledge information;

- stimulation for creative thinking by observation of some sorted knowledge information; and

- assistance to some kind of intelligent work and operations, etc.

In the following, some requirements and expectations are described with respect to the two aspects mentioned above.

As An Information Tool

Scientific document information has been used, constantly and/or as the need arises, to understand adequately the research trend and topics in the field of science concerned, and to obtain effective knowledge on individual scientific facts, methods, and techniques developed in the field. In addition to the content of the individual document, information such as the names of authors, his/her laboratory or institute, addresses, etc., may often be searched for. General-purpose information retrieval service of bibliographic data has already been in use widely in many fields of science and technology. These services are, however, not satisfactory, since they deal with only bibliographic data as pointed out by many users. Highly-developed service of a document information system is needed for effective use of unformatted information consisting of text, figures, graphs, images, etc.

General requirements for the usage of such a database from a user's viewpoint are:

(1) comprehensiveness, i.e. covering the full range of the field of science;

(2) completeness, i.e. being well supplied with full attributes of the data;

(3) flexibility, i.e. easy and fast access to expected data;

(4) operationability, i.e. having sufficient operations for process-ing, edition, etc., of complicated data; and

(5) intelligentness, i.e. meeting the needs of users of higher-level, etc.

Common dissatisfaction with most of the current systems is related to the points (3) and (4) above, and is concerned with the problems of data representation with respect to (2) and, in general, knowledge representa-tion of data in taking account of (5). Then, an advanced document infor-mation system in the sense of the above description has to be achieved through realization of more flexible access to data items and of various functions of data processing, especially of textual data. The most elemen-tary problems are to develop flexible user implementing interface realizing high-level functions for text processing and content access method, and to find an information representation model of document data constructed with multi-media information to make such operations possible.

As a Research Subject

In this subsection, we will focus on the problem of construction of a scientific document database and its information processing system, espe-cially the method of high-level usage of the system in a scientific working environment. The following points can be listed as very important factors in relation to the above discussion:

(1) adequate information representation of document contents, i.e. modelling of document data;

(2) content access method, i.e. usage of some content-oriented in-dexing method, etc.;

(3)   construction method of database, i.e. application of advanced DBMS technologies, etc.;

(4)   flexible and extended user interface, i.e. content-oriented data retrieval and its processing; and

(5)   personal document management with an access to a public database, etc.

Item (1) is a problem of how to represent unformatted conceptual information reflecting its contents together with formatted data such as bibliographic data in document information. More than simple key-word set representation is required as a matter of course. Item (2) is concerned with a tool for effective access and processing based on the information representation of (1). Though such a new and adequate system will be desirable for the most advanced stages (Lum et al., 1985; Rabitti, 1985), when (1) and (2) are resolved at some level, some of the existing DBMS or IRS with necessary modifications and extensions may be used effectively to implement such a database system in a restricted sense (Bancilhon and Richard, 1984; Haskin and Lorie, 1982; Schek, et al., 1982). With limited functions of existing commercial DBMS, system design including external and internal representation of document, especially for text data, is the basic problem in (3).

Item (4) is related to all of the above points, and may, also, need modelling study based on observation of problem solving processes of working scientists with document information of various forms in their field. Recent useful technologies in office automation (OA) such as multi-windows using a bit-mapped display and pointing devices may also be effective in our scientific document information system design, especially in its user interface design (Lee et al., 1985). Finally, just a personal management and manipulation of various data from both public databases and personal documents will be important in scientific working environments and flexible integration methods should be associated with (5) in relation to (4).

Design Consideration

As previously described, two aspects and functions of a document information system in a scientific working environment are very important guidelines in designing such a system. That is, the aspect of an information tool may indicate the access function to a public database, and the aspect of a research subject may lead us to a personal data manipulation function of the system. So far, these two types of functions have been developed for the so-called document database system and document preparation system, respectively.

A scientific document information system can be constructed as an integrated system of these two types of document information systems with more advanced functions, especially those in data manipulation for multi-media data. Such a system may be regarded as a personal document management system connected with an acess to a public database.

IMPLEMENTATION PROBLEMS

A small-scale document information system is under development as a pilot study of the scientific document information system. Information retrieval, in the usual sense, is an access function to a database and text processing is data manipulations. The latter is a typical example of unformatted information. In implementation of the system, existing commercial DBMS (ADABAS) is used, under a supporting system for database construction at Hokkaido Unive;rsity Computing Center (Amano and Mochida, 1985; Amano and Maeda, 1985), for reducing overload in making document databases and preparation of various utilities for data manipulation.

Some inconvenient features common to most commercial DBMSs are various constraints of the field and/or record length, which makes processing unformatted data such as text information very difficult. Furthermore, data manipulation language and retrieval language supplied by the DBMS are directed to formatted data, and do not match our purposes as they are.

The following three points are employed as design bases:

(1) appropriate partitioning of document information – to reduce redundancy of repeating information caused by creating one record for one document. But at the same time make each file useful for a user;

(2) preservation of meaning of data – to avoid destroying meaning of each record in a file and to find convenient units of data from the user's viewpoint; and

(3) flexible access method – to make good use of visual representation in the operation process by using most advanced input/ output devices, if possible.

File Organization of Document Information

It is difficult, in general, to formulate the information structure of scientific documents uniquely. We are concerned with the printed papers in scientific journals and proceedings of scientific conferences as the source of our primary document database, and those documents are to be characterized by the following attributive items:

Document-0[Document-ID, Title*, Author# (Author-Name, Address*), Source (Journal-Name, Volume, No, Publication-Year, Page), Classification-Code#, Key-Word#, Abstract* (Sentence*), Reference#, Language, Owner#]

In this scheme, and in the following, the symbol "*" indicates a textual attribute and "#" a set attribute, and "()" a set of complicated items, respectively.

It will not be so difficult, in principle, to map most of the scientific documents into such a framework of document information structure. But, the framework is redundant as its well known, especially in Bibliography, Classification-Code, Owner, and Author attributes. Design of file organization with suitable partitioning should be based on these features of the attributive item. At the same time, meaning preservation is also important as it was pointed out previously. The partitioning has to be made by taking into account these two requirements.

The results of the partitioning based on the above discussion are as follows:

(1) Document[Document-ID, Title*, Author# (N-th, Last-Name, Given-Name), Source (Journal-Id, Volume, No, Publication-Year, Page), Classification-Code#, Key-Word#, Reference-Id#, Language];

(2) Author[Author-Id, Last-Name, Given-Name, Address*];

(3) Journal[Journal-Id, Journal-Name, Publisher*, Owner-Id#];

(4) Abstract[Document-Id, Text# (Sentence*)];

(5) Term[Key-Word-Id, Key-Word, Related-Term# (Relation-Type, Related-Word#)];

(6) Owner[Owner-Id, Address*]; and

(7) Reference[Reference-Id, Document-Id#, Reference*].

Each of these files can be used independently. Three files of Document, Abstract, and Reference are closely related to each other, but the others may be modified and augmented by any arbitrary source of data, if necessary.

Document Information Database

So far, the following three journals in the field of information science have been put into our document information system and adding those in the artificial intelligence research to them is under preparation:

(1) Information Processing and Management (formerly Information Storage and Retrieval), Pergamon Press;

(2) Journal of The American Society for Information Science, (ASIS);

(3) The Journal of Documentation, Aslib.

The prototype database named AIRIS has been constructed using a commercial DBMS (ADABAS), especially its subsystem SOAR (Set Oriented Architecture of Request) developed for a general-purpose information retrieval system (Figure 1). AIRIS has a small collection of about 720 documents as a preliminary version under the scheme of "Document-0" described in the previous subsection without the Reference attribute. Later, the created file will be transformed into six files with necessary data processings and modifications.

Our concern is to be focused on two files, Document and Abstract. Text data of Title and Text attributes in these files have been stored in multiple occurrence fields of ADABAS by dividing into segments of a certain length.

Text Processing Facility

Powerful abilities of text processing are desirable in an advanced document information system with multi-media knowledge. There are three different levels of data manipulation of text information, i.e., word or string level, sentence or a sequence of strings, and text as a sequence of sentences. So far, at the first level text processing has mainly been performed literally in a word processing system (Meyrowitz and van Dam, 1982), some functions of processing at the second level are included in some text editors and in facilities of a few database systems (Stonebraker, et al., 1983), and processing at the third level has not been developed yet, but begins to attract interest in some fields (Bancilhon and Richard, 1984).

There are a number of text processing systems with text editing and formatting functions, most of them are at the first level (Furuta et al., 1982; Meyrowitz and van Dam, 1982). Text processing operations in these systems include SEARCH of location of specific word or substring of word in

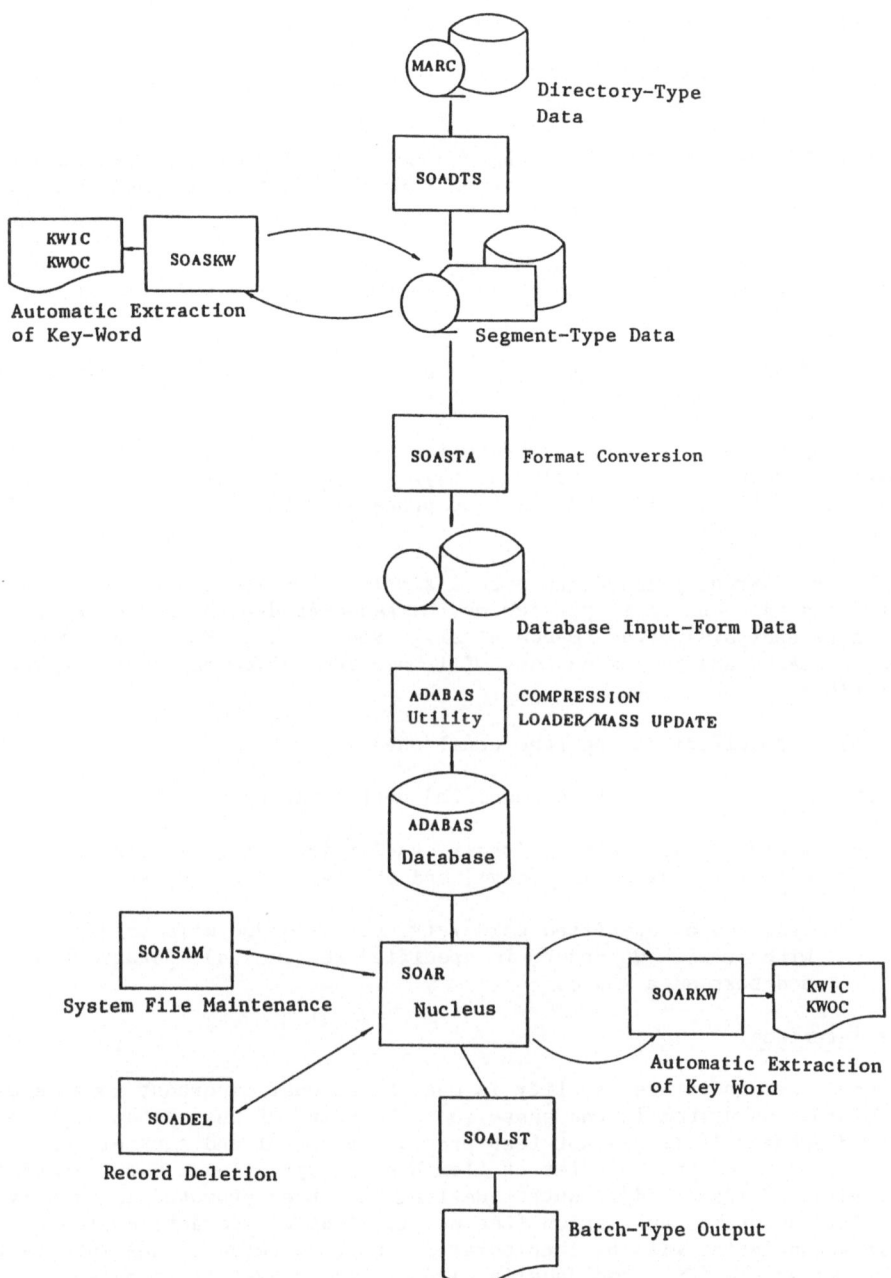

Figure 1. Database Construction Flow using SOAR Utility.

the target text, DELETE the word or substring in the text, INSERT a specific string into a particular part of the text, COPY and MOVE subtext within or to some location in another text, and REPLACE some string with other string in the text.

Extension of these primitive operations, especially SEARCH and REPJLACE to the second and third levels, is very important for the contextual text processing and its applications to document processing. The following directions of the extension are the most desirable:

(1) Syntax-directed, i.e. an extension of currently usable operations in many text editors;

(2) Grammar-based, i.e. using grammatical information of the target text, e.g., a part of speech information, sentence patterns, and text structures, etc.;

(3) Semantics-based, i.e. using semantic information, e.g., word meanings, various semantic relations of words and phrases, etc.; and

(4) Pragmatics-based, i.e. using pragmatic information, e.g., idioms and idiomatic expressions, etc.

The dictionary or some knowledge base in the fieflds concerned will be needed for approaches (2), (3), and (4). Realization of some of these extensions will provide advanced text processing capabilities for a wide range of applications.

We are currently concerned with a simple extension along the directions of (2) and (3), and this approach may be associated with the so-called text structure analysis method (Maeda et al., 1980; Maeda, 1981). Basic operation is SEARCH and the extensions will have the following as its object of operation:

(a) a specified string (the usual one);

(b) words belonging to a specified part of speech;

(c) repeating word/string itself, and/or including all its inflections, its synonym/antonym, and the related words; and

(d) sequence of specified words/strings (extended wild cards), with or without order, in specified sentence(s), paragraph(s), and text as a whole.

User Interface

Good user interface facility is one of the most important components of an information system in the sense that the value of the system might be reduced greatly if it has not been provided a useful and flexible user interface. Various technologies of flexible and operational user interface with advanced input and/or output devices have been promoted especially in the field of office automation (Lee et al., 1985). The application of these technologies will be incorporated even in a conventional information retrieval system (Frei and Jauslin, 1983). These systems prepare, for example, a bit-mapped display and pointing device and present visually a part of document text, so that it can be edited by manipulation of some icons in multi-windows.

Basic function of a good user interface facility is to enhance usability and flexibility of the information system.

The usability may be enhanced by providing proper functions for:

(a) access and manipulation of data including complicated ones;

(b) saving and activation of data of various types;

152

(c) backtracking of the process when necessary; and

(d) running multiple tasks concurrently, etc.

The flexibility may include

(e) visual representation and on-the-spot operation in the process;

(f) easy and simple manipulation of each operation and device; and

(g) mixed-initiative communication scheme, etc.

We are currently concerned mainly with (a) for the usability and (e) for the flexibility in a limited sense.

CONCLUDING REMARKS

Some design problems of an advanced scientific information system are discussed in this paper. There are two important guidelines of such a system in a scientific working environment, i.e., as an information tool and as a research object. These can be understood as a public database access function and a personal document manipulation function of the document information system, respectively. An approach to the implemention of the prototype system with these functions is presented. The prototype system is under development at Hokkaido University using existing DBMS.

Many problems in the development of an advanced scientific information system and scientific workstations are associated with diverse fields of science, especially computational linguistics, artificial intelligence, computer and information sciences. The most important and basic problems are in text information processing as an integral part of the so-called multi-media knowledge information, its modelling and conceptual representation scheme, and an advanced and extended database management system to deal with such diverse information. Cooperation of researchers in those fields of sciences is a necessity.

ACKNOWLEDGMENT

The authors would like to thank Prof. M. Kitamura of Dept. of Engineering Science, Hokkaido University, for his careful reading of the manuscript and helpful comments.

REFERENCES

Amano, K., and Mochida, A., 1985, "A Supporting System for Effective Construction and Sharing of Scientific Databases by General Researchers", Inform. Process. & Management, 21, (6), pp. 535-544.

Amano, K., and Maeda, T., 1985, "Database Management in Research Environment", in this issue.

Bancilhon, F., and Richard, P., 1984, "Managing Texts and Facts in a Mixed Database Environment", New Application of Databases, Gardarin, G. and Gelenbe, E. eds., Academic Press, pp. 87-107.

Crawford, R. G., 1981, "The Relational Model in Information Retrieval", J. ASIS, 32, (1), pp. 51-64.

Frei, H. P., and Jauslin, J.-F., 1983, "Graphical Representation of Information and Services: A User-Oriented Interface", Inf. Tech.: Research & Development, 2, (1), pp. 23-42.

Furuta, R., et al., 1982, "Document Formatting Systems: Survey, Concepts, and Issues", Computing Surveys, 14, (3), pp. 417-472.

Gardarin, G., 1984, "Towards the Fifth Generation of Data Management System", New Application of Databases, Gardarin, G., and Gelenbe, E., eds., Academic Press, pp. 3-15.

Haskin, R. L., and Lorie, R. A., 1982, "On Extending the Functions of a Relational Database System", Proc. ACM SIGMOD Conf., pp. 207-212.

Lee, A., et al., 1985, "User Interface Design", Office Automation Concepts and Tools, D. Tsichritzis, ed., Springer-Verlag, pp. 3-20.

Lum, V., et al., 1985, "Design of an Integrated DBMS to Support Advanced Applications", Proc. Intl. Conf. Found. Data Organization, Kyoto.

Maeda, T., et al., 1980, "An Automatic Method for Extracting Significant Phrases in Scientific or Technical Document", Inform. Process. & Management, 16, (3), pp. 119-127.

Maeda, T., 1981, "An Approach toward Functional Text Structure Analysis of Scientific and Technical Documents", Inform. Process. & Management, 17, (6), pp. 329-339.

Meyrowitz, N., and van Dam, A., 1982, "Interactive Editing Systems: Part I & II", Computing Surveys, 14, (3), pp. 321-352 and pp. 353-415.

Rabitti, F., 1985, "A Model for Multimedia Documents", Office Automation: Concepts and Tools, D. Tsichritzis, ed., Springer-Verlag, pp. 227-250.

Schek, H.-J., et al., 1982, "Data Structure for an Integrated Data Base Management and Information Retrieval System", Proc. VLDB-8, pp. 197-207.

Stonebraker, M., et al., 1983, "Document Processing in a Relational Database System", ACM Trans. on Office Information System, 1, (2), pp. 143-158.

Togashi, M., 1982, "Databox", RIMS Kokyuroku, 461, pp. 368-380.

Woo, D., et al., 1985, "Document Management Systems", Office Automation: Concepts and Tools, D. Tsichritzis, ed., Springer-Verlag, pp. 21-40.

A TECHNIQUE THAT SUPPORTS EVALUATION AND DESIGN OF USER INTERFACES[1]

I. Mistrik* and D. A. Nelson**

*Gesellschaft für Information und Dokumentation mbH(GID)
Tiergartenstr. 17
D-6900 Heidelberg 1
F. R. Germany
**Information Engineering
Elisenweg 12
D-8100 Garmisch-Partenkirchen
F. R. Germany

Abstract: We describe an initial attempt to incorporate results from the empirical evaluation of user interfaces in existing Interactive Information Systems (IISs) into a description of a generic User Interface (UI/F) of broad applicability. This generic UI/F is based on a display-screen-oriented user/system dialog that emphasizes the user's roles as pattern recognizer and selector and the IISs' roles as presenter of information and choices to the user.

The technique and its descriptive and representational abstractions have been applied to the evaluation and redesign of the UI/F for an existing IIS. The technique, as presented, employs a multi-level dialog description and generic, structured, screen representations of the state of the user/system dialog that are topologically consistent from state to state, but are adaptable to changing user needs and varying screen information content.

1. INTRODUCTION

One of the hallmarks of a mature branch of engineering is the capability of verifying and evaluating a product design before the product itself is constructed and installed. The accelerating growth in the development use of Interactive Information Systems (ISSs) signals a need to move beyond trial-and-error techniques in the design of user interfaces (UI/Fs) for IISs. This report describes the use of the concept of a generic UI/F (gUI/F) to obtain needed improvements in the design of these UI/Fs.

The UI/F for an IIS is a Virtual Machine that is operated by its users in order to gain access to the underlying functional capabilities of that IIS. It is now generally acknowledged that the UI/F must support access to an IIS without requiring that its users possess either general knowledge of

---

[1]Revision 1 (01/18/86).

computer technology or specific knowledge of the internal operation of that IIS. In this report, the UI/F for an IIS is treated as an active component of the IIS and not as an abstract, passive slice through the IIS. See Figure 1 and Moreland (1985) for an exposition of this view of the UI/F.

The user interface (UI/F) for an Interactive Information System (IIS) has an extraordinary role to play. It is, without exaggeration, the most important functional component of an IIS (Kay, 1984). The importance of the UI/F arises from these factors:

a) it provides the only means for invoking the underlying information processing functions of the IIS,

b) for users of the IIS, the user interface is the system (Kay, 1984), and

c) the quality of the UI/F is very often the critical factor

The primary objectives of such a UI/F are to provide the user of an IIS with unobtrusive, (user) task-oriented, easy-to-use access to, and transformations upon, the contents of that IIS.

Several projects devoted to developing UI/F generators have been reported (Friman, 1984; Olsen and Dempsey, 1983). Other researchers have reported on investigations of generic applications (Hansen and Hansen, 1982). Work that is more closely related to ours in its approach to the problem has been reported by Bass (1985), but he focuses on the support of traditional application programs and conventional programming language interfaces. What we believe is novel in our work is the development of a detailed design description for a generic user interface, or gUI/F. This gUI/F design can be particularized to yield a specific, concrete UI/F

```
+-------+-----------------------------------------------------------+
|       |                  User Interface Manager                   |
|       +-----------------------------------------------------------+
|       |                                                           |
|       |   Dialog Manager                                          |
|       |   Display Screen Manager                                  |
|       |           Entity/Index Window Manager                     |
|       |           System Replies Manager                          |
|       |           Supplementary Menu Manager                      |
|       |           User Input Window Manager                       |
|       |           Context Manager                                 |
|       |           Operations Manager                              |
|       +-----------------------------------------------------------+
|  IIS  |                  Modelbase Manager                        |
|       +-----------------------------------------------------------+
|       |                                                           |
|       |   Procedures for User Tasks                               |
|       |   Transaction Manager                                     |
|       +-----------------------------------------------------------+
|       |            Database (Objectbase) Manager                  |
|       +-----------------------------------------------------------+
|       |                                                           |
|       |   Directory Manager                                       |
|       |   Query Processor                                         |
|       |   Update Processor                                        |
|       |   Recovery & Restart Manager                              |
|       |   File Manager                                            |
+-------+-----------------------------------------------------------+
```

Figure 1. Global Architecture (Layering) in IISs.

in the acceptance or rejection of an IIS by its users.

design for a specific IIS and it can also be used to support the evaluation of existing concrete UI/F designs.

We believe that our work is more fundamentally concerned with the behavior of the UI/F as a system component than is evident in much of the work that has been done on UI/F generators. At the same time, we are also convinced that the development of the UI/F for an IIS must be decoupled from the development of the application or processing functions it facilitates (Gaines, 1981; Morland, 1985).

The use of a gUI/F as a basis for evaluating existing, concrete UI/Fs has these advantages:

a) the gUI/F exhibits, and illustrates characteristics that design guidelines can only allude to, and

b) the gUI/F provides a more flexible basis for comparison than is achieved when one concrete UI/F is used as the basis for evaluating another.

Thus using a gUI/F for evaluating either existing or proposed concrete UI/Fs, strikes a balance between the generality of guidelines and the, sometimes overwhelming, mass of detail embodied in a concrete UI/F. In particular, our experience indicates that system software developers respond very poorly to design guidelines ("they are just platitudes") and to using existing programs as models ("there are too many differences in detail").

Another advantage we expect to gain from the gUI/F approach is that the description of the gUI/F is deliberately designed for modification. Thus we anticipate that the model UI/F that is represented by the current gUI/F will be periodically revised and extended as new knowledge regarding UI/Fs becomes available. It should be noted that we regard the existence of a conventional UI/F generation as an impediment to the frequent revision and extension of a gUI/F. We feel very strongly that an object-oriented description of a gUI/F is inherently more maintainable and that its existence provides us with most of the benefits and few of the disadvantages of a UI/F generator.

In this report the focus is on: the user/system dialog structures, the objects that are manipulated by the user, and the display screen conventions that support dialoging. The design of the internal objects (and their data structures) to complete the gUI/F are not addressed due to their lesser importance and space limitations. Also, we have chosen not to present the design details of our approach to user task description, as that is a topic that deserves to be treated in a separate report.

2. REQUIREMENTS FOR A UI/F FOR IISs

The requirements for a UI/F that meets the objectives stated in Section 1 (above) are given in this section.

2.1 General Requirements

The requirements in this section are too general to be either stated or verified with precision and so they are presented here as design guidelines rather than as specific constraints. They are:

a) the UI/F should obey the (so-called) law of least astonishment (Thimbleby, 1983),

b) the UI/F should be consistent in its use of symbols and in its behavior from the user's perspective (Whiteside et al., 1985; Zisman, 1982),

c) the trade-off between complexity for the user versus complexity for the system shall be made in favor of simplicity for the user. (The digital or mechanical wrist watch is a good example, but IBM OC JCL is a violation of this guideline.) (See Zisman, 1982.),

d) don't make the user say anything more than once (e.g., if field length is given in file description, it should not be asked for in a report description),

e) the UI/F should be "bullet-proofed" against attempts to circumvent it to gain access to information or to internal functions (Smith et al., 1982),

f) the UI/F component of an IIS must be self-measuring to facilitate performance evaluations and tuning, i.e., it should be instrumented (Draper and Norman, 1984),

g) reliable operation (e.g., automatic error recovery) is necessary in order to give the users the confidence they need to reply on, and exploit, the IIS, (e.g., the UI/F should be designed and developed to support recovery from system crashes and file transcription errors) (Draper and Norman, 1984),

h) the UI/F must be integrated. The UI/F must be more than just the sum of its individual features. The UI/F must create, for the user, an integrated, coherent, consistent picture of the system. To do this, the UI/F must exhibit or support uniformity and consistency among, and the exchange, or sharing, of data between, its individual functions (Teitelbaum and Granda, 1983; Woodmansee, 1983). The current buzzword for uniformity and consistency is "modeless" (Tesler, 1983, p. 3). The current buzzword for sharing (or interchange) is "seamless" and several investigators stress its importance (Rutkowski, 1982; Smith et al., 1982),

i) User Friendliness shall characterize the UI/F.

   User Friendliness is a measure of the degree to which the user interface of an Information System: (1) directly supports the user's tasks, and (2) furnishes that support in the context of the object and operator domains of those tasks,

j) the UI/F shall facilitate the user's effort to create an effective User's Conceptual Model (or "user illusion"). The User's Conceptual Model may not be, and often is not, an accurate characterization of the system, but it can, and should, be workable (Carroll, 1982; Smith et al., 1982). "The 'user illusion' ... is the simplified myth everyone builds to explain (and make guesses about) the system's actions and what should be done next." (Kay, 1984),

k) the UI/F design shall be based on a specific, credible, model

of user behavior (the System's Conceptual Model of the User).
(Dagwell and Weber, 1983),

1) the User Services Model (USM) for the UI/F shall be derived
from the System's Conceptual Model (SCM) (Carroll, 1982;
Dagwell and Weber, 1983), and

m) the UI/F must directly support a high level user-task performance. (Don't keep the user busy operating the system, instead help that user to complete his/her task as rapidly as
possible (Fried, 1982; Zisman, 1982).)

2.2 Specific Requirements

These requirements are verifiable constrants on the design of the UI/F.

The UI/F must provide the following:

a) Direct Support for User Goals and Tasks.

User should access and transform information - not learn how
to operate a system (Benzon, 1985; Croft and Lefkowitz, 1984),

b) Direct Support for Task-Oriented Terminology and Objects.

"Technical choices irrelevant to the task at hand should be
eliminated from the user interface." (Rutkowski, 1982)

The user should focus on obtaining, or deriving, needed information - not on how to specify commands correctly (Benzon,
1985). E.g., to teach command syntax to the UI/F so that the
user does not have to learn that syntax,

c) Direct Manipulation of Task-Oriented Entities by the User.

"A person exerts the greatest leverage when his illusion can
be manipulated without appeal to abstract intermediaries such
as the hidden programs needed to put into action even a simple
word processor. ... direct leverage is provided when the
(user) illusion acts as a 'kit', or tool, with which to solve
a problem." (Kay, 1984)

The user feels, and actually is, more in control with a direct
manipulation UI/F than with an indirect (e.g., command-
oriented) UI/F (MacDonald, 1982; Teitelman, 1984; Tesler, 1983).
(See Figure 2.),

d) Multi-Dimensional and Multi-Media Facilities.

2-D displays deliver more information, faster, than 1-D (or
character-oriented) displays. 3-D is even better than 2-D.
Text, voice and especially image data are often more effective
than structured data (Benzon, 1985; Bolt, 1984; MacDonald, 1982;
Powell and Linton, 1983; Thalman, 1984),

e) Systematic Use of Embedded Knowledge.

Use embedded knowledge to minimize both learning and mental
recall by user (Jackson, 1983; Nelson, 1984). Support for
dynamic default replies and preferred values are two very elementary examples of the use of embedded knowledge (Apperley

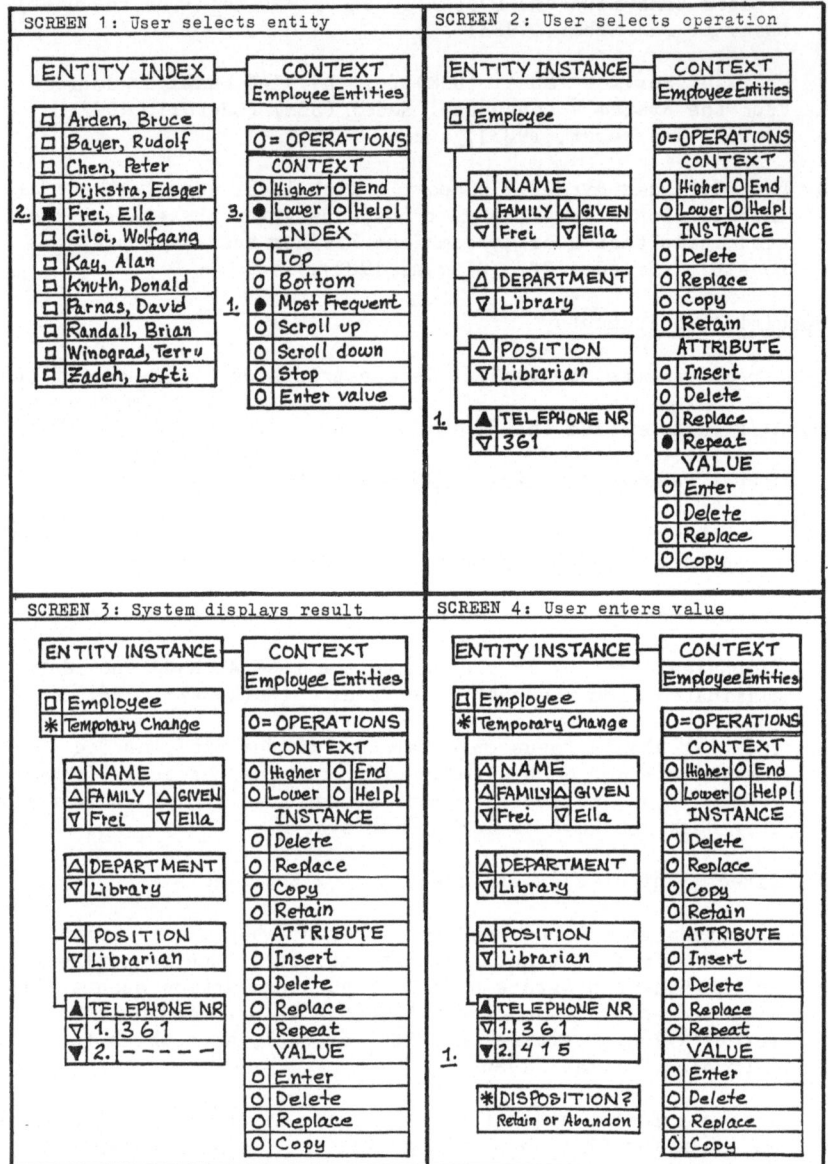

Figure 2. Illustration of Object-Oriented User Interface: an Additional Telephone Number.

and Spence, 1983; Shimomura, 1983), and

f) Selection as the User's Primary Role.

"Manipulating the image (on the screen) in a certain way immediately does something predictable to the state of the machine (as the user imagines that machine)." (Kay, 1984, p. 54)

"Can the user see what is to be done and simply go do it? (Kay, 1984, p. 57)

The User's roles are: 1) selector; and 2) pattern recognizer (Rutkowski, 1982; Tesler, 1983),

g) Transformation of Entitites as the System's Primary Role.

The UI/F's roles are: 1) symbol manipulator, and 2) offeror of choices to the user (Rutkowski, 1982),

h) Continuous Display of Status to User by System.

The UI/F remembers what the user was doing and displays the status of the system's responses so that the user is continuously being presented with context (Croft, 1984; Myers 1985),

i) "Un-Doing" of User-Initiated Actions.

UI/F must be capable of reversing the effect of any entity transformation (Apperley and Spence, 1983; Archer et al., 1984; Vitter, 1984),

j) Automatic Error Recovery.

The UI/F must insulate the user from the effects of errors that occur behind (below) the UI/F (Draper and Norman, 1984),

k) Customizing of the UI/F.

User leverage is increased by support of customizing and tailoring of the UI/F at both the user and organization levels (Cary, 1982; Mozeico, 1982), and

1) Self-Teaching Facilities.

The UI/F must teach the user about both the UI/F and the content of the IIS (Rutkowski, 1982; Houghton, 1984; Shapiro, 1984; Smith et al., 1982). A printed User's Manual should be regarded as a confession by the UI/F developers that they have failed to produce a UI/F that meets these requirements. "HELP!" menus and on-line tutorials are two examples of replacement technologies for printed user's manuals (Yestingsmeier, 1984).

3. DESIGN OF THE GUI/F

3.1 Introduction

In this section, a generic user interface (or gUI/F) for IISs is described. This gUI/F meets the requirements for a UI/F as stated in Section 2 (above) and, in fact, this gUI/F was derived directly from those requirements.

The basic premise underlying this design is that the user operates an IIS by conducting a user-directed dialog with that IIS. It is the function of the UI/F for an IIS to manage this dialog. A second premise is that the dialog between the user and the IIS will be represented on a workstation display screen as a combination of text, graphics, and structured data (See Figure 3).

This gUI/F also conforms to a specific style of UI/F that is known as "direct" or "direct-drive". Figure 2 contrasts this style with the

Characteristic	Direct	Indirect
targeted user	knowledge-worker	programmer
dialog form	menu selection (pointing device)	command language (keyboard)
demand upon user	recognize choices, options	recall command syntax, etc.
dominant user activity	selecting operands & operations	typing in commands
error exposure	all sections are valid	many combinations of commands & parameters are invalid
relative bandwidth	object-and operator-serial	character-serial
example	Macintosh (Apple Computer)	UNIX (AT&T)

Figure 3.   Contrasting User Interface Styles.

traditional, indirect, style. Note that Figure 3 is an example of the application of the "direct-drive" style.

,An IIS presents three basic kinds of information to its users:

a) meta-information (i.e., descriptive information concerning the primary content of the IIS),

b) information contained in (or derived from) the IIS's database(s), and

c) choices open to the end-user for manipulating the information and meta-information in the IIS.

In addition to offering information about both the types and instances of the constructs that it contains, the user interface acquires data about both the usage of its facilities and about the users themselves. Usage of each system facility is logged. Each user (or user identity) is represented by an entity that describes that user's access rights, usage patterns, stored procedures and administrative data.

3.2 Generic Dialog Structures

In this user-system dialog, each party makes requests of the other, and each party presents information to the other in response to those requests.

```
Object

    . ID (Identification or key) (Unique for each object)

    . State = Value(s)‡ (for entities and index entries,
                          state includes a user-declared
                          name or a system assigned default
                          name (eg employee-name))

    . Description

            . Type (eg Aggregate)

            . Validation rules‡

            : Conversion rules‡

                    . Presentation to Storage

                    . Storage to Presentation

            . Status

            . Authorization level

            . Help! (and tutorial material)

    . Operations (Methods)

        . User operations

        . UI/F internal operations
```

†source: NELSON

‡or name of procedure that returns, or invokes, them

Figure 4.   Generic Object Representation in the UI/F.

An example of the use of a display screen to represent a user–system dialog is illustrated in Figure 3. This example exhibits several characteristics of the gUI/F:

a) the context of the dialog is always visible (in summary form to the user,

b) the IIS entities being manipulated by the user are visible (as two-dimensional object structure diagrams where appropriate),

c) the currently valid operations on those entities are displayed (via selection menus), and

d) user selections are prominently displayed together with the choices from which those selections were made. (In Figure 3, the relevant tokens are darkened. Some UI/Fs use reverse video for this purpose.)

The generic structure of the user–system dialog is: a sequence of dialog segments where each segment consists of a user request for access to information followed by a series of (possibly nested) user–system request-reply pairs that specify (the user's role) and carry out (the system's role) transformations of the selected information. Note that this dialog structure is nested, but is not recursive. See Figure 4 for a description of the five primary levels of dialog in the gUI/F.

A user request for access to information, and the resulting dialog segments that specify and carry out the desired transformation on that information are illustrated in Figure 3.

On a more abstract level:

a) selection (by the user) of one or more sets of entities that contain the specific entity or entities to be operated upon,

b) presentation (by the system) of the contents of those sets,

c) selection (by the user) of the specific entities to be operated upon,

d) presentation (by the system) of the specific entities selected and the set of valid operations on those entities,

e) selection (by the user) of the specific operations to be performed on the previously selected objects, and

f) presentation (by the system) of the results of executing the selected operations (or, alternatively, a pledge by the system that those operations are being carried out so that the user is never in doubt as to dialog results).

Note that each of these six components of a dialog segment may, itself, consist of a series of dialog segments.

Wherever feasible, the process of identification is accomplished by presenting the user with an enumeration (e.g., index, selection menu) of the entities (or transformations) that are accessible to the user. Where presentation of an entire enumeration is not feasible (e.g., due to display screen size) then one of the following alternatives is to be employed:

a) a hierarchical index (or taxonomy) is used to support multi-step selection,

b) the user is prompted to select a selection mechanism from among those supported by the system, or

c) user is prompted to enter the name of the entity (or transformation) via a keyboard or other entry device.

3.3 Generic Presentation Layout for Dialoging

The display screen area is subdivided into as many as 5 non-overlapping windows. These windows are of variable dimensions and each is dedicated to one of the specific presentation functions listed below.

a) Dialog Context

Supplied automatically, and continuously, by the system. Summaries of previous dialog actions are presented in this window.

b) Current Entities of Interest

These may be text, graphic or structured data representations of entities. This window supplies the specific context (e.g., an entity instance or type) for the remaining two windows.

Dialog Level	Entity/Index (Operands)	Operations (Examples only)
1	**User Task List** . IIS lists the user tasks that are supported by the IIS . user selects specific task	**Operations on Task Description** . display description of selected task . display entity types index
2	**Entity Types Index** . IIS lists Entity Type IDs for all entity types defined for current application . user selects specific entity type(s)	**Operations on Entity Types Index** . find a specific entity type . instantiate an Entity Type
2	**Entity Type (Structure Diagram)** . IIS shows attribute structure of currently selected entity type . user selects specific attribute(s)	**Operations on Entity Types** . repeat attribute . instantiate attribute . delete attribute
3	**Entity Instances Index** . IIS lists Entity IDs of all entity instances of type selected . user selects specific entity instance(s)	**Operations on Entity Instances Index** . find a specific entity instance . instantiate an Entity . display selected entity instance(s)
4	**Entity Instance (Structure Diagram)** . IIS shows attribute structure of selected entity instance . user selects specific attribute(s)	**Operations on attributes of an Entity Instance** . display current value(s) of selected attributes
5	**Attribute Instances and Properties** . IIS shows current value(s) of selected attribute(s) . user selects specific value(s)	**Operations on properties of an attribute instance** . replace value(s) { enumeration / construction / entry by user } . reset to default value(s)

Figure 5. Generic Dialog Structure.

c) **Currently Valid Operations**

These are displayed in the form of a selection menu, and in order of expected frequency of selection.

d) **Supplementary Selection Menus or System Replies**

The supplementary menus support such functions as parameter specification. System Replies range from restatements of user requests to "answers" to user information transformation requests.

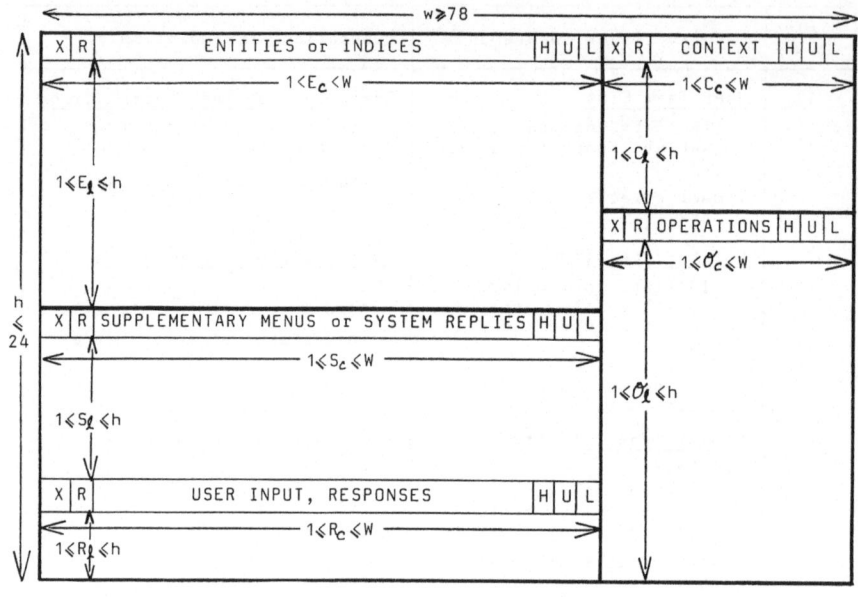

Figure 6. Generic Display Screen Layout.

e) **Entry of User Replies**

Used as a last resort and only when selection is not appropriate, e.g., when system cannot enumerate the appropriate responses. No internal, or coded, data are requested from users, and responses are brief (in terms of keystroke count).

This presentation structure is the basis for the generic display screen structure described in Figure 5. Note that windows can be expanded and contracted in size. Figure 3 illustrates the use of a concrete realization of this generic display screen structure.

3.4 Generic Operands

The operands that can be accessed and manipulated by the user are represented in the gUI/F as objects. The following operands are among the objects in the UI/F environment:

1) User task description (e.g., preparation of an employee telephone directory),

2) task-independent function supported by the modelbase of the
    IIS (e.g., database transactions),

3) Entity type (e.g., employees),

4) Index type (e.g., employee names),

5) Entity instance (e.g., description of a specific employee),

6) Index instance (e.g., names of employees of a specific firm), and

7) Attribute types (e.g., date of birth of an employee).

Note that attribute values, or properties, (e.g., "1947 April 21" is
the value of the date attribute in the "Frei, Ella" entity) are the only
components of an object that are represented in conventional databases. In
the gUI/F, properties are among the several components of an object.

See Figure 6 for a description of the generic object in the gUI/F.
Figure 2 shows concrete examples of two operand instances: an entity index
for employees and an entity instance of the type employee. Both concrete
examples are presented using Object Structure Diagrams.

3.5 Generic Operations

The gUI/F supports several generic, user-invocable, operations on both
system-declared and user-declared entities and entity types and their associated indexes or directories. Both entities and indexes and their types
are typically represented as objects in an IIS (see Figure 6). The generic
operations on these objects are shown in Figure 7.

Note that the user can also request the "un-doing" of the effects of a
previously invoked operation (Vitter, 1984). In addition, both entity
selection and the specification of selection criteria are supported as user
invocable functional capabilities. It should also be noted that, because
of the dialog structures employed, neither syntactically invalid nor
semantically invalid operations can be formulated at the gUI/F.

The set of operations that are presented to the user via an Operations
Menu are a subset of the operations in the object description(s) of the
current contents of the Entity/Index Window (the current operand(s)). The
operations specified in these object descriptions are further filtered to
remove operations that are:

a) not authorized for the current user, and

b) not consistent with current security and/or integrity
    constraints.

3.6 Generic Devices for User-System Communication

The basic purposes and primary functions of the physical components of
the UI/F are described below. Generic device technologies are listed in
order of preference.

3.6.1 Presentation

a) Primary functions: present selection menus, re-
                                trieved data and system in-
                                formation to user as request
                                by the user, or mandated by

Operation Category	Function
DISPOSITION[†]	RETAIN (make new version, replace any previous one) DISCARD (discard new version, retain previous one - "UNDO")
ENTITY or[‡] ATTRIBUTE	INSERT (instantiate) DELETE (de-instantiate) RESET (re-instantiate to default state) COPY (re-instantiate by replication - 2 operands) REPEAT (replicate - 1 operand) DISPLAY (present instances selected)
VALUE	ENTER (replace current (null or default) value) DELETE (replace current value with default value) COPY (replace current value with designated value)
INDEX SEARCHING	FIRST LAST MOST FREQUENT FIND BY ID (ie enter value of instance name or ID) FIRST HALF (BISECT HIGH) LAST HALF (BISECT LOW)
SCROLLING	UP - BY OBJECT UP - BY LINE DOWN - BY OBJECT DOWN - BY LINE LEFT - BY FIELD OR COLUMN LEFT - BY CHARACTER POSITION RIGHT- BY FIELD OR COLUMN RIGHT- BY CHARACTER POSITION STOP

[†] of object types, objects or attributes

[‡] operations on whole entities or whole attributes

Figure 7. Generic Operations.

the system.

b) Generic Device Technologies: bit-mapped display screen, char-
acter-generator display screen.

3.6.2 Selection

a) Primary Functions: provide pointing (cursor control)
capability.

b) Generic Device Technologies: touch-screen, puck, mouse, light
pen, special function keys, keyboard.

3.6.3 Entry

a) Primary Functions: provide character-serial input
capability for entering data, text
and parameters.

	Generic Device Type	Functions	Example (generic)
User Input	Token Entry	data, commands	keyboard
	Position Indicator	selection, cursor control	Mouse
	Free-form Drawing Instrument	data	Light-pen
	Voice	data, commands	Voice Recognizer
	Image Capture	data	Digitizing Camera
System Output	Interactive Display	data, system responses dialog management	CRT Monitor
	Hardcopy	data	Laser Printer
	Voice	data, system responses	Voice Synthesizer

Figure 8. Taxonomy of Devices that Support Human Interaction with an IIS.

b) Generic Device Technologies: keyboard, virtual keyboard.

3.6.4 Remote Data Presentation

a) Generic Functions: provide hard-copy data presentation for use away from system.

b) Generic Device Technologies: bit-mapped plotter/printer, character, line or page printer.

See Figure 8 for another view of generic device support for UI/Fs for IISs.

4. CONCLUDING REMARKS

By conscientiously incorporating widely accepted UI/F characteristics into a generalized model of a UI/F that we call a gUI/F, we hope to improve the quality of specific UI/Fs that are developed from the gUI/F. In this approach, each concrete UI/F is an instantiation of a gUI/F that exhibits both the characteristics of the gUI/F and the domain specific objects and operations of the particular IIS for which that concrete UI/F has been developed.

We have evaluated, and will continue to evaluate, existing UI/Fs and UI/F designs by comparing them with the gUI/F on the basis of the UI/F requirements stated in Section 2 of this report.

However, the ultimate evaluation of a UI/F can only be made by its users. Therefore, any UI/F produced by software developers must be considered, at best, as tentative and subject to change in order to more clearly meet the needs of those end-users.

ACKNOWLEDGEMENTS

The authors are grateful to the Gesellschaft fur Information und Documentation mbH (GID) and Information Engineering for supporting the development of the gUI/F and encouraging the preparation and publication of this report.

REFERENCES

Apperley, M. D., and Spence, R., 1983, "Hierarchical Dialogue Structures in Interactive Computer Systems", Software Practice & Exp., Wiley, 13, (9), pp. 777-790, September 1983.

Archer, J. E., Jr., et al., 1984, "User Recovery and Reversal in Interactive Systems", ACM Trans. Progr. Langs. & Systems, 6, (1), pp. 1-19, Jan. 1984.

Bass, L. J., 1985, "A Generalized User Interface for Applications Programs (II)", Comm. ACM, 28, (6), pp. 617-627, June 1985.

Becker, R. A., and Chambers, J. M., 1984, "Design of the S System for Data Analysis", Comm. ACM, 27, (5), pp. 486-495, May 1984.

Benbasat, I., and Wand, Y., 1984, "A Structured Approach to Designing Human-computer Dialogues", Int. J. Man-Machine Studies, 21, pp. 105-126.

Benzon, W. L., 1985, "The Visual Mind and the Macintosh", BYTE, 10, (1), pp. 113-130, January 1985.

Bolt, R. A., 1984, "The Human Interface", Lifetime Learning Publications, Belmont, CA.

Brown, J. W., 1982, "Controlling the Complexity of Menu Networks", Comm. ACM, 25, (7), pp. 412-418, July 1982.

Card, S., et al., 1983, The Psychology of Human-Computer-Interaction, LEA Publishers, Hillsdale, NJ.

Cary, T., 1982, "User Differences in Interface Design", Computer, IEEE, 15, (11), pp. 14-20, November 1982.

Carroll, J. M., 1982, "The Adventure of Getting to Know a Computer", Computer, IEEE, 15, (11), pp. 49-58, November 1982.

Croft, W. B., and Leftkowitz, L. S., 1984, "Task Support in an Office System", ACM Trans Office Info Syst, 2, (3), pp. 197-212, July 1984.

Croft, W. B., 1984, "The Role of Context and Adaptation in User Interfaces", Int. J. Man-Machine Studies, 21, pp. 283-292.

Dagwell, R., and Weber, R., 1983, "'System Designers' User Models: A Comparative Study and Methodological Critique", Comm ACM, 26, (11), pp. 987-998, November 1983.

Daniels, B., 1984, "The Architecture of the Lisa Personal Computer", Proc. IEEE, 72, (3), pp. 331-341, March 1984.

Draper, S. W., and Norman, D. A., 1984, "Software Engineering for User Interfaces", Proc. 7. ICSE, IEEE, pp. 214-221, March 26, 1984.

Fried, L., 1982, "Nine Principles for Ergonomic Software", Datamation, pp. 163-166, November 1982.

Friman, B., 1984, "MGEN - A Generator for Menu Driven Programs", Proc. 7. Int. Conf. Software Engr., IEEE, pp. 198-206, March 1984.

Gaines, B. R., 1981, "The Technology of Interaction-dialogue Programming Rules", Int. J. Man-Machine Studies, 14, (1), pp. 133-150.

Glinert, E. P., and Tanimoto, S. L., 1984, "Pict: An Interactive Graphical Programming Environment", Computer, IEEE, 17, (11), pp. 7-28, November 1984.

Hansen, M. R., and Hansen, B. S., 1982, A Generic Application Programming System, Masters Thesis, T.U. Denmark, Lyngby.

Hauptmann, A. G., and Green, B. F., 1983, "A Comparison of Command, Menu-Selection and Natural-language Computer Programs", Behavior & Info. Tech., 2, (2), pp. 163-178, Apr.-Jun. 1983.

Heckel, P., 1984, The Elements of Friendly Software Design, Warner Books.

Houghton, R. C., Jr., 1984, "Online Help Systems: A Conspectus", Comm ACM, 27, (2), pp. 126-133, Feb. 1984.

Jackson, M. D., 1983, "Constrained Languages Need Not Constrain Person/Computer Interaction", SIGCHI Bulletin, ACM, 15, (2-3), pp. 18-22, October 1983.

Kay, A, 1984, "Computer Software", Scientific American, 251, (3), pp. 52-59, September 1984.

MacDonald, A., 1982, "Visual Programming", Datamation, pp. 132-140, October 1982.

Moran, T. P., 1981, "An Applied Psychology of the User", Computer Surveys, ACM, 13, (1), pp. 1-11, March 1981.

Morland, D. V., 1983, "Human Factors Guidelines for Terminal Interface Design", Comm ACM, 26, (7), pp. 484-494, July 1983.

Moreland, D. V., 1985, "The Evolution of Software Architecture", Datamation, 31, (3), pp. 123-132, 1 Feb. 1985.

Mozeico, H., 1982, "A Human/Computer Interface to Accommodate User Learning

Stages", Comm ACM, 25, (2), pp. 100-104, Feb. 1982.

Myers, B. A., 1985, "The Importance of Percent-Done Progress Indicators for
Computer-Human Interfaces", Proc. CHI '85 Hum. Factors Comp. Systs,
Borman, L., and Curtis, B., eds., ACM, Apr. 1985.

Nelson, D. A., 1984, "A Software Development Environment Emphasizing Rapid
Prototyping", Approaches to Prototyping, Budde, R., ed., Springer
Verlag, 1984.

Norman, D. A., 1983, "Design Rules Based on Analyses of Human Error", Comm
ACM, 26, (4), pp. 254-258, Apr. 1983.

Norman, D. A., 1984, "Stages and Levels in Human-Machine Interaction", Int.
J. Man-Machine Studies, 21, pp. 365-375, 1984.

Olsen, D. R. Jr., and Dempsey, E. P., 1983, "SYNGRAPH: A Graphical User
Interface Generator", Computer Graphics, ACM, 17, (3), pp. 43-50.

Powell, M. L., and Linton, M. A., 1983, "Visual Abstraction in an Interactive Programming Environment", SIGPLAN Notes, ACM, 18, (6), pp. 14-21,
June 1983.

Rutkowski, C., 1982, "An Introduction to the Human Applications Standard
Computer Interface. Part 1: Theory and Principles", BYTE, 7, (11),
pp. 291-310, Oct. 1982.

Shapiro, E., 1984, "SoftOffice, the Integrated Software Package that Almost
Wasn't", BYTE, 9, (6), pp. 405-412, Jun. 1984.

Shimomura, T., 1983, "A Method for Automatically Generating Business
Graphs", IEEE CG&A, 3, (9), pp. 55-59, Sep. 1983.

Smith, D. C., et al., 1982, "The Star User Interface: An Overview", Proc.
NCC 1982, AFIPS Press.

Swezey, R. W., and Davis, E. G., 1983, "A Case Study of Human Factors
Guidelines in Computer Graphics", IEEE Comp. Graphics & Applications,
3, (8), pp. 21-30, Nov. 1983.

Teitelbaum, R. C., and Granda, R. E., 1983, "The Effects of Positional Con-
stancy on Searching Menus for Information, Proc. CHI '83 Hum. Factors
Comp. Systs, Janda, A., ed., ACM, pp. 150-153, Dec. 1983.

Teitelman, W., 1984, "A Tour Through Cedar", IEEE Software, 1, (2), pp.
44-73, Apr. 1984.

Tesler, L., 1983, "Object-Oriented User Interfaces and Object-Oriented
Languages", SIGPC Notes, ACM, 6, (2), pp. 3-5, 1983.

Thalman, D., 1984, "An Interactive Data Visualization System", Softw.
Pract. & Exp., 14, (3), pp. 277-290, Mar. 1984.

Thimbleby, H., 1983, "What You See is What You Have Got - a User Engineering Principle for Manipulative Display", Software-Ergonomie, Balzert,
H., and Teubner, B. G., eds., Stuttgart.

Thimbleby, H., 1983, "Guidelines for 'Manipulative' Text Editing", Behavior
& Info. Tech., 2, (2), pp. 127-164, Apr.-Jun. 1983.

Thompson, C. W., et al., 1983, "Building Usable Menu-Based Natural Language

Interfaces to Databases", Schkolnick, M., and Thanos, C., eds., <u>Proc.</u> <u>VLDB9</u>, VLDB Endow, pp. 43-55, 31 Oct. 1983.

Vitter, J. S., 1984, "US&R: A New Framework for Redoing", <u>IEEE Software</u>, <u>1</u>, (4), pp. 39-52, Oct. 1984.

Whiteside, J., et al., 1985, "User Performance with Command, Menu and Iconic Interfaces", <u>CHI '85 Conf. Proc.</u>, ACM SGICHI, pp. 185-193, 14 Apr. 1985.

Woodmansee, G., 1983, "Visi On's Interface Design", <u>BYTE</u>, <u>8</u>, (7), pp. 166-182, Jul. 1983.

Yestingsmeier, J., 1984, "Human Factors Considerations in Development of Interactive Software", <u>SIGCHI Bulletin</u>, ACM, <u>16</u>, (1), pp. 24-27, Jul. 1984.

Zisman, M. D., 1982, "Ease of Use", <u>Computerworld OA</u>, <u>16</u>, (39A), pp. 59-65, 29 Sep. 1982.

THE TERM ASSOCIATION THESAURUS: AN INFORMATION PROCESSING AID BASED ON

ASSOCIATIVE SEMANTICS

Annelise Mark Pejtersen*, Svend Erik Olsen**, and
Pranas Zunde***

*The Royal School of Librarianship
Copenhagen, Denmark

**Riso National Laboratory
Roskilde, Denmark

***Georgia Institute of Technology
Atlanta, GA   30332

Abstract: This paper describes the first phase of a project which is focused on the investigation of feasibility and utility of information processing aids and tools based on associative semantics and word association
techniques.   Emphasis is placed on the potential utility of such aids for
online information searching and retrieval in more complex cases, such as
browsing, for which the present methods are either not adequate or completely ineffective.   The construction of one kind of such aids, henceforth
called "Term Association Thesauri" or, briefly, TAThesaurus, is described
in some detail.

1.   INTRODUCTION

The growing involvement of information technology in the search for
literature from bibliographic data bases has created a need for more advanced (or "intelligent") systems to guide and facilitate user search
behavior.   This behavior can be supported by a wide range of possible automatic functions that help to formulate the user's needs and which also
present information in a way that best meets these needs and, at the same
time, his/her data-handling capabilities.   To achieve an optimal design,
however, we need a better understanding of the ways in which people process
information.

The main goal of the project, which is reported in this paper, is to
explore the extent to which the well-established technique of word association can be applied to the development of an aid in terms of a term association thesaurus for data base searching.

In a typical word association study, the participants are required to
respond to a given word (the stimulus word) with the first word that comes
to mind (the response word).   It seems reasonable to expect that people
with similar professional backgrounds or with similar goals and interests
will show common patterns of responses to stimulus words.   It is predicted

that there will be substantial between-group variation in the word associations elicited by the same set of stimulus words. Our hypothesis is that the networks of word associations obtained from these various groups are comparable to semantic networks, and could thus be usefully incorporated into advanced information systems to aid search, user-system dialogues, and the design of question-answering devices.

The network proposed in this project will also encompass the user's point of view, his/her previous experience, and various other pragmatic factors of which the user may not be aware, but which contribute to more complex cases, such as browsing, for which the present methods are either not adequate or completely ineffective.

2. WORD ASSOCIATION STUDIES

Word association studies have been very popular for the last one hundred years. This popularity can be ascribed partly to the relative ease with which the tests can be undertaken. Another source of their popularity is undoubtedly their supposed ability to expose the subjects' mental structures and processes. Galton (1880), who in the past century began experimental research with word association with himself as a subject, concluded that it would be instructive to compare and statistically treat the results gleaned from many experiments.

Although the word association method has a long and honorable history in psychology and in philosophy, the theories behind the word association are very varied (Hormann, 1979).

The following assumptions have been made about the word association technique:

1. Word associations may be seen as a kind of shorthand for complex semantic relations. All associations have as their basis a semantically deep propositional structure in which the stimulus is the predicate and the response the subject. The response "good" to the stimulus "bad" reveals an underlying propositional structure, which might be expressed like "good is the opposite of bad" (Deese and Hamilton, 1974).

2. The associative processes must be studied with a whole battery of methods; the word association test will be one of these. The word may be conceived as as three-component temporal pattern, namely as 1) an act of reference and a sustained process of representation, 2) an emotive process, and 3) an associative process. Operationally, these components can be partly assessed by such procedures as 1) request for definition, 2) semantic-differential scalings, and 3) word association tests (Rommetveit, 1968).

For our present purposes, the most important theoretical points are: 1) that word association tests appear to provide information about certain connections between the stimulus word and the response word that, in some sense, is important to the subject and, 2) that a given group of people with certain common features will also evidence similarities in their word associations.

Deese (1962, 1965) has suggested, in regard to the correlation between the stimulus word and the response word, that the distribution of response words to a given stimulus word be designated as the stimulus word's "associative meaning".

If the associative meaning of a stimulus is given by the distribution of responses to that stimulus, then two stimuli may be said to have the same associative meaning when the distribution of associates to them is identical. Two stimuli overlap or resemble one another in associative meaning to the extent that they have the same distribution of associates. By comparing the distribution of response words to any two stimulus words, one can make quantifiable judgements how similar or dissimilar any two stimulus words are.

It is this overlap in the distributions of responses to various stimulus words which we will utilize when constructing a Term Association Thesaurus (TA-Thesaurus).

3. THE TA-THESAURUS

Since the amount of terms used in documentation language are too numerous to memorize, aids are available in the form of thesauri. By definition, a thesaurus is a compilation of terms showing synonyms, hierarchical and other relationships and dependencies, the function of which is to provide a standardized controlled vocabulary for information storage and retrieval. It tells the user whether a particular word has been accepted as a descriptor, i.e., allowed term or, if not, show the user how the word is expressed in the indexing language. In addition to assisting the user in the choice of search terms, a thesaurus also functions as a help in the formulation of the conceptual context of the knowledge of a specific subject area.

A thesaurus is constructed on the basis of referential and/or denotative meaning of the terms by means of lexicographical tools. These structures are expressed in the logical hierarchical subject relationships in the form of cross-references such as generic to specific, part to whole, etc. For instance, a generic relationship can be presented in this way:

FEAR
Narrower term: Fear of life

FEAR OF LIFE
Broader term: Fear

A part whole relationship can be specified as follows:

DENMARK
Narrower term: Copenhagen

COPENHAGEN
Broader term: Denmark

The relationship between subjects in conventional thesauri may also cut across hierarchical categories. They occur when two terms are mentally connected without being part of the same hierarchy. These are the so-called related terms, i.e.

BIRDS
Related term: Ornithology

In order to reduce subjectivity, the notion of relatedness is usually restricted in conventional thesauri by the requirement that one of the terms in an association relationship be a necessary component in any definition of the other. In general, though, use of related terms has a low priority due to their potential subjectivity.

The essential difference between a conventional thesaurus and the proposed TA-Thesaurus is that the structure of the latter is based only on the relationships in associative meaning of the subject terms or descriptors in its vocabulary. The associative meanings of these subject terms are determined in word association experiments, in which subject terms are used as stimulus words. The cross-references between subject terms are based on the relationships, which reflect the overlap of the associative meanings of these subject terms. In our pilot study, three relationships of this kind are to be considered between any two subject terms with overlapping associative meanings, namely:

1. strong associative overlap (SAO),

2. medium associative overlap (MAO), and

3. weak associative overlap (WAO).

In order to define these three relations of overlap in associative meaning, we need to introduce first a measure of overlap of associative responses to any two stimulus terms. A number of such measures have been described by Marshall and Cofer (1963). We chose to develop a measure of similarity of associative responses different from those described in the above mentioned paper, since none of them turned out to be quite satisfactory for our purpose.

The measure of similarity of associative responses used in this study is defined as follows. Let S_x and S_y be two stimulus words (i.e. subject terms of a TA-Thesaurus) and let R_1, R_2,.....,R_k be the terms which are common response terms to stimulus terms S_x and S_y. Let n_i^x be the number of occurrences of response word R_i in the set of responses to the stimulus words S_x and n_i^y be the number of occurrences of the same response word R_i in the set of responses to the stimulus word S_y, $i = 1, 2,.....,k$. Finally, let N_x be the total number of responses to the stimulus word S_x and N_y the total number of responses to the stimulus word S_y. The measure of similarity of associative responses to stimulus words S_x and S_y is

$$\sigma_{xy} = \frac{1}{(N_x + N_y)/2} \sum_{i=1}^{k} \left(\min\{n_i^x, n_i^y\} + \frac{\min\{n_i^x, n_i^y\}}{\max\{n_i^x, n_i^y\}} \left| n_i^x - n_i^y \right| \right)$$

We illustrate the computation of this measure by an example. Let S_1 = HOUSE and S_2 = MOTHER. Assume that word association experiments produced the following response data for these two stimulus words. For the stimulus word HOUSE, presented to 38 subjects, the responses and their frequencies, i.e. the number of occurrences, are

HOME   18

MOTHER   10

CHILD   6

ROOF   2

RED   1

LAKE   1

and for the stimulus word MOTHER, presented to 50 subjects, the response words and their frequencies are

CHILD	24
FLOWER	12
LOVE	8
HOME	3
LAKE	1
VACATION	1
CANDY	1

We further assume with Deese (1962) that each stimulus word first triggers itself as a response (so-called 'implicit response'), an assumption, which is suggested by the common notions about the association experiment as well as by the analysis-by-synthesis approach (Hoermann, 1979). Accordingly, we add to the response data for the stimulus word HOUSE the response item ('implicit response')

HOUSE	38

and to the response data for the stimulus word MOTHER the item ('implicit response')

MOTHER	50

where the associated frequencies 38 and 50 are equal to the number of subjects in the experiments. For this data we now have:

* common response words to stimulus words S_1 and S_2:
R_1 = HOME, R_2 = MOTHER, R_3 = CHILD, R_4 = LAKE.

* $n_1^1 = 18$, $n_2^1 = 10$, $n_3^1 = 6$, $n_4^1 = 1$

* $n_1^2 = 3$, $n_2^2 = 50$, $n_3^2 = 24$, $n_4^2 = 1$,

and the coefficient of similarity of associative meaning of the words S_1 and S_2 is

$$\sigma_{12} = \frac{1}{(76 + 100)/2} \left[(3 + \frac{3}{18} \cdot |3 - 18|) + (10 + \frac{10}{50} \cdot |10 - 50|) = \right.$$

$$(6 + \frac{6}{24} \cdot |6 - 24|) + (1 + \frac{1}{1} \cdot |1 - 1|) = \frac{1}{88} \left[5.5 + \right.$$

$$\left. 18 + 10.5 + 1 \right] = 0.3977$$

The proposed measure of similarity of associative responses has very attractive properties, which none of the measures described by Marshall and Cofer (1963) possessed in their totality. The proposed measure σ_{xy} takes values in the closed interval $0, 1$. Its value is equal to zero if and only if the two sets of associative responses have no response word in common, and it is equal to 1 if and only if the two associative response sets are completely identical. If the response sets are identical except for the 'implicit responses' and the 'implicit response' word to the one stimulus term does not occur as an explicit response word to the other, then the value of the similarity coefficient σ_{xy} is equal to 0.5. This is, again, an intuitively satisfactory result, since in the latter case the overlap between the two response sets is exactly half the number of their elements. Finally, the proposed measure can be applied even to associative response sets of different cardinalities and, if a response word common to both associative response sets has different response frequencies, its contribution to the similarity of the corresponding two stimulus terms is appropriately weighted.

Using the similarity measure σ_{xy}, we now define the three relations of associative overlap, i.e., the three relations of similarity in associative meaning on a set of subject terms as follows. Let x and y be two arbitrary subject terms, elements of the set S. Let T_1 and T_2 be real numbers and such that $0 \leq T_1 < T_2 \leq 1$. Then

1. The pair (x,y) of subject terms is related in the sense of weak associative overlap or simply WAO-related if and only if $\sigma_{xy} \in [0,T_1)$.

2. The pair (x,y) of subject terms is related in the sense of medium associative overlap or simply MAO-related if and only if $\sigma_{xy} \in [T_1,T_2]$.

3. The pair (x,y) of subject terms is related in the sense of strong associative overlap or simply SAO-related if and only if $\sigma_{xy} \in (T_2,1]$.

A literature search on the application of the word association method in this context resulted in references only to the "associative thesaurus" of A. Kiss (1975). The goal of that project was an "associative thesaurus" for a greater part of the English vocabulary. Kiss concludes that word associations have a direct relationship to "relevance", explicated by Kiss as "what goes with what".

There are, however, several differences bestween Kiss' associative thesaurus and the TA-Thesaurus of this study. Firstly, there is an essential difference in the methodology. Kiss used not only response words to a series of selected stimulus words as the basis for his word association network, but he also compiled the response words to the initial response words – up to several "steps" removed from the original stimulus words. Whatever interest this method may have, it is not applicable to this project. Kiss was concerned with associative stimulus response relations and hence he did not have a well-defined practical area of application – a lack which makes testing of the actual usefulness of the results difficult.

4. THE EXPERIMENTAL DATA BASE FOR THE STUDY OF ASSOCIATIVE SEARCH METHODS

The experimental data base, which was selected for this study, is the AM2 data base developed at the Library School of Copenhagen (Pejtersen, 1983). The AM2 data base is composed of 171 Danish novels written by authors publishing for the first time between 1918 and 1938, including their subsequent publications up to 1980. The 171 novels are classified according to a multidimensional classification system designed as part of a study of fiction retrieval (Pejtersen, 1983, 1984). Library users' fiction inquiries and needs, obtained in a series of user-librarian dialogues, formed the basis for this system. The novels are classified into a number of user-relevant dimensions such as subject, time, place, milieu, emotional experience, recognition, information, readability, etc. The content of each novel is classified according to this scheme, and is represented by an annotation in natural language and by a number of controlled subject terms. The documents in the AM2 data base can be searched online with the Boolean operations. Only searching by controlled subject terms or descriptors is of interest in the context of the present study. Controlled subject terms were selected as the basis for the construction of the TA-Thesaurus, and only search entries by controlled subject terms of the data base will be used. Examples of subject terms from the AM2 data base are: school, puberty, generation gaps, workers, white collar workers, families, the occupation, depressions, and anxiety.

. The AM2 data base has been chosen for two major reasons. Economic considerations necessitated selecting a data base of a more moderate size and selecting a modest number of terms as stimulus words. It will also be easier to make the first evaluation of the efficiency of the TA-Thesaurus assuming that the effect of such aids will be more pronounced using a less specialized vocabulary of a fiction data base compared to a scientific data base. The formulation of possible design modifications for the improvement of the search function is perhaps easier in this type of experimental search system. Nevertheless, the use of the AM2 data base in the first experiment does not mean abandoning the intention of generalization of the results so that they would still be applicable to the design of dialogues and interfaces for use in man-machine communication in a wider context.

5. COMPILATION OF WORD ASSOCIATION DATA FOR THE TA-THESAURUS

Word associations have been established for various speaker communities and are referred to as word association norms. There exists today a number of norm lists covering an extensive number of words and encompassing quite a few groupings of people. Most of these studies are American (Bousfield, 1961; Gerow & Pollio, 1965; Kent and Rosanoff, 1910; Postman and Keppel, 1970). However, norms do also exist in other countries.

A review of published word association norms indicated that the existing norms cannot be used for this project.. Only about 30% of the controlled subject terms of the AM2 data base can be found in the existing word association norms. It is also doubtful, from a methodological point of view, whether American word association norms compiled at different historical periods can be generalized to include Danish word associations in the 1980's. Therefore, it was decided to conduct word association experiments and obtain more associations as responses to the subject terms in the AM2 data base used as stimulus words. This procedure was methodologically more sound and yet feasible and not too costly.

Two data files were established on the Library School's Nord 100 computer for the compilation of word associations. The file was called "association program" and consisted of 223 controlled subject terms from the AM2 data base. The "association synonyms" file consisted of 179 synonyms of the controlled terms. The subject terms in the "association program" file were used as stimulus words presented to the subject in a different and random order. The subject terms in the "association synonyms" file were also presented to all the subjects as stimulus words, but in a fixed order. According to Szalay and Deese (1978), the frequency distribution of response words stabilizes itself at the level of approximately 50 subjects. The subjects in this experiment were 50 library school students. By choosing student librarians we were assured of a relatively homogeneous group of subjects. Word association data was collected online, each person entering his or her response words directly into the computer. The subjects were presented with each stimulus word three times. Each time they responded with one response word . Thus, every stimulus word has

Subject No.	Time	Response Time/Secs.	Stimulus Word No.	Response Word No.
24	10:13:34	8	222 Marriage	1 Love
24	10:13:42	11	222 Marriage	2 Happiness
24	10:13:54	7	222 Marriage	3 Fidelity
24	10:23:30	6	45 Divorce	1 Sadness
24	10:23:37	10	45 Divorce	2 Infidelity
24	10:23:48	5	45 Divorce	3 Hate
21	14:11:26	13	81 Jobs	1 Identity
21	14:11:39	5	81 Jobs	2 Social Role
21	14:11:45	5	81 Jobs	3 Education
21	14:16:16	20	172 W. Germany	1 Discipline
21	14:16:36	7	172 W. Germany	2 Diligence
21	14:16:44	21	172 W. Germany	3 Factor of Power

Figure 1. A Sample of Stimulus Words and Associated Responses.

three different responses associated with it, and each response word is numbered as either number one, number two, or number three. Figure 1 shows a couple of stimulus words and their respective associative response words (response time includes writing time).

The subjects generated word associations to all the 223 subject terms and to the 179 synonym words. Altogether it took the subjects from five to seven hours to produce and enter into the computer a total of 1206 response words to the 402 stimulus words. Because of the great number of stimulus words, every shift to a new stimulus word was marked by a graphic sign.

Prior to the experiment, each subject received written instructions and an oral briefing about the experiment, followed by a demonstration of the procedure on the computer and a short training session. Essentially, the instructions addressed the following issues:

1. The purpose of the experiment, i.e. the development of a term association thesaurus as a new retrieval aid for on-line searching of bibliographic data bases.

2. The subjects' task, i.e. to record spontaneously the first word that comes to mind when he/she is exposed to a stimulus word which is a subject term of the AM2 data base. Three different response words for every stimulus word were to be entered into the computer. The subject was permitted to relax a short while after each new stimulus word so as to receive the next stimulus word with an open mind. The subjects were told that there were no correct or incorrect associations.

3. Special situations requiring subjects attention. The subjects were instructed to avoid sentences and long digressions, to avoid associations to response words which they had previously produced instead of associations to the stimulus word, and to avoid taking recourse to routine answers such as word-rhyming. Though they were told that there were no right

or wrong answers, they were requested to avoid very private
responses or responses which derived from the working
environment of the experiment.

The subsequent interviews with the subjects revealed that they found
the task an easy one despite the great number of stimulus words. The first
response words usually came quickly while difficulties with the third word
sometimes occurred. The participants felt that they revealed something
interesting about their inner life. They often found their own responses
surprising, which suggests that word association studies actually tap
something of psychological importance.

On the other hand, our pilot studies revealed the importance of knowing
the subjects' reaction to computer messages during the experiments. For
instance, we experienced that subjects might perceive messages from the
machine as the computer's value judgements of their associations instead of
procedural or error messages related to their operations of the computer.
This situation was remedied by changing the computer's messages and by a
careful briefing of the subjects about these messages.

Also, we experienced an error rate or usage deviation of the language
of about 15%, which might affect the viability of a computer based analysis
of the extent of overlap of the responses to the subject terms. Therefore,
all the subjects' associations were manually proofread in order to eliminate trivial errors before the statistical analysis.

The main morphological and technical inconsistencies encountered were
for instance: singular vs. plural, adjectives vs. substantives, definite
vs. indefinite articles, compound words written as one instead of two
words, the number of spaces between words, the use of complete sentences,
ordinary typing errors, and, finally, various (acceptable or erroneous)
ways of spelling.

Another problem, also relevant, although not touched upon here, is the
use of obvious synonyms. Unfortunately, this problem cannot be eliminated
just by giving the subjects appropriate instructions. The appearance of
synonyms will, therefore, be the subject of a selective, manual analysis
later in the experiment in order to understand their frequency, character,
and potential influence on our results.

6. PRELIMINARY ANALYSIS OF THE DATA

The first analysis of the response data was focused on the question to
what extent there existed overlapping responses to the stimulus words,
i.e., the subject terms of the thesaurus. To begin with, only the response
words to the 223 stimulus terms from the AM2 data base were analyzed.
Therefore, the results discussed below do not incude the response words of
the 179 synonyms. Each subject's associative responses were printed together with the stimulus words in the numerical order of response words
together with response/writing time for each response word. The data was
sorted according to a key that compiled all the identical response words in
alphabetical order.

Figure 2 gives an example of seven stimulus words selected from 40 different stimulus words which all had the response word "Suppression" in
common. Suppression occurred 83 times in total, and the figure shows the
stimulus words with associative response "Suppression" occurring with a
frequency greater than 4.

Thus, the TA-Thesaurus will contain mutual cross references between the

Stimulus Words	Response Words	Frequency of Occurrence
Display of Force	Suppression	8
Revolt	Suppression	7
Struggle for Liberty	Suppression	7
Absolute Monarchy	Suppression	6
Fascism	Suppression	4
Imperialism	Suppression	4
Servants	Suppression	4

Figure 2. A Sample of Stimulus Words (Subject Terms) with
a Common Response Word SUPPRESSION.

seven subject terms by means of their relatedness due to overlap in
response words. If, for example, "absolute monarchy" is the entry, the
the references will appear as illustrated in Figure 3.

If every one of the 223 stimulus words were connected to the other 222
stimulus words through overlap in associative meaning – then the number of
related pairs of stimulus words would be 24,753 (or 223x222/2). We did not
expect that the actual amount of overlap would be anything near the 24,753.
Surprisingly, the number of pairwise overlapping responses turned out to be
very great, namely 20,385. This means that more than 4/5 of the stimulus
words had some degree of overlap in associative meaning with other stimulus
words. Naturally, this number includes also the weakest possible overlap
between any two stimulus words, namely, one subject giving the same
response words to two different stimulus words. Therefore, the next step
in the analysis of the data was to find out how many different response
words contributed to any one of the 20,385 overlaps. This analysis showed
that associative relatedness occurred between all the 223 stimulus words
with a threshold of 5 different response words in common.

7. FUTURE RESEARCH DIRECTIONS

Before developing a term association thesaurus it is necessary to
determine a threshold for the number of response words that are necessary
in order to accept a relationship between two subject terms. Such a
threshold for the degree of relatedness between subject terms can only be
determined in relation to the character of the data.

Absolute Monarchy

Related Terms: Display of Force
Fascism
Imperialism
Revolt
Servants
Struggle for Liberty

Figure 3. Terms Related in Associative
Meaning to ABSOLUTE MONARCHY.

Once the TA-Thesaurus has been developed, experimental procedures for searching the AM2 data base will be developed in order to test the efficiency of a TA-Thesaurus as an aid in browsing, in query formulation, and information retrieval. The experiment will include browsing and searching the AM2 data base assisted by the traditional thesaurus, with the assistance of both the traditional thesaurus and the TA-Thesaurus, and searches assisted only by the TA-Thesaurus. Searches of the AM2 data base will be followed up by the searcher's online evaluation of the formulation of the query and the retrieved items. The analysis of the searches will include variables of thesaurus type, inquiry type, and user type. Although it has been considered to use recall and precision measurements, the other methods for evaluation of the efficiency of the different thesauri types will be considered.

ACKNOWLEDGEMENTS

This project is supported by grants from the Danish Research Council for the Humanities, the Scandinavian "Nordinfo" Research Council, the Royal School of Librarianship, Risø National Laboratory, and the School of Information and Computer Science, Georgia Institute of Technology, Atlanta.

REFERENCES

Bousfield, W. A., et al., 1961, The Connecticut Free Associational Norms, The University of Connecticut, Technical Report No. 35.

Cramer, P. W., 1968, Word Association, Academic Press, New York, NY.

Deese, J., 1962, "On the Structure of Associative Meaning", Psychological Review, 69, pp. 161-175.

Deese, J., 1965, The Structure of Association in Language and Thought, John Hopkins Press.

Deese, J., and Hamilton, H. W., 1974, "Marking and Propositional Effects in Associations to Compounds:, American Journal of Psychology, 87, pp. 1-15.

Find, S., and Pejtersen, A. M., 1984, Manual til AMP-, AM2- og ABC-databaserne, The Royal School of Librarianship, Copenhagen.

Galton, F., 1880, "Psychometric Experiments", Brain, 2, pp. 149-162.

Gerow, J. R., and PJollio, H. R., 1965, Word Association, Frequency of Occurrence, and Semantic Differential Norms for 360 Stimulus Words, The University of Tennessee, Department of Psychology, Technical Report No. 1.

Glucksberg, S., and Danks, J. H., 1975, Experimental Psycholinguistics, Lawrence Earlbaum Association, Hillsdale, NY.

Hormann, H., j1979, Psycholinguistics, Springer Verlag, New York, NY.

Hutchins, W. J., 1975, Languages of Indexing and Classification - a Linguistic Study of Structures and Functions, Peter Peregrinus, Stevenage, Herts.

International Organization for Standardization, 1981, Guidelines for the Establishment and Development of Monolingual Thesauri, ISO 2788, Draft

2nd Edition. (Published by Unesco as Document P61-81/ns15, 1981.)

Kent, H. G., and Rosanoff, A. J., 1910, "A Study of Association in Insanity", 67, pp. 37-96 and pp. 317-390.

Kiss, A., 1975, "An Associative Thesaurus of English: Structural Analysis of a Large Relevance Network", Studies in Long Term Memory, Kennedy, A., and Wilkes, AJ., eds., Wiley & Sons, London.

Marshall, G. R., and Cofer, C. N., 1963, "Associative Indices as Measures of Word Relatedness: A Summary and Comparison of Ten Methods", Journal of Verbal Learning and Verbal Behavior, 1, pp. 408-421.

Palermo, D. S., and Jenkins, J. J., 1964, Word Association Norms: Grade School through College, Minneapolis, University of Minnesota Press, p. 40.

Pejtersen, A. M., 1984, "Design of a Computer-Aided User-System Dialogue Based on an Analysis of Users' Search Behaviour", Social Science Information Studies, (4), pp. 167-173.

Pejtersen, A. M., and Austin, J., 1983/4, "Fiction Retrieval: Experimental Design and Evaluation of a Search System Based on Users' Value Criteria. Part 1 and 2", Journal of Documentation, 39, (4), pp. 230-246 and 40, (1), pp. 25-35.

Postman, L. L., and Keppel, G., 1970, Norms of Word Association, Academic Press, New York, NY.

Szaley, L. B., and Deese, J., 1978, Subjective Meaning and Culture, Lawrence Earlbaum Association, Hillsdale, NY.

USE OF COMPUTER GAMES TO TEST EXPERIMENTAL TECHNIQUES AND COGNITIVE MODELS

J. Rasmussen

Riso National Laboratory
DK 4000 Roskilde, Denmark

Abstract: In design of computer systems, one attempts to match the interface to the needs of the users by a careful consideration of the mental representations and information processing strategies which will be effective for the various tasks of the users. In this effort, it is important to consider that the task repertoire will include familiar work routines as well as occasional requirements for problem solving and, in addition, that the system should be able to support a novice without frustrating the highly skilled users.

For this purpose, an experimental technique is needed which is less time consuming than, for instance, analysis of verbal protocols. The paper discusses the requirements to an experimental setup suited to study mental strategies, their evolution with training, and the related error mechanisms. It is concluded that computer games are well suited for this purpose due to their well structured, closed world and to the amount of data that can be collected from subjects while acquiring a high level of skill.

INTRODUCTION

In design of computer based decision support systems, one attempts to match display contents and formats to the needs of the users during their varying work conditions. In executive management as well as supervisory process control, decision making involves resource management including information processing tasks such as state identification and diagnosis, goal setting, and planning. Each of these tasks can be performed by a variety of mental processing strategies leading to the same ultimate product but having very different process characteristics in terms of requirements for processing capacity, prior experience, memory load, etc.

A systematic design, therefore, has to be based on a careful consideration of the mental representations and information processing strategies which will be effective for the various decision tasks by users in different work situations. The basic design problem will be to predict the subjective performance criteria that will control the users' choice of mental processing strategies during the actual work situations, i.e., whether the set of normative strategies chosen as a basis for system design does in fact match the set chosen by the user group. In this effort, it is important to consider that the task repertoire will include familiar work routines as well as occasional requirements for problem solving, and, in addition, the system should be able to support a novice without frustrating the highly skilled users.

Management information systems as well as industrial process systems are becoming increasingly centralized and, consequently, effects of decision errors are increasingly serious. Concurrently, there is a tendency towards decision support systems tailored to the requirements of the individual application. This leads to a severe need for tools to verify the design basis, and to demonstrate that design targets are met.

To this end, an experimental technique is needed to identify the mental information processing strategies applied in a complex task environment in which the subjects are exposed to familiar as well as less familiar problems. Verbal protocols have been used for this purpose, but their collection and analysis are extremely time consuming, and more systematic and effective methods for analysis of human-computer interaction data are needed. The present paper describes our effort to design an experimental setup to test the use of systematic algorithms for identifying strategies in terms of patterns in sequences of interaction data. To plan this experiment, it will be necessary to consider a framework for modeling human performance.

MODELING SYSTEM USERS

For evaluation of interface design, it will be important to identify and analyze the errors which are made by the system users. When considering a highly adapted human in error-free performance, a model of the performance will, in the ultimate consequence, be a model of the task requirements to which the human has adapted during training. How specifically this representation will reflect task characteristics depends on the dynamic characteristics of the task and the human controller. For slow task categories, i.e., slow compared with the human response times, the representation of the task may be very rudimentary, since proper performance can be based on simple feed-back tactics. When delay of feed-back information about the outcome becomes long compared to the pace of action, more effective responses in terms of stored behavioral patterns which can be released in an open-loop control mode becomes necessary, and the representations of task characteristics becomes more complex. In this way, the "decision model" representing error-free performance is independent of human characteristics, and can, in principle, be found from analysis of the task itself, although observation of the actual performance of skilled subjects may be very fruitful for identification of effective "tricks" and heuristics.

A performance model will be a model of a human user, only when a representation of error performance is included. Research on human error clearly indicates that, in addition to reflecting limits of capability, basic error mechanisms are closely related to the mechanisms behind learning and adaptation. Frequently, errors reflect interference from the vast repertoire of trained behavior patterns, possibly disturbing the actual performance in a particular, less familiar situation. This means that the manifestation of the error mechanism in terms of actual performance depends not only on the present task, but on the total background of routines relevant for the actual task context. In consequence, a model of human performance during less familiar task environment will have to include a representaion of the total, available performance repertoire.

Therefore, development of models of human performance, including unfamiliar task requirements, in a real life work context is a nearly unbounded

enterprise, and it will be very difficult to test an experimental concept
or a model, unless a limited task ensemble can be found that has little
similarity to general everyday activities (in order to avoid uncontrolled
interference) and which, nevertheless, gives a person the opportunity to
develop high skill. Several modern computer games appear to present such a
task environment, which in particular is exciting enough to make a subject
willing to spend the time needed for skill development.

Another advantage of computer games is the amount of behavioral data
which can be collected systematically. In general, research to identify
the mental strategies used in a task requires the use of verbal protocols,
interviews, etc. Such methods are time consuming and interfere with performance. More automatic analysis of systematically recorded activity
sequences will be helpful to detect and identify different behavioral
patterns, and the development of patterns during training periods. In
addition, on-line analysis will be useful to focus interviews and discussion with subjects after an experimental session on the relevant aspects
of the session. This should support the identification of the decision
strategies in terms of higher level information processing concepts by
means of a joint analysis of the data patterns found in the records and of
the rules of the game. Probably, on-line analysis could be arranged with
automatic alert of the experimentator to question the player.

In general, several different strategies may be chosen to perform a
given task, and the one chosen will depend on the performance criteria
chosen by the person considering the actual task demand—mental resource
margins. In complex or dynamically demanding tasks, the one chosen will
reflect human limiting properties, and the errors made when requirements
are increased may be important data for model development. In consequence,
test of a model of human error mechanisms will also be facilitated by the
amount of data and the bounded repertoire of routines which is found in
computer games.

MODES OF HUMAN INFORMATION PROCESSING

In order to establish the context of the development of data analysis
algorithms, a discussion will be useful of the adaptation mechanisms in
terms of three levels of cognitive control derived from analysis of human
errors (Rasmussen, 1980).

In this model, the final stage of adaptation is the skill-based level
where automated routines are based on subconscious time-space manipulations
of objects of symbols in a familiar scenery. During training, the necessary sensorimotor patterns develop while the activity is controlled by
other means. From a control point of view, two problems must be solved
during training. First, the activity must be synchronized with the behavior of the environment in order to meet the proper purpose at all.
Secondly, the activity must be optimized to form a smooth and efficient
pattern within the boundary of the task.

A good example illustrating the synchronization and optimization problem is learning to ride a bicycle. The control of the activity during the
initial phases of synchronization and formation of the sequence of acts can
be obtained in various ways. It may happen directly at the skill-based
level by imitation and trial-and-error, as for instance,, learning to play
an instrument by ear or children learning to talk, etc. In some cases,
synchronization presents a problem – as by walking, riding a bicycle – and
an external assistant with a hand-on-the-saddle kind of support will be
effective. In other cases, control at the rule-based behavioral level will
be efficient during development of the automated skill. At this level,

behavior is controlled by a set of rules of know-how, e.g., cook-book
recipes, which is activated by association from stereotype signs. The
rules may be obtained from an instructor or a textbook, as is typically the
case in learning to drive a car, to operate tools and technical devices
supplied with an instruction manual, or to manage social interactions from
"rules of good manners". And, finally, persons with a basic knowledge of
the structure and functioning will be able to generate themselves, by
thought experiments at the <u>knowledge-based level</u>, a set of rules to control
activities related to various purposes during early phases of learning.

An important point is that it is <u>not</u> the behavioral patterns of the
higher levels that are becoming automated skills. Automated time-space
behavioral patterns are developing while they are controlled and supervised
by the higher level activities - which will eventually deteriorate - and
their basis as knowledge and rules may deteriorate. In fact, the period
when this is happening may lead to errors due to interference between a not
fully developed sensorimotor skill and a gradually deteriorated rule system. This kind of interference is known also to highly skilled musicians
when they occasionally start to analyze their performance during fast pas-
sages. It seems to be plausible also that this effect can play a role for
pilots of about 100 hours flying experience, which is known among pilots to
be an error-prone period.

Anderson (1982) discusses a similar distinction between knowledge-based
behavior which he labels the "declarative" stage, and the rule/skill-based
level, called the "procedural stage", a distinction, which is identical
with that discussed above, being based on the distinction between control
by a structural model and by rules. Anderson describes the transfer of
control by the computer metaphor knowledge "compilation", which, however,
should be used with some caution. According to the view argued in the
present paper, "rules" may not be derived from higher level knowledge by
"compilation" but based on an entirely different information collected and
organized during the knowledge-based control period.

During the first phases of skill acquisition, the activity will be controlled by separate cues which are defined individually and related to
rules controlling very elementary acts. As skill develops, cues of more
global nature in terms of the data pattern they include and depending on
temporal and situational aspects will be adopted, and rules will be related
to activity patterns rather than acts, i.e., intentions are expressed in
terms of goals rather than acts to perform. Finally, the whole task is
automated and is performed without conscious awareness as long as unexpected deviations do not occur, and the higher the skill, the less probable
will unexpected occurrences be. In this phase, the initial expression of a
rule as "it's now 25 mph and I have to change gear" is replaced by the
overall intention: "it's four o'clock and I have to go home", and the conscious mind can start planning the weekend activities while the skill
brings you home through rush hours.

A typical computer game scenario may be illustrative for a more detailed discussion of the features in a behavioral sequence to identify by
the data analysis.

One scene is the following: You are piloting a space craft which can
be placed translatorily according to order and fire a laser gun horizontal-
ly in the flight direction. Enemy crafts are descending from the upper
right-hand corner of the display and have to be shot down before gaining
too much speed, in which case you will not be able to aim your gun without
being involved in a head-on collision. The initial attempt will typically
be a feed-back mode attack in which you dynamically aim at an enemy craft
and then fire. This is possible in the first rounds of combat, but in

later phases the speed makes this mode difficult. Playing the game, you
rapidly realize the stereotypical behavior of the enemy, and by trial-and-
error, i.e,. rule identification directly in the rule-based domain, find a
very effective open-loop strategy:

- Position your ship in the upper left corner, a couple of centimeters
  below the top.

- Shoot a couple of rounds starting at the whining entry sound of the
  first enemy craft - and you won't miss.

- Move your craft downwards one centimeter or so and wait for the
  entry sound of the next craft, and so on.

Another scene involves an enemy craft which is aiming at your ship and
firing rounds from two guns immediately when aligned. The speed of response of the enemy craft is too high to allow a simple feed-back strategy,
but noticing the control law of the craft and the time constant of responses you may, by knowledge-based reasoning, find an effective open-loop
strategy which is:

- Position your craft at the bottom of the display.

- When the enemy enters at the top, start moving upwards and shoot
  continuously in passing (since the enemy only shoots on aligned
  crafts, they will miss a moving target).

- If you miss, keep moving up and down and shoot in passing.

That the strategy is entirely open-loop is proved by the fact that it
is effective even though the enemies are moving more rapidly and become
invisible during later scenarios of the game.

In both cases, the players' responses will initially be more or less
random control actions to get information on the working of control keys
and response patterns of the elements of the game display. Gradually,
stereotype action sequences will emerge, with a continuous development also
of a stereotype timing pattern, which reflects the basic rules of the game
and is synchronized with, but not necessarily controlled by, elements of
the game.

The identification of the successful strategies will require pattern
identification algorithms that are capable of finding recurrent sequence
patterns in the recorded response data with greatly varying timing properties in the initial learning phases.

The credibility of the analysis will be higher if alternative strategies are possible in a game, and can be found by the analysis program.
Too many degrees of freedom in the game may, however, be a disadvantage in
the initial development phases, since too many different hypotheses may be
formed by the player, and cause switching back and forth in the strategy
forming experiments.

To cope with the complexity of data sequences, it may be necessary to
convert the raw data to a higher "semantic" level in terms referring to the
game content, not to be forced to identify also the basic transformation
from joystick movements to game context by the analysis program. The basic
idea is to find recurrent relationship between problems and action (not
movement) patterns, i.e., a set of production rules: if (state) - then
(action), at the detailed tactical level which then by analysis of verbal
reports could be related to higher level strategies.

If the game is simple, and only invites one or a few competing strategies, it may not be necessary to analyze at a semantic level in the initial analyses. If it is assumed that with training, strategies develop which are to a large degree "open-loop tactical sequences" which reflect the stereotypical rules behind the behavior of the "sprite" of the game, it should be possible to detect the stages in adaptation by analyzing only the elementary movement patterns. If, however, several different strategies are possible, depending upon the game content, recoding to higher semantic levels, and concurrent analysis of the state of the game and of the action sequence will be necessary to separate different strategical approaches.

CONSIDERATION OF ERROR MECHANISMS

An analysis of the <u>successful</u> strategies will lead to a model of a "perfect player". It is, in fact, a model of the game rather than a model of the player. It will be converted to a model of human performance by introducing a representation of typical human heuristics and error mechanisms. Since the game context is planned to be a tool for verification of models suited for simulation of human behavior and for development of experimental tools, it is essential to focus on identification of the conditions when acts or sequences of acts are erroneous or counterproductive.

Simulation of successful performance is, in consequence of the arguments above, no test of the validity of a model. Only test of the limits of proper performance is an acceptable test (compare Popper's arguments). In the experiments, errors are to be defined as variations with reference to patterns of behavior which have previously proven effective, not with reference to the formally correct response. In addition, errors are found when the habitual responses are ineffective due to variations in the game scenario compared with the more frequent settings.

Identifications of typical errors as a function of the degrees of adaptation can be very important, considering the arguments that errors are necessary parts of the learning process (Rasmussen, 1985; Reason, 1985). Different errors should be expected during phases when the player is making experiments in order to identify effective heuristics at the rule-based level, and, respectively, to fine-tune skills at the sensorimotor level. This means, however, that the pattern identification algorithms should be able to establish reference for identification of the individual erroneous acts, and for their categorization.

METHODS FOR IDENTIFICATION OF SEQUENTIAL PATTERNS

Several methods for systematic (automatic) identification of patterns in records of human-computer interaction sequences are being considered in the present experiment. In studies of animal ethology and human non-verbal behavior, several approaches have been taken to systematic identification of sequential patterns.

Different temporal clustering techniques have been used: Delius (1969) aimed at the problem of detecting patterns in the behavior of skylarks by searching for a sequential, temporal relationship between two behavior elements whatever might occur between them. In order to solve this problem, correlational techniques were used to assess the tendency of the elements to have a certain time distance. By varying the length of the distance, Delius was able to show strong temporal correlations between behaviors for certain interval lengths. Dawkins (1976), on the other hand, aimed only at an identification of frequent sequential "chunks" in order-only records of behavior. The behavior records were long sequences of symbols, signifying the order of occurrence of a number of mutually exclusive categories of behavior elements, and the algorithm then counts the frequency of all different pairs of symbols. By repeating this process, a hierarchical structure can be identified. Based on these approaches, Magnusson (1982) developed an algorithm for temporal configuration analysis which has been used to analyze non-verbal communication of children. The algorithm is based on an assumption of a Posion distribution of elements in a sequence, and detects in a hierarchical structure, sequences which are violating this assumption in a statistically significant degree. The method is especially adapted for effective use of small data samples, and the level of significance accepted for the analysis can be varied.

The data used in our previous analysis of verbal protocols from electronic maintenance (Rasmussen and Jensen, 1973) have been analyzed by this program, but the amount of data was insufficient for conclusive judgement of the applicability of the method. Some very preliminary indications may be worthwhile for a closer look: the program (analyzing for temporal distances irrespectively of elements in-between, and with the order of elements interpreted as uniform temporal ordering) did not identify the strategies previously identified by manual analysis, (due to the complexity of protocols compared with the amount of data?) but found some sequential order in those parts of the protocols where subjects were in difficulties, and the task content, therefore, lost control of performance (resort to stereotypical human patterns of cursing and taking coffee breaks). With caution, the conclusion may be that the human computer interaction sequences from our game experiments should be analyzed for more free temporal patterns during phases controlled by elementary human traits as well as for more strictly sequential order during phases controlled by game characteristics.

An interesting possibility will be to correlate the results of an automatic pattern identification with the contents of verbal protocols or interviews: To what extent are subjects consciously aware of their strategies, and realize their shifts between different strategies? To this end, verbal protocols will be taken for some of the sessions, and the records analyzed manually and by means of visual pattern identification from graphical computer logs of coded records.

LEARNING CURVES

For evaluation of a new interface system, a quality measure to consider may be related to the learning process, e.g., to the speed with which users develop effective heuristics, and to the characteristics of these heuristics with respect to errors and error recovery when task conditions are changing.

An interesting study, therefore, will be the use of computer games and algorithms for identification of recurrent sequences for analysis of learning curves. Several classic studies are considering the shape of learning curves. These studies have led to a discussion of the question whether or not learning curves have plateaus, and whether the shape is most adequately represented by a mathematical power law or an exponential function. A recent review is given by Newell et al. (1981). The focus of previous studies of learning curves has been behavioristic analyses only considering the product of behavior in terms of, e.g., speed-accuracy measures, no attention has been paid to an analysis of the strategical structure of mental processing tasks. Furthermore, the tasks studied typically have been perceptual-motor tasks such as cigar making, mirror tracking, scanning for visual targets, etc. In consequence, learning (practice learning) may largely involve optimization and reorganization of behavior within the same level of behavioral control by chunking elements of a large repertoire (hence the "mixture" and "chunking" explanation of power curves). The classical context, for instance, for arguments against plateaus has been the learning of Morse codes. If, however, learning involves shifts in the level of cognitive control because the task may be solved by basically different mental strategies, learning curves with pronounced plateaus should be expected. In the present analysis of computer games by methods aiming at a description of the process characteristics also of the mental task, a closer look at learning curves should be possible.

CONCLUSION

In conclusion, computer games appear to be very well suited as research vehicles in development of methods for data collection and analysis serving identification of mental strategies and human error modes and their changes during learning. The initial experiments have proved it possible to connect data collection routines to professional games (like Summer Games) for on-line data recording within a usual home computer system (Commodore 64 with standard floppy disk station) without impairing the pace of the games. The experiments also have shown that a kind of taxonomy of games according to the semantic significance of the players actions will be useful to be able to choose games and plan data recoding, according to the aim of the particular experiments. This work is now in progress.

REFERENCES

Anderson, J. R., 1982, "Acquisition of Cognitive Skills, Psychological Review, 89, (4), pp. 369-406.

Dawkins, R., 1976, "Hierarchical Organization: A Candidate Principle for Ethology", Growing Points in Ethology, Bateson, P. P. G. and Hinde, R. A., eds., Cambridge University Press, London.

Delius, J. D., 1969, "A Stochastic Analysis of the Maintenance Behaviour of Skylarks", Behaviour, 33, pp. 137-178.

Magnusson, M., 1982, Temporal Configuration Analysis: Detection of a Meaningful Underlying Structure Through Artificial Categorization of a Real-Time Behavioural Stream, Presented at AI-Workshop, University of Uppsala, (private communication).

Newell, A., and Rosenbloom, P. S., 1981, "Mechanism of Skill Acquisition and the Law of Practice", Cognitive Skills and Their Acquisition, Anderson, J. R., ed., Lawrence Erlbaum Associates, Hillsdale, New Jersey.

Rasmussen, J., 1980, "What Can be Learned from Human Error Reports?", Changes in Working Life, Duncan, K., Gruneberg, M., and Wallis, D., eds., John Wiley and Sons, London.

Rasmussen, J., 1985, Human Error Data, Facts or Fiction?, Riso-M-2499, Riso National Laboratory, Roskilde, Denmark.

Rasmussen, J., and Jensen, A., 1974, "Mental Procedures in Real-Life Tasks: A Case Study of Electronic Trouble Shooting", Ergonomics, 17, (3), pp. 293-307.

Reason, J., 1985, "Generic Error-Modelling System (GEMS): A Cognitive

Framework for Locating Common Human Error Forms", <u>New Technology and Human Error</u>, Rasmussen, J., Duncan, K., and Leplat, J., eds., John Wiley and Sons, London (in press).

USERS' OPINION OF THEIR WORK, LANGUAGE, AND COMPUTERIZED SYSTEM[1]

Gunhild Sandström

Lund University
Department of Information and Computer Sciences
The Lund University Research on Information Systems Group
Sölvegatan 14 A, S-223
62 Lund, Sweden

Abstract: With the help of Osgood's semantic differential method, I have made an empirical study in a manufacturing company in Sweden. Almost all the people in a department participated in the study. A team-working group, who handle export orders and the ensuing shipping documents by means of a computerized information system, gave their opinions of the existing "computer display-language", "decision support basis", "computer", "professional knowledge after computer" and "work after computerizing" in their own everyday jobs. Five different groups of professionals participated. With this material as a foundation, I discuss how to improve the measuring method for possible further uses within the field of information sciences.

1. REALMS AND CONTEXTS

The research is part of a program named "User Oriented Information Systems - Their Use and Development" (Nissen et al., 1982). The aim of my work as a whole is to develop ideas that make it possible for people to be more aware of what a computerized system can offer and how such a system can constrain. The realm of this work concerns the use of information systems and this report is about an initial part of an evaluation phase from a broader work. My example is a particular computerized information system used by an export team that handles all papers concerning import and export at a manufacturing company.

The workers at the department inform themselves on

- available means of transport,

- kinds of customers,

- kinds of agents available,

- different countries' rules,

---

[1]This study was supported by the Swedish Work Environment Fund and the National Swedish Board for Technical Development.

- sales conditions and so on.

in order to make correct invoices; to get profitable freight for the customers and, thereby, gain good-will for the company; to make alterations when the customer changes his mind; and to make co-transports, etc.

The research was empirical and, as written above, this evaluation was part of broader work. In the enterprise, I started the research work by informing the people I was going to work with about my intentions with the research during my stay at their place of work. I was at their place 4 hours, 2 times a week during 20 weeks in total, so I knew the participants rather well before the investigation described in this paper took place. The main activities during the whole 20 week period were the following:

		Users' Time	Researcher's Time
*	Introducing	15	5
*	Observing	2	40
*	Participating	3	10
*	Explaining	45	30
*	Free Telling	10	20
*	Evaluating Activities	30	20

The time devoted, in man-hours, to each phase for the users and myself are indicated in the columns. The figures are averages for this and four other areas studied. The figures do not include time for discussions among the users afterwards as a result of my visits, for travels, or for documentation.

The introductory phase was mostly devoted to finding out what the users were doing; their work as a whole; their different working situations; the special working situations concerning their information system; where they wanted support from their own system; the intentions with their searching for information; what problems they were solving; and whom they thought they were helping.

The physical use of their "own" information system was the object of my observation in the second phase. I found it important to describe how the users actually and practically worked by

- observing and interpreting what they were doing, and

- asking and listening to what they thought they were doing with the help of the information system.

The participation and explanation phases were main ones in the research as a whole and I will not describe them in great detail in this paper, but just tell that they were necessary in order to make possible an increased understanding of what the users were doing and of the concepts that stand for phenomena in their work and that are mediated by their information bank or databases. The users also told me rather freely about the use and the non-use of their system.

This paper concerns the last activity mentioned above, the evaluation.

2. MEASURING BY SEMANTIC DIFFERENTIAL

2.1 Performance

By Osgood's semantic differential (Osgood et al., 1957), I made an evaluation on the basis of the user's opinions in a diagram concerning

- computer display language,

- computer based decision support,

- their computer,

- professional knowledge after acquiring their data system,

- their work after acquiring their data system,

in order to find some common positive or negative attitudes towards the use of computerized information systems.

The evaluation was made during 2 hours at the same time for the whole group. They got a form of six pages as shown in the Appendix. The form was of course in Swedish and there might be differences of nuances due to the translation.

After this formal and voiceless investigation, the participants started to discuss the investigation, the method, the form, the pair of adjectives (see the form in the Appendix), their work, their language, and their computer system. First they did this very aggressively in critical terms, but later on also in a rather constructive way. I asked them if I could stay and listen. They were confident with me and I got their permission to do so and also to make notes.

2.2 A "Mixed" Method

In order to collect and analyze people's opinions about their work and their computerized environment, I used, as I said before, "the semantic differential", a method frequently used in social sciences studies (Kerlinger, 1964). I used it for two reasons.

One reason is that I wished to try a quantitative method that is combined with measuring quality values to see how it worked. I call this a 'mixed' method because of its two-fold features. There is need for both quality and quantity values when doing research and the semantic differential is an instrument, which can be used to get both values.

The other reason is that I wanted to know the users' opinions through an anonymous investigation within the work group.

"The semantic differential is a method of observing and measuring the psychological meaning of concepts" (Kerlinger, 1964, p. 566). In all concepts there must be some common core of meaning. Osgood invented the semantic differential to measure the connotative meanings of concepts as points in what he has called °semantic space° (Osgood, et al., 1957).

A semantic differential consists of a number of scales, each of which is a bipolar adjective pair. The bipolar adjectives are usually seven point rating scales, where the underlying nature has to be determined empirically. In this investigation, after the fill-in-phase, I clustered the bipolar pairs into evaluation and potency adjectives. I have chosen my own pairs of adjectives for this investigation (see Appendix) based upon an

```
inexact       :_____:_____:_____:_____:_____:_____:     exact

rich          :_____:_____:_____:_____:_____:_____:     poor

incompre-                                               intelli-
hensible      :_____:_____:_____:_____:_____:_____:     gible

entertaining  :_____:_____:_____:_____:_____:_____:     boring

correct       :_____:_____:_____:_____:_____:_____:     invalid

fragmentary   :_____:_____:_____:_____:_____:_____:     complete

                                                        full of
stereotyped   :_____:_____:_____:_____:_____:_____:     nuances

fuzzy         :_____:_____:_____:_____:_____:_____:     clear

angular       :_____:_____:_____:_____:_____:_____:     flexible

wrong         :_____:_____:_____:_____:_____:_____:     correct
```

Figure 1. Form for Measuring Opinions on Display Language.

intuitive and experienced knowledge of 'users and their data systems'.

To illustrate the method, I chose the following example. In a working group in one department, the members were asked to fill in five forms about different concepts regarding their own work. One of the forms concerned the "computer display language". I asked them to associate spontaneously with "computer display language", something between a pair of evaluating and action-related adjectives (see Figure 1). The results obtained were then grouped according to kinds of end-users and to closely related adjectives for presentation and discussion. This will be shown in the next section.

2.3 Different Kinds of Results

One of the diagrams concerns the "computer display language". I asked them to associate spontaneously with "computer display language", something between the pair of evaluating and action-related adjectives (see Figure 2). The pairs of adjectives in Figure 2 were arranged in another way when the investigation was made. All the 'positive' values were not on the same side as in Figure 2, when I needed to show results in a more lucid way. The results collected from 20 people (of 28 in all, 5 were absent and 3 did not response) are marked as follows:

SP   typical value from the sales personnel, three people, who use computer-based results indirectly;

OP   typical value from the order personnel, six people who take care of the orders from customers;

FA   typical value from the four forwarding agents, who tell the assistants what to do;

SA   typical value from the five shipping assistants, who are face-to-display workers; and

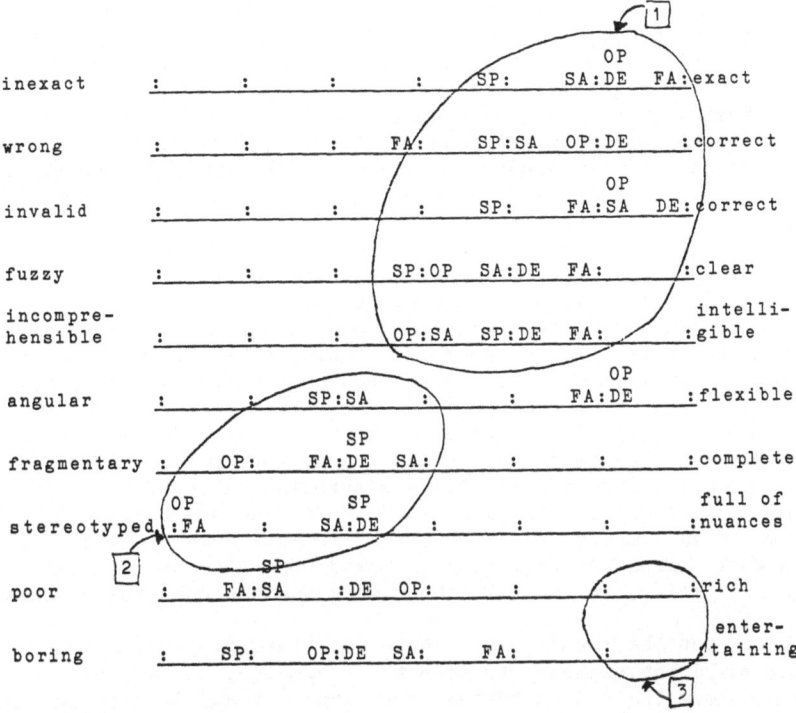

```
                                              OP
inexact   :      :      :      :     SP:     SA:DE  FA: exact

wrong     :      :      :     FA:    SP:SA   OP:DE    : correct
                                              OP
invalid   :      :      :      :     SP:     FA:SA  DE: correct

fuzzy     :      :      :    SP:OP   SA:DE   FA:       : clear

incompre-                                            intelli-
hensible  :      :      :    OP:SA   SP:DE   FA:      : gible
                                              OP
angular   :      :    SP:SA    :       :     FA:DE    : flexible
                            SP
fragmentary :   OP:   FA:DE  SA:     :       :        : complete

            OP         SP                            full of
stereotyped :FA    :   SA:DE   :       :       :      : nuances
                   SP
poor      :    FA:SA   :DE   OP:    :       :        : rich

                                                     enter-
boring    :    SP:    OP:DE  SA:    FA:     :         : taining
```

Figure 2.   Opinions About "Computer Display Language".

DE   typical value from the two data experts, who handle the computer
     system and the statistics.

There were no surprising results from this study. The users of this
data system agreed on the fact that their "computer display language" is
mainly "exact, clear, correct and intelligible" [1] but is also "fragmen-
tary and stereotyped" [2]. It is neither "rich" nor "entertaining" [3].

Four similar studies have been made with the same group about:

    "computer-based decision bases";

    "computer";

    "your professional knowledge"; and

    "your job".

The results, comprised in the same kind of diagrams, are presented in the
Appendix. The interpretations are the following:

The group of people handling exports found their computerized decision
bases to be very "useful, interesting, and important" [4]. They really
trusted the material mediated by the computer system [5], and they found it
"objective" if they belonged to the ordinary users, but as data experts the
decision bases in question were rather "subjective" [6]. The extreme
groups - the shipping assistants and the sales personnel - did not find the
material as engaging as the middle group people, who actually worked out
the material [7].

The "computer" is an "important, indispensable, well-known, comprehensible and reliable" [8] machine, which is rather "foolish and expensive" [10]. Maybe this is due to the fact that the group was, from my point of view, exactly the right size and that the computer was placed in the same premises where they worked. They could both see and hear it. The computer was a machine of their own and they had to pay for it out of their own budget. For most of the group, the computer also was fast and facilitated their work [9]. However, the shipping assistants found it rather tiring. They fed it with data most of the time.

Their opinions on whether computerization has changed their professional status or not were extremely different. In cases where it did change, quite new jobs were created and people became data feeders and computer maintainers. Almost everyone thought that their professional status got a positive contribution through computerization both regarding activity [11], and the contents [12]. The work seemed to be "important and responsible" [13], and "rich and entertaining" [14]. There seemed to be no conflict between freedom and security. Their work was "both free and safe" and "both creative and formal" [15] - a surprising result. It was due to different definitions of what was meant to be free and safe. The shipping people saw it as a matter of "to be free" in work demands first "to be safe" in work. From the beginning I looked upon them as competing phenomena. Finally, in general, their work was not especially heavy.

Looking upon the results as a whole for these people, it can be seen that they would not be happy to lose their computerized system. Even if they do not love their data system, they trust it and feel secure using it. Maybe they have got so used to it that they do not want to lose it or exchange it because that would disturb the routines. In spite of this - as a result of my visit - many of the people expressed enthusiastically that "the system has to be altered; it is possible to do a lot more" and as an example of the other extreme, resignedly, that "I could do nothing about the machine". Their use of and the utility of the computerized information system was focused through my investigation and there were several discussions on if and how to improve the system and if the system could be improved and some people also questioned computerization as such.

Studies with the help of Osgood's semantical differential are worth repeating in other work groups. They are not soft and well-organized; they are sufficiently anonymous and not too time-demanding. They could serve as triggers in order to intervene.

3. EARLIER RESEARCH

In order to assess attitudes toward information systems there have been very few investigations. Katzer (1972) measured attitudes among library science students with the help of the semantic differential toward one specific system. He was possibly the first to use the semantic differential for measuring purposes within the field of information science.

To concentrate the measuring on effectiveness, instead of on the efficiency, is an important task for Pearson & Bailey (1980), who say

"..., there is a need for quantitative measures of effectiveness to counterbalance the influence of efficiency only measures." (Pearson & Bailey, 1980, p. 59).

They also see "user satisfaction" as a multi-dimensional attitude and Pearson defines it as

"the sum of feelings or affective responses to distinguishable factors of the computer-based information products and services that
are provided within the organization" (ibid, p. 59).

The base for Pearson and Bailey's study is the semantic differential,
by which they developed and evaluated a questionnaire. The evaluation took
place among 32 middle managers and gave as a result that the questionnaire
was both reliable and valid. It was also objective and economical to
administer.

Studies on different types of communications such as comparisons between various media, with and without differences in time and space, have
been made in close fields. For example, Shorts, Williams, and Christie
have done such a study in the middle of the seventies to measure the relative degree of social presence, among some media, from face-to-face to
business letter (Christie, 1981).

The semantic differential has also been successfully utilized by
Gingras and McLean (1982) to measure profiles of the designer, the user,
and the "ideal" user of an operational information system. From 17 (of 17)
designers and 52 (of 111) users they got opinions, through 17 quite different pairs of adjectives and a seven-points scale, about the partici-
pant's self-image, their image of each other, and their image of the
"ideal" user and made some interesting comparisons.

Ives, Olson and Baroudi (1983) made measurements with the help of the
semantic differential with other purposes. They used user information
satisfaction as an evaluation mechanism to determine whether an information
system was needed or if an implemented system functioned properly. Their
user has been the manager. User information satisfaction measured how managers view their information system. Others involved are not encountered
in this study.

4. USE OF RESULTS GAINED THROUGH INTERVENING

All these good studies described in the last section have other objectives and were done differently than mine regarding:

- people involved;

- how to cluster and present the material;

- how to choose and arrange the bipolar adjectives; and

- the perspective behind or stated goals for each investigation.

In my study the people involved were in a whole, one and the same department and all the people were asked to participate. They got an opportunity to have their discussions noted, discussions of what they had done
in the study and the meaning of it. They might themselves (as representatives for "users" groups) have improved the method (for me) and their own
work situation with respect to their information system. The research was
directly connected to the reality. The other cases described in section 3
concentrated their studies on a special group of users - often managers in
several enterprises or students using an overall system - instead of a team
of workers using a dedicated system.

Instead of having the "good" adjectives to the left and the "bad" ones
to the right on the scale, I mixed them up stochastically. I also chose
very close adjectives in the same form while the others chose, as far as I

can see, not overlapping adjectives. The clustering of the adjectives and the naming of the clusters was made beforehand in the other studies, but afterwards, when ordered, and without real etiquette in my study. They search for reliance, objectivity, validity, effectivity factors, while I looked for possibilities to intervene and discuss conflicts; at the same time I got some valuable quantitative information.

The form in my study has functioned as an initating factor to a very important process for the users who have got a "legal" reason to "criticize" and "create" their own work. I think this is an extremely good opportunity to see what is wrong in a department. Besides the formal measurement with a good method there will be results from the involved persons. They start to dispute about words, forms and methods - the researcher gets feed-back. They go on disputing about the work, the display, the decision bases, the routines, the computerization, their wages and so on - the workers involved at the working place and the enterprise get feedback.

5. SOME THEMES TO DISCUSS

I take the liberty to suggest some themes that interest me regarding measuring people's opinion of and the effectiveness of "their" computerized information system:

• The need for these kinds of measurements within the realm of information and software sciences.

• Improvements of similar studies for future uses.

• Research ethics and intervention in connection with such studies.

• Different layouts of forms for measuring opinions about information systems and computerization.

• The possibility to develop a kernel of the semantic differential method for various uses, with necessary adaptations depending on whether it is going to be used

   - for practical applications or in research,

   - for developing an information system or for information systems use,

   - for measuring or also for intervening purposes, and

   - for getting quantitative results or for improving the quality.

REFERENCES

Christie, B., Face to File Communication - A Psychological Approach to Information Systems, John Wiley & Sons, Ltd., New York.

Gringas, L., and McLean, E. R., 1982, "Designers and Users of Information Systems: A Study in Differing Profiles", Proceedings of the Third International Conference on Information Systems, eds., Ginzberg and Ross, Ann Arbor, Michigan.

Ives, B., Olson, M. H., and Baroudi, J. J., 1983, "The Measurement of User Information Satisfaction", Communications of the ACM, 26, (10), October, 1983.

Katzer, J., 1972, "The Development of a Semantic Differential to Assess Users' Attitudes Towards an On-line Interactive Reference Retrieval System", Journal of the American Society for Information Science, March-April 1972, pp. 122-127.

Kerlinger, F. N., 1964, Foundations of Behavioral Research, Holt, Rinehart and Winston, New York, 1973 (reprint).

Nissen, H.-E., Carlsson, S., Flensburg, P., Holmberg, K.-A., Sandström, S., and Wormell, I., 1982, User Oriented Information Systems - A Research Program, Department of Information and Computer Sciences, Lund University, Sweden.

Osgood, C. E., Suci, G. J., and Tannenbaum, P. H., 1957, The Measurement of Meaning, University of Illinois Press, Urbana, Chicago, and London, 1967 (reprint).

Pearson, S. W., and Bailey, J. E., 1980, "Measurement of Computer User Satisfaction", Performance Evaluation Review, ACM, 9, (1).

Sandström, G., 1985, Towards Transparent Data Bases - How to Interpret and Act on Expressions Mediated by Computerized Information Systems, PhD Thesis, Studentlitteratur Chartwell-Bratt, Lund, Sweden.

APPENDIX

APPENDIX

Gunhild Sandström   October 1984
Information and Computer Sciences
Lund University

INVESTIGATION OF WORK, LANGUAGE AND COMPUTER SYSTEM

PLEASE, DO NOT TURN THE PAGE a) UNTIL YOU ARE CONVINCED THAT YOU UNDERSTAND WHAT IS ON THIS PAGE!

I am a researcher in information and computer sciences and am paid by The Swedish Work Environment Fund and The National Swedish Board for Technical Development and Lund University. I have got permission to make an investigation at some departments in "xxx" company concerning the use of computer system and language. I am going too question some people who work directly or indirectly with the system "aaa". On the following pages you will see some diagrams looking like this:

WRITING TABLE

full   *   *   *   *   *   *   * empty

orderly *   *   *   *   * messy

and so on with 10-12 such lines.

In these diagrams you shall mark what you associate with WRITING-TABLE if you primarily think of WRITING-TABLE as tremendously 'full' put a mark

a) Next page is A3 (in this presentation).

at the sign nearest 'full' or as completely 'empty' put a mark at the sign nearest 'empty'. Almost 'empty' could be shown next furthest to the right. An example of a mark is given at the line "orderly......messy". This is about values that you give and you decide yourself the meaning of 'empty' and "full" and the five possible places between on the line. There are about ten lines for each CONCEPT and five in total concepts On each line you may show where you want to associate between the two extremes. Answer spontaneously – do not think too long! It does not matter if it looks constraining. Do not bother if you see the same things appear again.

When answering have your own work in mind and it is the computer system "aaa" which is referred to where approriate.

Thank you for your help.

Before you turn the page b) write down your position, function or title at the department:

_____

In other respects this investigation is anonymous.

(The following empty diagrams are shown compressed in this appendix. In the real investigation there was one diagram with triple line distances on each page)

b) Next page is A3 (in this presentation).

© G Sandström 7.3.85

APPENDIX (Continued)

COMPUTER DISPLAY LANGUAGE

inexact	*	*	*	*	*	*	*	exact
rich	*	*	*	*	*	*	*	poor
incomprehensible	*	*	*	*	*	*	*	intelligible
entertaining	*	*	*	*	*	*	*	boring
correct	*	*	*	*	*	*	*	invalid
fragmentary	*	*	*	*	*	*	*	complete
stereotyped	*	*	*	*	*	*	*	full of nuances.
fuzzy	*	*	*	*	*	*	*	clear
angular	*	*	*	*	*	*	*	flexible
wrong	*	*	*	*	*	*	*	correct

COMPUTERIZED DECISION BASES

trivial	*	*	*	*	*	*	*	interesting
actual	*	*	*	*	*	*	*	inactual
useless	*	*	*	*	*	*	*	useable
correct	*	*	*	*	*	*	*	wrong
fuzzy	*	*	*	*	*	*	*	clear
unimportant	*	*	*	*	*	*	*	important
naive	*	*	*	*	*	*	*	sofisticated
subjective	*	*	*	*	*	*	*	objective
boring	*	*	*	*	*	*	*	engaging
reliable	*	*	*	*	*	*	*	unreliable
old	*	*	*	*	*	*	*	new
imperative	*	*	*	*	*	*	*	unconstraining

COMPUTER

cheap	*	*	*	*	*	*	*	expensive
easy to handle	*	*	*	*	*	*	*	hard to handle
unknown	*	*	*	*	*	*	*	wellknown
important	*	*	*	*	*	*	*	unessential
time-consuming	*	*	*	*	*	*	*	fast
dispensable	*	*	*	*	*	*	*	indispensable
incomprehensible	*	*	*	*	*	*	*	comprehensible
reliable	*	*	*	*	*	*	*	crafty
tiring	*	*	*	*	*	*	*	facilitating
intelligent	*	*	*	*	*	*	*	foolish
time-demanding	*	*	*	*	*	*	*	time-consuming

YOUR PROFESSIONAL KNOWLEDGE AFTER THE COMPUTER SYSTEM WAS INTRODUCED INTO THE DEPARTMENT

altered	*	*	*	*	*	*	*	unaltered
creative	*	*	*	*	*	*	*	paralyzing
specialized	*	*	*	*	*	*	*	broadened
overtaken	*	*	*	*	*	*	*	enriched
passive	*	*	*	*	*	*	*	active
strengthened	*	*	*	*	*	*	*	weakened
facilitated	*	*	*	*	*	*	*	burden
bad	*	*	*	*	*	*	*	good
engaging	*	*	*	*	*	*	*	monotonous
blunted	*	*	*	*	*	*	*	extended

207

APPENDIX (Continued)

<u>YOUR WORK</u> AFTER THE COMPUTER SYSTEM WAS INTRODUCED INTO THE DEPARTMENT

dull	*	*	*	*	*	*	* rich
safe	*	*	*	*	*	*	* unsafe
unimportant	*	*	*	*	*	*	* significant
good	*	*	*	*	*	*	* bad
entertaining	*	*	*	*	*	*	* boring
free	*	*	*	*	*	*	* limiting
heavy	*	*	*	*	*	*	* easy
without responsibility	*	*	*	*	*	*	* responsible
informal	*	*	*	*	*	*	* formal
conservative	*	*	*	*	*	*	* creative
important	*	*	*	*	*	*	* indifferent

<u>SUMMARIZED TYPICAL VALUES</u>
from the groups: sales personnel (SP)
order personnel (OP)
forwarding agents (FA)
shipping assistants (SA)
data experts (DE)

COMPUTER DISPLAY LANGUAGE

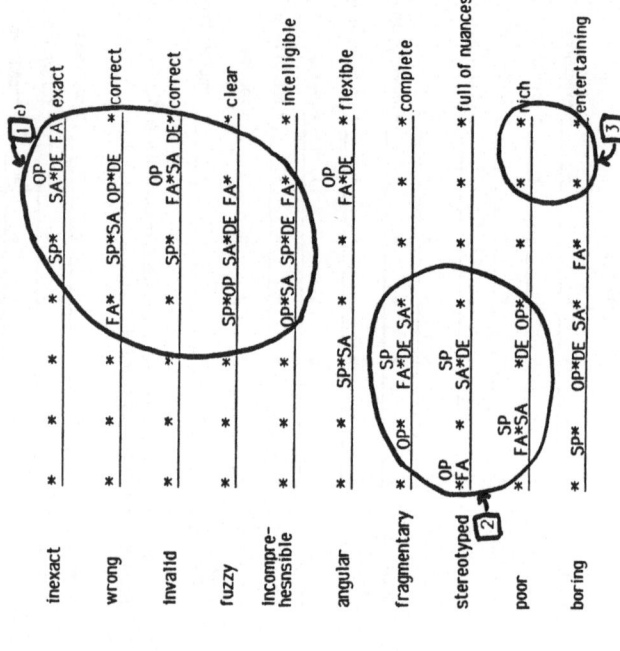

inexact	*	*	SP*	*	OP SA*DE FA	exact [c) / 1]
wrong	*	FA*	SP*SA	OP*DE	*	correct
invalid	*	*	SP*	OP FA*SA DE*		correct
fuzzy	*	SP*OP	SA*DE FA*			clear
incomprehensible	*	OP*SA	SP*DE FA*			intelligible
angular	*	SP*SA	*	OP FA*DE	*	flexible
fragmentary	*	OP*	SP FA*DE SA*	*	*	complete
stereotyped	OP *FA [2]	SP FA*SA	*	SP SA*DE	*	full of nuances
poor	*	*	*DE OP*	*	*	rich [3]
boring	*	SP*	OP*DE SA*	FA*	*	entertaining

c) These encircled fields are commented on in the main text.

COMPUTERIZED DECISION BASES^d)

COMPUTER

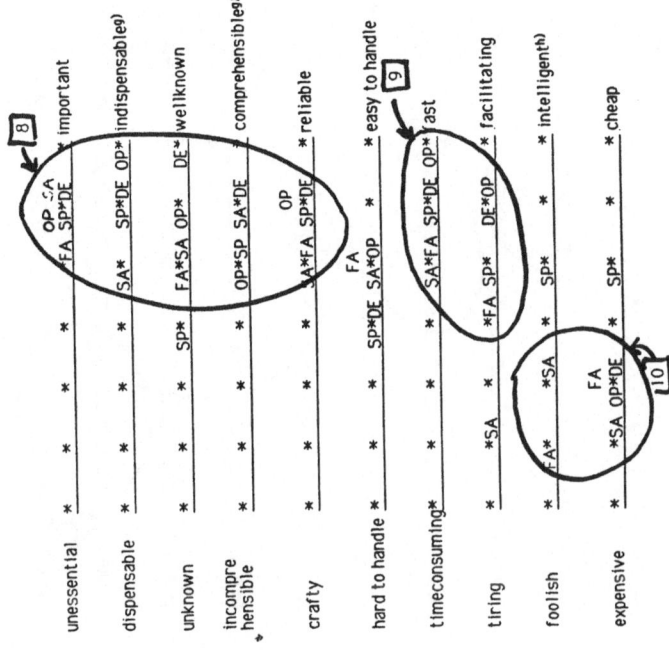

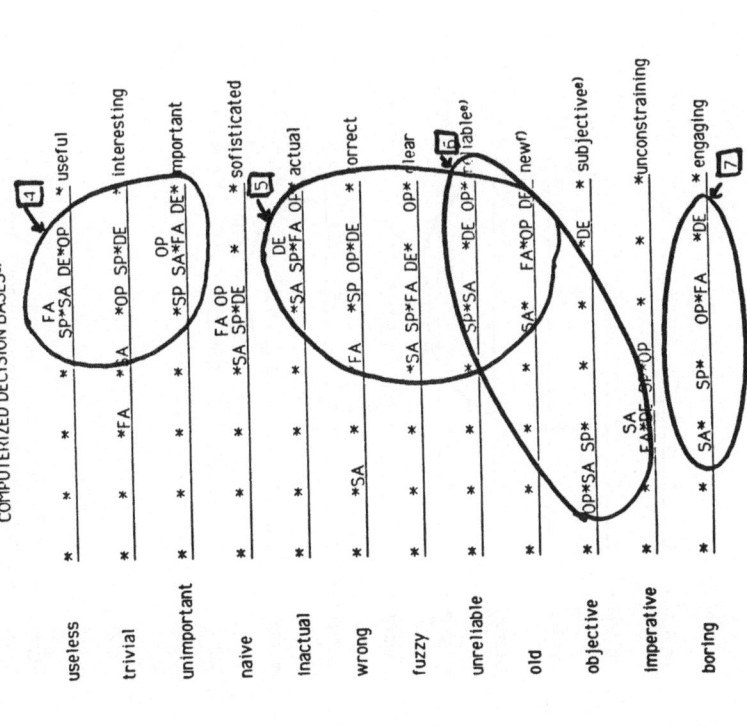

d) Two people from the SA-group have not answered at all
e) In the FA-group the same amount of people answered both - and.
f) In the SP-group they answered both - and, to the same extent.

g) In the FA-group they answered both - and, to the same extent.
h) In the groups OP and DE they answered both and to the same extent.

APPENDIX (Continued)

YOUR PROFESSIONAL KNOWLEDGE AFTER THE COMPUTER SYSTEM WAS INTRODUCED INTO THE DEPARTMENT[i]

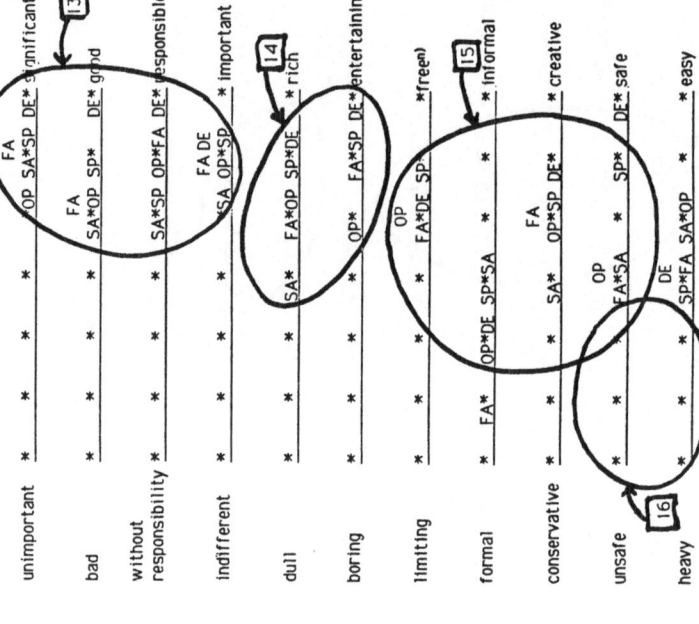

altered					FA* unaltered[i]
paralyzing					* creative[k]
overtaken					enriched[k]
passive					active
weakened					strengthened[l]
monotonous					engaging[l]
blunted					extended
specialized					broadened[l]
burden					facilitated[m]
bad					good

YOUR WORK AFTER THE COMPUTER SYSTEM WAS INTRODUCED INTO THE DEPARTMENT

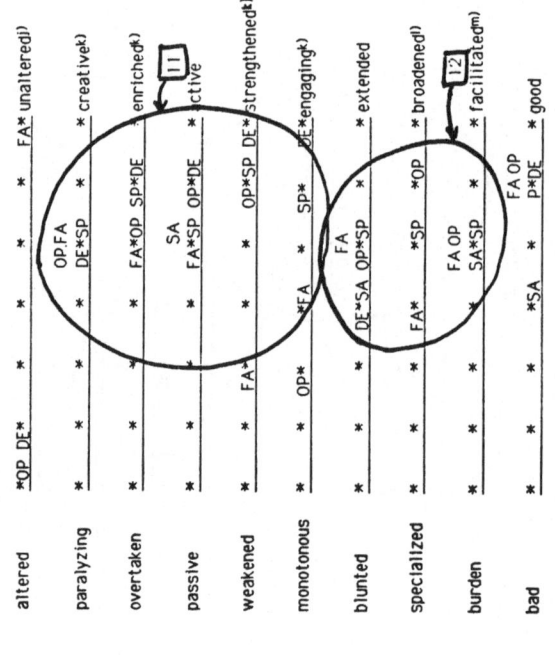

unimportant					significant
bad					good
without responsibility					responsible
indifferent					important
dull					rich
boring					entertaining[n]
limiting					free[n]
formal					informal
conservative					creative
unsafe					safe
heavy					easy

i) One person in the FA-group had just two marks.
j) In the groups SA and SP they answered both – and, to the same extent.
k) In the SA-group they answered both – and, to the same extent.
l) In the groups SA and SP they answered both – and, to the same extent.
m) In the DE-group they answered both – and, to the same extent.
n) In the SA-group they answered both – and, to the same extent.

210

EARLY SOFTWARE SIZE ESTIMATION: A CRITICAL ANALYSIS OF THE SOFTWARE
SCIENCE LENGTH EQUATION AND A DATA-STRUCTURE-ORIENTED SIZE ESTIMATION
APPROACH[1]

A. S. Wang* and H. E. Dunsmore**

*AT&T Bell Laboratories
 Piscataway, New Jersey 08854
**Department of Computer Science
 Purdue University
 West Lafayette, Indiana 47907

Abstract: Estimating the effort involved in software development is one of
the most important tasks in any software project. Using current estimation
techniques, early size estimation is typically a critical component of
early effort estimation. In this paper the size estimation approach based
on the Software Science length equation is critically examined. This is
followed by the presentation of a new size estimation approach based on the
early estimation of a data-structure metric. This approach is derived from
the assumption that programs can be constructed in a regulated fashion such
that most data structure decisions can be made during program design. The
feasibility of this approach was demonstrated by a size estimation experiment involving small, but non-trival, programming tasks. Size estimates
using this approach were as good as or significantly better than subjective
estimates made by the experimental subjects.

1. INTRODUCTION

Estimating the amount of effort required for software development is
one of the most important and yet most difficult aspects of any software
project undertaken today (DeMarco, 1982). Virtually all effort estimation
models proposed so far require project size as the dominant parameter for
determining project effort (Wolverton, 1974; Mohanty, 1981; Boehm, 1981).
Unfortunately, however, empirical results (as well as anecdotal evidence)
have suggested that early size estimation is nearly as difficult as early
effort estimation (DeMarco, 1981; Boehm, 1981; Boehm, 1984). Therefore,
our study focused on the issue of early software size estimation. We
attempted to develop techniques for estimating program size at an early[2]
stage in the software development process.

The remainder of this paper is divided into six sections. The basic
idea of early size estimation approaches is introduced in Section 2. A

---

[1]This paper is based upon work previously done at the Department of Computer Science, Purdue University, West Lafayette, Indiana, USA.
[2]The specific early stage considered in our study is the end of the design
 stage.

critical analysis of one early size estimation approach, the Software
Science length equation, is given in Section 3. Our proposed size estimation approach based on the early estimation of a data-structure metric is
presented in Section 4. To investigate the feasibility of this new approach, a size estimation experiment involving small, but non-trivial,
programming tasks was conducted. This empirical investigation is described
in Section 5. Section 6 reports major findings from this experiment.
Finally, a summary and conclusion is contained in Section 7.

2. INDIRECT EARLY SIZE ESTIMATION

The size estimation approach undertaken in this study is what we call
an indirect approach. First, we conjecture that program size can be approximated as a function of some other measurable quantities related to the
program. Second, we assume that a program can be developed in such a way
that these quantities can be measured early. Then, it follows that the
early estimation of size can be obtained indirectly by measuring and combining these quantities at an early stage.

Several researchers have suggested a number of ways for estimating program size indirectly from measurable program quantities. For example,
Halstead (1977) introduced a formula called the "length equation" to estimate program size from program vocabulary. More recently, Itakura and
Takayanagi (1982) suggested a size estimation model based on input and
output data elements that can be determined at the end of the design stage
based on specification documents and design documents. Furthermore,
Albrecht (Albrecht and Gaffney, Jr., 1983) proposed to estimate software
size based on a measure called "function points", i.e., a weighted sum of
the number of "inputs", "outputs", "master files", and "inquires" to be
used or provided by the software.

Halstead's length equation has been shown to work reasonably-well for
programs written in several languages and within different organizations
(Christensen, Fitsos, and Smith, 1981; Shen, Conte, and Dunsmore, 1983).
In addition, several software analyzers that compute Halstead's metrics are
available to us.[3] Therefore, we chose to use Halstead's length equation as
a starting point for our study.

Halstead's measure for program size is the Software Science program
length N, the count of total occurrences of operators and operands contained in a program. As defined in Software Science (Halstead, 1977),
there are four basic quantities which can be measured in a program:

n_1 = number of unique operators

n_2 = number of unique operands,

N_1 = total occurrences of operators, and

N_2 = total occurrences of operands.

Operands include variables, constants, and character strings. An operator

---

[3]At Purdue University there are software analyzers that compute Halstead's
metrics and other metrics such as lines-of-code and McCabe's "cyclomatic
number" v(G) (McCabe, 1976) for the languages Fortran, Pascal, Cobol, and
C.

is anything that acts upon the operands.[4] Program vocabulary n includes n_1 and n_2; i.e., $n = n_1 + n_2$. Program length N is defined as the total occurrences of all operators and operands:

$$N = N_1 + N_2 \tag{1}$$

Halstead conjectured that <u>program length N</u> is a function of n_1 and n_2 alone and could be estimated even before N_1 and N_2 were available. The formula he proposed for estimating N based on vocabulary is the following:

$$\text{Estimated length} = \hat{N} = n_1 \log_2 n_1 + n_2 \log_2 n_2 \tag{2}$$

Equation (2) will be referred to as "Halstead's length equation". This relationship cannot be justified on purely theoretical grounds. In fact, it is possible to construct a pathological program to make $\hat{N}$ a poor predictor of N. Nevertheless, a substantial amount of empirical evidence supporting the validity of this relationship has been collected for a number of languages over the past several years (Christensen, Fitsos, and Smith, 1981; Shen, Conte, and Dunsmore, 1983). The metric $\hat{N}$ has been observed to be an acceptable estimator of N when applied to a wide range of programs (Christensen, Fitsos, and Smith, 1981).

Given the assumption that program size measured in N can be approximated as a function of unique operators and unique operands, the next step is to investigate how these two components of $\hat{N}$ can be predicted early.

<u>Early Estimation of Unique Operators (n_1)</u>. As suggested by Christensen, Fitsos, and Smith (1981), and Shen, Conte, and Dunsmore (1983), for large programs written in languages such as Pascal and PL/S where the use of direct transfers (i.e., GOTO statements) are discouraged, n_1 can be approximated by a constant. That is, there is a standard set of operators (verbs, arithmetic operators and the like) used by most Pascal programmers that is somewhat independent of the program being written. Thus, the early estimation of program size can be predicted solely based on the early estimation of n_2.

<u>Early Estimation of Unique Operands (n_2)</u>. The metric n_2 is the number of unique operands contained in a program. We conjecture that programs can be constructed in such a way that n_2 can be estimated early in the development process. One way to accomplish this is through what we call the "top-down data-structure-first" development strategy. Using this strategy, the program design process includes the following three activities: (1) identifying the underlying structure and major components of the program, (2) specifying procedural and data connections among the components, and (3) establishing a detailed layout of data representations and developing basic algorithms to manipulate them. From these activities, most data structures and variables should be developed by the end of the design stage.

In summary, the early size estimation approach using the length equation is based on three assumptions: (I) the length equation works reasonably well; (II) the metric n_1 can be approximated by a pre-determined constant; and (III) the metric n_2 can be estimated well at an early stage. Since Pascal programs were used in the empirical investigation of our study, the validity of each of these three assumptions for Pascal programs was examined and is reported in the following sections.

---

[4]Detailed counting rules for operands and operators in Pascal programs can be found in Burch (1982).

3. CRITICAL ANALYSIS OF THE SOFTWARE SCIENCE LENGTH EQUATION

   Since empirical studies supporting the length equation have focused
primarily on Fortran (Halstead, 1977), PL/1 (Elshoff, 1978), PL/S (Fitsos,
1980), and Cobol (Shen and Dunsmore, 1981) programs, it was necessary to
confirm the validity of the length equation for Pascal programs in our
study. The Software Science study by Johnston and Lister (1979) provided
some empirical support for the length equation based on the analysis of a
large number (12,886) of small (less than 50 lines-of-code) student programs. However, in their later study (Johnston and Lister, 1981), some
questions were raised concerning the validity of the length equation for
nine large Pascal programs. The estimated size obtained using the length
equation underestimated the actual size by an average of 37%.

   In order to further investigate the validity of the length equation for
Pascal, we gathered data on some 78 large programs (21 from a 1982 experiment, 33 from a database class, and 24 large programs from the Department
of Computer Science and the Purdue University Computing Center). These
programs ranged in size from 215 lines-of-code[5] to more than 4500. They
were analyzed using our Pascal program analyzer (Burch, 1982). The estimated size obtained using the length equation consistently underestimated
the actual size by a significant amount (42% on average). This seems to
confirm the findings of the study by Johnston and Lister (1981) mentioned

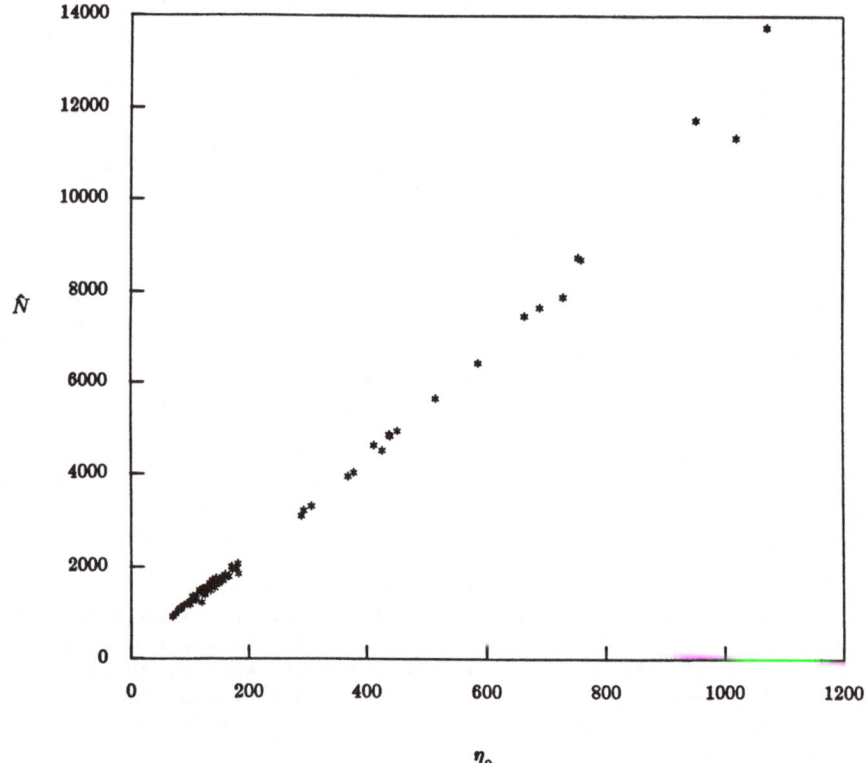

Figure 1. $\hat{N}$ vs. n_2 (78 Pascal programs).

---

[5]In this paper, (the number of) lines-of-code is defined as the number of
 total text lines excluding comment lines and blank lines.

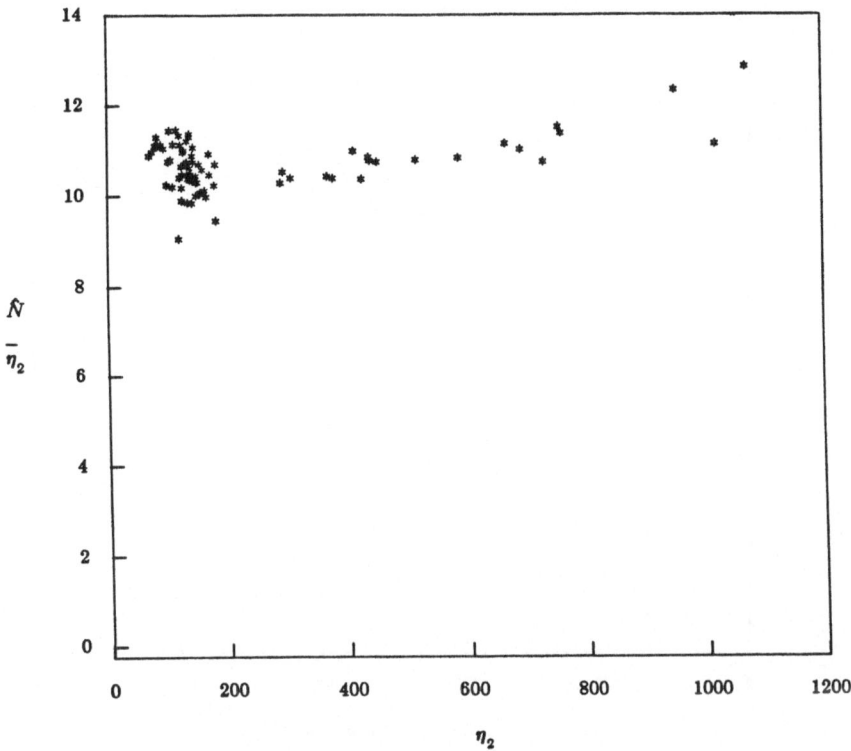

Figure 2. $\hat{N}/n_2$ vs. n_2 (78 Pascal programs).

above. These results led us to reexamine the nature of the length equation.

We first examined the relationship between $\hat{N}$ and n_2. Figure 1 shows the scatter plot of $\hat{N}$ vs. n_2 for the 78 Pascal programs we analyzed. It should be clear that $\hat{N}$ increases approximately linearly with n_2. This result led us to examine the relationship between the ratio $\hat{N}/n_2$ and n_2. The scatter plot of $\hat{N}/n_2$ vs. n_2 is shown in Figure 2. It was found that 95% of the time $\hat{N}/n_2$ fell within the range between 9.5 and 11.5. The mean value of $\hat{N}/n_2$ was 10.6. This observation suggested that for this set of Pascal programs, using the length equation to compute $\hat{N}$ is similar to multiplying n_2 by an appropriate constant (in this case, 10.6). The following analysis attempts to explain why.

Dividing both sides of the length equation by n_2, we get

$$\hat{N}/n_2 = (n_1 \log n_1)/n_2 + \log_2 n_2 \tag{3}$$

For a fixed n_1, the ratio $\hat{N}/n_2$ becomes a function of n_2. As n_2 increases, the value of the first term on the right hand side of Eq. (3) decreases, while the value of the second term increases. Therefore, it is conceivable that for a certain range of n_2, the range of $\hat{N}/n_2$ will be relatively small. An example plotting $\hat{N}/n_2$ vs. n_2 is given in Figure 3 where n_1 is fixed at 60 and n_2 varies from 70 to 1000. In this example, the ratio $\hat{N}/n_2$ varies approximately between 9.4 and 11.2. In other words, with $n_1 = 60$ and $n_2 = 70$ to 1000, the range of $\hat{N}/n_2$ is relatively small and thus may very well be approximated by a constant. Table 1 shows the ranges of $\hat{N}/n_2$ for different

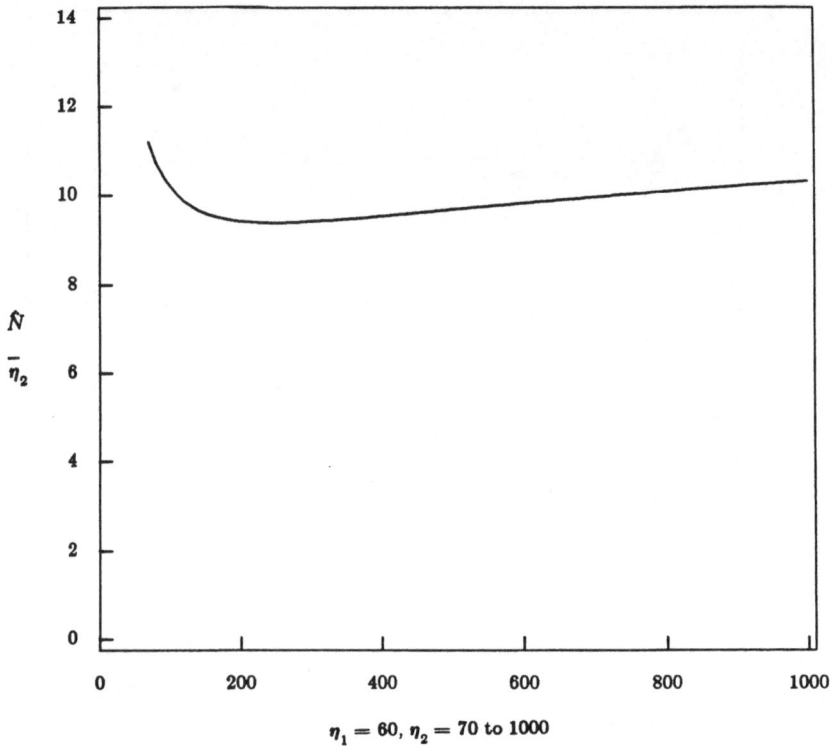

$$\eta_1 = 60,\ \eta_2 = 70 \text{ to } 1000$$

Figure 3. $\hat{N}/n_2$ vs. n_2.

combinations of some n_1 and n_2 values. For example, as shown in the third
row of Table 1, when n_1 is fixed at 60, as long as n_2 falls within the
range of 60 to 1000, $\hat{N}/n_2$ will always fall within the range of 9.1 to 10.6.
It should be noted that the lower bound value of n_2 shown in the table was
chosen to make the size of N/n_2 range not to exceed 2.0.

In addition to the 78 Pascal programs mentioned before, we also observed the ranges of $\hat{N}/n_2$ and N/n_2 for 223 PL/S programs, 271 Cobol programs, and 86 Fortran programs. These programs were collected from a
variety of applications at different industrial and university settings.
Table 2 summarizes the results. From the small standard deviation shown in
the fourth column of the table, it should be clear that the range of $\hat{N}/n_2$
is relatively small. It should also be noted that the mean of N/n_2 is
close to that of $\hat{N}/n_2$ for PL/S, Cobol, and Fortran. But this is not true
for Pascal (19.8 vs. 10.6).

From the above analysis, we concluded that

"When the values of n_1 (number of unique operators) and n_2
(number of unique operands) fall within a certain range,
using the Software Science length equation to compute
(the estimated size) is equivalent to multiplying n_2 by an
appropriate constant to compute $\hat{N}$."

Since this constant is too small for large Pascal programs to predict
actual program size, the length equation is apparently not suitable for
large Pascal programs. That is, Assumption (I) described in Section 2 is
not valid for this set of Pascal programs.

Table 1

Range of $\hat{N}/\eta_2$

η_1	range of η_2	range of $\hat{N}/\eta_2$	size of range
30	30 to 1000	8.2 to 10.1	1.9
40	40 to 1000	8.7 to 10.6	1.9
50	60 to 1000	9.1 to 10.6	1.5
60	70 to 1000	9.5 to 11.2	1.7
70	80 to 1000	9.7 to 10.7	2.0
80	100 to 1000	10.0 to 11.7	1.7
90	110 to 1000	10.2 to 12.1	1.9
100	130 to 1000	10.4 to 12.1	1.7
110	140 to 1000	10.5 to 12.5	2.0
120	160 to 1000	10.7 to 12.5	1.8
130	180 to 1000	10.8 to 12.6	1.8
140	190 to 1000	11.0 to 12.8	1.8
150	210 to 1000	11.1 to 12.9	1.8

4. DATA-STRUCTURE-ORIENTED SIZE ESTIMATION APPROACH

In order to validate Assumptions (II) and (III) stated in Section 2, an exploratory study involving a program construction experiment was conducted.

In this experiment, programs with sizes on the order of 500 lines-of-code were constructed over three-week periods. A detailed description of this preliminary study can be found in Wang (1984), Chapter 2.

Two of the major findings of this experiment were: (estimating η_2 using an appropriate constant was quite accurate, but (2) estimating η_2 at the end of the design stage was difficult (the <u>early</u> η_2 values were only

Table 2

Range of $\hat{N}/\eta_2$ and N/η_2

		$\hat{N}/\eta_2$		N/η_2	
	no. of programs	mean	std. dev.	mean	std. dev.
Pascal	78	10.6	.6	19.8	6.0
PL/S	223	8.4	1.1	9.6	4.6
Cobol	271	10.1	1.3	10.5	3.0
Fortran	86	9.3	1.4	10.0	3.6

about 42% of the final n_2 values on average, instead of a high percentage as expected). This result led us to reexamine the components that constitute n_2.

n_2 is composed of three major items: variables, constants, and character strings. Let us refer to the first component "variables" as VAR.[6] Using the "top-down data-structure-first" development strategy as described before, most VAR should be created during the design stage and the remaining portion of n_2 (constants and character strings) should be added when the actual code is developed. Therefore, it is more intuitively appealing to determine VAR rather than n_2 at an early stage. Thus, a new size estimation approach based on VAR (the number of unique variables) was suggested as a replacement for the size estimation approach based on the length equation. Since the metric VAR can be determined from data structures and variables developed early during program design, we call this size estimation approach a data-structure-oriented approach.

Having identified the metric VAR as an attractive candidate for <u>early</u> estimation, we needed a size model to relate VAR to size. We will explain later how we constructed such a size model in our study.

5. EMPIRICAL INVESTIGATION

To investigate the feasibility of our data-structure-oriented size estimation approach, a size estimation experiment was conducted.[7] The participants in this experiment were forty-four students enrolled in a course concerning software metrics during the summer of 1983 at Purdue University. Most of them were Computer Science graduate students. As class assignments, each subject was required to write two Pascal programs over a five-week period. The completed programs varied in size from about 200 to about 800 lines-of-code and required from about 10 hours to more than 50 hours development time. We asked each subject to construct the programs in a "top-down data-structure-first" manner as described before. At the end of various phases of their construction process (including the end of the design phase) each subject was required to report to the experiment administrator for a "milestone interview". The only concern to us in this paper are the early milestone interviews conducted before and at the end of the design stage.

At each "milestone-interview", each subject was required to turn in a syntax-error-free version of the program. This intermediate version was analyzed right away in order to obtain metric counts (such as VAR and program size in lines-of-code) at that point. The experimenter then asked the subject to estimate the final values of these metrics based on the actual values "in place". The subjects made their best estimates with such information in mind, in addition to their knowledge about the status of program development. Therefore, the subjective estimates gathered in this experiment should be considered "structured" subjective estimates as opposed to <u>ad-hoc</u> guesses. The subject's estimate of the final program size will be referred to as $\hat{S}_{PGMR}$. Later in the next section, it will be shown that the subjective estimates of VAR were used to produce the indirect size estimates (which below we refer to as $\hat{S}_{VAR}$) to be compared with the direct size estimates ($\hat{S}_{PGMR}$).

---

[6]VAR is the unique variable count and is computed by subtracting the number of numeric constants and character strings in the program from the count. Detailed counting rules can be found in Burch (1982).

[7]A detailed description of this experiment can be found in Wang (1984), Chapter 3.

Table 3

Early Estimation of Size

Program	estimate	$\overline{MRE}$	ranking
1	$\hat{S}_{VAR}$	.20	same
	$\hat{S}_{PGMR}$	.23	same
2	$\hat{S}_{VAR}$	.30	1
	$\hat{S}_{PGMR}$	.42	2

6. EXPERIMENT RESULTS

As introduced in Section 2, the general approach to an early indirect size estimation involves two steps: (a) establishing a size model which approximates size as a function of measurable program quantities, and (b) identifying development strategies that encourage the early development of such quantities. Since in our preliminary study we identified the metric VAR as an attractive candidate for early estimation, the next step was to find a size model for VAR.

The size model for VAR was constructed based on the 78 large Pascal programs we mentioned before. We first observed that for this set of programs, VAR and program size in lines-of-code were highly correlated (correlation coefficient = .94). As a consequence, linear regression was applied to this set of data and it led to the following relationship relating VAR to S (size in lines-of-code):

$$\hat{S}(VAR) = 102 + 5.31 \; VAR \tag{4}$$

Thus, the equation suggests that the addition of any new variable in a program leads to an estimate of a little more than 5 additional lines-of-code − with a base of about 100 lines-of-code to begin with. We are not prepared to defend this as a relationship that will hold up in other organizations, but we did decide to use it in analyzing our experiment results as a means of objectively producing a size estimate $\hat{S}$ from a subject's estimate of the number of unique variables VAR which we refer to as $\hat{S}_{VAR}$.

In this paper, the performance of an estimation will be evaluated in terms of its ability to predict actual values. Thus, the direct size estimates ($\hat{S}_{PGMR}$) will be compared to the indirect size estimates ($\hat{S}_{VAR}$) according to the accuracy in predicting the actual size. Table 3 shows the results of this comparison.

Since all subjects in the experiment constructed two different programs, our early size estimation approach based on VAR was evaluated separately using the two sets of data associated with these two programs. The first half of Table 3 corresponds to the size estimation results for the first program; the second half corresponds to the results for the second one.

Entries in the third column of Table 3 (under the label "$\overline{MRE}$") summarize the estimation performance in terms of the evaluation criteria $\overline{MRE}$. $\overline{MRE}$ is the average absolute relative error between the predicted and actual values. The smaller $\overline{MRE}$, the more accurate the estimation. Entries in the last column of the table (under the label "ranking") are the performance rankings for the two estimation methods according to the paired t-test results of their mean $\overline{MRE}$ values (Nie, Bend, and Hull, 1975).

In our study, we consider that the difference between two estimation methods is statistically significant at a certain level if the paired t-test results indicated that, at that significance level, the mean MRE value of the first method is significantly different from that of the second. Thus in Table 3, if two estimations are given different rankings, their performances are significantly different at α < .10. If they are ranked the "same", their performances are not significantly different at α ≥ .10.

As shown in the first half of Table 3, for program-1, the two methods for estimating size at the end of the design stage were not significantly different from each other. The MRE values were all relatively small (i.e., smaller than .25). It should be recalled that the subjective estimates we collected were "structured" ones, which were made based on the actual value "in place" at the time of estimation. This probably explains the satisfactory performance of the subjective size estimation for program-1.

However, the subjective size estimation method was not as good for program-2. Its performance was significantly worse than that of the indirect method. In the post-experiment interviews, most subjects indicated that when they first read the specification for program-2, it appeared to be a very difficult program. They did not realize that the program was not as difficult as they thought until midway through the construction process. This miscalculation was reflected by their overestimation of program size. In fact, this is a good demonstration that even "structured" subjective estimates can also be unreliable.

Comparing the program-1 results with the program-2 results, it is clear that the method based on early estimation of VAR was as good as or significantly better than the subjective method. This suggests that our proposed size estimation method can be used as a reliable "backup" for the "structured" subjective method.

7. SUMMARY AND CONCLUSION

In this paper we presented two approaches to indirect early size estimation. The first approach was based on Halstead's length equation and early estimation of the metric n_2 (the number of unique operands). The results of our preliminary study suggested that (a) Halstead's length equation may not be a good size model for large Pascal programs, and (b) the metric n_2 may not be appropriate for early size estimation. Our second approach was a data-structure-oriented approach based on the early estimation of the metric VAR (a subset of n_2) and a size model which approximated program size as a linear function of VAR. The feasibility of the second approach was demonstrated by a size estimation experiment where the indirect size estimates using this approach were as good as or significantly better than the subjective estimates made by the programmers.

Based on these findings, we believe that early estimation of program size can be improved at the end of the design stage. In spite of the encouraging findings in our study, caution must be taken in the application of these results. We must emphasize that these results should be considered "laboratory" results at this point. Our subjects were student programmers (although they were upper-level undergraduate and graduate Computer Science students). The software constructed was not nearly as large as that produced in industry. Furthermore, our results pertain primarily to the coding process after specifications and high level design had been completed. It is well-known that as much as 50% (or more?) of total effort may be expended before entering the code development phase. However, we believe that an ability to predict program size accurate at the beginning of this phase is a start toward the goal of achieving better software size and effort estimation at earlier points in software development.

8. REFERENCES

Albrecht, A. J. and Gaffney Jr., J. E., November 1983, "Software Function, Source Lines of Code, and Development Effort Prediction: A Software Science Validation", IEEE Transactions on Software Engineering, pp. 639-648.

Boehm, B. W., 1981, Software Engineering Economics, Prentice-Hall, Inc., Englewood Cliffs, NJ.

Boehm, B. W., January 1984, "Software Engineering Economics," IEEE Transactions on Software Engineering, pp. 4-21.

Burch, D. C., May 1982 (available upon request), Purdue Pascal Software Metrics Analyzer User's Manual, Dept. of Computer Science, Purdue University.

Christensen, K., Fitsos, G. P., and Smith, C. P., 1981, "A Perspective on Software Science", IBM Systems Journal, (4), pp. 372-387.

DeMarco, T., September 1981, Yourdon Project Survey: Final Report, Yourdon, Inc., New York, NY.

Elshoff, J. L., February 1978, "An Investigation into the Effect of the Counting Method Used on Software Science Measurements", ACM SIGPLAN Notices, 13, pp. 30-45.

Fitsos, G. P., January 1980, Vocabulary Effects in Software Science, IBM Santa Teresa Lab., Tech. Report 03.082.

Halstead, M. H., 1977, Elements of Software Science, Elsevier North Holland, Inc., New York, NY.

Itakura, M., and Takayanagi, A., September 1982, "A Model for Estimating Program Size and Its Evaluation", Proceedings, Sixth International Conference on Software Engineering, pp. 104-109.

Johnston, D. B., and Lister, A. M., September 10-11, 1979, "An Experiment in Software Science", Proceedings, Symposium on Language Design and Programming Methodology, Sydney, Australia, pp. 195-215.

Johnston, D. B., and Lister, A. M., 1981, "A Note on the Software Science Length Equation", Software - Practice and Experience, 11, pp. 875-879.

McCabe, T. J., December 1976, "A Complexity Measure", IEEE Transactions on Software Engineering, pp. 308-320.

Mohanty, S. N., 1981, "Software Cost Estimation: Present and Future", Software - Practice and Experience, 11, pp. 103-121.

Nie, N. H., Bend, D. H., and Hull, C. H., 1975, SPSS: Statistical Package for the Social Sciences, McGraw Hill, Inc., New York, NY, 2.

Shen, V. Y. and Dunsmore H. E., August 1980, revised September 1981, Analyzing Cobol Programs via Software Science, Dept. of Computer Science, Purdue University, Report CSD TR-348.

Shen, V. Y., Conte S. D., and Dunsmore, H. E., March 1983, "Software

Science Revisited: A Critical Analysis of the Theory and its Empirical Support", IEEE Transactions on Software Engineering, pp. 155-165.

Wang, A. S., August 1984, The Estimation of Software Size and Effort: An Approach Based on the Evolution of Software Metrics, Ph.D. Thesis, Purdue University, West Lafayette, IN.

Wolverton, R. W., 1974, "The Cost of Developing Large-Scale Software", IEEE Transactions on Computers, 23 (6), pp. 615-636.

SOFTWARE SYSTEMS FOR MANAGERIAL WORK: SOME CONCLUSIONS FROM INFORMATION RESEARCH

Tom Wilson

Department of Information Studies
University of Sheffield, UK

Abstract: The nature of managerial work is examined from the point-of-view of the suitability of software systems designed for (or advertised as being designed for) managerial level workers in organizations. It is suggested that the assumptions underlying much existing software do not hold true for managerial behavior. In particular, the preference for oral communication, signifying the social nature of managers' work, is not catered for, nor is fragmentation of work and the limited time managers have available for learning. It is suggested that software designers will need to pay more attention to the context of information behavior in organizations if systems are to be widely adopted.

INTRODUCTION

The worlds of information science and computer science appear to intersect only at a single very narrow theme of common interest - information retrieval. Even here there does not appear to be a very high degree of interaction (at least to the casual reader of the literature). It is of no surprise, therefore, to discover very little in the way of common ground between the human factors literature in computer science and the literature on information seeking behavior (ISB) in information science. The former appears to be largely concerned with 'micro' aspects of the human use of machine systems, such as the design of screen menus or proper seating for the keyboard operator, light levels for work at a terminal and so forth. (For example, see the papers of a recent conference, Janda, 1984). The latter is concerned more with aspects of human behavior in an organizational or social context.

Information science has been biased in two other respects: it has been excessively concerned with scientific research workers and their ISB, and it has been concerned chiefly with the use made of scientific research literature, rather than with 'information' in general. The first bias may have arisen because it is relatively easy to gain access to such workers whose ethos supports the idea of research. The second bias probably results from the concern of librarians and scientific information workers to ensure that their collections meet the 'needs' of their clients.

This paper gives a view of information use by 'practitioners' (for want of a better word), rather than researchers, and a view of ISB in the

context of communication in organizations such as local government departments and businesses. The focus is on managerial levels of work in these
organizations and, hence, there will be an attempt to relate the ideas to
current concepts of software aids for managers.

SOFTWARE FOR MANAGERS - THE TARGETS

Everyone in an organization is a manager to some extent - everyone has
to manage his or her time to allow for the performance of those tasks that
are part of the total job. The term is usually restricted, however, to
identify those people who have responsibility for supervising the work of
others, or for directing non-line functions, or who have overall responsibility for directing the organization. The terms used are various, but
'strategic management' and 'operational management' are frequently used, as
are top management, middle management, and lower management.

The term 'manager', therefore, is not a very useful one from the point
of view of developing software to aid his work. It hides the fact that
some managers are 'generalists', while others are very specialized in the
range of tasks they perform - for example, personnel managers, managers of
finance sections or accounts departments, computer services managers,
corporate management services managers, etc.

Much software is devised especially for specialists in organizational
management - accounting packages, database systems for personnel records,
orders, stock records, etc. And studies on the response to office-automa-
tion show that specialists in virtually any category are likely to be keen
users of the technology. It fits them; they have often been accustomed to
using other forms of keyboards or equipment such as calculators and the
step to a computer terminal or microcomputer is not a very big one, and in
large organizations they may have become accustomed to some degree of computer use already. For the general manager, however, this is often not the
case. There is also a tendency for resistance to the technology to increase with age, and the more senior managers in organizations are likely
to be the older managers.

Unfortunately for the software designer, it is this last category of
manager who has to be convinced of the desirability of the hardware and
software because it is at that level that decisions on buying are made,
particularly if organization-wide systems are to be implemented. An
individual section head may have authority to purchase a 500 British pounds
microcomputer out of petty cash, but installing, say, DEC's 'All-in-one' at
perhaps 100,000 British pounds for 15 to 20 screens is a different matter
altogether. It is necessary, therefore, to look at the nature of managerial work to see how far the assumptions implicit in much software and in
its promotion tally with reality.

MANAGERIAL WORK AND SOFTWARE DESIGN

Sufficient knowledge now exists on the nature of managerial work to
provide software engineers with adequate guidelines for the design of systems for managers. There is little evidence in the human factors literature, however, to suggest that this body of knowledge is being tapped. The
micro level of analysis prevails and the broader view of ISB appears to be
completely absent.

A number of assumptions appear to underlie current practice in the
design of software and these assumptions are very much at odds with the
communication behavior and general work behavior of managers. The

Table 1. Meetings.

Work Role	No. of Staff	No. of Meetings	Ave. Duration (hours)	Ave. hours Per Person
Directorate	5	60	1.4	16.8
Line Managers	6	43	1.8	13.0
Advisers	4	21	1.2	6.5
Social Workers	5	14	1.4	3.8
Admin. Support	2	3	0.4	0.6

assumptions, and the opposing facts, are:

Assumption 1

Managers engage in desk-bound tasks as the greater part of their work.

A number of the other assumptions discussed below are dependent on this first assumption. The very idea of an all-purpose 'executive work-station' assumes that the manager is going to spend a good deal of time at a desk, with the work-station sitting there, ready to deliver the information goods whenever they are required. Of course, the situation is complicated by the fact that many managers at different levels of the organization, particularly in middle and lower management, will spend time at their desks and it is likely that the more specialized the role of the manager, in respect of the main line or staff functions of the organization, the more time will be spent at the desk. But managers do other things.

Facts. Mintzberg's (1973) managers spent a lot of time talking with other people and a good deal of this talking time was spent in scheduled and unscheduled meetings, in fact 69% of their time. The amount of time our managers in local government spent in meetings is shown in Table 1. This table illustrates two of the points being made in this paper: managers do not perform stereotyped roles - their behavior varies and, to some extent, is different from that of those they manage. Secondly, managing is a social activity, not a solitary activity. Indeed, the manager who becomes a solitary figure is probably unlikely to remain a manager for long.

Another aspect of the social nature of managerial work is the amount of time managers spend away from their own offices. Mintzberg (1973) recorded that the managers he observed spent 38% of their time away from the organization altogether, and only 39% of their time in their own offices.

Assumption 2

Managers are mainly text generators and processors.

In spite of advertising hype to the contrary there is really very little in the way of true 'decision support systems' for managers. This is partly due to a lack of understanding as to the nature of decision-making, partly because of an assumption that decisions are necessarily rational, and partly because the integration of diverse information types from many sources into a single system is a difficult task. So, office automation systems have little to offer the manager in this sector. But, because they have to sell through management, word processing, database systems, and spreadsheets are glossily presented as aids to management decision making. Add communication facilities to permit the use of electronic mail and messaging and, one way or another, you have systems which assume the manager is going to sit down at a keyboard and generate symbols on a

Table 2. Oral Communication.

Communication Type	%
Telephone calls	6
Scheduled Meetings	59
Unscheduled Meetings	10
Organizational Tours	3
Other Media	22
Total -	100

screen.

The publicity material includes statements such as:

"[System X] The all-in-one business software system
for managers and professionals."

and then goes on to promise integration of all the elements:

"You can view and make changes in letters, graphs,
and spreadsheets, simultaneously on the same screen."

Facts. As Mintzberg (1973) noted, "The manager's work is essentially
that of communication..." and in this work the dominant medium is the
voice. Oral communication face-to-face with others or via the telephone
accounts for the greater proportion of all communication acts by managers:
in Mintzberg's study many managers spent in the order of 80% of their time
in oral communication. Table 2 shows the results of Mintzberg's analysis.

Other work (Wilson and Streatfield, 1980) suggests that managers and
other levels in local government show similar patterns of activity. Oral
communication constituted 62% of directorate level activity and 58% of line
managers' activity. Interview respondents, including the social worker
grade as well as managers, reported an average of 69.3% of time in oral
communication. 53% of respondents reported more than 71% of their time
going in oral communication.

This is not to say that managers do not process text, of course they
do, but written communications often enter or leave the manager's world via
intermediaries who prepare brief reports or who take dictation and produce
text for signature. The social world of the manager remains one mainly of
oral communication rather than written communication.

Assumption 3

Managers have time available for learning how to use software.

This assumption is rarely spelled out explictly in any promotional
material for managerial software - indeed, the extent to which the words
"user-friendly" are used promotes quite the opposite set of expectations.
The game is given away, however, by the proliferation of text-books on how
to use system X, Y or Z (Lotus 1-2-3, dBase II or III, or any other package
you care to name), and by the number of training courses offered by organizations specializing in the field. In fact, anyone sitting down to try to
use a multi-purpose package for the first time is advised by the package
publishsers to read at least the introductory manual and, before long, will
be expected to read and assimilate practically every other bit of paper in
the package. This takes time - lots of it. There is also the assumption,

Table 3. Duration of Communication Events.

Duration	% 'Events' (N=5839)	Cumulative Total
2 minutes or less	53.0	53.0
3 - 5 minutes	21.7	74.7
6 - 10 minutes	10.5	85.2
11 - 15 minutes	3.7	88.9
16 - 20 minutes	1.9	90.8
more than 20 minutes	4.4	95.2
not recorded	4.9	100.1*

*Rounding Error

again unstated, that the user will be using the package often enough for
the initial learning to stick. 'Learning is easy', says the copywriter
and, of course, it is not all easy. 'User-friendliness' is claimed for the
most appallingly unfriendly systems. For example, one of the word processing packages for the IBM PC requires five keystrokes to start underlining
and five to switch it off again! And that kind of learning load is
repeated for other functions, some of which are more complex still.

Facts. Time is of the essence to the manager. To quote from Mintzberg
again:

> "Because of the open-ended nature of his job, the manager
> feels compelled to perform a great quantity of work at an
> unrelenting pace."

> "In contrast to activities performed by most non-managers,
> those of the manager are characterized by brevity, variety
> and fragmentation."

An impression of the time constraint is given by our results from local
government (see Table 3). The data are not broken down by work role, but,
in fact, there was little variation among the strata. Again, Mintzberg's
results are in line with ours. Although his definition of 'activity' is
not the same as our 'event', he found that only 10% of activities lasted
longer than one hour. The absence of managers from their own offices,
noted above, also has clear consequences for the amount of time the manager
has available for learning how to use systems.

Assumption 4

The search for 'hard facts' and data constitutes the whole of managerial ISB.

Throughout the history of attempts to apply computers to the information needs of managers there has been a tendency to assume that the dominant need is for organizational data. Hence, in the early days of ill-
fated management information systems, large piles of computer printout
arrived on managers' desks - to be promptly ignored - except for the one or
two critical pieces of data the manager had managed to discover and to
which he always turned. The view that 'information' = 'data' is still
common today. Witness a number of the Department of Trade and Industry
office automation test-site developments. Almost universally, when management levels have been the targets, there has been an assumption that
corporate data will be needed. Interestingly, in one of the test-sites the

Table 4. Analysis of Communication Activity.
(Wilson & Streatfield, 1977, p. 290)

Activity	% of Events
Receiving Information	27.8
Receiving Requests	14.2
Receiving Opinion	0.7
Receiving Request for Opinion	0.4
Other Receiving Acts	0.8
Giving Information	12.7
Giving Opinions	0.7
Giving Instructions	0.7
Seeking Information	9.2
Requesting Action	3.3
Seeking Opinion	0.4
Document Handling	10.7
Other	19.1
Total —	100.1*

*Rounding Error

information service got permission to mount on the management viewdata system a database of news information from the specialist press relating to the industry. The pages containing that database turned out to be the most used pages on the system, partly because of their intrinsic usefulness, partly because the most enthusiastic users were not the top-management targets, but middle management.

Facts. The final point made above makes the point that the assumption is ill-founded. There is other evidence: Table 4 above shows an analysis of the communications events engaged in by one social services department manager. In other words, advice and opinion are significant parts of the whole of management communication. Mintzberg makes a similar point which is worth quoting at length:

> "In categorizing the chief executive's information...
> we saw that some comes in the form of pressures. Sub-
> ordinates seek to extend their own influence; directors
> attempt to impose their opinions of decisions; members
> of the public bring special pressures to bear...These
> pressures form a special part of the organization's in-
> formation system. They represent the value positions
> of those who seek some measure of control over the ac-
> tions of the organization in order to satisfy special
> needs." (Mintzberg, 1973, p. 73.)

In our studies of local government managers we found that two types of information were perceived as useful, to the extent of being needed daily. These were 'Names, addresses, and telephone numbers', and 'News of developments'. More recently, in a study of medium sized businesses we have found a consistent level of stated need for 'news' information. For example, news of potential market opportunities, and news of the activities of competitors in the field. In other words, corporate data is only one of the inputs into management decision-making. Environmental information, which is often not readily available in the form of hard data, may be as useful for some decisions as the hard facts on production levels, new orders, or the rate of the British Pound against the U.S. Dollar.

It is not intended that these facts should determine the <u>nature</u> of management information software, but it is suggested that they ought to inform software designers of the context in which systems will be used. They also explain why so much of management communication is oral: in speaking to others, even when ascertaining facts, it is possible to seek advice on the meaning of those facts for the organization or for a specific decision, or to seek opinions on associated matters. Until expert systems are better developed and <u>appropriate</u> to general management functions, computer-based systems are likely to contribute little to these aspects of the manager's job.

THE LESSONS FOR SOFTWARE DESIGN

It is possible to draw some lessons from the research outlined above, and from related research. The very fact of the predominance of oral communication points, for example, to the need for devices such as ICL's "One-per-desk", with telephone and other messaging facilities, rather than, say, a dumb terminal or a microcomputer with a load of applications packages. The development of computer-based voice messaging systems would certainly expedite the take-up of the technology. As Pye and Young (1982) note:

"Research finding   Service implication

90% of manager's time   For managerial acceptance
is spent communicating   communication orientation
                                is important"

As to learning time, Fischer (1984) suggests that:

"The time needed to learn how to use functions should be
short, particularly for busy users who have little time
to spare. The aim should be 'no threshold and no ceiling':
...This can be achieved by constructing systems that grow
with the experience of the user."

The problem with this approach, so far as managers are concerned, is that they have <u>no</u> time to spare for learning and, probably, use the systems insufficiently frequently to retain what is learned beyond a fairly low level of performance. Any increase in the complexity of functions, therefore, must be made transparent to the user. 'Improvements' to systems, which usually connote increasing complexity, must be associated with genuine improvements in 'user friendliness' (to use that over-used word again).

The overall conclusion from the evidence is that producing software systems that will be used by managers is no easy task. The problems to be overcome <u>may</u> be intractable because embedded in the stereotypical behavior pattern revealed by research is very idiosyncratic behavior on the part of the individual manager - all have different styles, different ways of doing things, within the stereotype. The further complication is that these patterns are themselves embedded in the social worlds of organizations with their own mores and customs which vary from organization to organization and which managers learn to negotiate. Getting systems used, therefore, is not a matter or persuading the individual, but a matter of organizational change.

REFERENCES

Fischer, G., 1984, "Human-Computer Communication and Knowledge-Based Systems", The Managerial Challenge of New Office Technology, Otway, H. J., and Peltu, M., eds., Butterworths, London, pp. 54-79.

Janda, A., ed., 1984, Human Factors in Computing Systems: Proceedings of the CHI '83 Conference..., North-Holland, Amsterdam.

Mintzberg, H., 1973, The Nature of Managerial Work, Harper & Row, New York.

Pye, R., and Young, I., 1982, "Do Current Electronic Office System Designers Meet Users Needs?", Emerging Office Systems, Based on Proceedings of the Stanford University International Symposium on Office Automation, Ablex, Norwood, NJ, pp. 73-94.

Wilson, T. D., and Streatfield, D. R., 1977, Information Needs in Local Authority Social Services Departments: An Interim Report on Project INISS, Journal of Documentation, 33, pp. 277-293.

Wilson, T. D., and Streatfield, D. R., 1980, You Can Observe A Lot ...: A Study of Information Use in Local Authority Social Services Departments, University of Sheffield, Department of Information Studies, Sheffield.

INFORMATION AND ITS RELATIONSHIP TO DECISION MAKING: THE INFORMATION

PROFILE AND OTHER QUANTITATIVE MEASURES;   A BRIEF SUMMARY

M. C. Yovits, A. de Korvin, R. Kleyle, and M. Mascarenhas

Purdue University School of Science
Indiana University-Purdue University
Indianapolis, IN 46223

Abstract: In previous work the basic concepts of a fundamental theory of
information flow and analysis were developed. Some important measures were
defined explicitly and quantitatively. The basis of the previous work
rested upon the use of a Generalized Information System, the relating of
information to the certainty in making a decision, and the consideration of
average decision makers, thus permitting the development of unique relationships. This paper is a brief summary of some of our more important
research results. We have recently extended earlier theoretical results to
a much wider set of situations for which external documentation plays the
dominant information role. This involves the consideration of the way external documentation changes an average decision maker's effectiveness for
a particular problem. This in turn leads to the concept of an information
profile which is the relationship giving the change in decision maker effectiveness as a function of the decision maker effectiveness for a specific document. A number of additional quantities are also defined explicitly and quantitatively. The definition of information developed in earlier
work is extended and generalized quantitatively. Information is decision
maker dependent and is related to the certainty in choosing various courses
of action to solve a particular problem. Information is shown to be pro-
portional to the sum of the squares of the probabilities of choice and is
defined in terms of binary choice units or BCU's. The previous work also
has been extended to include the situation where the decision maker does
not initially know the viable courses of action and must learn them.

INTRODUCTION

This paper presents a summary of some research results which have recently been obtained by our group. We have been working for some time now
toward developing a fundamental theory of information flow and analysis.
We believe that this theoretical development is important and we expect
that it can be effectively applied to practical and useful situations.

In the development of a significant framework it is necessary to define
quantifiable terms and then to establish explicit relationships among them.

In our approach we are concerned with information and its relationship to decision making inasmuch as we point out that information must be <u>utilized</u> by a decision maker if it is to be a significant quantity. While our formulation may somewhat delimit the total range of interest in an intellectual sense, it does have virtually universal applicability with regard to any potential applications for information. We believe that any more general approach would not readily be amenable to quantification and to the establishment of meaningful relationships.

The ultimate goal of our approach is to establish an empirical basis for the design and development of information systems. However, before appropriate empirical data can be gathered we must first understand what data are needed, how the data are to be used, and what we can learn from the data. Furthermore, we hope that eventually, if we are able to measure and quantify the <u>value</u> of a piece of data, this measure can be an important parameter in helping us to design and organize our data base efficiently.

In this paper, we briefly summarize several recent important results which we have obtained that enable us to extend previous work. In particular:

1. We have explicitly defined a quantitative measure for external documentation and show how to relate this to information;

2. We have refined and extended the definition of information, relating it to the information state of the decision maker as originally suggested in previous work (Yovits and Abilock, 1974; Yovits, Foulk and Rose, 1981);

3. We have extended the general model of decision making in a "closed system" to the situation where the structure of the system is also unknown; and

4. We have shown how external documentation relates to our previous model of a closed system.

Although this paper is relatively brief, we nevertheless believe that it is quite descriptive and that it summarizes our concepts accurately and satisfactorily. The details which become rather lengthy, are provided in other papers which are to be published elsewhere.

Information has in the past been defined and used in many different ways, almost always in a broad context. Quantitatively, <u>information</u> is generally defined in the "information theory" or "communication theory" context of Shannon and Weaver (1949). This approach is concerned with the probability of receipt of a particular message without regard to the value or use of that message. Other approaches have considered the semantics or meaning of the message as important in defining "information". Winograd (1972) for example, attempts to quantify the semantic content of simple declarative sentences within a restricted language system.

On the other hand our approach focuses, as stated earlier, on the relationship between information and decision making and how important or valuable that information is to the resulting decision. Thus the significance of the information is in its <u>use</u>. As we have shown in previous work, information in our context then is defined explicitly and quantitatively. Specifically our approach defines information inversely relative to the uncertainty in making a decision. That is, information is a function of the certainty involved in choosing a course of action to meet certain goals or objectives.

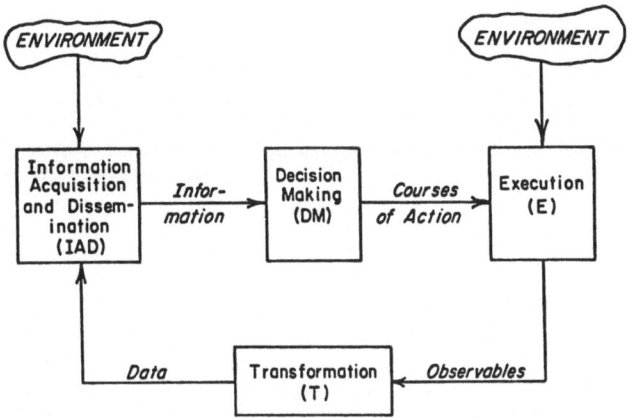

Figure 1. The Generalized Information System Model.

BACKGROUND

The necessary background is described in detail in Yovits, Foulk and Rose (1981). A brief summary is given here. The basis is the model of a Generalized Information System (GIS) (See Figure 1.).

This model follows from our formulation relating information to decision making. Information and decision making are intimately connected and one cannot exist without the other. Decision makers use this model or a similar one (at least in part) in making decisions. On the basis of his current assessment of the total situation, the decision maker (DM) must choose a best course of action (COA) from among many available to him. As the DM makes more decisions and obtains feedback from these decisions, he becomes a more effective decision maker. In the process he learns more about the entire situation and his confidence increases as well. External documentation may of course also modify the DM's decisions. We had in previous work (Yovits, Foulk, and Rose, 1981) not considered the effects and significance of external documents although they are of course almost always used and are certainly important.

The DM chooses all COA's probabilistically where the probabilities are some function of his assessment of the expected values of all the COA's. As he becomes more effective he tends to choose the COA with the greatest expected value with greater and greater probability until he becomes completely certain and chooses the COA with certainty. Most decision makers will have some implicit (if not explicit) probability distribution in mind at any time in the decision making process. Although the finer details of decision making may depend on the precise model of optimization used by the DM, the broad features we believe are still applicable.

As the DM becomes more effective his estimates of the expected value (EV) of various courses of action approach the _actual_ expected values which we call EV*. On the _average_, over many executions of a single COA the value obtained in fact will be the _actual_ expected value, EV*. In this way using an average learning rule which we have developed, we can examine the _average behavior_ of decision makers.

Furthermore, although the behavior of an individual DM may differ (it may even differ significantly) from the average, the average of many DM's of equal effectiveness, learning, and confidence will be that of the average DM with that particular learning and confidence. Thus we are able to establish _unique_ relationships involving the _average_ decision maker and his behavior. It is our concern with the behavior of the average DM that permits the discussion of unique and useful relationships.

As stated above the DM's choices among the various COA's are probabilistic. Thus on the average we can define the performance of a DM simply as the sum of all the EV*'s weighted by the probability of choice of each COA. We further define the decision maker effectiveness (DME) as performance divided by the maximum possible performance, namely, the maximum EV*. Thus

$$DME = \sum_{i} P(a_i) EV_i^* / (EV_k^*)_{max} \text{,} \tag{1}$$

where $P(a_i)$ is the probability of choosing the $i\underline{th}$ COA, EV_i^* is the actual expected value for the $i\underline{th}$ COA, and $(EV_k^*)_{max}$ is the maximum actual expected value. We note that DME is dimensionless and ranges from zero to one.

A QUANTITATIVE MEASURE FOR EXTERNAL DOCUMENTATION: THE INFORMATION PROFILE

In our previous work (Yovits, Foulk, and Rose, 1981) we considered only a closed system where the only information available to the DM was feedback from the data generated as the result of his choices of courses of action. With this information feedback the DM is able over time to become more effective and to choose the "best" COA with a high probability. In more recent work (Yovits and Foulk, 1985) we developed some experimental results which provided values for some of the parameters and at the same time generally validated our approach.

However, a completely closed system is unrealistic and generally artificial, inasmuch as external documentation consisting of documents, books, messages, datasets advice, etc. is generally available and will be used by the DM. As a consequence we have now extended our development to include a quantitative treatment of the use of external documentation.

In our approach we relate information to decision making. In particular we define information quantitatively in terms of the uncertainty (more accurately the certainty) which a decision maker has in choosing a COA for a particular situation. By _information_ or _quantity of information_ we thus mean the _internal information state_ or simply the _information state_ of the decision maker.

The external documentation, on the other hand, does not in itself contain information. It has the _potential_ to become information when used by a decision maker. For want of a better term we will call what is contained in external documentation, _knowledge_.

Thus to consider the potential for information in a document we must necessarily consider decisions to be made by a DM using this document. Use of the external documentation leads to a change in the information state of the DM. This change is of course dependent in a significant way on the characteristics of the user of the document. Clearly, the measure of information cannot be absolute and must depend on the recipient and the effectiveness of the recipient, i.e., it is a _relative_ measure. A measure of information which does not possess this relative property can have only limited application. In particular the entropy approach of Shannon and Weaver (1949) and others is really not adequate nor is it even appropriate to use for this type of situation. Our approach relates information to decision making and defines its value or effectiveness by how much it changes the _effectiveness_ of a decision maker. In other words, the _use_ of the information is _the_ important factor. By considering the _average_

234

decision maker we are able to establish <u>unique</u> relationships.

External documentation will change the capability or effectiveness of a decision maker. How much it changes the effectiveness is in turn a function of the effectiveness of the DM who uses the information. The decision maker effectiveness (DME) is quantitatively defined by Equation 1. We can thus define:

<u>Information Profile</u> for a given document is the relationship between ΔDME and DME,

where ΔDME is the change in decision maker effectiveness resulting from the external documentation for the DM using that documentation. The use of external documentation changes the information state of a DM. This in turn leads to the change in his DME. In other words the external documentation is the driving force in this relationship.

There are two major factors upon which the development of a profile rests:

First, there is the amount of knowledge in the document being considered which is already known by the decision maker. For example, a research scholar will likely know most of the material in an introductory text, whereas a beginning student would know little in a research monograph.

Second, there is the capability of the DM to learn the knowledge available. A beginning student would have little capability to learn much from a research monograph, whereas a research scholar would be able to learn easily what he does not already know of the contents and would find the document useful.

We have suggested that, at least in essence, we may represent these factors by exponentials of the DME. For example, we can represent the first factor by a term DME^r and the second by DME^n where r and n are parameters yet to be determined with r generally greater than n. Thus we have (defining G(DME) and α below)

$$\Delta DME = \alpha DME^n (1-DME^r)/G'(DME). \tag{2}$$

This is the analytical definition of an <u>information profile</u>. We call n the learning exponent and r the exponent representing what is already known. These are related to k_λ and k_c, the learning and confidence coefficients discussed in Yovits, Foulk and Rose (1981). Further experimental data gathering is necessary to establish values for n and r and to determine their relationship to k_λ and k_c.

The function G(DME) relates Decision Maker Effectiveness to Information. The internal information state I and DME are <u>on the average</u> related by a unique function. A DM will have a specific information state at any particular time. This will give rise <u>on the average</u> to a specific and unique DME. We find it more convenient rather than dealing with DME as a function of I, however, to deal with I as a function of DME. This function we call G. Thus we may represent information as a function of DME; that is, I = G(DME), and G'(DME) is the derivative of G with respect to its argument. We need experimental data to determine the precise behavior to G. We have, nevertheless, without experimental data been able to establish some of the specific properties of the G function.

The quantity α represents the fraction of the total knowledge required to solve that problem by some <u>idealized</u> DM, and it has a value between zero and two. The value two means that the document can solve the problem completely; the value one means that it can solve half the problem, etc. More explicitly, the quantity α represents the <u>maximum amount of information</u> that could <u>ideally ever be obtained from a document</u> (and that, of course, only by a highly idealized DM).

As we have noted, in order to study in detail the behavior of Information Profiles, we of course need experimental data which provides data regarding G(DME) as well as typical values for n and r. Nevertheless, we are able to determine some of the necessary properties of these profiles and also to draw some typical curves representing these relationships.

For example, we have shown that:

1. There is a maximum value for α for which the profile is meaningful;

2. The value and slope of the profile at the extremes must fall within certain constraints;

3. A fundamental profile is unimodal;

4. There are certain constraints which must be satisfied for which the external documentation can be divided into several independent pieces, the sum of which still give essentially the same profile as the initial external material; and

5. For the Information Profile to be meaningful, the average decision maker must not have previously utilized that external documentation.

Finally, we emphasize that all of this discussion holds for only a <u>single</u> problem or situation. Clearly, a document which solves one problem may well be useless for a greatly different problem, and a DM who has a high effectiveness in one area may likely have low effectiveness in some different area. Information and decision making are highly situation dependent. They are not absolute as are physical quantities and relationships. However, once it is recognized that we are referring to a single problem or situation which in itself may be relatively well defined, this should cause no problem. Further, it is consideration of the average decision maker which gives rise to the unique relationships we develop.

EXAMPLES OF INFORMATION PROFILES

As we have indicated we need data regarding G(DME) to understand better the shape of these profiles. However, we do have a number of constraints which have been established for G. We have made several reasonable simplifying assumptions for G(DME) and have accordingly obtained the following typical information profiles. Two illustrative examples are shown in Figure 2 and Figure 3. Typical values are shown in Table 1 and Table 2.

A QUANTITATIVE MEASURE FOR INFORMATION

In the process of formulating the basic relationships involved for the information profile, we must consider the quantitative relationships for information itself. Our approach, as we have stated, relates information to decision making and we define information quantitatively in terms of the certainty which a DM has in choosing a course of action for a particular situation. Information is then a function of the probabilities of choice.

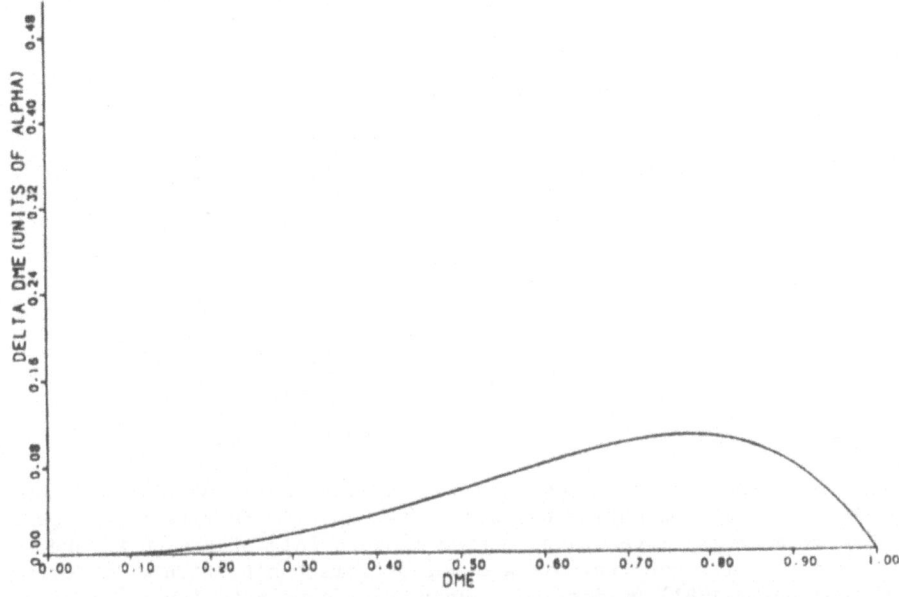

Figure 2. Example of Profile, $\alpha = 1$, $DME_R = 3.16$,
$n = 3$, $r = 4$

More precisely, by information we mean the internal information state of
the decision maker, or simply the information state of the decision maker.
Both the information state of the DM and the decision maker effectiveness
are functions of the probabilities of choice, and there is a relationship
between information and DME. By treating <u>average</u> DM's we are able to

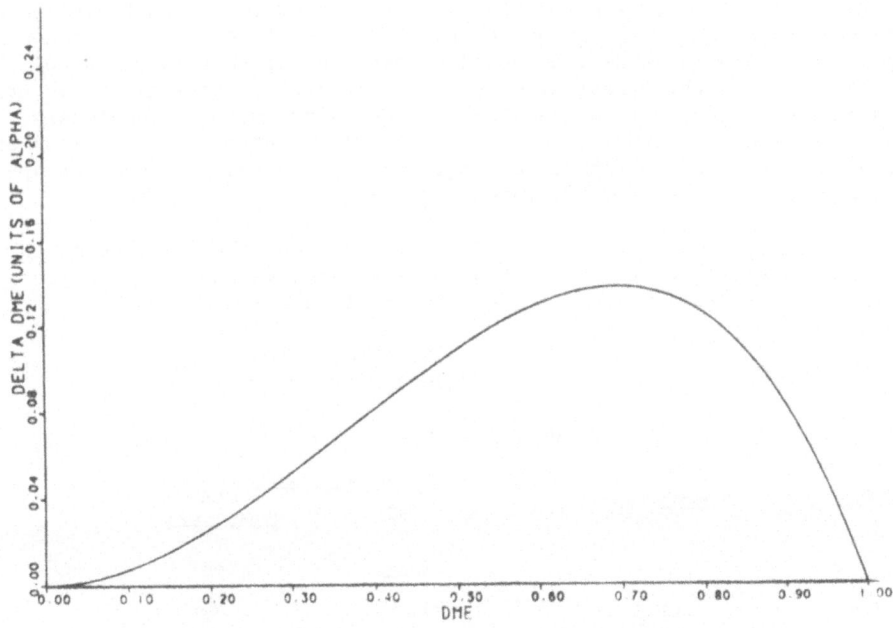

Figure 3. Example of Profile, $\alpha = 1$, $DME_R = 1.68$,
$n = 2$, $r = 3$

Table 1

QUADRATIC G,mDME$_R$ = 3.16

n	r	Maximum Co-ordinates DME	DME (Units of α)
2	3	0.6901	0.1269
3	4	0.7901	0.1078
4	5	0.8000	0.0976
100	101	0.9940	0.0745

develop <u>unique</u> relationships between those two quantities.

We again emphasize that the information state is a function of time and, of course, of the entire history of the DM. It is situation dependent inasmuch as a DM may have a high degree of certainty of choice in one situation and be quite uncertain in another different situation. In Yovits, Foulk, and Rose (1981) we derived a quantitative measure for information and showed that it was a function of the squares of the probabilities of choice. This treatment was essentialy correct, but incomplete, and we extend it here. We briefly summarize our approach.

First, we recognize that there are two discrete aspects to the information state. One situation to be considered is the case where all of the COA's are known by the DM, but the relationship among the expected values of the various COA's is not known by the DM. This results in the choice of each COA being probabilistic. We call this case relational uncertainty or structural certainty.

The other aspect involves the situation where the COA's themselves are not known, nor is any relationship among them known. It remains to be determined which COA's have no value and should be discarded and which COA's appear to have some value and should be considered; that is which COA's are viable. We call this phase structural uncertainty. Certainly it is true that neither structural nor relational uncertainty will be completely separated from each other in any real situation, and ultimately these approaches should be combined in a single model. We believe that our approach does give the major features however.

In Yovits, Foulk, and Rose (1981) we considered the information for relational uncertainty only and noted that when the variance of the probabilities of choice is a maximum, the certainty is a maximum (or the

Table 2

QUADRATIC G, n = 2, r = 3

mDME$_R$	Maximum Coordinates DME	DME (Units of α)
1.2	0.7000	0.1509
1.68	0.6950	0.1386
3.16	0.6901	0.1269
3.6	0.6600	0.1261

uncertainty is a minimum) and when the variance is minimum so is the certainty. In fact the variance is maximized when one COA has probability of one and the others are zero (certainty). It is minimized when all the probabilities are the same (random choice).

We further note that two situations with the same variance but different means have different uncertainties depending on the value of the mean. It is the size of the variance compared to the mean which is the important factor. Thus we define our information measure to be

$$I_{relational} \propto \frac{\text{mean square variance of probabilities}}{\text{mean of probabilities}}$$

Note that this is somewhat different from the relationship suggested in Yovits, Foulk, and Rose (1981). Recognizing that the mean of the probabilities is just one divided by the number of courses of action, and adopting a proportionality factor of 2 we have

$$I_{relational} = 2(\sum_{i=1}^{m} P(a_i)^2 - 1/m), \text{ in units of BCU,} \tag{3}$$

where $P(a_i)$ is the probability of choice of the $i\underline{th}$ course of action and m is the number of viable courses of action.

Note that, when one probability is one and the others are zero (certainty), then $I_{relational}$ becomes $(2 - 2/m)$. When m equals two, the binary case, $I_{relational}$ becomes one. That is, for the deterministic binary situation the amount of information resulting from learning the relations is one BCU; thus the unit BCU is used.

We further note when all the probabilities are equal then $I_{relational}$ is identically zero. This will be the case for structural certainty, where nothing is known of the relationships among the COA's and their probabilities of choice must then all be equal. For this case as we show in the next section, the quantity of information is simply two divided by the number of COA's remaining at time t, represented by N(t). That is,

$$I_{structural} = 2/N(t). \tag{4}$$

Then since I_{total} is simply the sum of $I_{structural}$ and $I_{relational}$ we have

$$I_{total} = 2\sum_{i=1}^{m} P(a_i)^2, \text{ in BCU's.} \tag{5}$$

For the case of certainty this expression becomes 2 BCU's. If there is any uncertainty then I_{total} is always less than 2 BCU's. Since the relational information is one BCU for the binary case, we see that half the information has been the result of the structure and half the result of learning the relationships among the values of the COA's. For 3 viable COA's these two BCU's are divided 2/3 for structure and 4/3 for relationships, etc.

THE MODEL FOR STRUCTURAL UNCERTAINTY

In the previous section we briefly discussed the two aspects of the decision making spectrum, recognizing that they will overlap in any real situation and that the transition in reality is smooth. These are structural uncertainty and relational uncertainty.

During the structural uncertainty phase one of the main functions of the DM is to eliminate non-viable COA's. This elimination will proceed at a decreasing rate since non-viable COA's can be eliminated relatively easily, but eventually it becomes difficult to decide which (if any) of the remaining COA's are non-viable. To simplify the mathematical modeling of this phase, we assume that all those COA's still remaining at any time in the structural uncertainty phase of the process are equally likely to be chosen. (The DM is assumed not to have any relational knowledge of the COA's.)

Once the structure of the model has been established, the DM concentrates on determining the correct selection probabilities for those COA's still under consideration, as we discussed in the section on background. As the DM learns which COA's give better results, these selection probabilities continually change. Eventually the best COA achieves a very high selection probability, while the probabilities associated with the remaining COA's become very low.

With this procedure we are able to develop Equation (4) for the information measure for structure uncertainty. We also can show that for structural uncertainty

$$DME_{structural} = mDME_{random}/N(t). \tag{6}$$

where $N(t)$ is the number of COA's remaining at time t and DME_{random} is given by Equation (15) of Yovits, Foulk, and Rose (1981).

CONCLUDING REMARKS

In this paper, we have summarized briefly some important results which have extended previous ongoing work leading toward a conceptual and theoretical approach to information flow and analysis. The material which has been presented is available in considerable detail in a number of journals.

Our conceptual formulation is an important effort to define information flow and various associated systems quantitatively and measurably. Furthermore, a number of terms, generally used loosely, have been defined in terms of their significance and use, again quantitatively and measurably. For example, we have defined information entirely as a decision oriented measure; we have explicitly quantified external documentation; we have defined such terms as decision maker effectiveness as well as other similar terms.

We have described an approach which permits us to assess quantitatively the effects of external documentation on decision makers through a relationship we call an information profile. This is a direct extension of previous research which considered a closed system only, involving a decision maker who chooses a course of action to achieve certain results and has only feedback information from his choice available to update his next choice.

In previous work we considered only the situation for which the decision maker knows all of the viable courses of action, but initially does not know the relationships among them. This situation we call relational uncertainty or structural uncertainty. We have in this paper extended the model to the situation where the decision maker does not know the various courses of action; this case we call structural uncertainty.

Experimental verification of our concepts and model is an important task remaining. It is only through further experimentation that we can as well obtain specific values for important parameters which are involved.

It is our ultimate goal to apply this theory to real and useful situations and to describe and measure the significance and value of information in these situations. We hope to apply this work to information systems development, database management systems, information retrieval, and to decision systems in general.

ACKNOWLEDGEMENT

Research supported in part by the National Science Foundation under Grant Number IST 83-12728 and Grant Number IST 83-03900. Any opinions, findings, and conclusions expressed herein are those of the authors and do not necessarily reflect the views of the National Science Foundation.

REFERENCES

Langefors, B., 1972, Theoretical Analysis of Information Systems, Auerback, Philadelphia, PA (also Student Litteratur, Lund, Sweden).

MacKay, D. M., 1969, Information, Mechanism and Meaning, MIT Press, Cambridge, MA.

Pearson, C., and Slamecka, V., 1983, "Perspectives on Informatics as a Semiotic Discipline", The Study of Information: Interdisciplinary Messages, Machlup, F., and Mansfield, U., eds., J. Wiley & Sons, New York, pp. 141-148.

Shannon, C. E., and Weaver, W., 1949, The Mathematical Theory of Communication, The University of Illinois Press, Urbana, IL.

Winograd, T., 1972, "Understanding Natural Language", Cognitive Psychology, 3, pp. 1-191.

Yovits, M. C., and Abilock, J. G., 1974, "A Semiotic Framework for Information Science Leading to the Development of a Quantitative Measure of Information", Information Utilities, Proceedings of the 37th ASIS Annual Meeting, 11, Atlanta.

Yovits, M. C., Foulk, C. R., and Rose, L. L., 1981, "Information Flow and Analysis: Theory, Simulations and Experiment, Part 1. Basic Theoretical and Conceptual Development, Part II. Simulation, Examples, and Results", Journal of the American Society for Information Science, 32, pp. 187-210.

Yovits, M. C., and Foulk, C. R., 1985, "Experiments and Analysis of Information Use and Value in a Decision-Making Context", Journal of the American Society for Information Science, 36, (2), pp. 63-81.

INFORMATION SCIENCE LAWS AND REGULARITIES: A SURVEY*

Pranas Zunde

Georgia Institute of Technology
Atlanta, GA 30332

Abstract: This paper catalogs laws and regularities of empirical nature
which are in the domain of study of information science and which have been
published in professional literature. No attempt has been made to critically assess or evaluate their validity in terms of reported empirical
evidence. Selected applications of some of these laws and regularities are
listed at the end.

1. INTRODUCTION

It has been argued elsewhere (Zunde, 1984) that information science is
an empirical science of informative texts. More explicitly, information
science is the study of the nature and properties of informative texts with
the ultimate objective of establishing - through laws and theories - general principles by which phenomena related to generation, transmission,
transformation, and storage of such texts can be explained, accounted for,
and predicted. By the generic name of a text we mean a structured collection or sequence of signs of a sign system (language), either formal or
interpreted.

Observable properties of informative texts can be grouped, with respect
to the mode of observability, into two major categories: (1) directly observable properties or phenomena; and (2) indirectly observable properties
or phenomena.

Directly observable properties of informative texts are physical,
chemical and other properties of their sign vehicles, syntactic properties
of texts, and effects of semantic and pragmatic properties of informative
texts on the interpreters.

Indirectly observable properties of informative texts are their semantic and pragmatic effects on interpreters as reported by the interpreters,
eventually with some subjective bias.

The purpose of this article is to survey laws and regularities of the

*This study was supported in part by the National Science Foundation,
 Grant No. DSI77-05297, which is gratefully acknowledged.

above mentioned types of observables as reported in information science literature. An attempt is also made to systematize these laws and regularities to some extent to facilitate the overview.

2. STATUS OF INFORMATION SCIENCE LAWS

The principal objective of an empirical science is, other than the description of empirical phenomena, to establish, through laws and theories, general principles by means of which empirical phenomena can be explained, accounted for, and predicted. The explanatory and predictive principles of a scientific discipline are stated in its hypothetical generalizations and its theories; they characterize general patterns or regularities to which the individual phenomena conform and by virtue of which their occurrence can be systematically anticipated (Hempel, 1952).

We call a proposition of science an empirical law if it contains only constructs that refer to observables or are operationally definable, and if it has been extensively verified and found to hold under a variety of conditions. Thus, empirical laws derive their support wholly from their observable instances and not at all from any theoretical or other considerations which may be involved.

It is clear from the nature of observables mentioned in the introduction, that quantitative laws of information science may be expected to be laws relating some aspects of the behavior of interpreters to other behavioral aspects or to characteristics of informative texts, or conversely.

There is no agreement among scientists, whether or not confirmed, verified regularities governing various phenomena of human behavior are laws in the sense of the laws of "hard sciences" like physics or chemistry. The laws of physics or chemistry are considered universal in terms of their validity and invariant in time. In other words, these laws, such as Ohm's law and others, are generally assumed to have been true millions of years ago and to remain true for millions of years to come. On the other hand, laws of human behavior obviously cannot be older than the human species itself, have obviously changed in the past and may change in the future. Therefore, so the argument goes, it makes no sense at all to consider laws of human behavior and laws of, say, physics as birds of the same feather.

We adopt here the viewpoint of Kendall (1961) that "man is a short-lived animal who is still, sociologically speaking, in a rapid phase of development. The laws which control his social actions and interactions may themselves be subject to rapid change. To such an organism the laws of Nature, with their vaster time-scale, appear unchanging, and may indeed be so. But the difference is possibly one of degree rather than kind."

In particular, from the viewpoint of engineering applications, what matters is the _relative_ stability of these laws, but not their ultimate ontological status. After all, the lifetime of systems engineered on the basis of insights provided by such laws is not a million years, and not even a thousand. The lifetime of many of the present day systems is perhaps 25 or 50 years. Relative to this kind of planning horizon, these "soft" laws, if sufficiently verified, can be expected to be sufficiently stable and reliable to serve a useful purpose in system engineering.

On the other hand, it is true that in the domain of study of information science there are, as yet, very few observed regularities which have been sufficiently verified and confirmed. One reason for this state of affairs is that information science still is in the very early stages of its development as a scientific discipline. It is beyond the scope of this survey to critically evaluate the extent of produced evidence in support of postulated relationships among various observables. It is, therefore, quite possible that some of the hypothesized laws may not survive a more rigorous experimental testing. We have, therefore, chosen to refer here to all reported observations of empirical relationships as regularities rather than laws, thus withholding, by implication, a judgement on their scientific status.

3. CLASSIFICATION OF SURVEYED REGULARITIES

The regularities surveyed and reported here are classified into nine major categories, namely

1. Syntactic regularities of use of natural languages.

2. Syntactic regularities of use of artificial languages.

3. Semantic regularities of use of natural languages.

4. Regularities relating syntactic indicators to semantic and pragmatic features.

5. Regularities of information representation.

6. Regularities of information acquisition and processing.

7. Regularities of structure and behavior of information sources.

8. Regularities of use of information sources and information transfer.

9. Regularities of growth of recorded information and knowledge.

Each main category is in turn subdivided into two types of regularities. Type I is a subcategory which consists of observed regularities of statistical nature, i.e. frequency distributions of entities or events. This subcategory is in turn subdivided into two classes, (A) the class of rank-frequency distributions, and (B) the class of other kinds of distributions.

Rank-frequency distribution is a very common type of regularity in the domain of information science. Briefly, a rank-frequency distribution is defined as follows. Let E be some finite set of events, $E = \{e_1, e_2,...,e_n\}$, and let $f(e_i)$ be the frequency of occurrence of event e_i. Let the events be ordered by nonincreasing frequency of occurrence and assign rank 1 to the event with the highest frequency of occurrence, rank 2 to the event with second highest frequency of occurrence, and so on. Events with equal frequencies of occurrence are assigned consecutive ranks arbitrarily. The best known example of a regularity with underlying rank-frequency distribution is the Zipf's law relating word frequencies to their ranks. In this example the rank-frequency distribution is close to a hyperbolic distribution law (Zunde, 1984).

The second class in the Type I subcategory contains statistical regularities of all other kinds with probability laws of frequency distributions such as negative binomial, Poisson, or gamma distribution.

The Type II subcategory of each main category lists postulated relationships linking two or more directly observable variables. In most cases this dependency is not strictly deterministic, but is obtained as a result of a linear or nonlinear regression of a set of statistical data. Hence the name "Correlational Dependencies" for the regularities grouped under that subcategory.

4. SYNTACTIC REGULARITIES OF USE OF NATURAL LANGUAGE

4-IA. Rank-frequency Distribution of:

phonemes (Krevitt and Griffith, 1972);

letters (Krevitt and Griffith, 1972; Good, 1969; Resnikoff and Dolby, 1970);

words (Zipf, 1949; Mitsevich and Solov'ev, 1969; Mandelbrot, 1953; Edmundson, 1977; Good, 1969; Brookes and Griffiths, 1978; Belonogov, 1962; Neshitoi, 1977);

phrases (Smith and Devine; 1985);

words in journal article titles (Heaps, 1972);

words in document titles (Krevitt and Griffeth, 1972);

descriptor terms in bibliographic data files (Kim, 1982);

nouns (Good, 1969);

word stems (Belonogov, 1962);

surnames (Fokker and Lynch, 1974); and

morphemes (Zipf, 1949).

4-IB. Probability Distribution of:

word types by frequency of occurrence (Zipf, 1949; Parker-Rhodes and Joyce, 1956; Booth, 1967; Simon, 1955; Good, 1953; Sichel, 1975; Herdan, 1964; Kraus, 1972);

word types by length in phonemes (Guiraud, 1971; Herdan, 1958; Edmundson, 1977);

word types by length in letters (Edmundson, 1977);

word types not occurring in text of a given length by length of text (Serebrianyi, 1978);

word types by the number of morphological derivatives (Guiraud, 1971);

word tokens by their length in phonemes (Guiraud, 1954; Herdan, 1958; Guiraud, 1965(a); Edmundson, 1977; Dolby and Resnikoff, 1971);

word tokens by length in letters (Herdan, 1958; Edmundson, 1977);

word tokens by number of syllables (Ludvikova, 1971; Fucks, 1955; Tarnoczy, 1961; Bartkowiakowa and Gleichgewicht, 1962);

text vocabulary size over the length of text (Gani, 1975);

surname occurrences by their length in letters (Healy, 1968);

sentences by their length in word tokens (Gaddum, 1945; Dolby and Resnikoff, 1971; Edmundson, 1977);

article titles by their length in word tokens (Chernyi, Kuznetsova and Matsak, 1969; Bird and Knight, 1975);

gaps between two successive occurrences of a particular word type by length of gaps in word tokens (Zipf, 1949; Kralik, 1977; Edmundson, 1977);

bibliographic records by number of substantive words contained in them (Dayton et al., 1977); and

lines in PERMUTERM type title indexes by length in words (Chernyi, Kuznetsova and Matsak, 1969).

4-II. Correlational Dependencies of:

average length in phonemes of a word type occurring with a given frequency on that frequency (Zipf, 1949; Pearson and Slamecka, 1977);

average length in syllables of a word type occurring with a given frequency on that frequency (Zipf, 1949; Pearson and Slamecka, 1977);

number of word types on the number of word tokens in a text (Carroll, 1938; Zipf, 1949; Good and Toulmin, 1956; Herdan, 1964; Kherts, 1969; Webster, 1969; Brainerd, 1972; Heaps, 1972; Gor'kova, 1972; Gani, 1975; Pearson, 1978; Edmundson, 1977);

number of word types on the number of word tokens in titles (Heaps, 1972);

number of word types and number of word tokens in subject headings (Heaps, 1972);

number of lexical word types on the total number of word types in a text (Kuhlen, 1975);

number of lexical word types on the total number of word tokens in a text (Kuhlen, 1975);

number of formal word types on the total number of word types in a text (Kuhlen, 1975);

number of formal word types on the total number of word tokens in a text (Kuhlen, 1975);

number of word stem types on the total number of word types in a text (Kuhlen, 1975);

number of word stem types on the total number of word tokens in a text (Kuhlen, 1975);

number of lexical functions of a word type on its frequency (Andrukovich and Korolev, 1977);

median of noun frequencies in a text on the length in words of that text (Williams, 1970);

mean and the variance of the distribution of word types by their length in phonemes on the mean and the variance of the word token distribution of their length in phonemes (Herdan, 1964);

average length of word types on the average length, in word tokens, of sentences in a text (Weiss, 1967; Srinivasan, 1977);

average rank of a word type in an ordered list by nonincreasing frequency of occurrence on the length in phonemes of that word type (Guiraud, 1963);

rank of a character in a play and the number of lines spoken by the character in that play (McCurdy, 1953; Brainerd, 1973);

mean word length in oral and written behavior (Portnoy, 1973);

relative use of most of the grammatical word classes in oral and written behavior (Portnoy, 1973); and

verb-adjective ratio in oral and written behavior (Portnoy, 1973).

5. SYNTACTIC REGULARITIES OF USE OF ARTIFICIAL LANGUAGES

5-IA. Rank-frequency Distribution of:

distinct entities in algorithms (Zweben, 1977);

operands in computer program codes (Zweben, 1977);

operators in computer program codes (Zweben, 1977); and

computer instruction types (Resnikoff and Dolby, 1970); and

commands in human-computer dialogs (Ellis and Hitchcock, 1986).

5-II. Correlational Dependencies of:

length of a computer program and the total number of distinct operators as well as the total number of distinct operands (Bulut, Halstead, and Bayer, 1974).

6. SEMANTIC REGULARITIES OF NATURAL LANGUAGE USE

6-IB. Probability Distribution of:

word types by the number of their lexical meanings (Pap, 1967; Krylov and Yakubovskaya, 1977; Korolev, 1977; Zunde, 1981); and

word types by frequency of occurrence as associative responses to a given stimulus word (Skinner, 1936).

6-II. Correlational Dependencies of:

co-occurrence of word types related in meaning and the distance between them in word tokens (Lewis, Baxandale, and Bennett, 1967; Korolev, 1977);

co-occurrence of synonymous word types in different sentences and the similarity of their contexts (Lewis, Baxandale, and Bennett, 1967);

difference in meaning of two morphemes and the similarity of their environments (Harris, 1954; Rubenstein and Goodenough, 1965);

number of meanings (senses) of a word type and the frequency of its occurrence (Zipf, 1949; Guiraud, 1965(b); Guiraud, 1971);

number of meanings of a word type and the number of phonemes in that word (Guiraud, 1965(b));

number of meanings of a word type and the length in letters of that word type (Baker, 1950);

number of lexical meanings of a word type and its rank in a list ordered by nonincreasing frequency of occurrence of word types (Zipf, 1949);

number of synonyms of a word type in a given text and the number of occurrences of that word type in text (Andrukovich and Korolev, 1977);

structural similarity and the associative similarity of scientific concepts (Johnson, 1969);

structural similarity and judged similarity of scientific concepts (Johnson, 1969);

meaningfulness of a word and its perceptual stability (Terwilliger, 1968);

speed of recognition of meaning related words and their pronunciation (Meyer and Schvaneveldt, 1976; Becker and Killion, 1977); and

fraction of cognates shared by two daughter languages and the duration of their development (Edmundson, 1977).

7. REGULARITIES OF SYNTACTIC INDICATORS OF SEMANTIC AND PRAGMATIC FEATURES

7-II. Correlational Dependencies of:

time required to program a preconceived one module algorithm, and the total number of distinct operators as well as the total number of distinct operands (Bulut, Halstead, and Bayer, 1974);

program implementation time in machine language and the total number of distinct operators and operands (Halstead, 1977);

total number of delivered errors in a computer program and the total number of distinct operators as well as the total number of distinct operands (Halstead, 1977);

number of resource types being managed by an operating system and the number of machine language instructions required to control these resources (Halstead, 1977);

rank of a word type and the probability of it being selected as an indexing term for a given document (Brookes, 1978);

title length and the number of keywords it contains (Chernyi, Kuznetsova, and Matsak, 1969);

total length in words of an indexed collection of document abstracts and the total number of keywords in the index to that collection (Chernyi, 1968);

position of a keyword on frequency ranked list and its effectiveness for searching KWIC and KWOC indexes (Gor'kova and Naumycheva, 1970);

position of a word type on frequency ranked list of word types and the value of that word type as content identifier of the document (Pao, 1978);

functional role of a word type and its value as content identifier of a document (Briner, 1976);

total number of keyword types and the total number of keyword tokens in an indexed text (Neshitoi, 1977);

amount of information lost per message and the length of the message as well as the number of symbols in the vocabulary (Pollack, 1952);

number of books published on some life event and the amount of semantic information in that event (Levine, 1977);

indicativity of a catalog field and the length of that field in word tokens (Marcus, Kugel, and Benenfeld, 1978);

value of a journal and its rank on a list ordered by nonincreasing number of citations (Dalziel, 1937);

information value and the amount of information processed (Leimkuhler, 1977);

subjective information content of a text and the number of errors made in guessing that text character by character (Kauffman et al., 1974);

informativeness of titles and time of publication (Ghosh, 1977);

scientific productivity in terms of the number of publications and scientific recognition (Ashton and Oppenheim, 1978);

total influence score of a university's publications and the peer rating of that university (Anderson, Narin and McAllister, 1978); and

presence of a colon in the title of a paper and the scholarship of the author (Perry, 1985).

8. REGULARITIES OF INFORMATION REPRESENTATION

8-IA. Rank-frequency Distribution of:

keywords in queries (Petrenko, 1974);

index terms by the number of posted documents (Brookes, 1978; Nelson and Tague, 1985); and

library classification subject matter categories by the number of books assigned (Houston and Wall, 1964).

8-IB. Probability Distribution of:

titles by number of keywords (Bird and Knight, 1975);

data element types over indexes and bibliographies (Marulli and Koenig, 1979);

subject matter categories in library classifications by the number of volumes catalogued (Krevitt and Griffeth, 1972);

indexing terms by the number of postings (Houston and Wall, 1964);

citations by the number of unique nomenclature word types (Dayton et al., 1977);

connections (in terms of domain overlap) between subject categories of a classification system by authorship (Akhmerov, 1969); and

weights assigned to documents based on the degree of agreement of the set of indexing terms assigned to the document and the set of terms chosen in the search query formulation (Heine, 1977).

8-II. Correlational Dependencies of :

number of keywords assigned to a text and the length of the text in words (Chernyi, 1968; Gor'kova and Naumycheva, 1970; Dubovikov, Markova, and Sol'ts, 1976);

size of an index vocabulary (i.e. the total number of distinct indexing terms used) and the total number of postings in the index file (Houston and Wall, 1964);

size of an index vocabulary and the total number of documents indexed (Houston and Wall, 1964);

size of an index vocabulary and both the number of documents indexed (i.e. the collection size) and the average number of documents retrieved per search (Rolling and Plette, 1968);

thesaurus growth by number of descriptors and time (Heine, 1977);

rate of growth of an index vocabulary and the number of documents indexed (Houston and Wall, 1964);

set of documents clustered by co-citation patterns and the same set of documents clustered by natural classification, in terms of the degree of coextensionality (Small and Koenig, 1977);

problem representation alternatives and the amount of information that can be processed during problem solving (Mayer, 1976); and

knowledge based on the concensus of experts and the knowledge expressed in the literature of that field (Kim and Kim, 1977).

9. REGULARITIES OF INFORMATION PROCESSING AND ACQUISITION

9-II. Correlational Dependencies of :

comprehensibility of words in spoken and written language and the length of the words in letters (Portnoy, 1973);

comprehensibility of a sentence and the distance between the subject and predicate in that sentence (Fry, 1977);

comprehension and the level of education of the human subject (Lowry and Marr, 1974);

comprehension and the degree of prior subject familiarity by the human subject (Lowry and Marr, 1974);

reading time and selected properties of sentences (Garrod and Sanford, 1977);

readability of a text and the degree of text condensation (Dronberger and Kowitz, 1975);

achievement of learning by heart and the information content of the text learned (Strizenec, 1965);

error rate in reconstruction of sequences of characters and the "strangeness" of these sequences of characters (Pearson, 1979);

amount of information gained and the number of possible alternatives (Pollack, 1952);

choice-reaction time and the number of alternatives (Hick, 1952);

amount of information lost in messages and the length of the length of the messages (Pollack, 1952);

affective connotation of words and word frequency (Zajonc, 1968);

frequency of exposure and the affective connotation of nonsense words and symbols (Zajonc, 1968);

word frequency and subject's attitude to their referents (Zajonc, 1968);

size of a vocabulary and the recognition of symbols selected from the vocabulary (Miller, Heise and Lichten, 1951);

delay between stages in a multistage information processing task and the reaction time (Leonard, 1958);

semantic distance between two signs and the reaction time (Mynatt, 1977);

types of signs (icons, symbols, etc.) and the reaction time (Banks and Flora, 1977);

processing different parts of a sentence and the semantic level of processing (Reynolds and Flagg, 1975);

information demand and the amount of information processed (Leimkuhler, 1977);

subject's uncertainty about the time of stimulus of occurrence and simple reaction time (Klemmer, 1957);

quality of recall and the type of sentence (abstract, concrete, etc.) (Reynolds, 1972);

semiotic information contained in a message vs. the emotional intensity and the amount of "hard" information (Levine, 1977);

openness of information and relevance judgement (Davidson, 1977);

information content of a word and the number of senses which enter into its composition (Guiraud, 1971); and

    reaction time of a stimulus and information contained in that stimulus (Hyman, 1953).

10. REGULARITIES OF STRUCTURE AND BEHAVIOR OF INFORMATION SOURCES

10-IA. Rank-frequency Distribution of:

    scientific journals by number of articles published on a given subject (Vickery, 1948; Bradford, 1950; Cole, 1962; Kozachkov and Khursin, 1968; Brookes, 1968; Brookes, 1969(a); Brookes, 1969(b); Lawani, 1973; Chonez, 1974; O'Neill, 1974; Loiferman, Volkov and Duzhenko, 1975; Mitsevich, 1975; Fernandez and Saracevic, 1977; Leimkuhler, 1977; Smol'kov, 1977; Hubert, 1978; Leimkuhler, 1980; Sichel, 1985);

    publishers by the number of monographs published on a particular subject (Brookes, 1969(b); Worthen, 1975);

    journals by the number of papers which were presented at a scientific meeting and published by these journals (Garvey, Lin, and Nelson, 1970); and

    journals by the number of their contributions to a specialized abstracting service (Gorkova and Mellion, 1968).

10-IB. Probability Distribution of:

    periodicals by number of articles (Neshitoi, 1977); and

    university libraries by size (Dolby and Resnikoff, 1971).

10-II. Correlational Dependencies of:

    dynamics of the population of scientist and time (Martino, 1969);

    dynamics of organizations and time (Starbuck, 1965);

11. REGULARITIES OF USE OF INFORMATION SOURCES AND INFORMATION TRANSFER

11-IA. Rank-frequency Distribution of:

    journals by the number of citations to publications in these journals (Brookes, 1969(a));

    cities by number of references to publications produced in these cities (Barker, 1966);

    indexed periodicals by the number of references to these periodicals (Brookes, 1969(a); Brookes, 1969(b));

    use of abstracting serials (Brookes, 1969(a); Brookes, 1969(b));

    books in a library by the number of times a book was checked out (Fairthorne, 1969); and

    journal use in a library (Goffman and Morris, 1970; Mayes, 1975).

11-IB. Probability Distribution of:

articles being cited by other articles (MacRae, 1969);

citations by time of publication of citing documents (Burton and Kebler, 1960; Barker, 1966; Brookes, 1970; Clark, 1976);

citations by journals (Donohue, 1973; Meadows, 1974);

citations to articles over time (MacRae, 1969);

references to an issue of a periodical over time (Brookes, 1971);

articles by the number of citings (Margolis, 1967);

citations in any given year over all the previous articles which are cited at least once (Cawkell, 1976);

cited articles by age of the articles at the time of first citing (MacRae, 1969, Gilbert and Woolgar, 1974);

readers on library circulation lists over popularity ranked journals (Mayes, 1975);

time-lag periods of items published in secondary publications by duration (Zhurek, 1969);

frequency of user demands by sources which are likely to satisfy the demands (Kashafutdinova, Grishina, and Mial'dizina, 1975);

demand of a library item over time (Morse and Elston, 1969; Beheshti and Tague, 1984);

library users by the length of stay during a single visit in the library (Bush, Galliher, and Morse, 1956);

library users by number of tasks they perform during a single library visit (Bush, Galliher, and Morse, 1956);

number of requests for a given title being made during a single loan period in a library (Buckland and Woodburn, 1969; Lau, 1977);

book use during any given year after its publication (Jain, Leimkuhler, and Anderson, 1969);

frequency of use of journals in a library (Morse and Leimkuhler, 1977; Sichel, 1985);

titles in an information store by demand rate (Parker, 1982(a));

scientists by the number of significant contacts within the scientific community (Griffith, Jahn, and Miller, 1971);

scientists by the number of significant contacts with scientists outside the specialty under consideration (Griffith, Jahn, and Miller, 1971); and

periodicals by the number of requests from outside organizations for journal loans from a national library (Sichel, 1985).

11-II. Correlational Dependencies of:

expected number of citations and the publication date of the cited papers (Dieks and Chang, 1976; Gilbert and Woolgar, 1974);

rate of change in the total number of published titles and the total number of citations to publications in a given subject area (Ivanov, Kapustin, and Makhotenko, 1973);

average number of references in a paper and the time of publication of that paper (Cawkell, 1968; Gilbert and Woolgar, 1974);

person's contribution to science and the number of citations to his publications (Cole et al., 1974);

usage and age of a periodical (Cole, 1963; Parker, 1982(b));

size of a personal document collection and the average number of references in the papers authored (Soper, 1976);

residual utility of a set of periodicals and their age (Brookes, 1970);

use of scientific and technical literature and the period of time elapsed since their publication (Oliver, 1971; Brookes, 1973);

intensity of circulation of a library item and the "softness" of the subject (McGrath, 1978);

intensity of circulation of a library item and its ranking on "basic-applied" scale of the subject field (McGrath, 1978);

communication pressure and the number of requests for information (Browning, 1978);

communication patterns and the effects of various parameters (such as duration and attitude of communicants) on them (Browning, 1978); and

information diffusion dynamics in terms of potential contributors, individuals contributing, and individuals who have contributed in the past (Goffman, 1966; Coadic, 1974).

12. REGULARITIES OF GROWTH OF RECORDED INFORMATION AND KNOWLEDGE

12-IA. Rank-frequency Distribution of:

scientists by publication productivity (Shreider and Osipova, 1969).

12-IB. Probability Distribution of:

scientists-authors by the number of their published contributions (Williams, 1944; Simon, 1955; Price, 1963; Mantell, 1966; Nalimov and Mul'chenko, 1969; Krisciunas, 1977; Neshitoi, 1977; Coile, 1978; Rao, 1980; Brookes, 1983; Sichel, 1985; Nicholls, 1986);

scientists in a research laboratory by their productivity in terms of scientific publications (Shockley, 1957);

authors by the number of their contributions to a single scientific journal (Schorr, 1974; Radhakrishnan and Kernizan, 1979);

independently made discoveries or inventions by the number of scientists contributing (Simonton, 1978); and authors-chemists by the number of their publications during the first six years after receiving their doctorates (Sichel, 1985).

12-II. Correlational Dependencies of:

number of periodicals publishing articles on a specific subject and the number of authors contributing to these periodicals (Goffman and Warren, 1969);

average number of publications produced by the universities and the amount of research funding (Narin, 1976);

increase of the output of scientific activities and the rate of increase of scientists as well as the total number of scientists working in a research area (Nalimov and Mul'chenko, 1969);

volume of produced scientific literature and time (i.e., growth of the literature of science) (Baker, 1961; Zvorykin, 1967; Holt and Schrank, 1968; Kochen, 1969; Nalimov and Mul'chenko, 1969; Krauze and Hillinger, 1971; Oliver, 1971; Brookes, 1971; Mitsevich, 1973; Nowakowska, 1973; Gilbert and Woolgar, 1974; Gubankov, 1975);

degree of exhaustivity of content representation of a document and the number of indexers contributing (Zunde and Dexter, 1969); and

presence of selected research method criteria in the published literature of a subfield and the growth rate of published literature of that subfield (Stephenson, 1985).

13. SOME REPORTED APPLICATIONS OF SURVEYED REGULARITIES

To Library and Information Center Management

*   Determination of the potentially most useful stock pattern (Aridaman, 1967; Brookes, 1972; Douglas, 1973);

*   Optimal allocation of limited funds to acquisitions and storage (Goffman and Morris, 1970; Buckland and Woodburn, 1969);

*   Verification of the comprehensiveness of a subject area of an abstracting or indexing service (Brookes, 1971(a));

*   Determining titles which constitute the "core" periodicals of a subject so far as quantity, not quality, of papers is concerned (Brookes, 1971(a));

*   Determination of the number of periodical titles required to cover a specified fraction of the total periodical literature of a given subject (Brookes, 1971(b));

*   Determining at what point substitution of photocopies of relevant papers in periodicals relating to a subject is cheaper than subscribing to the periodicals (Bubel, 1973; Dikeman, 1975);

*   Planning the acquisition of periodicals within a hierarchical network of libraries (Lawani, 1973);

*   Costing library services (Leimkuhler, 1977);

*   Discarding and relegating older materials in libraries (Line and Sandison, 1974);

*   Dislocation of books on storage shelves in libraries (Booth, 1967); and

*   Retention policies of periodicals (Meadows, 1974; Line and Sandison, 1974).

To Information Processing and Information Storage and Retrieval

*   Design of automatic indexing systems (Briner, 1976; Dietze, 1975; Fukunaga, Morikawa, and Kasai, 1976);

*   Selection of weights for keywords in information retrieval (Neshitoi, 1977; Novikov and Yakushin, 1972; Robertson and Sparck Jones, 1976);

*   Design and automated construction of thesauri (Krautwurst, 1969; Korolev, 1977, Kim and Kim, 1977);

*   Design of PERMUTERM indexes (Chernyi, Kuznetsova, and Matsak, 1969);

*   Verification of the completeness of a bibliography (Brookes, 1971(a));

*   Design of information search strategies, such as zone searching (Leimkuhler, 1977);

*   Modeling structural connections in the classification of information flows (Gor'kova and Shishova, 1978);

*   Automatic conversion of user requests to search queries (Pschenichnaya and Shzamko, 1976);

*   Data base design (Fokker and Lynch, 1974; Fedorowicz, 1982; Heaps, 1974); and

*   Man-machine interface design (Kuhlen, 1975; Sager, 1976).

Miscellaneous Applications

*   Characterization of style and discrimination of authorship (Greenblatt, 1978; Srinivasan, 1977);

*   Discrimination of subject fields and identification of subfields of especially rapid development (Wyllys, 1975);

*   Detection of abnormalities in the results of literature use surveys (Cole, 1962);

*   Comparison of programming language levels (Halstead, 1972);

*   Estimating programming time (Halstead, 1972); and

*   Estimating the effects of modular programming (Halstead, 1972).

REFERENCES

Akhmerov, F. R., 1969, "Characteristics of Links Between Authors and Their Utilization for Classification Purposes, Nauch.-Tekh. Inf., Series 2, 10, pp. 6-9. (In Russian.)

Anderson, R. C., Narin, F., and McAllister, P., 1978, "Publication Ratings versus Peer Ratings of Universities", J. Am. Soc. Inf. Sci., 29, pp. 91–103.

Andrukovich, P. F., and Korolev, E. I., 1977, "The Statistical and Lexico-grammatical Properties of Words", Autom. Doc. Math. Linguist., 11, (2), pp. 1–11. Also in Nauch.-Tekh. Inf., Series 2, 11, (4), pp. 1–9.

Aridaman, K. H., et al., 1967, Statistical Study of Book Use, Purdue University, Lafayette, Indiana.

Ashton, S. V., and Oppenhein, C., 1978, "A Method for Predicting Nobel Prizewinners in Chemistry", Social Studies of Science, 8, pp. 341–348.

Baker, D. B., 1961, "Growth of Chemical Literature: Past, Present, and Future", Chem. Eng. News, pp. 78–81, July 17, 1961.

Baker, S. J., 1950, "The Pattern of Language", Journal of General Psychology, 42, (1), pp. 25–66.

Banks, W. P., and Flora, J., 1977, "Semantic and Perceptual Processes in Symbolic Comparisons", J. Exp. Psychol., Human Perception and Perfor-mance, 3, (2), pp. 278–290.

Barker, D. L., 1966, Characteristics of the Scientific Literature Cited by Chemists of the Soviet Union, Ph.D. Thesis in Library Science, University of Illinois, Urbana.

Bartkowiakowa, A., and Gleichgewicht, B., 1962, "On the Length of Expressions in the Texts of Polish Authors", Zastosowania Matematyky, 5, pp. 309–319. (In Polish.)

Becker, C. A., and Killion, T. H., 1977, "Interaction of Visual and Cognitive Effects in Word Recognition", J. Exp. Psychol., Human Perceptions and Performance, 3, (3), pp. 389–401.

Beheshti, J., and Tague, J. M., 1984, "Morse's Markov Model of Book Use Revisited", Journal of the ASIS, 35, (5), pp. 259–267.

Belonogov, G. G., 1962, "On Some Statistical Regularities in Written Russian, Voprosy Iazykoznania, 7. (In Russian.)

Bird, P. R., and Knight, M. A., 1975, "Word Count Statistics of the Titles of Scientific Papers, Information Scientists, 9, (2), pp. 67–68.

Booth, A. D., 1967, "A 'Law' of Occurrences for Words of Low Frequency", Inform. and Control, 10, pp. 386–393.

Bradford, S. C., 1950, Documentation, Public Affairs Press, Washington, D.C., pp. 144–159.

Brainerd, B., 1972, "On the Relation Between Types and Tokens in Literary Text", J. Appl. Prob., 9, pp. 507–518.

Brainerd, B., 1973, "On the Number of Words a Character Speaks in the Plays of Shakespeare", Computer Studies in the Humanities and Verbal Studies, 4, pp. 57–63.

Briner, L. L., 1976, "Identifying Keywords in Text Data Processing", Fifteenth Annual Technical Symposium Directions and Challenges, June 17, 1976, National Bureau of Standards, Gaithersburg, Maryland, pp. 85–90.

Brookes, B. C., 1968, "The Derivation and Application of the Bradford-Zipf Distribution, J. of Documentation, 24, (4), pp. 247-265.

Brookes, B. C., 1969(a), "Bradford's Law and the Bibliography of Science", Nature, 224, (5223), pp. 953-956.

Brookes, B. C., 1969(b), "The Complete Bradford-Zipf 'Bibliograph'", J. of Documentation, 25, (1), pp. 58-60.

Brookes, B. C., 1970, "The Growth, Utility, and Obsolescence of Scientific Periodical Literature", J. of Documentation, 26, (4), pp. 283-294.

Brookes, B. C., 1971(a), "Optimum P% Library of Scientific Periodicals", Nature, 232, (5311), pp. 458-461.

Brookes, B. C., 1971(b), "Usage and Obsolescence", J. of Documentation, 27, (4), p. 306.

Brookes, B. C., 1972, "The Aging of Scientific Literature", Problems of Information Science, Chernyi, A., ed., FID478, VINITI, Moscow, pp. 66-90.

Brookes, B. C., 1973, "Numerical Methods of Bibliographic Analysis", Libr. Trends, 22, (1), pp. 18-43.

Brookes, B. C., 1978, "Characteristic Profiles of Developing Information Systems", Int. Forum Inf. Doc., 3, (4), pp. 3-6.

Brookes, B. C., 1983, "The Empirical Law of Natural Categorization", J. of Information Science, 6, (5), pp. 147-157.

Brookes, B. C., and Griffiths, J. M., 1978, "Frequency-Rank Distributions", J. Am. Soc. Inf. Sci., 29, (1), pp. 5-13.

Browning, L. D., 1978, "A Grounded Organizational Communication Theory Derived from Qualitative Data", Communication Monographs, (45), pp. 93-109.

Bubel, S. L., 1973, "Determination of the Extent of Duplication in Collecting and Storing Periodicals and Sserials, Nauch.-Tekh. Inf., 3, (6), pp. 12-17. (In Russian.)

Buckland, M. K., and Woodburn, I., 1969, "An Analytical Study of Library Book Duplication and Availability", Inform. Storage and Retrieval, 5, (2), pp. 69-79.

Bulut, N., Halstead, M. H., and Bayer, R., 1974, "Experimental Validation of a Structural Property of Fortran Algorithms", Proceedings of the National Conference, Assoc. for Computing Machinery, San Diego, pp. 207-211.

Burton, R., and Kebler, R., 1960, "The Half-Life of Some Scientific and Technical Literatures", Amer. Document, 11, (1), pp. 18-22.

Bush, G. C., Galliher, H. P., and Morse, P. M., 1956, "Attendance and Use of the Science Library at MIT", J. Am. Soc. Inf. Sci., 7, pp. 87-109.

Carroll, J. B., 1938, "Diversity of Vocabulary and the Harmonic Series Law of Word-Frequency Distribution", Psychological Record, 2, pp. 379-386.

Cawkell, A. E., 1968, "Documentation Notes -- Citation Practices", Journal of Documentation, 24, (4), pp. 299-303.

Cawkell, A. E., 1976, "Documentation Note: Citations, Obsolescence, Enduring Articles, and Multiple Authorships", <u>Journal of Documentation</u>, <u>32</u>, (1), pp. 43-58.

Chernyi, A. I., 1968, "General Structures of Thesauri", <u>Nauch.-Tekh. Inf.</u>, Series 2, (5). (In Russian.)

Chernyi, A. I.,. Kuznetsova, E. E., and Matsak, N. M., 1969, "Permutation Indexes: Some Considerations Regarding Their Effectiveness, Areas of Application, and Structure", <u>Nauch.-Tekh. Inf.</u>, Series 2, (10), pp. 12-23. (In Russian.)

Chonez, A., 1974, "Scattering of Periodical Literature in Informatics, or the Pseudo-scientific Bradford's Law", <u>Documentaliste</u>, <u>11</u>, (4), pp. 175-184. (In French.)

Clark, C. V., 1976, "Obsolescence of the Patent Literature", <u>Journal of Documentation</u>, <u>32</u>, (1), pp. 32-52.

Coadic, Y. F., 1974, "Information Systems and the Spread of Scientific Ideas", <u>R&D Management</u>, Pearson, A. W., ed., <u>4</u>, (2), pp. 97-111.

Coile, R. C., 1978, <u>Lotka's Frequency Distribution of Scientific Productivity</u>, Center for Naval Analyses, Arlington, VA.

Cole, J. R., et al., 1974, "Citation Analysis", <u>Science</u>, <u>183</u>, pp. 28-33.

Cole, P. F., 1962, "A New Look at Reference Scattering", <u>Journal of Documentation</u>, <u>18</u>, (2), pp. 58-64.

Cole, P. F., 1963, "Journal Usage Versus Age of Journal", <u>Journal of Documentation</u>, <u>19</u>, (1), pp. 1-11.

Dalziel, C. F., 1937, "Evaluation of Periodicals for Electrical Engineers", <u>Library Quarterly</u>, <u>7</u>, pp. 369-372.

Davidson, D., 1977, "The Effect of Individual Differences of Cognitive Style on Judgments of Document Relevance", <u>J. Am. Soc. Inf. Sci.</u>, <u>28</u>, pp. 273-284.

Dayton, D. L., et al., 1977, "Comparison of the Retrieval Effectiveness of CA Condensates (CACon) and CA Subject Index Alert (CASIA)", <u>J. Chem. Inf. Comput. Sci.</u>, <u>17</u>, (1), pp. 20-27.

Dieks, D., and Chang, H., 1976, "Differences in Impact of Scientific Publications: Some Indices Derived from a Citation Analysis", <u>Social Studies of Science</u>, <u>6</u>, pp. 247-267.

Dietze, J., 1975, "A Frequency-Statistical Method of Automatic Indexing", <u>Nauch.-Tekh. Inf.</u>, <u>1</u>, pp. 223 233. (In Russian.)

Dikeman, R. K., 1975, "A Use of Bibliometric Techniques in Serials Management for Libraries", <u>Information Revolution</u>, Husbands, C. W., Tighe, R. L., eds., Proceedings of the 38th American Society for Information Science Annual Meeting, Boston, Massachusetts, October 26-30, <u>12</u>, American Society for Information Science, Washington, pp. 55-56.

Dolby, J. L., and Resnikoff, H. L., 1971, "On the Multiplicative Structure of Information Storage and Access Systems", <u>Interfaces</u>, <u>1</u>, pp. 23-30.

Donohue, J. C., 1973, <u>Understanding Scientific Literatures: A Bibliometric</u>

Approach, MIT, Cambridge, MA, p. 101.

Douglas, I. A., 1973, "Optimum Size of a Library of Monographs, Aust. Libr. J., 22, (10), pp. 404-407.

Dronberger, G. B., and Kowitz, G. T., 1975, "Abstract Readability as a Factor in Information Systems", J. Am. Soc. Inf. Sci., 26, (2), pp. 108-111.

Dubovikov, M. S., Markova, L. F., and Sol'ts, N. A., 1976, "The Application of a Statistical Method to the Analysis of Document Information Flows", Nauch.-Tekh. Inf., Series 2, 1, pp. 22-25. (In Russian.)

Edmundson, H. P., 1977, "Statistical Inference in Mathematical and Computational Linguistics", International Journal of Computer and Information Sciences, 6, (2), pp. 95-129.

Ellis, S. R., and Hitchcock, R. J., 1986, "The Emergence of Zipf's Law: Spontaneous Encoding Optimization by Users of a Command Language", IEEE Transactions on Systems, Man., and Cybernetics, SMC-16, (3), pp. 423-427.

Fairthorne, R. A., 1969, "Empirical Hyperbolic Distributions (Bradford-Zipf-Mandelbrot) for Bibliometric Description and Prediction", Journal of Documentation, 25, (4), pp. 319-343.

Fedorowicz, H., 1982, "The Theoretical Foundations of Zipf's Law and Its Application to the Bibliographic Database Environment", J. of the American Society for Information Science, 33, (5), pp. 285-293.

Fernandez, R. P., and Saracevic, T., 1977, "Intercommunication Among Physics Research Groups in Latin America", Information Processing and Management, 13, (1), pp. 57-68.

Fokker, D. W., and Lynch, M. F., 1974, "Application of the Variety-Generator Approach to Searches of Personal Names in Bibliographic Data Bases. Part I. Microstructure of Personal Authors' Names", Journal of Library Automation, 7, (2), pp. 105-118.

Fry, E., 1977, "Fry's Readability Graph: Clarifications, Validity, and Extension to Level 17", Journal of Reading, 21, (3), pp. 242-252.

Fucks, W., 1955, Mathematical Analysis of Speech Elements, Style, and Languages, Arbeitsgemeinschaft Fuer Forschung des Landes Nordrhein - Westfalen, Oekln und Opaden. (In German.)

Fukunaga, K., Morikawa, T., Kasai, T., 1976, "Recognition of Words with Semantic Information", Electronics and Communications in Japan, 59, (1), pp. 12-19.

Gaddum, J. H., 1945, "Lognormal Distributions", Nature, 156, (3964), pp. 463-466.

Gani, J., 1963, "Formulae for Projecting Enrollments and Degrees Awarded in Universities", Journal of the Royal Statistical Society, Series A, 126, pp. 400-409.

Gani, J., 1975, "Stochastic Models for Type Counts in a Literary Text", Perspectives in Probability and Statistics, Gani, J., ed., Applied Probability Trust, NY, pp. 313-323.

Garrod, S. S., and Sanford, A. A., 1977, "Interpreting Anaphoric Relations: The Integration of Semantic Information While Reading", <u>Journal of Verbal Learning and Verbal Behavior</u>, <u>16</u>, pp. 77-90.

Garvey, W. D., Lin, N., and Nelson, C. E., 1970, "Some Comparisons of Communication Activities in the Physical and Social Sciences", <u>Communication Among Scientists and Engineers</u>, Nelson, C. E., and Pollock, D. K., eds., D. C. Heath and Co., Lexington, MA, pp. 61-84.

Ghosh, J. S., 1977, "The Information Content of Titles in Contraception Literature", <u>J. Chem. Inf. Comput. Sci.</u>, <u>17</u>, (1), pp. 36-40.

Gilbert, G. N., and Woolgar, S., 1974, "The Quantitative Study of Science: An Examination of the Literature", <u>Science Studies</u>, <u>4</u>, pp. 279-294.

Goffman, W., 1966, "Mathematical Approach to the Spread of Scientific Ideas -- the History of Mast Cell Research", <u>Nature</u>, <u>212</u>, (5061), pp. 449-452.

Goffman, W., and Morris, T. G., 1970, "Bradford's Law and Library Acquisitions", <u>Nature</u>, <u>226</u>, (5249), pp. 922-923.

Goffman, W., and Warren, K. S., 1969, "Dispersion of Papers Among Journals Based on a Mathematical Analysis of Two Diverse Medical Literatures", <u>Nature</u>, <u>221</u>, (5178), pp. 1205-1207.

Good, I. J., 1953, "The Population Frequencies of Species and the Estimation of Population Parameters", <u>Biometrika</u>, <u>49</u>, pp. 237-264.

Good, I. J., 1969, "Statistics of Language", <u>Encyclopedia of Linguistics, Information and Control</u>, Meetham, A. R., and Hudson, R. A., eds., Pergamon Press, Oxford, pp. 567-581.

Good, I. J., and Toulmin, G. H., 1956, "The Number of New Species, and the Increase of Population Coverage, When a Sample is Increased", <u>Biometrika</u>, <u>43</u>, pp. 45-.

Gor'kova, V. I., 1972, "Statistical Estimates of Parameters of Statistical Sets of Documentary Information Flows", <u>Nauch.-Tekh. Inf.</u>, Series 2, (12), pp. 14-20. (In Russian.)

Gor'kova, V. I., and Mellion, S. P., 1968, "Regularity of the Distribution of Publications in Periodicals and Serials on Electrotechnology and Power Engineering (Using as an Example the Abstract Journal <u>Elektrotekhnika i Energetika</u>), <u>Nauch.-Tekh. Inf.</u>, Series 2, (11), pp. 3-7. (In Russian.)

Gor'kova, V. I., and Naumycheva, K. I., 1970, "Frequency Distribution of Sets of Keywords", <u>Nauch.-Tekh. Inf.</u>, Series 2, (6), pp. 3-8. (In Russian.)

Gor'kova, V. I., and Shishova, L. A., 1978, "Simulation Models of Structural Links in Classifications of Information Flows", <u>Nauch.-Tekh. Inf.</u>, Series 2, (6), pp. 1-7.

Greenblatt, D. L., 1978, "Variable Rules and Literary Style", <u>Computers and the Humanities</u>, <u>11</u>, pp. 193-197.

Griffith, B. C., Jahn, M. J., and Miller, A. J., 1971, "Informal Contacts in Science -- Probabilistic Model for Communication Processes", <u>Science</u>, <u>173</u>, (3992), pp. 164-166.

Gubankov, V. N., 1975, "Some Time Relationships in the Patterns of the Quantitative Changes of Cited Scientific Documents", Autom. Doc. Math. Linguist., Series 2, (3), pp. 3-6.

Guiraud, P., 1954, "Language and Communication. Informational Substance of Semantization", Bulletin de la Societe de Linguistique de Paris, 49, pp. 119-133. (In French.)

Guiraud, P., 1963, "Oleatoric Structures of Double Articulation", Bulletin de la Societe de Linguistique de Paris, 58, pp. 135-155. (In French.)

Guiraud, P., 1965(a), "Diacritical and Statistical Models for Languages in Relation to the Computer", The Use of Computers in Anthropology, Hymes, D., ed., Mouton and Co., London, pp. 235-254.

Guiraud, P., 1965(b), "Elementary Structures of Signification", Bulletin de la Societe de Linguistique de Paris, 60, pp. 97-114. (In French.)

Guiraud, P., 1971, "The Semic Matrices of Meaning", Essays in Semiotics, Kristeva, J., Rey-Debove, J., and Umiker, D. J., eds., Mouton, Paris, pp. 150-159.

Halstead, M. H., 1972, "Natural Laws, Controlling Algorithm Structure?", ACM Special Interest Group on Programming Languages: SIGPLAN Notices, 7, pp. 19-26.

Halstead, M. H., 1977, Elements of Software Science, Elsevier North-Holland, New York, NY.

Harris, Z., 1954, "Distributional Structure", Word, (10), pp. 146-162.

Healy, M. J., 1968, "The Lengths of Surnames", Journal of the Royal Statistical Society, Series A, 131, pp. 567-568.

Heaps, H. S., 1972, "Storage Analysis of a Compression Coding for Document Data Bases", INFOR Journal, 10, (1), pp. 47-61.

Heaps, H. S., 1974, "Data Compression of Large Document Data Bases", Journal of Chemical Information and Computer Sciences, 15, (1), pp. 32-39.

Heine, M. H., 1977, "Incorporation of the Age of a Document Into the Retrieval Process", Information Processing and Management, 13, (1), pp. 35-37.

Hempel, C. G., 1952, "Fundamentals of Concept Formation in Empirical Science", International Encyclopedia of Unified Science, 2, (7), University of Chicago Press, Chicago, IL.

Herdan, G., 1958, "The Relation Between the Dictionary Distribution and the Occurrence Distribution of Word Length and Its Importance for the Study of Quantitative Linguistics", Biometrics, 45, pp. 222-228.

Herdan, G., 1964, Quantitative Linguistics, Butterworth's, Washington, D.C.

Hick, W. E., 1952, "On the Rate of Gain of Information", Q.J. Exp. Psychol., 4, pp. 11-26.

Holt, C. C., and Schrank, W. E., 1968, "Growth of the Professional Literature in Economics and Other Fields, and Some Implications", J. Am. Soc. Inf. Sci., 19, pp. 18-26.

Houston, N., and Wall, E., 1964, "The Distribution of Term Usage in Manipulative Indexes", J. Am. Soc. Inf. Sci., 15, pp. 105-114.

Hubert, J. J., 1978, "A Relationship Between Two Forms of Bradford's Law, J. Am. Soc. Inf. Sci., 29, (3), pp. 159-161.

Hyman, R., 1953, "Stimulus Information as a Determinant of Reaction Time", J. Exp. Psychol., Human Perception and Performance, 45, pp. 188-196.

Ivanov, Y. B., Kapustin, V. M., and Makhotenko, Y. A., 1973, "One Approach to the Evaluation of the Growth of Document Information Flows Over Time", Nauch.-Tekh. Inf., Series 2, (2), pp. 3-5. (In Russian.)

Jain, A. K., Leimkuhler, F. F., and Anderson, V. L., 1969, "A Statistical Model of Book Use and Its Application to the Book Storage Problem", J. Am. Stat. Assoc., 64, pp. 1211-1224.

Johnson, P. E., 1969, "On the Communication of Concepts in Science, Journal of Educational Psychology, 60, (1), pp. 32-40.

Kashafutdinova, E. S., Grishina, F. E., and Mal'dizina, M. N., 1975, "Analysis of Demands for Journals on Power and Energy Technology from the Collections of the Reference Center of VINITI", Nauch.-Tekh. Inf., Series 2, (8), pp. 8-11. (In Russian.)

Kauffman, D., et al., 1974, The Empirical Derivation of Equations for Predicting Subjective Textual Information, Arizona State University, Report No. AD-788 427.

Kendall, M. G., 1961, "Natural Law in the Social Sciences", Journal of the Royal Statistical Society, Series A, 124, pp. 1-19.

Kherts, M. M., 1969, "On the Representativeness of a Text of Given Length", Nauch.-Tekh. Inf., Series 2, (6), pp. 25-28.

Kim, C., 1982, "Retrieval Language of Social Sciences and Natural Sciences: A Statistical Investigation, J. of the ASIS, 33, (1), pp. 3-7.

Kim, C., and Kim, S. D., 1977, "Consensus vs. Frequency: An Empirical Investigation of the Theories for Identifying Descriptors in Designing Retrieval Thesauri", Information Processing and Management, 13, pp. 253-258.

Klemmer, E. T., 1957, "Simple Reaction Time as a Function of Time Uncertainty", J. Exp. Psychol., Human Perception and Performance, 54, (3), pp. 195-200.

Kochen, M., 1969, "Stability in the Growth of Knowledge", Amer. Document, 20, (3), pp. 186-197.

Korolev, E. I., 1977, "The Use of the Distributive Statistical Method in the Language Apparatus of Automated Information Systems", Autom. Doc. Math. Linguist, 11, (1), pp. 31-37.

Kozachkov, L. S., and Khursin, L. A., 1968, "Models of Growth of Scientific Publications Based on Lotka-Bradford-Zipf Law", Nauch.-Tekh. Inf., Series 2, (7), pp. 3-10. (In Russian.)

Kralik, J., 1977, "An Application of Exponential Distribution Law in Quantitative Linguistics", Prague Studies in Mathematical Linguistics, 5, pp. 223-235.

Kraus, J., 1972, "On the Stylistic-Semantic Analysis of Adjectives in Journalistic Style (A Quantitative Approach)", Prague Studies in Mathematical Linguistics, 4, The Univ. of Alabama Press, pp. 95-106.

Krautwurst, J., 1969, "Evaluation of a Thesaurus by Means of Information-Theoretical Tools", Nachr. Dokum., 20, (2), pp. 68-72.

Krauze, T. K., and Hillinger, C., 1971, "Citations and References, and the Growth of Scientific Literature", J. Am. Soc. Inf. Sci., 22, pp. 333-336.

Krevitt, B., and Griffith, B. C., 1972, "A Comparison of Several Zipf-Type Distributions in Their Goodness of Fit to Language Data", J. Am. Soc. Inf. Sci., 23, pp. 220-221.

Krisciunas, K., 1977, "Lotka's Law -- Year by Year", J. Am. Soc. Inf. Sci., 28, pp. 65-66.

Krylov, Yu. K., and Yabubovskaya, M. D., 1977, "Statistical Analysis of Polysemy, As a Language Universal and the Problem of the Semantic Identity of the Word", Autom. Doc. Math. Linguist., 11, (1), pp. 80-87. Also in Nauch.-Tekh.Inf., Series 2, 11, (3), pp. 1-6.

Kuhlen, R., 1975, "Quantitative Problems in Dictionary Construction", Nachr. Dokum., 26, (4-5), pp. 163-167. (In German; English Summary.)

Lau, W., 1977, Library Book Duplication, Working Paper, Georgia Institute of Technology, Atlanta, GA.

Lawani, S. M., 1973, "Bradford's Law and the Literature of Agriculture", International Library Review, 5, (3), pp. 341-350.

Leimkuhler, F. F., 1977, "Operational Analysis of Library Systems", Information Processing and Management, 13, (2), pp. 79-93.

Leimkuhler, F. F., 1980, "An Exact Formulation of Bradford's Law", J. of Documentation, 36, (4), pp. 285-292.

Leonard, J. A., 1958, "Partial Advance Information in a Choice Reaction Task", British Journal of Psychology, 49, pp. 89-96.

Levine, D. M., 1977, "Multivariate Analysis of the Visual Information Processing of Numbers", Journal of Multivariate Behavioral Research, 12, (3), pp. 347-355.

Lewis, P. A., Baxendale, P. B., and Bennet, J. L., 1967, "Statistical Discrimination of the Synonymy/Antonymy Relationship Between Words", Journal of the ACM, 14, (1), pp. 20-44.

Line, M. B., and Sandison, A., 1974, ""Obsolescence' and Changes in the Use of Literature with Time", Journal of Documentation, 30, (3), pp. 283-350.

Loiferman, P. G., Volkov, V. N., and Duzhenko, V. S., 1975, "An Experimental Study of Rank Distribution of Documentary Sources According to the Role They Play in the Formation of the Information Flow", Nauch.-Tekh. Inf., Series 2, (12), pp. 8-13. (In Russian.)

Lowry, D. T., and Marr, T. J., 1974, Clozentropy as a Measure of International Communication Comprehension, Paper presented at 57th Annual Meeting of Association for Education in Journalism, San Diego,

California, August 18-21, 1974.

Ludvikova, M., 1971, "Quantitative Syllable Analysis of Words in Czech", Prague Studies in Mathematical Linguistics, 3, pp. 28-34.

MacRae, D., 1969, "Growth and Decay Curves in Scientific Citations", Am. Sociol. R., 34, pp. 631-635.

Mandelbrot, B., 1953, "An Informational Theory of the Statistical Structure of Language", Communication Theory, Jackson, W., ed., Butterworth Sc. Publ., London, pp. 486-502.

Mantell, L., 1966, "On Laws of Special Abilities and the Production of Scientific Literature", Amer. Document, 17, pp. 8-16.

Marcus, R. S., Kugel, P., and Benenfeld, A. R., 1978, "Catalog Information and Text as Indicators of Relevance", J. Am. Soc. Inf. Sci., 29, (1), pp. 15-30.

Margolis, J., 1967, "Citation Indexing and Evaluation of Scientific Papers, Science, 155, pp. 1213-1219.

Martino, J. P., 1969, Science and Society in Equilibrium", Science, 165, pp. 769-772.

Marulli, L., and Koenig, M. E., 1979, "Bradford Distribution of Data Elements", J. Am. Soc. Inf. Sci., 30, pp. 7-8.

Mayer, R., 1976, "Comprehension as Affected by Structure of Problem Representation", Memory and Cognition, 4, (3), pp. 249-255.

Mayes, P. B., 1975, "The Use of the Bradford-Zipf Distribution to Estimate Values for a Journal Circulation System", Journal of Documentation, 31, (4), pp. 287-289.

McCurdy, H. G., 1953, The Personality of Shakespeare, Yale Univ. Press, New Haven, Conn.

McGrath, W. E., 1978, "Relationships Between Hard-Soft, Pure-Applied, and Life-Nonlife Disciplines and Subject Book Use in a University Library", Information Processing and Management, 14, pp. 17-28.

Meadows, A. J., 1974, Communication in Science, Butterworth's, London.

Meyer, D. E., and Schvaneveldt, R. W., 1976, "Meaning, Memory Structure, and Mental Processes", Science, 192, (4234), pp. 27-33.

Miller, G. A., Heise, C. A., and Lichten, W., 1951, "The Intelligibility of Speech as a Function of the Context of Test Materials", J. Exp. Psychol., Human Perceptions and Performance, 41, pp. 329-335.

Mitsevich, A. T., 1973, "Analysis of Information Flows in Shipbuilding and Allied Fields", Nauch.-Tekh. Inf., Series 1, (6), pp. 21-28. (In Russian.)

Mitsevich, A. T., 1975, "Investigation of the Structure of Flows of Scientific and Technical Information on Machine Construction", Nauch.-Tekh. Inf., Series 2, (5), pp. 3-16. (In Russian.)

Mitsevich, A. T., and Solov'ev, N. K., 1969, "Analysis of Certain Regularities of Flows of Scientific-Technical Information on Machine

Construction", Nauch.-Tekh. Inf., Series 2, (9), pp. 3-7. (In Russian.)

Morse, P. M., and Elston, C., 1969, "A Probabilistic Model for Obsolescence", Oper. Res., 17, pp. 36-47.

Morse, P. M., and Leimkuhler, F. F., 1977, Exact Solution for the Bradford Distribution and Its Use in Modelling Informational Data, Working Paper, MIT, Operations Research Center, OR 068-77.

Mynatt, B. T., 1977, "Reaction Times in a Bisensory Task: Implications for Attention and Speech Perception", J. Exp. Psychol., Human Perceptions and Performance, 3, (2), pp. 316-324.

Nalimov, V. V., and Mul'chenko, Z. M., 1969, Scientometrics. Study of the Development of Science as an Information Process, Nauka, Moscow. (In Russian.)

Narin, F. 1976, "The Use of Publication and Citation Analysis in the Evaluation of Scientific Activity", Evaluative Bibliometrics, Computer Horizons, Inc., Cherry Hill, NJ for NSF Contract NSF-C627.

Nelson, M. J., and Tague, J. M., 1985, "Split Size-Rank Models for Distribution of Index Terms", J. of the ASIS, 36, (5), pp. 283-296.

Neshitoi, V. V., 1977, "Distribution of Keywords in Text", Cybernetica, 13, pp. 277-287.

Nicholls, P. T., 1986, "Empirical Validation of Lotka's Law", Info. Processing and Management, 22, (5), pp. 417-419.

Novikov, A. I., and Yakushin, B. V., 1972, "Algorithm for Indexing a Text by Semantically Weighted Keywords Using Method of Semantic Filters", Nauch.-Tekh. Inf., 2, (6), pp. 15-20. (In Russian.)

Nowakowska, M., 1973, "An Epidemical Spread of Scientific Objects: An Attempt of Empirical Approach to Some Problems of Meta-Science", Theory and Decision, 3, pp. 262-297.

Oliver, M. R., 1971, "The Effect of Growth on the Obsolescence of Semiconductor Physics Literature", Journal of Documentation, 27, (1), pp. 11-17.

O'Neill, E. T., 1974, "A Stochastic Scattering Model", Proc. of the 37th Annual Meeting of the Am. Soc. Inf. Sci., Zunde, P., ed., Atlanta, Georgia, Oct. 13-17, 1974, 11, pp. 155-159.

Pao, M. L., 1978, "Automatic Text Analysis Based on Transition Phenomena of Word Occurrences", J. Am. Soc. Inf. Sci., 29, pp. 121-124.

Pap, F., 1967, "On Some Quantitative Characteristics of a Language Vocabulary", Annales Instituti Philologiae Slavicae Universitatis Debreceniensis, 7, pp. 51-58. (In Russian.)

Parker, R. H., 1982(a), "Bibliometric Models for Management of an Information Store. I. Differential Utility Among Items", J. of the ASIS, 33, (3), pp. 124-128.

Parker, R. H., 1982(b), "Bibliometric Models for Management of an Information Store. II. Use as a Function of Age of Material", J. of the ASIS, 33, (3), pp. 129-133.

Parker-Rhodes, A. F., and Joyce, T., 1956, "A Theory of Word-Frequency Distribution", _Nature_, _178_.

Pearson, C., 1978, "Quantitative Investigation into the Type-Token Relation for Symbolic Rhemes", _Proceedings of the Semiotic Society of America, 1976_, pp. 312-328.

Pearson, C., 1979, _Semiotics and the Measurement of Shape_, Working Paper, Georgia Institute of Technology, Atlanta, GA.

Pearson, C., and Slamecka, V., 1977, _Semiotic Foundations of Information Science_, Final Report, Jan. 1974 - Dec. 1976, Report GIT-ICS-77-01, NTIS PB-265 897.

Perry, J. A., 1985, "The Dillion Hypothesis of Jitulor Colonicity: An Empirical Test from Ecological Sciences", _J. of the ASIS_, _36_, (4), pp. 251-258.

Petrenko, B. V., 1974, "Documentary Information Flow Study Based on the Analysis of Information Users' Requests", _Nauch.-Tekh. Inf._, Series 2, (10), pp. 3-8. (In Russian.)

Pollack, I., 1952, "The Information of Elementary Auditory Displays", _J. of the Acoustical Society of America_, _24_, pp. 745-749.

Portnoy, S., 1973, "A Comparison of Oral and Written Verbal Behavior", _Studies in Verbal Behavior: An Empirical Approach_, Salzinger, K., and Feldman, J. S., eds., Pergamon Press, New York, NY, pp. 99-151.

Price, D. J., 1963, "A Calculus of Science", _International Science and Technology_, _1963_, pp. 37-42.

Radhakrishnan, T., and Kernizan, R., 1979, "Lotka's Law and Computer Science Literature", _J. Am. Soc. Inf. Sci._, _30_, (1), pp. 51-54.

Rao, I. K. Ravichandra, 1980, "The Distribution of Scientific Productivity and Social Change, _J. of the ASIS_, _31_, pp. 111-122.

Resnikoff, H. L., and Dolby, J. L., 1970, _Economic Accumulation of Book Indexes and Information Theory_, Working Paper.

Reynolds, A. G., 1972, _Coding, Ordering, and Retrieving Information from Sentences_, Final Report, Dartmouth College, Hanover, NH, EDRS.

Reynolds, A. G., and Flagg, P. W., 1975, _Recognition Memory for Elements of Sentences_, EDRS.

Robertson, S. E., and Sparck Jones, K., 1976, "Relevance Weighting of Search Terms", _J. Am. Soc. Inf. Sci._, _27_, (3), pp. 129-146.

Rolling, L., and Plette, J., 1968, "Mechanized Information Storage, Retrieval and Dissemination", _Interaction of Economics and Automation in a Large-Size Retrieval System_, North-Holland, pp. 367-386.

Rubenstein, H., and Goodenough, J. B., 1965, "Contextual Correlates of Synonymy", _Communications of the ACM_, _8_, (10), pp. 627-633.

Sager, N., 1976(b), "Perspective Paper: Computational Linguistics", _Natural Language in Information Science Perspectives and Directions of Research_, Walker, D. E., Karlgren, H., and Kay, M., eds., Skriptor, Stockholm, Sweden, FID Publication 551, pp. 75-100.

Schorr, A. E., 1974, "Lotka's Law and Library Science", <u>RQ</u>, <u>14</u>, (1), pp. 32-33.

Schwartz, S. P., et al., 1977, "State and Process Limitations in Informamation Processing: On Additive Factor Analysis", <u>J. Exp. Psychol. Human Perceptions and Performance</u>, <u>3</u>, (3), pp. 402-410.

Serebrianyi, A. I., 1978, "On the Problem of Automatic Construction of an Indexing Algorithm", <u>Nauch.-Tekh. Inf.</u>, Series 2, (5), pp. 7-16. (In Russian.)

Shockley, W., 1957, "On the Statistics of Individual Variations of Productivity in Research Laboratories", <u>Proceedings of the IRE</u>, <u>45</u>, (3), pp. 279-290.

Shreider, Yu. A., and Osipova, M. A., 1969, "On Some Dynamic Models in Informatics", <u>Nauch.-Tekh. Inf.</u>, Series 2, (8), pp. 15-18. (In Russian.)

Sichel, H. S., 1975, "On a Distribution Law for Word Frequencies", <u>J. Am. Stat. Assoc.</u>, <u>70</u>, (352), pp. 542-547.

Sichel, H. S., 1985, "A Bibliometric Distribution Which Really Works", <u>J. of the ASIS</u>, <u>36</u>, (5), pp. 314-321.

Simon, H. A., 1955, "On a Class of Skew Distribution Functions", <u>Biometrika</u>, <u>42</u>, pp. 425-440.

Simonton, D. K., 1978, "Independent Discovery in Science and Technology" A Closer Look at the Poisson Distribution", <u>Social Studies of Science</u>, <u>8</u>, pp. 521-532.

Skinner, B. F., 1936, "The Verbal Summation and a Method for the Study of Latent Speech", <u>The Journal of Psychology</u>, <u>2</u>, pp. 71-107.

Small, H. G., and Koenig, M. E., 1977, "Journal Clustering Using a Bibliographic Coupling Method", <u>Information Processing and Management</u>, <u>13</u> (5), pp. 277-288.

Smith, F. J., and Devine, K., 1985, "Storing and Retrieving Word Phrases", <u>Information Processing and Management</u>, <u>21</u>, (3), pp. 215-224.

Smol'kov, N. A., 1977, "An Equation for the Scattering of Publications in Periodicals", <u>Autom. Doc. Math. Linguist.</u>, <u>11</u>, (1), pp. 1-6.

Soper, M. E., 1976, "Characteristics and Use of Personal Collections", <u>Lib. Q.</u>, <u>46</u>, (4), pp. 397-415.

Srinivasan, D., 1977, "Style in Syntax: A Computer Aided Quantitative Study", <u>Computing in Humanities</u>, Lusignan, S., and North, J. S., eds., Univ. of Waterloo Press, pp. 85-97.

Starbuck, W. H., 1965, "Organizational Growth and Development", <u>Handbook of Organizations</u>, March, J. G., ed., Rand McNally and Co., Chicago, IL, pp. 451-532.

Stephenson, M. S., 1985, "The Research Method Used in Subfields and the Growth of Published Literature in Those Subfields: Vertebrate Paleontology and Geochemistry", <u>J. of the ASIS</u>, <u>36</u>, (2), pp. 130-133.

Strizenec, M., 1965, "Information and Mental Processes, <u>Entropy and</u>

Information in Science and Philosophy, Kubat, L., and Zeman, J., eds., Elsevier, Amsterdam, pp. 149-153.

Tarnoczy, T., 1961, "A Jeloszlas es a Hirtartalcm Nyelveket Meghataroza Tulajdon Tulajdonsagairol", *Nyelvtudomanyi Kozlemenyek*, 63, pp. 161-178.

Terwilliger, R. F., 1968, "Meaning and Mind", Oxford Univ. Press, New York.

Vickery, B. C., 1948, "Bradford's Law of Scattering", *Journal of Documentation*, 4, (3), pp. 198-203.

Webster, R. J., 1969, "Communication in Man as a Random Process", *Kybernetik*, 6, (2), pp. 72-74.

Weiss, H., 1967, *Statistical Studies of Sentence Length and Structure as Style Attributes of Author*, Ph.D. Dissertation, Aachen. (In German.)

Williams, C. B., 1944, "The Numbers of Publications Written by Biologists", *Annals of Eugenics*, 12, pp. 143-146.

Williams, C. B., 1970, *Style and Vocabulary: Numerical Studies*, Griffin, London.

Worthen, D. B., 1975, "The Application of Bradford's Law to Monographs, *Journal of Documentation*, 31, (1), pp. 19-25.

Wyllys, R. E., 1975, "Measuring Scientific Prose with Rank-Frequency ('Zipf') Curves: A New Use for an Old Phenomenon", *Information Revolution: Proceedings of the 38th ASIS Annual Meeting*, 12, Boston, Massachusetts, October 26-30, 1975, pp. 30-31.

Zajonc, R. B., 1968, "Attitudinal Effects of Mere Exposure", *Journal of Personality and Social Psychology Monograph Supplement*, 9, (2), pp. 1-27.

Zipf, G. K., 1949, *Human Behavior and the Principle of Least Effort*, Addison-Wesley Press, Cambridge, Mass.

Zunde, P., 1981, *On Empirical Foundations of Information Science*, Research Report, Georgia Institute of Technology, Atlanta, GA, NTIS Access No. PB82-125998.

Zunde, P., 1984, "Empirical Laws and Theories of Information and Software Sciences", *Information Processing and Management*, 20, (1-2), pp. 5-18.

Zunde, P., and Dexter, M., 1969, "Indexing Consistency and Quality", *Amer. Document.*, 20, (3), pp. 259-267.

Zhurek, J., 1969, "On Certain Measurable Indicators of Information Service Effectiveness", *Akt. Probl. Inf. Dokum.*, 14, (2), pp. 1-8. (In Polish.)

Zvorykin, A. A., 1967, "Science as Structure: Quantitative Methods to Its Studies", *Vsesoyuznoe Soveshchanie po Kolichestvennym Metodam v Sotsiologii*, (Sbornik Dobladov). (In Russian.)

Zweben, S. H., 1977, "A Study of the Physical Structure of Algorithms", *IEEE Trans. Software Eng.*, SE-3, (3), pp. 250-258.

INDEX

Behavior
  managerial, 223

Causal net, 21
Communication
  oral, 223
Complex system, 21
  design, 21
Complexity measure, 13, 81
Computer games, 187
Control, 21
  behavior, 26

Data-structure metric, 211
Database
  integrated, 145
  legal, 54
  management, 3, 45
Debugging, 63
Decision
  making, 22, 123, 231
  support, 196
Decision Monitoring Model (DEMON), 123
Design
  specification, 229
  top-down, 115
Diagnostics
  medical, 29
Dialog structure, 165
Dynamic Environment Simulation
    System (DESSY), 24

Effort estimation, 211
Empirical laws, 213
Error
  correction, 63
  mechanisms, 191
Evaluation, 99
  methods, 100
Exitialization, 135, 136
Expert system
  distributed, 73
External documentation, 234

File organization, 149

Human factors

Information
  acquisition, 244, 251
  growth, 255
  measures, 231
  processing, 223, 244, 257
    aids, 175
    human, 187
  profile, 231
  representation, 244, 255
  retrieval, 3, 145, 257
  source, 244, 252
  transfer, 244, 253
Information science, 243
  laws, 213, 244
Information System, 196
  design, 145
Initialization, 136
Instruction
  knowledge based, 10
Integration, 3, 145
Interaction, 99
  patterns, 192
Interface, 152
  design, 155
  evaluation, 188

Knowledge,
  distribution, 78
  representation, 250, 256

Learning, 21
  curves, 193
Library management, 256
Logging, 99

McCabe metric, 17
Measurement
  of association, 180
  of complexity, 13
  of data-structure, 211
  of similarity, 182
  theory, 13
Medical diagnostics, 29
Metacognitive function, 123

Modeling, 21, 74, 123, 156
  british economy, 28
  cognitive, 187
  conceptual data, 45
  system users, 188
MONSTRAT, 73

Parallelism, 83
Playback, 99
Pragmatics, 249
Problem solving, 187
Program
  design, 134
    methodology, 138
  management, 5, 9
  planning, 109
  testing, 65
  validity, 63
  verification tools, 99
Programming
  aids, 110
  computer-aided, 109
  environment, 73, 116
  strategy, 114
PROTEVS project, 34
Protocol
  verbal, 99
Prototyping, 3, 33, 73, 109

Rank-frequency distribution, 245
Resource monitoring, 123

Screen layout, 167
Semantics, 249
  associative, 175, 177
  differential, 196
Signals detection, 63
Software
  complexity, 13
  design, 224, 229
  development, 211
  engineering, 110, 135
  errors, 63
  size estimation, 211
  validation, 63
Specification of requirements, 33
Strategy
  mental, 187
  selection, 123
Syntactics, 246, 248
System
  design, 21, 33
  development, 37
    user controlled, 37
  evaluation, 198
  interactive, 99

Test data analysis, 68
Text
  classification, 46
  electronic, 49

Text (Continued)
  environment, 45
  processing, 45, 150, 251
Thesaurus, 175
  of term associations, 175
Triform structure, 136
Type-token relation, 213

Uncertainty
  structural, 240
User
  interface, 152, 187
    design, 155
    evaluation, 155
    styles, 160
  needs, 225
  prototyping, 35
  study, 196
User-system dialog, 155

Workstation
  scientific, 145